JASPER WHITE'S COOKING FROM NEW ENGLAND

JASPER WHITE'S
COOKING FROM NEW ENGLAND

More than 300 Traditional and

Contemporary Recipes

JASPER WHITE

DECORATIVE PAINTINGS BY DEBORAH HEALY
TECHNIQUE DRAWINGS BY STEPHEN SCHINDLER

 HarperPerennial
A Division of HarperCollins*Publishers*

First HarperPerennial edition published 1993.

Designed by Patricia Dunbar

LIBRARY OF CONGRESS CATALOG CARD NUMBER 89-45074

ISBN 0-06-092399-7

93 94 95 96 97 DT/MPC 10 9 8 7 6 5 4 3 2 1

For Nancy and J. P.

Acknowledgments

I typed this book, but I did not write it. I doubt if anyone has ever really written a cookbook. I believe that the creative process in cooking is a matter of transforming small parts of a much greater body of folk knowledge into new variations, however slight the differences. This ties all good cooks to the past, to each other and, hopefully, to the future. As I try to remember all the people (an impossible task) who have inspired me as a chef, and who have helped me with my career and with this book, I realize what a truly rich experience this life of cooking has given me.

In particular, I would like to thank the following people:

- Pat Brown, who convinced me I could and should write this book and who has guided me from the beginning.
- Susan Derecskey, whose clear focus and attention to detail has transformed my thoughts into a book. She has amazed me.
- Larry Ashmead and Margaret Wimberger, my editors, and all the dedicated people at Harper & Row.
- Dean Paris, Mark Cupolo, Stan Frankenthaler, Nam Van Tran, Helen Browne and all the staff at my restaurant, whose professionalism afforded me the time to write this book.
- Lydia Shire, my cooking partner and dear friend, with whom I have shared so much hard work and even more good food.
- Elizabeth Laing and Lenny Pepe, who believed in my restaurant from day one.
- The chefs of New England who have contributed to this book. Their recipes have enriched this manuscript and added credence to my belief that we are all in this together.
- The farmers, fishermen, foragers and other food producers of New England, without whom there would be no reason for this book.
- All my friends and neighbors, who have already tasted their way through this book.
- Muriel and Trevor Thom, my in-laws, who made me feel at home in New England.
- Paul Morgan, whose entrepreneurial philosophy had a profound affect on the direction I chose in life.
- All of my family, especially Mom, Dad, Mike, Matt, Nina and Pop, for their love and support.
- And my wife, Nancy, whose deeds are too numerous to count.

Contents

Introduction

It was no accident that I chose to become a professional chef; it was in my stars. My great-grandfather, Giuseppe Padagrosi, was a chef who emigrated from Rome to New York and later New Jersey in 1903. In the rigid and chauvinistic American culture of those times, the Padagrosis, like many other immigrants, used food within the privacy of their home as an expression of love for the homeland they missed and their love for each other. Nothing was too much work when it came to dinner. No detail was too small. Although I never knew my great-grandparents, their daughters, Josephine and Ida (my grandmother), reflected the philosophy of their parents in the way they lived. Food was the center their family life revolved around and was always held in high esteem. As Nina (our name for my grandmother, Ida) became more American, the same respect was extended to corn on the cob and other American dishes as to the traditional Italian dishes from her childhood. This passion for good food was passed along to my father, who expressed his closeness to food by hunting and farming.

Considering this introduction to food, you may wonder why my style of cooking did not develop more along the lines of my Italian grandmother. But that is not what I learned from her. What I learned was the connection between the land and the food and how one adapts to a new environment. I also learned an uncompromising attitude that disdains anything but the very best.

My mother's side of the family was Irish and had a somewhat different relationship with food. They knew hard times and taught us to thank God for every morsel of food we got. My mother somehow managed to balance the tendencies of the two families, learning a lot about cooking from her Italian mother-in-law but tempering it with a more practical outlook. She always set a good meal in front of us, every night.

As a child I learned to hunt and fish. We lived on a farm near the New Jersey shore. At a young age I gained an important understanding of the connection between the land and the sea and the table. Rather than the isolation from food that many Americans of my generation suffered, I was exposed to a wide variety of foods in the unadulterated state. In my family it was normal to love good food and dwell on it. There was no disappointment when I announced my chosen profession at the age of eighteen.

So how did an Irish-Italian kid from New Jersey become a self-appointed spokesman for New England cooking? It's a long story; here is the short version of it. After graduating from culinary school, I headed to the West Coast. When I was living in San Francisco, I met a girl named Nancy Thom from Providence, Rhode Island. Today she is my wife. We have lived together in New England for eleven years, and now we have a son named J. P. (Jasper Paul). We have a restaurant and a home in Boston and another house on Sawyer's Island near Boothbay Harbor, Maine. I could not be more settled. I have made New England my home, and I am here to stay.

As I have come to love the region that is now my home, I have made a study of New England food, from the historical and cultural vantage point to the reality of what, when, where and how local foods are available to us. I needed this knowledge to perfect my craft. What I have found is a region that is rich in ingredients, history, cultural diversity and a tradition of both good cooking and sound teaching of the culinary arts. Fannie Merritt Farmer, Julia Child and Madeleine Kamman all chose Boston at one point or another of their lives to spread the gospel of good cooking.

In this book I have made an attempt to relay what I have learned about cooking and specifically cooking in New England. The book is organized by ingredients, which enabled me to focus on what I consider the be-all and end-all of good cooking. New England is a remarkable region for food. From our rocky coast come the greatest variety and best quality of shellfish in America. From the rivers, bays and ocean come an abundance and a multitude of species of fish that are also unrivaled. The rolling hills and valleys of New England are home to some of America's oldest fruit orchards, vegetable, grain, meat, poultry and dairy farms. Almost all of the world's cranberries come from New England and the beach plums and wild berries can be found in every corner. As a farmer friend once told me, "You can't swing a dead cat around here without hitting a berry patch." The woodlands are abundant in sugar maples, wild mushrooms and fiddleheads. Other treats you will find are freshly milled flours, handmade Cheddars, cob-smoked hams, apple cider and old-fashioned fruit wines. The list goes on and on.

Seasonal changes in New England are dramatic; there always seems to be something coming and something going. The cool climate makes for a short and often late growing season, but when it's in its full glory, there is a wealth of both summer and fall foods that rarely coincide in other areas. When summer vegetables get scarce, we change our focus to the roots and winter squash that are so often identified with our cooking. And we always look forward to the shellfish that is at its peak in the cold winter months.

Aside from the actual ingredients, seasonal changes also take into consideration the style of food preparations. Many of the classic New England dishes are cold-weather dishes; many of the dishes in this book are too. I offer these richer dishes without apology, but with qualification. Any dish taken out of context can be an abomination, so I urge you to use common sense and also to refer to the recipe headnotes and chapter introductions, which help place things in perspective. I have also compiled some seasonal menus to demonstrate the stylistic changes that are appropriate as the weather changes over the year.

Lastly, one cannot take an in-depth look at cooking in New England without considering the historical and cultural aspects of this region. Early colonial cooking was a mix of American Indian and Anglo-Saxon cooking. Dishes like steamed brown bread, succotash, baked beans and the clambake all stem from the original people of New England, the Indians. Fruit, meat and seafood pies, boiled dinners and chowders can be clearly traced back to England. Shortly after the settlement of New England, a bustling shipping industry based on the export of salt cod made exotic fruits, spices and animals from the Caribbean and the Orient frequently available, if not commonplace. The Shakers, who were anything but boring cooks, also had a significant effect on the cooking of this region. Later migrations of Irish, Italians, Chinese, Eastern Europeans, Greeks and Portuguese contributed to the diversity of food in New England. The Italians and Portuguese, in particular, have had a most profound influence. New migrations of people from Central America and Southeast Asia are making their mark today in our marketplaces and on our ever-changing art of cookery. And talented young American chefs all around New England have continually reworked and expanded this region's cooking repertoire. Recipes from some of the best are included in this book.

Instead of the provincial and stodgy stereotype that is all too often associated with New England, I have discovered an eclectic and exciting region, full of complexities and contrasts. So with a view to the present and a view to the past, I invite you to discover or rediscover New England by this tour. Welcome to my kitchen!

Jasper White
Boston, Massachusetts

Shellfish

Oysters

Oysters on the Halfshell

Jasper's Mignonette for Oysters

Fresh Horseradish and Lemon with Oysters

Apple Cider Mignonette for Wild Maine Oysters

Oyster Stew

Crispy Batter-Fried Oysters

Oyster, Ham and Wild Mushroom Tartlets

Baked Oysters with Leeks and Pancetta

Broiled New England Shellfish

Clams

Clams on the Halfshell

Green Tomato Cocktail Sauce for Clams

Juan's Sauce for Clams

Wasabi and Ginger with Clams

New England Clam Chowder

Steamers

Fried Clams

Clam Fritters

Pasta with Green Clam Sauce

Stuffed Quahogs

The Clambake

Mussels

Mussel and Ham Bisque

Cold Mussels

Mussels Steamed with White Wine, Garlic and Fresh Herbs

Portuguese-Style Steamed Mussels

Scallops

Raw Cape Scallops with Lemon, Onion and Capers

Salad of Scallops, Pear and Celery

Cape Scallops Sautéed with Garlic and Sundried Tomatoes

Fried Scallops

Batter-Fried Scallops

Breaded Fried Scallops

Flash-Fried Scallops

Grilled Sea Scallops

Grilled Sea Scallops with Green Onions and Curry

Curry Butter

Periwinkles

Periwinkles Poached in a Spicy Saffron Broth

Periwinkles with Escargot Butter

Blanched Periwinkles

Sea Urchins

Squid

Squid and Olive Salad

Fried Squid, North-End Style

Maine Shrimp

Shrimp Bisque with Shrimp Toasts

Shrimp Toasts

Saffron Noodles with Maine Shrimp, Country Bacon and Pine Nuts

Nam Tran's Shrimp and Cabbage Salad

Shrimp Stock with Tomato

Shrimp Butter

Maine Crab (Rock Crab)

Antipasto with Maine Crab and Prosciutto

Garden Tomatoes with Maine Crab

Maine Crabmeat Turnovers

Crab Cakes

Crab or Lobster Salad

Lobster

Lobster and Corn Chowder

Chunky Lobster Stew

Tomalley Croutons

Warm Salad with Lobster, Foie Gras and Papaya

Lobster Sausage with Savoy Cabbage

Warm Savoy Slaw

Lobster Sautéed with Spring Vegetables

Panroasted Lobster with Chervil and Chives

Grilled Lobster

New England is the world's premier shellfish region. I do not know of any other place that can compare, not only in terms of the abundance but also the quality and variety of shellfish. Lobsters, crabs, scallops, oysters, clams, mussels, periwinkles, sea urchins, squid and even shrimp all live in our icy waters. They are the stars of New England cookery, and many of the classics, as well as new dishes are inspired by them.

Tales of plenty were told by the early settlers: six-foot walls of lobsters piled on the beach after a storm; farmers using lobsters as fertilizer; fishermen using lobster and crabs as bait. They go on and on. For certain, lobster was so abundant that it was regarded as food for the lower classes. And I myself, 350 years later, have seen mussels piled almost three feet high on the beach after a hurricane.

Our colonial forefathers were very fond of oysters and clams but never ate mussels and rarely ate the other shellfish. They were an odd bunch, living out the winter on salt pork and beans while good shellfish rotted on the beach. Unlike contemporary man, however, they did not intentionally destroy or overlook the destruction of the natural habitat.

We are still blessed with abundance, but that is changing at an alarmingly fast pace. The problem with shellfish is singular. Oil spills, ocean dumping of waste and other forms of manmade pollution are poisoning the shallow waters that are the natural habitat of most shellfish. Bivalves—oysters, clams, scallops and mussels—are like filters; they strain micro-organisms from the ocean water that passes through their bodies. Their flavor is the flavor of the sea. And if that sea tastes like diesel fuel, so will they. If there is bacteria from human waste in the water, it will infect the shellfish. At the present rate of pollution of our coastal waters, our grandchildren will have to go to museums to view relics of the foods we once highly cherished. We must do whatever we can to stop the reckless pollution of our waters; they are too precious a resource to let them be destroyed.

Here are a few general rules that are helpful when cooking shellfish:

- Cook only the freshest of shellfish, from unpolluted waters. Cooking will not destroy the elements in bad shellfish that are harmful to man; you can get just as sick eating a bad clam cooked as one that is raw. If there are any abnormalities in color, odor, flavor or shape, discard the shellfish. If you are not sure but think something is wrong, go with your instincts.
- Never overcook shellfish. If they are suitable for eating raw, like clams, oysters and scallops, cook them just until they are warmed through. Other shellfish should be cooked until the meat is set. Overcooking destroys the natural flavor and texture of shellfish.
- Be very careful with the use of salt. Many shellfish impart enough so that no additional salt

is needed; all release some salt of their own. Oversalting can mask the delicate flavor of shellfish.

- Buy for quality, not for price. If you want to save money, eat pasta and beans; if you want good shellfish, pay the price. I am not saying that you should not be conscious of prices; you should be. I only want to stress that price should not be the determining factor in buying. Pick the quality you want, then haggle or check around to see if someone else is offering the same quality at a lower price.

The reality is that when it comes to shellfish, there are no bargains to be had. What is to be had, however, are the tastiest, briniest clams and oysters imaginable, the sweetest scallops and shrimp you have ever tasted, and the most succulent lobsters in the world. All are well worth the expense. All are worth saving for future generations.

OYSTERS

I can think of no better way to start a meal—or a book—than with oysters. Ice-cold freshly opened oysters arouse the appetite and the taste buds; some people say they stimulate even more. I can't comment on that, but I do know that a dozen oysters definitely give you a burst of energy.

Two types of oysters are harvested and consumed in New England; both can be found cultivated and in the wild. By far the most abundant and popular is the native Eastern oyster, which ranges from Nova Scotia to Florida. This oyster takes on different names as well as characteristics, depending on its waters of origin. In the South, it is known as the Carolina, the Chincoteague, the Chesapeake and so on. In the Mid-Atlantic states, it is most often called a Blue Point. New England oysters take on the name of the nearest bay or town, and there are many different ones; Cedar Points, Pemaquids, Cotuits, Wellfleets and Sheepscotts are a few of the most popular. The names are important to remember because the oysters are truly different from one place to the next. Wellfleet is considered one of the world's great oyster beds. In fact, the oysters from this bay were so popular during colonial times that they were completely depleted by the year 1820. The beds were reseeded shortly afterward with oysters from the Chesapeake region, and to this day the demand is still greater than the supply. What makes them special is that Wellfleet's shallow bay has an incredibly fast-moving twelve-foot tide that washes in a phenomenal amount of fresh ocean water and feed twice a day. The strong current and the abundant feed cause the oysters to grow large and elongated. It is very easy to distinguish a true Wellfleet; if the opportunity to taste it arises, don't miss it.

The second type of oyster to grace our shores is a fairly recent import from France, the European flat, often referred to as a Belon. Properly speaking, however, Belon is the name for a European flat oyster found off the coast of Brittany. This is like giving French names (Chablis, Burgundy) to American wines: not correct but there's not much you can do about it once the names take hold. French oyster seedlings were first brought to Maine about twenty years ago for commercial cultivation. Acceptance of this very briny, somewhat bitter-flavored oyster was slow, and production often outweighed demand, forcing some pioneer farmers out of business. The oyster itself adapted extremely well and flourished. Beds of wild European flat oysters are not uncommon, though if discovered, they are rarely left undisturbed. Producers are finding a bigger market today for Belons; it looks as if they are here to stay. I personally consider them to be among the tastiest of all our New England oysters.

This country was once blessed with an extraordinary abundance of seafood, but in recent times our magnificent coastal waters have become fatally polluted through greed and carelessness and apathy. New England oysters are becoming scarcer with every passing year. What is most frightening is the devastation caused by oil spills. About eight years ago, the Cotuit oyster beds were closed by a spill. It took five years before the oysters could be harvested again, and they are not the fabulous Cotuits they once were. Just last year a spill off Martha's Vineyard ruined the wonderful oyster beds of Tisbury, another of my favorites. Farther south the problem is even worse. New Jersey, once a major supplier of oysters and clams, is all but completely shut down and the Chesapeake region is not far behind. Sometimes I fear that in my lifetime the experience of eating fresh shellfish will exist only in memory.

How to Buy and Store Oysters

There is an old saying that oysters are good only during months with the letter R. This belief is based on the fact that oysters spawn in summer. (Oysters are protected by law during the spawning season in New England.) But I hold that New England oysters are better in May than in September. In May the waters are still very cold and most oysters have not yet begun to spawn; in September the spawning is over, but the waters are still warm. Oysters from warmer waters have a certain flabbiness as they say in the wine trade, that is, a loss of definition of taste, and a less appealing texture than those from icy cold waters. Spawning also gives oysters a mushy texture.

On a recent trip down South, I was fortunate to partake in an oyster roast. Oysters were the big topic of conversation and my cold water theory was shot down as chauvinistic by my Carolina friends who, not surprisingly, considered their oysters the greatest. My reply was, "If y'all's oysters are so good, why do y'all cook 'em?" I omitted the fact that we cook oysters up North as well. I do believe, however, that the single greatest way to eat oysters is raw, on the halfshell. It is the true test of an oyster's merit.

With oysters, as with all seafood, freshness equals quality. The best way to tell if an oyster is fresh is to feel the weight. A very fresh oyster feels heavy for its size and is full of liquid that tastes like the sea, for obvious reasons. This briny taste is the most beautiful flavor an oyster can have. Purchase your oysters from a reputable fishmonger, but make no assumptions. The only way to get the best is to know what the best is and demand it.

Store oysters (and other bivalves) refrigerated and pressed very tightly against each other to keep them from opening. The best container is a sack made of burlap or some other porous material, tied tightly. Any oyster found open is dead and must be discarded.

How to Open an Oyster

Opening an oyster is strictly a matter of leverage. No brute strength is required or necessary.

At least one hour before opening, scrub the oysters under cold running water. Place them flat on a pan in the refrigerator, allowing them to relax. Remember, they are living creatures; too much shaking or handling will make them tense and harder to open.

Hold the oyster, flat side up, in a cloth or towel, pressed firmly against the work surface. Do not try to open an oyster in midair as you would a clam. Keep your hand out of the area where the knife could slip: I have seen an oyster knife go right through the palm of a hand. Place the tip of the knife in the Achilles' heel (see diagram) and turn your hand as if you were turning the throttle of a motorcycle, pushing in with steady pressure until you feel the snap. Now give a full twist to make enough of an opening to slide the knife along the top of the shell, cutting the muscle. The top of the shell is now off and all that is left to do is cut the bottom muscle. Keep the oyster level at all times, so as not to lose any of the juice. Always serve on crushed ice, which holds the oyster level and keeps it cold. For shucked oysters simply slide the oyster and its juices into a small container and keep refrigerated until ready to use.

Oysters on the Halfshell

The purest, simplest way to serve oysters is raw with a squeeze of lemon and a twist of freshly ground pepper from the mill. To elaborate on this a little, you could cut a whole lemon into six or eight wedges. Then slice the wedges crosswise into paper-thin triangles and soak these for a few minutes in a bit of fresh lemon juice. Open the oysters and place on crushed ice. Put a slice of lemon and a little lemon juice on each oyster. Grind a bit of pepper over each and serve immediately. Real pepper lovers may prefer freshly cracked pepper (page 325). If desired, sprinkle with a small amount of chopped fresh parsley or chervil.

Jasper's Mignonette for Oysters

This mignonette is the one we serve most often at my restaurant. It works very well with Cape Cod and other Eastern oysters, which are the ones most readily available for us. The finely diced carrot adds a little sweetness and crunch; the champagne vinegar gives a crisp, clean bite.

MAKES ENOUGH FOR
THIRTY-SIX OYSTERS

2 tablespoons finely chopped
  shallots
1 tablespoon finely chopped
  carrot
2 tablespoons finely chopped
  fresh parsley
1 tablespoon freshly cracked
  black pepper (page 325)
¾ cup champagne vinegar
36 oysters, scrubbed

1. Combine all the shallots, carrot, parsley, pepper and vinegar and chill for at least 20 minutes.
2. Open the oysters as directed on page 6 and place on crushed ice. Spoon a little mignonette over each one.

VARIATION

Caviar with Oysters

This may not be the best way to eat caviar, but it certainly is the best way to eat oysters. Go light on the mignonette and finish with a dollop of your favorite caviar on each oyster. At the restaurant we usually use osetra, the medium-size (and medium-priced) caviar.

Fresh Horseradish and Lemon with Oysters

A simple but excellent preparation for raw oysters that is especially well suited to Wellfleets and other Eastern oysters. Although horseradish is certainly an assertive flavor, it will not mask the true flavor of the oyster when used in small amounts.

MAKES ENOUGH FOR
THIRTY-SIX OYSTERS

4 tablespoons finely grated fresh
  horseradish
1 tablespoon sour cream
2 tablespoons lemon juice
freshly ground black pepper
36 oysters, scrubbed

For Serving
lemon wedges, visible seeds
  removed
common crackers

1. Mix the horseradish, sour cream and lemon juice. Season to taste with pepper.
2. Open the oysters as directed on page 6 and place on a bed of crushed ice. Put a small dollop of the horseradish mixture on each oyster and serve with lemon wedges and common crackers.

Apple Cider Mignonette for Wild Maine Oysters

This mignonette is especially good with wild European flats, sometimes called Belons. These oysters were introduced for commercial cultivation and have taken so well to these parts that they can now be found growing wild along the Maine coast. They are famous for their strong, somewhat bitter flavor and their brininess. Essential to this dish, after very fresh oysters of course, is excellent quality apple cider vinegar; you can usually find it in a good natural foods store. The sauce gets its tartness from the vinegar, its sweetness from the apple, spice from the pepper and aroma from the shallots. Spoon just a little over the freshly opened oysters so as to enhance them, not drown them.

MAKES ENOUGH FOR
THIRTY-SIX OYSTERS

1 tablespoon finely chopped
   shallots
3 tablespoons finely chopped tart
   apple, such as Granny Smith
1 tablespoon cracked black
   pepper
1/3 cup apple cider vinegar
36 oysters, scrubbed

1. Combine the shallots, apple, pepper and vinegar and chill for at least 20 minutes.
2. Open the oysters as directed on page 6 and place on a bed of crushed ice. Spoon a little mignonette over each one.

Oyster Stew

Shellfish stew is so traditional I consider it a must for a proper Thanksgiving feast or other family holiday. On some occasions I serve this oyster stew; on others, Chunky Lobster Stew (page 47). Since shellfish stews are usually made with milk and butter, with just salt and pepper as seasoning, they remain very true to the flavor of whatever shellfish is used. In both my recipes I have elaborated on the ingredients to enrich the flavor while keeping the original premise of a clean and natural-flavored broth. First I make a stock to heighten the flavors, then I add heavy cream; together they equal the consistency of a stew made only with milk. The added benefit of using heavy cream is that it almost never breaks (curdles) the way milk often does.

SERVES SIX AS A STARTER

1 pint shucked oysters and their
   liquid
1/2 cup onion, cut in small
   (1/4 inch) dice
1/2 cup celery root or peeled
   celery cut in small (1/4 inch)
   dice
6 tablespoons unsalted butter
1 1/2 cups heavy cream

1. Pick through the oysters very carefully, removing any bits of shell. Place in a small saucepan with their liquid and 2 cups water. Heat slowly until the oysters begin to curl. Remove and set aside. Strain the liquid and set aside.
2. Slowly simmer the onion and celery root in butter in a soup pot until tender (about 6 minutes). Add the oyster-cooking liquid and heavy cream. Heat almost to the boiling point and simmer for 10 minutes. Add oysters, parsley and chervil. Season to taste with pepper. Simmer 1 minute more.

2 tablespoons chopped fresh
   parsley
1 tablespoon chopped fresh
   chervil
freshly ground pepper
common crackers for serving

3. Ladle into soup plates or bowls and serve with common crackers.

Crispy Batter-Fried Oysters

Fried oysters are wonderful as a snack or appetizer. Some late nights I frequent a little place in Boston's Chinatown called the Lucky Dragon. One of my favorite dishes is their very crisp fried oysters served with cassia-flavored salt, which you sprinkle on the oysters with your fingers. It is typical of the Chinese genius with food to add something as simple as a seasoned salt to make a dish complete. (Cassia is sometimes called Chinese or poor man's cinnamon.) Batter-fried oysters are great as a garnish with grilled steak or poultry as long as there is something to tie the two together, as in the Old-fashioned Club Steak with Oysters (page 172) for example.

SERVES FOUR AS AN APPETIZER

20 large oysters
Beer

Batter
¾ cup beer (½ bottle)
1 egg
2 tablespoons peanut oil
1 cup cornstarch
1 tablespoon chopped scallion or
   chives (optional)
salt (optional)
freshly ground black pepper

peanut oil for deep-frying
cornstarch for dredging

For Serving
Rémoulade or Tartare Sauce
   (page 333) or cassia salt (see
   Note)

1. Scrub the oysters and open them as directed on page 6. Drain well.
2. Combine the beer, egg and oil with the cornstarch. Whip to a smooth batter, stir in the scallions or chives, if using, and season to taste with salt and pepper. Omit the salt if serving the oysters with cassia salt.
3. Pour 3 inches of peanut oil into a deep-sided heavy pot and heat to 360 degrees. Dredge the shucked oysters lightly in cornstarch then dip in batter, dipping only as many at one time as you can fry in one batch. Do not crowd the pot or the oysters may stick together.
4. Fry a few at a time in the hot oil. Drain on paper towels and serve with sauce or flavored salt. It is always nice to serve hot oysters or any fried foods on a folded white napkin.

NOTE. To make cassia salt, mix ½ cup kosher salt with 1 teaspoon ground cassia. Heat very slowly in a dry skillet or wok until the salt starts to discolor slightly. Remove to a jar and allow to sit for at least 1 day for the flavors to marry. (You can buy ground cassia at spice shops and oriental markets.)

Oyster, Ham and Wild Mushroom Tartlets

If you read old cookbooks from New England, you will come across many recipes for oyster, scallop, lobster and clam pies. I find the old-fashioned seafood pie, a double-crusted concoction filled with shellfish and béchamel sauce, a bit heavy for the modern palate. A warm pastry shell filled with shellfish that has been cooked separately seems more suitable to me. This arrangement also ensures that the shellfish is not overcooked.

SERVES FOUR AS AN APPETIZER

½ recipe Thin Butter Crust
(page 284)
20 large oysters
2 tablespoons chopped shallots
1 cup sliced chanterelles or other
wild mushrooms
1 tablespoon unsalted butter
¼ cup dry white wine
¾ cup heavy cream
¼ cup Vermont or other cooked
smoked ham cut in medium
(½ inch) dice
juice of ½ lemon
freshly ground black pepper
1 tablespoon chopped fresh
parsley

1. Prepare the butter crust as directed on page 284 and line 4 tartlet tins (3½-inch or 4-inch size) and bake blind until fully cooked. Unmold the shells and place on a sheetpan. This can be done earlier in the day.

2. Shortly before serving, preheat the oven to 325 degrees. Open the oysters as directed on page 6, saving the juices and being careful not to mix any chips of shell in with the oysters.

3. Sauté the shallots and mushrooms slowly in butter in a small saucepan. After 5 minutes add the wine, cream and all of the juice from the oysters. Bring to a slow boil and continue simmering for about 8 minutes. Meanwhile, place the tartlets in the preheated oven. Add the ham and oysters to the mushroom mixture and simmer until the oysters curl (about 2 minutes).

4. Remove the tartlets from the oven and put on small plates. With a slotted spoon, remove the oysters and other solids from the pan and place in the tartlet shell. Put the saucepan back on the heat. Season to taste with lemon juice and pepper. Add the chopped parsley. The sauce should lightly coat a spoon; reduce it a bit more if necessary. Spoon over mixture in the pastry shells and serve immediately.

Baked Oysters with Leeks and Pancetta

This recipe works well with most oysters, provided they are not too small (at least three inches long). Best are the more full-flavored oysters, like Malpeques or Belons. If pancetta (Italian rolled unsmoked bacon) is not available or if you would prefer a smokier dish, use smoked bacon. The pancetta does allow more of the oyster flavor to come through, though.

SERVES FOUR AS AN APPETIZER

20 large or medium-size oysters
4 ounces pancetta, cut in very
fine julienne
4 medium leeks, trimmed,
washed and cut in very fine
julienne (3 cups)
2 tablespoons sweet butter
freshly ground black pepper
½ cup dry breadcrumbs
½ cup freshly grated romano
cheese
2 tablespoon chopped fresh
parsley
lemon wedges for serving

1. Wash and scrub the oysters thoroughly. Set aside in the refrigerator.

2. Render the pancetta in a sauté pan until crisp. Add the leeks and butter, turn down the heat and simmer until leeks are tender (5 to 8 minutes). Season to taste with pepper. Allow to cool.

3. Open the oysters as directed on page 6 and place on a pan of rock salt to hold them level. Spread a thin layer of the pancetta and leek mixture over each oyster. Spoon some of the juices over each one as well.

4. Preheat the broiler or preheat the oven to 450 degrees. Mix the breadcrumbs, cheese and parsley together and sprinkle over the oysters. Broil or bake in the preheated oven until the topping is lightly browned and the oysters plump (about 6 to 8 minutes in the oven, 4 to 5 minutes under the broiler). Transfer to oyster dishes or plates with rock salt. Serve with lemon wedges.

Broiled New England Shellfish

This is a wonderful appetizer. Most of the preparation can be done early in the day, so that all you have to do at the last minute is open a few clams and oysters and broil the shellfish. I can guarantee that you and your guests will be glad you took the trouble. The dish can be adapted to any combination of shellfish. For instance, if you do not want to bother with periwinkles or cannot find any, omit them and add a few extra clams, mussels or oysters.

SERVES FOUR AS AN APPETIZER

16 mussels
½ cup white wine
1 cup periwinkles (about 30)
6 tablespoons Garlic Butter
    (page 330)
¼ pound smoked bacon, cut in
    small (¼ × 1 inch) strips
8 slices (½ inch thick) baguette
    (long French bread)
8 medium-size oysters
12 littleneck or cherrystone
    clams
freshly ground black pepper
½ lemon
1 tablespoon chopped fresh
    parsley

1. Steam the mussels in white wine until just barely opened. Reserve the broth. Remove half of the shell. Cover the mussels on the halfshell with a damp towel, wrap in plastic and refrigerate until needed.

2. Blanch the periwinkles as described on page 31. Prepare the garlic butter. Refrigerate both.

3. Render the bacon only until partially cooked; it should be very limp. Set aside.

4. Toast the baguette slices on both sides. Leave out to dry.

5. Scrub the oysters and clams thoroughly and open them as directed on page 6 and page 13; save any juices that escape. Leave the oysters and clams on the halfshell.

6. Preheat the broiler. Line up the oysters, clams, mussels and periwinkles in a shallow roasting pan or on a sheetpan with sides. Put a small dollop of garlic butter on each piece of shellfish. Scatter the strips of bacon at random over the oysters, clams and mussels. Pour the mussel broth and juices from the oysters and clams over the shellfish. Most of this will reach the bottom of the pan. Grind pepper over the shellfish.

7. Place the pan of shellfish under the broiler and broil for about 4 to 5 minutes. The shellfish will cook, the bacon will crisp and the garlic butter will melt.

8. Put 2 slices of dry toast in the bottom of each soup plate. Quickly transfer the shellfish to the plates, distributing them evenly and keeping them level. The toast will help to keep the oysters level.

9. Squeeze the juice of half a lemon into the pan. Add the chopped parsley. Spoon the pan juices over the shellfish and serve at once.

CLANS

No longer the slave of ambition,
I laugh at the world and its shams
As I think of my pleasant condition,
Surrounded by acres of clams.
—ANONYMOUS

As the unknown author of the above verse, quoted by Evan Jones in his brilliant and prophetic book, *American Food,* suggests, clams have an earthy appeal, which makes them a favorite not only of New Englanders but of most Americans. Nearly everyone can relate to the traditional clam dishes—clam chowder, steamers, fritters; they need no justification. The clam works well with a variety of foods and seasonings, and most of the ethnic groups that have migrated to our shores have made good use of it. Of course, the clam was not a stranger to them.

How to Buy and Store Clams

Like an oyster, a clam should feel heavy in relation to its size. Clams should be stored refrigerated, wrapped tightly in a sack made of burlap or some other porous material. Their shells should be closed or stay closed when squeezed. Any that are open should be discarded.

The clam family is so complex and the nomenclature so varied that I would not even attempt to categorize or explain all the different types. I will limit myself to the common clams that are sold commercially, excluding some great local species, like the mahogany clam from Maine. These break down into three categories: the various quahogs or hard-shell clams, soft-shell clams and razor clams.

The quahog (pronounced co'hog) family includes many of the most popular and useful clams for cooking and eating raw. All have a very hard, rocklike shell. The largest of this family is the giant sea clam, harvested from deep ocean floors; it is usually processed for commercial use. It is also the clam of choice for traditional clam pie, but for general cooking purposes the sea clam is inferior to its smaller relatives. For this reason I have not included any recipes using them. It is important to note, however, that the sea clam represents an incredible food resource; as smaller clams from shallower beds are destroyed by pollution, this clam will become more and more important. The next size down is known as the quahog (although they are all quahogs). The larger quahog is used mostly in chowders or for stuffing.

Next by size is the cherrystone, the largest clam that is normally eaten raw. It is also excellent for cooking. The smallest of the quahog family are the littlenecks and the special count or count littlenecks. Count littlenecks are simply the smallest littlenecks, which are culled from the littleneck harvest. Littlenecks and counts are the best for eating raw, but are also very useful for cooking. They should always be just barely cooked, never overcooked.

The second type is soft-shell clams. They can be recognized by their long neck (siphon) and their soft, almost egglike textured shell. They are also known as steamer clams, piss clams and frying clams (when sold shucked for frying). These clams are very abundant and less expensive than hard-shell clams. Because they do not bury themselves very deeply in the sand, they are also the easiest to dig for.

The last type is the razor clam, an elongated species which is harvested almost completely for export to Japan, where it is used for sashimi. Although I have not included any recipes using this clam, it is very tasty and can be substituted in many of the recipes that follow, especially chowder. Razor clams are easy to shuck; I have seen it done using a spoon.

Clams are available year round but are best when the waters are the coldest. Be especially careful during the summer months when clams can contain very high levels of bacteria that are harmful to man.

How to Open a Clam

Scrub the clams under cold running water at least an hour before opening; lay them flat in the refrigerator. Think of the clam as a harp: the shapes are similar. Hold the clam upright (like a harp) firmly in the palm of your hand. The hinge should be at the top. Hold the clam knife at the base with your other hand. This hand only holds and guides the knife; the hand holding the clam does most of the work. Line up the blade of the clam knife with the Achilles' heel and parallel to the edge where the two shells meet. Curl the fingers of the hand holding the clam around the dull edge of the knife and exert steady pressure until the knife slides in. Now turn the clam so it is level and the juices don't escape. Twist the wrist of the hand holding the knife to make an opening wide enough to cut the top muscle. Keep the knife above the clam so as not to cut it when cutting the muscle. Break off the top shell and cut the bottom muscle. Keep the clam as level as possible to avoid spilling the juice. If serving on the halfshell, place the clams on crushed ice to keep the clams level and well chilled. If not, drop the clams into a container; be sure to save the juice. Keep refrigerated until ready to use.

Clams on the Halfshell

Ice-cold clams on the halfshell are very refreshing, and like oysters they awaken rather than dull the palate. The briny and robust flavor of clams makes them easy to pair with all kinds of flavors, especially acids. Most preparations are so easy that by offering a few or all of these toppings, you could make the next occasion you serve clams a very festive one, with little extra effort. Many people like cherrystones on the halfshell, but I prefer littlenecks and especially count littlenecks because of their size and texture. Open the clams as instructed and always serve on crushed ice.

Green Tomato Cocktail Sauce for Clams

The tartness of pickled green tomatoes blends well with horseradish in this unusual sauce.

MAKES ENOUGH FOR
THIRTY-SIX CLAMS

½ cup Pickled Green Tomatoes
   (page 340)
2 tablespoons finely grated
   horseradish
juice of ½ lemon
freshly ground black pepper
hot-pepper sauce or Chinese
   hot-chili oil
36 clams, littlenecks or
   cherrystones

1. Remove as much seed and pulp as possible from the tomatoes, then chop until very fine, almost pureed. Mix with the horseradish and lemon juice and season to taste with pepper and hot-pepper sauce or hot-chili oil. Chill for at least 20 minutes.

2. Open the clams as directed on page 13 and place on crushed ice. Put a small dollop of sauce on each clam and serve immediately.

Juan's Sauce for Clams

Like many other areas of the United States, New England has a new community of Central Americans. Kitchen work is often the easiest kind of work to find for immigrants because the language barrier is not as much of a problem. American chefs teach them to produce food in our style, but at the same time some of their style rubs off on us.

Juan Paiz came to Boston from El Salvador and has been the garde-manger at my restaurant since we opened in 1983. He is very talented with food and often brings me samples of his native cooking that he prepares at home. Knowing my passion for oysters and clams, he sometimes surprises me during the evening with a little plate of one or the other. The first time Juan served me these clams, I flipped. They were so good that I put them on the menu. Is this New England cookery? It is now!

MAKES ENOUGH FOR
THIRTY-SIX CLAMS

*2 tablespoons finely chopped red
  radish
2 tablespoons finely chopped red
  onion
2 tablespoons finely chopped
  fresh cilantro
1 teaspoon finely chopped fresh
  chilies, or more to taste
juice of 4 limes
36 clams, littlenecks or
  cherrystones*

1. Combine the chopped radish, onion, cilantro and chilies with the lime juice. Chill for at least 20 minutes.

2. Open the clams as directed on page 13 and place on crushed ice. Spoon a little sauce on top of each clam.

Wasabi and Ginger with Clams

Clams are excellent with this version of a traditional Japanese garnish. The grenadine turns the ginger a light shade of pink, which makes a nice contrast with the green horseradish; if you prefer the natural color of ginger, use sugar instead.

MAKES ENOUGH FOR
THIRTY-SIX CLAMS

*2 teaspoons wasabi powder
sugar
1 teaspoon white rice wine
  vinegar
1 piece (2 inches) ginger
grenadine syrup
36 clams, littlenecks or
  cherrystones*

1. Mix the wasabi powder with a pinch of sugar, a few drops of the rice wine vinegar and enough water to make it the consistency of wet sand.

2. Peel the ginger and cut into julienne strips as fine as possible. Simmer 2 minutes in enough water to cover. Flavor the water with rice wine vinegar and a few drops of grenadine. Cool and keep in liquid.

3. Open the clams as directed on page 13 and place on crushed ice. Put a few pieces of ginger on each clam and top with a very small dab of wasabi.

New England Clam Chowder

No one New England dish has been subjected to more abuse than clam chowder. My recipe may not be the definitive or only authentic recipe for this famous dish, but it has the virtue of being very true to spirit and style of the original. Chowder is a one-pot dish, more of a stew than a soup. It should be thick but not thickened, except by the starch released from the potatoes during the cooking.

Chowder is a perfect main course for lunch or a light supper. Serve it with common crackers, biscuits or Clam Fritters. Fritters and chowder are great together. With my Lobster and Corn Chowder (page 46), I usually serve Corn Fritters (page 267).

SERVES EIGHT AS A MAIN COURSE

10 pounds quahogs in the shell
scraps of onion, celery, thyme
 and bay leaf (optional)
¼ pound smoked bacon or salt
 pork, cut in small (¼ inch)
 dice (see Note)
2 medium onions, cut in medium
 (½ inch) dice (2½ cups)
2 bay leaves
1 tablespoon chopped fresh
 thyme
2 tablespoons unsalted butter
5 or 6 red or white new
 potatoes, roughly cut in
 ½-inch dice
2 cups heavy cream
freshly ground black pepper
2 tablespoons chopped fresh
 parsley

For Serving
common crackers
Cream Biscuits (page 269)
Clam Fritters (page 18)

1. Scrub the quahogs thoroughly and place in a large pan with 2 cups water and any scraps of onion, celery, thyme and bay leaf you may have around. Cover and place on high heat until the quahogs are steamed completely open.

2. Pour off liquid and reserve. Remove the clams from their shells; roughly chop (about ⅜-inch pieces); set aside. Carefully pour the liquid (about 3 cups) through a fine strainer; set aside.

3. Slowly render the bacon or salt pork in a soup pot until slightly crisp. Add the onions, bay leaves, thyme and butter. When the onions are translucent, add the potatoes and the broth from the quahogs. Simmer until potatoes are cooked (about 12 minutes).

4. Add the chopped clams and cream and simmer 5 minutes more. Season to taste with pepper and add chopped parsley. Ladle into soup plates or cups. Serve with common crackers, cream biscuits and clam fritters.

NOTE. Salt pork is traditional, but I prefer the smoky flavor the bacon imparts.

Steamers

My favorite scenario for steamers is a drizzly afternoon at an oceanside bar or restaurant. Draft beer, steamers, a few friends, a few side orders of clam fritters and not having to work; one of life's truly important moments. The best restaurant for steamers is one that keeps the clams in salt-water tanks.

Steamers are easy to make at home, and they are the perfect starter for an outdoor barbecue. I like to steam the clams in beer and water, but it is fine to use all water. Figure on one pound of clams per person. You will need a big table with enough room for the bowls of steamers, broth and drawn butter for each person and empty bowls for the shells. You will also need lots of napkins and plenty of beer.

Most people peel the little skin off the neck of the clam and then, holding the neck with their fingers, dip the clam into the broth to heat and rinse it. Then it goes into the butter and is popped in the mouth, all in one motion. After the clams are all gone, you drink some of the broth. There is usually a little sand in the bottom of the cup, so don't drink it all.

SERVES SIX AS AN APPETIZER OR SNACK

6 pounds soft-shell clams
Drawn Butter
12 tablespoons (1½ sticks) unsalted butter
juice of ½ lemon
salt and freshly ground black pepper

1 bottle or can (12 ounces) beer
1 onion, roughly chopped
2 celery stalks, roughly chopped
4 cloves garlic, finely chopped
4 bay leaves
1 tablespoon black peppercorns

1. Soak the clams in a big pot of cold water. Mix them around a bit and remove to another pot of cold water. Repeat this several times until the clams are very clean.

2. For the drawn butter, put the butter in a pan in a warm spot on the stove. If your stove has no such place, put the pan on low heat and melt the butter. Season with lemon juice and salt and pepper to taste; stir well to mix the components of the butter (fat, liquid and milk solids).

3. Combine the beer with 1 cup water, the onion, celery, garlic, bay leaves and peppercorns in a large steam pot. Bring to a boil. After 5 minutes, carefully add the clams and cover the pot. Check in about 5 minutes. The clams should be completely opened and cooked through.

4. Quickly remove the clams to bowls and rush to the table. Pour the broth through a strainer, stopping before the little bit of sand at the bottom of the pot goes into the strainer. Pour the broth into hot cups, pour the drawn butter into small bowls and bring both to the table. Dig in!

Fried Clams

Follow these directions for perfectly crisp fried clams. They are relatively inexpensive and are great for snacks or for lunch. Serve with one or more of the mayonnaise-based sauces or just with lemon wedges. Frying clams are soft-shell clams that are sold already shucked. Be sure to get nice fresh ones.

SERVES SIX AS AN ENTREE

2 pounds frying clams
2 cups milk
1 cup all-purpose flour
1 cup johnnycake meal or cornmeal
1 teaspoon salt
1 teaspoon cayenne pepper
peanut oil for deep-frying

For Serving
lemon wedges
mayonnaise-based sauces (page 333)

1. Pick over the clams for fragments of shell and put in the milk to soak. Mix the flour, johnnycake meal or cornmeal, salt and cayenne pepper together.

2. Preheat 3 inches of oil to 375 degrees. Lift the clams out of the milk with a wire basket or slotted spoon, drain thoroughly and place in the flour mixture. Be sure all the clams are well coated.

3. Drop about a third of the batch at a time in the hot oil. They will take only 1 minute to cook. Drain on paper towels and serve immediately. Garnish with lemon wedges and sauce.

Clam Fritters

Clam fritters or clam cakes are most commonly served as a side dish with New England Clam Chowder (page 16); they are also good with Steamers (page 16) or on their own with one of the mayonnaise-based sauces (page 333). They make a welcome addition to a summer buffet or other informal occasions. The basic recipe is perfect for fritters served with chowder, but the batter can be embellished with all sorts of things, like diced bacon (cooked), corn kernels, chopped onions or fresh herbs.

MAKES ABOUT TWO DOZEN FRITTERS

5 pounds quahogs or
   cherrystones
2 cups all-purpose flour
1 cup johnnycake meal or
   cornmeal
2 teaspoons baking powder
4 eggs, lightly beaten
1 cup milk
4 tablespoons unsalted butter or
   bacon fat
½ cup chopped scallions
salt and freshly ground pepper
corn oil for deep-frying

1. Wash the clams and steam open in ½ cup of water; chop and set aside. Reserve 1 cup of the juice.
2. Combine the flour, johnnycake meal or cornmeal, baking powder and eggs. Mix well.
3. Heat the milk, clam juice and butter or bacon fat until the fat melts. Slowly add to the flour and egg mixture.
4. Fold in the chopped clams and scallions and season to taste with salt and pepper. Refrigerate for at least 1 hour.
5. Heat the oil in a deep-fat-fryer to 375 degrees. Drop the batter by the tablespoonful into the hot oil and fry until golden brown. Drain on paper towels and serve hot.

Pasta with Green Clam Sauce

The city of Boston is a monument to the talented Italian masons who built many of the grand hotels, homes and other buildings around the city. Italian immigrants also had a profound influence on cuisine in New England. Much of the cooking brought from Italy, however, has become bastardized over the years. Rather than throw these dishes away, I like to try to restore them. This is a variation on linguine with red or white clam sauce, a standard in many Italian restaurants in the Northeast.

While fresh noodle dough is necessary for stuffed and flavored pastas, only top-quality dry pasta gives a true al dente effect. At my restaurant we dry our own homemade noodles when flavored noodles are needed, but when plain semolina noodles are the order of the day, we buy them at one of the many Italian food markets around the corner in Boston's North End. For this dish, use top-quality linguine or spaghetti.

SERVES FOUR AS AN APPETIZER

30 small littleneck clams
   (3½ pounds)
½ pound dry linguine or other
   pasta
⅓ cup olive oil

1. Clean and shuck the clams as directed on page 13, saving the juice. Bring a pot of salted water to a boil. Put the pasta in the boiling water.

2 bay leaves
*2 tablespoons finely chopped
    garlic (6 to 8 cloves)*
1 medium onion, finely chopped
½ teaspoon crushed red pepper
¼ cup dry white wine
*3 tablespoons chopped Italian
    parsley*
*2 tablespoons chopped fresh
    basil*
*2 tablespoons chopped fresh
    chives*
2 tablespoons unsalted butter
*½ cup freshly grated parmesan
    or romano cheese*
freshly ground black pepper

2. Heat the olive oil and bay leaves in a 10-inch sauté pan. Add the garlic, onion and crushed red pepper; cook on high heat. When the onions and garlic start to brown (4 minutes), add the wine, the clams and their juice, the parsley, basil and chives. Simmer 1 minute. Taste the pasta; it should be al dente. Drain and add to the pan; add the butter and cheese. Remove from the heat. Season with ground pepper; no salt is necessary. Serve in soup bowls or plates.

Stuffed Quahogs

This is street food, sold at festivals, fairs and roadside stands. At home it can be served as a snack or as a side dish for a cookout or casual buffet. This stuffing is made with finely diced bread rather than breadcrumbs. By using small cubes of dried bread and mixing gently, you keep the stuffing light and crisp.

SERVES SIX AS AN APPETIZER

*1 baguette (long French bread),
    cut in ¼-inch dice (4 cups)*
*¼ pound pancetta or bacon,
    finely diced*
12 quahogs
⅓ cup olive oil
3 tablespoons chopped garlic
*2 medium onions, finely chopped
    (2 cups)*
½ teaspoon crushed red pepper
2 eggs
*2 tablespoons chopped fresh
    basil*
*1 tablespoon chopped fresh
    oregano*
*2 tablespoons chopped fresh
    parsley*
*⅔ cup grated parmesan or
    romano cheese*
salt and freshly ground pepper
*6 tablespoons unsalted butter,
    sliced thin*
lemon wedges for serving

1. Preheat the oven to 300 degrees. Place the bread in the preheated oven and toast until completely dry (15 minutes). Set aside.

2. Render the pancetta or bacon in a sauté pan until it begins to crisp slightly. Drain on paper towels and set aside.

3. Scrub the quahogs well, then steam with ⅔ cup of water in a tightly covered pot until they open (about 6 minutes). Strain the broth through a fine strainer and set aside. Chop the clams into small (¼- to ½-inch) pieces and set aside. Clean the shells thoroughly by boiling in water.

4. Heat the olive oil in a sauté pan and add the garlic, onions, and crushed red pepper; cook until the onions are translucent. Allow to cool.

5. Combine 1 cup of clam broth with 2 eggs in a large mixing bowl; mix well. Add the onion mixture, the chopped clams, the pancetta and the basil, oregano and parsley; toss well. Add the cheese and bread and fold everything together so that it is mixed but not overmixed. Season to taste with salt (very little will be needed) and pepper; do this early in the mixing so the seasoning gets distributed evenly.

6. Preheat the oven to 400 degrees. Fill each shell with stuffing. Place a thin slice of butter on each one. Arrange on a sheetpan (rock salt helps keep the clams level, but it is not necessary). Bake in the preheated oven for 25 minutes or until golden brown. Serve with lemon wedges.

The Clambake

The clambake, "the most colorful, joyous and festive of American feasts," as Craig Claiborne once called it, is more than just a Northeast tradition. It is one of the few American Indian rituals to be assimilated into American culture. This way of steaming food with hot rocks and seaweed in a pit dug in the sand is a tribute to the Indians' ingenuity and their harmony with nature. Everything new in New England cookery seems to pale by comparison. Today's clambake is probably not much different from the clambakes of four hundred or maybe even a thousand years ago. Animal skins have been replaced by tarps, and cheesecloth has been added for convenience. Melted butter is new as is beer. Other additions, such as *linguiça* and *chouriço,* have been contributed by later settlers. I can't help thinking that if we had applied more of this kind of adaptation to American Indian culture, we all would have benefited from it.

The basic ingredients of a clambake vary a bit from place to place. Chicken is found at some clambakes, sausage and even hot dogs at others. I have heard of placing a few giant sea clams amid the hot rocks in order to flavor the steam. In Maine the meal is called a lobster-bake, in honor of the most popular ingredient found at every clambake. Corn on the cob is an absolute must, as are clams (littlenecks or soft-shells). New potatoes are also very common, but a mixture of potatoes and sweet potatoes is not unheard of. Other ingredients might include boiling onions or other root vegetables, fresh crabs, mussels, oysters or even whole fish. The important thing is that the food be layered from bottom to top according to the amount of heat needed to cook each one. Those requiring the longest cooking time are put at the bottom, closest to the source of heat. Even for a small clambake, a lot of seaweed is needed. The best is the very common and abundant rockweed, which has small bumps filled with sea water. When heated they burst and give off steam. If you are unable to gather it yourself, most lobster dealers will sell you some. In addition to that, you will need shovels for digging the pit, tarps for lining it, cheesecloth for packaging the food and brooms for sweeping the stones. A clambake is an all-day affair, so bring along a full day's worth of drinks and a few snacks to nibble on during the morning. (And don't forget to pack some watermelon and homemade pies for dessert.) It is wise to dig the pit and gather the wood and driftwood and stones the day before if possible. For enough food for twenty-four, the pit should be 4 feet deep, 3 or 4 feet wide and 6 feet long.

You can have a clambake on a rocky beach as well as a sandy beach. I learned to make a rocky beach clambake from my friend John Stevens from Boothbay Harbor, Maine, and it is my favorite setting. The heat from solid rocks is so intense, it seldom takes longer than an hour for the food to cook; I think the results are superior. Because it is difficult to dig a deep pit on a rocky beach, the layers may come a foot over the ground. You will need a larger tarp, but it will still work.

SERVES ABOUT TWENTY-FOUR

6 to 8 pounds small Maine
   potatoes
½ bushel cherrystone or
   littleneck clams
4 dozen ears of corn

1. Cover the bottom of the pit with large stones, gathered from the beach. Build a roaring fire with wood and driftwood. Keep stoking the fire for 2 hours. Now, allow the wood to burn off. This will take at least 2 more hours. The stones should be red-hot. Sweep away any embers from the stones.

2. While the fire is blazing, package the foods (except the lobsters and crabs) in cheesecloth. Make flat packages, 1½ by 2 feet

5 pounds boiling onions
½ bushel freshly picked mussels
6 to 8 pounds linquiça *or other sausage*
24 live lobsters, about 1 pound each
live crabs (optional)

For Serving
drawn butter (page 330)
lemon wedges
salt
pepper
hot-pepper sauce
Anadama Bread (page 274) or Boston Brown Bread (page 270) or rolls

square. Anything that requires rinsing should be rinsed in the ocean prior to packaging.

3. Once the stones are ready, you must work quickly. Cover the red-hot stones with a thick (8 to 10 inches) layer of seaweed. Place the packages of potatoes and clams on top of the seaweed. Add a thinner layer of seaweed (6 inches) and place the corn and onions on top. Add another thin layer of seaweed and place the mussels and sausages on top. Finally, add a thin layer of seaweed and top it with the live lobsters and crabs, if using. Place the lobsters so the tails point toward the center. Since lobsters walk backward, they will stay put as they back into one another. Cover with seaweed and place a large, thick, wet tarp over the pit. Secure the tarp with stones and sand so the pit becomes airtight.

4. After 1 hour, check the lobsters. If they are ready, the bake is ready, but most likely they will take another 30 minutes or so.

5. Remove the lobsters, crabs and packages of food and serve with lots of drawn butter, lemon wedges, salt and pepper, hot-pepper sauce, other condiments and bread or rolls.

MUSSELS

You never have to look very far along the New England coast to find mussels. They are incredibly abundant. When you pick your own, there is obviously no reason to worry about quality and freshness, just be sure they are from clean waters and that there is no "red tide" in your area. ("Red tide" occurs when certain microscopic organisms turn the water yellow or brown or red in a so-called algae bloom. Fish and especially shellfish become contaminated and risk being toxic to man.)

I have spent many a morning or afternoon, depending on the tide, with my wife and our dearest friends gathering mussels along the rocky beaches of Little Compton, Rhode Island. It is always a group effort, which we all enjoy later in the day in an eating orgy. Big bowls of freshly picked mussels steamed with white wine and garlic are our starter. Later we may grill some lobsters or bluefish and serve them with all sorts of summer salads, but the mussels always seem the most important because we gathered them ourselves. It is all very tribal, the sharing of work followed later by the sharing of food and friendship. It is what good food is really all about.

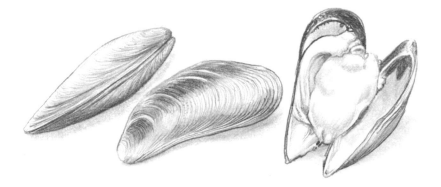

When buying mussels, the rules are the same as for oysters and clams: they should feel heavy for their size; the shell should be closed or stay closed when squeezed; they should have no perceptible odor; and their shells should be neither too soft nor too brittle. I prefer uncultivated mussels, which are more full flavored; they are usually smaller than the cultivated ones. Store mussels in a tight-fitting porous sack in the refrigerator.

Shortly before cooking (mussels are always cooked), scrub the mussels under cold running water and remove the "beard" by tearing it away from the shell. This job is made easier if a kitchen towel is used instead of bare hands.

Occasionally during the summer months you find tiny crabs inside mussels and oysters. I have heard these referred to as "oyster crabs." They are not parasites; on the contrary, they are feed for the shellfish. They are harmless and even considered a delicacy by some people. I personally find them a nuisance and disagreeable in appearance, but there is no way to remove the crabs and still deliver the mussels to the table steaming hot.

Mussel and Ham Bisque

When I carve a bone-in ham or shoulder, I am never too precise; I always leave some meat attached to the bone for future use. You will see a number of pork and shellfish dishes in this book. The type of pork—ham, bacon, pancetta, salt pork or fresh pork—and the ratio of pork to shellfish determine the final outcome: no two dishes taste alike. This soup is my down-home (or should I say Down East?) version of that suave modern French classic, mussel and saffron bisque.

SERVES EIGHT AS A STARTER

3 pounds uncultivated mussels
1 cup dry white wine
4 tablespoons olive oil
2 medium onions, cut in small
    (¼ inch) dice (2 cups)
2 tablespoons finely chopped
    garlic (6 to 8 cloves)
2 medium carrots, peeled and
    finely chopped (1 cup)
1 teaspoon whole black
    peppercorns
2 bay leaves
½ teaspoon Spanish string
    saffron
3 tablespoons all-purpose flour
1 small meaty ham bone
1 ripe tomato, roughly chopped
2 cups heavy cream
salt and freshly ground pepper
chopped chives or parsley for
    garnish

1. Scrub and debeard the mussels, Discard any that are open.

2. Bring the white wine and 2 cups of water to a boil in a large pot. Add the mussels and cover tightly. Steam the mussels until open (6 minutes). Strain the broth through a fine strainer; set aside. Remove mussels from their shells; set aside.

3. Heat the olive oil in a soup pot, then add the onions, garlic and carrots. Simmer for 5 minutes or until the onions are translucent. Add the peppercorns, bay leaves, saffron and flour. Continue to cook for 5 minutes, stirring constantly.

4. Slowly add 5 cups of broth (if you do not have 5 cups, make up the difference with water) a little at a time, allowing the soup to thicken before adding more broth. When all the broth has been blended in, add the ham bone and tomato. Simmer slowly for 1 hour, skimming the foam off the top occasionally.

5. Remove the ham bone and any pieces of ham that have fallen off the bone. Dice the ham into very small (¼ inch) pieces. Pour the soup through a medium strainer. Bring the strained soup back to a boil. Skim the soup again, add the cream and turn down to a simmer. Add the mussels and diced ham. Simmer 2 minutes. Season to taste with salt (very little will be needed) and ground pepper. Serve in soup plates or bowls and sprinkle a little chopped chives or parsley on each.

Cold Mussels

Mussels are not eaten raw, but cooked and chilled mussels have a very appealing flavor and texture. They can be served in the shell as an hors d'oeuvre or removed from the shell and mixed with other foods in a cold salad. Pasta, beans, potatoes; vegetables, greens, lettuces; curry, basil, saffron and lemon—all are suitable. There is a lot of room for creativity. For example, take the components of any good hot mussel dish, such as the Portuguese-style Steamed Mussels (page 24), and transform them into a salad. Or serve mussels in the shell, atop a small bed of chilled wilted spinach with some Aïoli (page 332). Or mix cold cooked rice with mussels, shrimp, roast peppers, olives and tomatoes and toss in a savory vinaigrette. Use your imagination.

One cup of white wine or water is enough to steam open five pounds of mussels. Use seasonings that are compatible with the final dish. Scrub and debeard the mussels first; discard any that are open. They should take about six minutes in a tightly covered pot. Save the broth and try to incorporate it into whichever preparation you choose. For instance, if you are making a mayonnaise-based sauce, whip a little of the broth into the mayonnaise. Many cold mussel dishes can be prepared well in advance, but you should sauce them just before serving.

Mussels Steamed with White Wine, Garlic and Fresh Herbs

This is the way we usually eat mussels that we pick ourselves at the beach in Rhode Island. It is always casual and we eat them like steamers, with a little broth and drawn butter. This is the fun way; for a more serious presentation see the note at the end of the recipe.

SERVES FOUR AS AN ENTREE

3½ pounds uncultivated mussels
½ cup dry white wine
3 tablespoons finely chopped
    garlic (about 10 cloves)
12 whole black peppercorns
½ cup coarsely chopped mixed
    fresh herbs, such as thyme,
    basil, chervil, parsley and
    chives
drawn butter (page 330)

1. Scrub and debeard the mussels. Discard any that are opened.
2. Combine the wine, garlic, peppercorns and herbs in a large pot. Bring to a full boil, add the mussels and cover tightly. Steam until opened (about 6 minutes). Rush the steaming hot mussels to the table along with bowls of broth and drawn butter. You will also need extra bowls for the empty shells.
3. Remove each mussel by hand, dip it into broth, then into butter, then into your mouth, all in one swift motion. After the mussels are gone, drink the broth.

NOTE. Finish the dish in the kitchen if a less casual presentation is desired. Steam the mussels, omitting the whole peppercorns, transfer them to individual bowls and cover temporarily to keep hot. Pour the broth with the garlic and herbs into a hot frying pan and reduce by half. Remove from the stove and whip in 8 tablespoons of butter. Season to taste with salt and pepper, spoon over the mussels and serve immediately.

Portuguese-Style Steamed Mussels

New England has a large Portuguese population, which is concentrated in large fishing centers like New Bedford, Gloucester and Provincetown, Massachusetts. Most of the Portuguese who immigrated to New England were experienced fishermen, and they are the dominant ethnic group in the fishing industry today. Many Sunday afternoons I have observed Portugese families gathering mussels and other shellfish off the rocky beaches of southern Massachusetts and Rhode Island. Later in the day they cook the mussels with white wine and lots of garlic, and small pieces of onion, bell pepper, and *chouriço* sausage. In Portugal there is a special oval-shaped pot for cooking mussels or clams, called the *cataplana*.

SERVES FOUR AS AN ENTREE

3 pounds uncultivated mussels
4 tablespoons olive oil
3 small bay leaves
1 tablespoon finely chopped garlic (3 or 4 cloves)
1 medium onion, cut in small (¼ inch) dice (1 cup)
1 small bell pepper, green or red, cut in small (¼ inch) dice
2 medium tomatoes, peeled, seeded and finely chopped
¼ pound chouriço *or* linguiça *sausage, thinly sliced (see Note)*
1 cup dry white wine
2 tablespoons chopped Italian parsley
2 tablespoons chopped fresh cilantro
freshly ground black pepper

1. Scrub and debeard the mussels. Discard any that are open.
2. Heat the olive oil and bay leaves in a large pot. Add the garlic, onion and bell pepper. Cook 5 minutes until vegetables are tender. Add the tomatoes, *chouriço* and wine. Simmer 5 minutes. Add the mussels and cover tightly. Steam the mussels until open (6 minutes).
3. Transfer the mussels to bowls and return the sauce to the heat. Add the parsley and cilantro and season to taste with ground pepper. Spoon the sauce over the mussels and serve immediately. Provide empty bowls for the shells.

NOTE. *Chouriço* is a garlicky dry sausage, similar to the more widely available chorizo, which may be substituted for it. *Linguiça* is similar to *chouriço*, but thinner.

SCALLOPS

Scallops are so versatile I hardly know where to begin. They can be served raw, cured (as in seviche), smoked, fried, stir-fried, sautéed, grilled, broiled, poached or steamed. They work well with many different spices, vegetables, other seafoods and even meat and poultry. If you are creative, you will never run out of ways to prepare scallops for appetizers, soups, salads or main courses.

New England scallops come in three different sizes, each lending itself to different methods of cooking. New Bedford, Massachusetts, claims to be the largest center for scalloping in the entire world. Scallops are unloaded there every morning by the ton to be distributed all over the country. The scallops brought into New Bedford are sea scallops, the largest variety; they are gathered by dragging a special net along the ocean floor. Sea scallops can be deep-fried, poached, steamed, broiled or grilled; they are awkward to sauté. They are at their very best when grilled. Sea scallops are available year-round.

The bay scallop is a medium-size scallop that is gathered in the large bays from Long Island to Digby in Nova Scotia. Because of their size, they are the most versatile and can be cooked successfully by almost any method. They are also quite good raw. If they are grilled, it must be done very quickly to prevent overcooking. Do not confuse New England or Canadian bay scallops with the tiny southern calico scallop that is also called bay. The southern scallop is sometimes passed off as a small bay or cape scallop, but don't be fooled: it is an inferior specimen. New England bays are almost the same width as height; southern bays are elongated. Bay scallops are in season from October to May.

Although all New England scallops are tasty and sweet, the cape scallop is the most highly prized. Cape scallops are available only during the winter months (December, January and February). They are gathered close to the shore. The very best come from Nantucket Island. Cape scallops are best eaten raw or just barely cooked. Quick sautés, stir-frys and flash-frying are the best methods for cooking these scallops.

Scallops in New England are, unfortunately, almost always sold shucked without the roe. What we call a scallop is just the muscle from the bivalve; the rest is discarded. If you are lucky enough to find some scallops in the shell (they are easy to shuck), leave the coral-colored roe intact and save the beautiful shell for serving. Beware of scallops sold with the roe attached, though: they are usually imported from Europe and are of questionable quality by the time they reach here. Scallop roe is very delicate and needs to be cooked very gently (poached or steamed).

Fresh scallops should be a clear white color and have a sweet pleasant aroma. Very fresh scallops are somewhat dry; any found swimming in juice are usually a few days old. Always remove the little crescent-shaped strap and pick through for small fragments of shell. Do not wash fresh scallops.

Raw Cape Scallops with Lemon, Onion and Capers

Small sweet cape scallops are delicious raw. Although inspired by seviche, this dish differs in that the scallops are flavored, not cured, by the lemon or lime. Here I have kept the flavors on the mild side, without being bland, to capture the full beauty of the tiny scallop's flavor. For a more Oriental effect, I sometimes use celery, pickled ginger and cilantro instead. Serve on scrubbed scallop shells if you have them; otherwise use small plates.

SERVES SIX TO EIGHT
AS AN APPETIZER

1½ pounds fresh cape scallops
juice of 1 lemon
1 lemon, seeded and cut into
    small (¼ inch) dice
⅓ cup first-press olive oil
½ small to medium red onion,
    cut in very small (less than
    ¼ inch) dice (¼ cup)
2 tablespoons capers
3 tablespoons coarsely chopped
    Italian parsley
1 head romaine lettuce
salt and freshly ground black
    pepper

1. Pick through the scallops, removing the straps and any particles of shell. Chill thoroughly.

2. Mix the lemon juice, lemon dice, olive oil, onion, capers and parsley. Also chill this mixture thoroughly.

3. Wash the yellow inner leaves of the romaine and slice very fine (chiffonade). Keep chilled.

4. About 10 minutes before serving, mix the scallops and the lemon mixture. Season to taste with salt and pepper. Keep chilled.

5. Make a little nest with the chiffonade of romaine in each scallop shell or on each plate. Toss the scallops to distribute ingredients evenly and divide equally among the nests. Spoon any extra juice over the scallops and the lettuce. Serve at once.

Salad of Scallops, Pear and Celery

On a culinary tour of China last year, I was introduced to two dishes that gave me the idea for this salad. One chilly November afternoon outside Beijing, we were served a simple salad of julienned pear and celery. The celery in China is much thinner and more flavorful than the celery we are accustomed to, and pears (and other fruits) have a fragrance that is very floral. The salad was absolute perfection. Later during the trip I was served scallops set on disks of pear with a little mousse to bind the two, then deep-fried. Another amazing dish! And the idea for this salad came to me.

SERVES FOUR TO SIX
AS AN APPETIZER

1 pound bay scallops
2 tablespoons peanut oil
salt and freshly ground black
    pepper
2 tablespoons cider vinegar
2 Bosc or other flavorful pears
4 medium stalks celery
3 scallions
½ cup celery leaves, yellow inner
    leaves only, picked and
    coarsely chopped
juice of 1 lemon
⅓ cup peanut oil
1 tablespoon sesame oil
1 head Boston or Bibb lettuce

1. Pick through the scallops, removing the straps and any particles of shell. Heat a sauté pan to a medium temperature. Add the 2 tablespoons of peanut oil. Season the scallops with salt and pepper and add to the pan, turning the scallops so that they cook evenly. They can take on a little color, but not too much. After 2 minutes add the vinegar and continue cooking for 1 minute more. Pour the scallops into a bowl with the pan juices. Chill.

2. Peel, core, and cut the pears into fine julienne strips, the size of wooden matches. Peel the celery and cut in the same fashion. Slice the scallions on the diagonal, very thin.

3. Combine the scallops with the pear, celery, scallions, celery leaves, lemon juice, ⅓ cup peanut oil and the sesame oil. Chill for 1 hour.

4. Wash and dry the lettuce. Make a small bed on each of 4 plates. Toss the scallop mixture and check the seasoning. Divide the mixture among the plates. Spoon any extra sauce over the top. Serve at once.

Cape Scallops Sautéed with Garlic and Sundried Tomatoes

The flavor of scallops works perfectly with garlic and tomatoes. Since cape scallops are available only in the winter months, I match them with sundried tomatoes. Be sure the pan is extremely hot before adding the scallops and work very quickly so as not to overcook the scallops. If necessary, make the dish in two sauté pans at the same time.

SERVES FOUR AS AN ENTREE

1½ pounds cape scallops
salt and freshly ground black
   pepper
3 tablespoons olive oil
2 tablespoons finely chopped
   garlic
1 cup julienned sundried
   tomatoes (see Note)
juice of ½ lemon
2 tablespoons unsalted butter
3 tablespoons chopped Italian
   parsley
risotto or buttered pasta for
   serving

1. Pick through the scallops, removing the straps and any particles of shell. Place the scallops in a colander so that they are as dry as possible. Prepare, measure and have all of the ingredients ready to go. The cooking time for this dish is very short.

2. Heat the sauté pan (or pans) until smoking hot. Season the scallops with salt and pepper. Add the oil and then the scallops to the pan, leaving a little space for the garlic. As soon as the scallops hit the pan, add the garlic. Do not move the pan or stir the scallops.

3. After 30 seconds, add the sundried tomatoes and toss. Cook for 30 seconds more. Add the lemon juice, butter and parsley. Remove from heat and toss or stir until butter melts. Check the seasoning. Serve immediately.

NOTE. If you use sundried tomatoes in oil, you will just need to slice them. If you buy tomatoes that are completely dried, you will need to steam or poach them first.

Fried Scallops

There are basically three ways to deep-fry scallops: with batter, with breading and with a dusting of flour, cornmeal or cornstarch. The size of the scallops and the ultimate flavor and presentation will determine which method you choose. The nicest way to present fried scallops is on a folded napkin with a little parsley. I like to serve an oyster fork with cape scallops.

Batter-Fried Scallops

This method is most appropriate for large bay scallops or sea scallops; follow the recipe for Crispy Batter-fried Oysters (page 9). Batter-fried scallops are always good with the traditional mayonnaise-based sauces, like Tartare or Rémoulade Sauce (page 333), but if you want something a little different, you might try a Chinese-style dipping sauce or a flavored salt like the one described in the Crispy Batter-fried Oysters recipe. Batter-frying also lends itself to a mixed fry (fritto misto) using other seafood, vegetables or a mixture of both. Use peanut oil at 360 degrees for batter-frying.

Breaded Fried Scallops

This is another excellent way to fry large bay scallops and sea scallops. Dredge the scallops in flour, dip in egg wash, then roll in breadcrumbs (see page 69 for more details on breading). I like to season the breadcrumbs well with herbs and sometimes cheese and serve only wedges of lemon with the scallops. It is important that scallops, or any food for that matter, be breaded just minutes before frying. When the scallops are freshly breaded, the breading forms an airtight seal. The scallops actually steam inside the breading; properly done, they puff. The breading is all that is actually fried. If the scallops are breaded too far in advance, the oil penetrates the breading and makes the scallops greasy. Frying at too low a temperature can also cause greasiness. Any high-quality vegetable or peanut oil will do, but the best by far is olive oil. Fry at 350 degrees.

Flash-Fried Scallops

This method is best for cape scallops or small bay scallops, which require a short cooking time (one minute for capes). Dust the scallops in seasoned flour, cornmeal, cornstarch or a combination of these, then fry in very hot oil (375 degrees) for a very short time. Scallops fried in this manner can be served with a multitude of sauces and garnishes or served plain with lemon.

Grilled Sea Scallops

Once you have tasted sea scallops grilled over charcoal or wood, you will forget forever about poaching, braising, frying or sautéing them. Those methods are more suitable for the smaller bay or cape scallops. I recommend using a skewer for any small items that are going to be grilled: it gives better control during the cooking. (Be sure to soak bamboo skewers in water at least overnight; the water-soaked skewers can take a lot of heat before they begin to burn.) The variations on grilled scallops are endless, from the foods that are skewered with the scallops to the different sauces, compound butters, chutneys or relishes used to finish the dish. And the garnishes are just as numerous. So take this concept and adapt it to seasonal foods whose flavors complement the scallops and each other. Here are a couple of suggestions.

Bacon is one of the most traditional partners for scallops. Instead of wrapping the scallop in bacon, use thick slices of slab country bacon (partially rendered) cut into pieces about the size of the scallop. Alternate bacon, scallops and green onion on the skewers. (You will notice that I never use the words *scallion* and *scallop* in the same sentence or in the name of a dish.) Let the fire burn down to medium heat, season the brochettes, dredge in oil and grill about two minutes on each side. Brush with lemon butter.

Scallops can also be skewered with pieces of sweet pepper and onion or with fresh shrimp and cherry tomatoes. Finish the brochettes with brown butter (page 329) and garlic or with a fresh tomato and mint sauce.

VARIATION

Broiled Sea Scallops   If you do not have a grill, use the broiler. After skewering and seasoning the scallops, dredge them in oil, then roll them in fresh white breadcrumbs. You will need about 1 cup of crumbs for a recipe serving 4. Place close to the heat in a preheated, very hot broiler. After 1 minute the breadcrumbs should turn golden brown. Turn the scallops and cook 1 minute more.

Grilled Sea Scallops with Green Onions and Curry

While New Yorkers tend to be francophiles, many New Englanders are enamored with British life-styles. Curry has retained some of its popularity in our region, perhaps because of its association with English cookery. Unfortunately the English version of curry is often an abomination having little to do with the cooking of India. This recipe does not pretend to be Indian or even Anglo-Indian; it simply borrows some of the flavors of India to enliven our own tasty local scallops. I usually serve the dish with small Wild Rice Pancakes. Any neutral-flavored rice, grain or pasta dish would make a good accompaniment.

SERVES FOUR AS AN ENTREE

24 large sea scallops (about 1½
    pounds)
6 scallions
salt and freshly ground pepper
⅓ cup vegetable oil
Curry Butter, melted (recipe
    follows)
Wild Rice Pancakes (page 266)
    for serving

1. Pick through the scallops, removing the straps and any particles of shell. Cut the scallions into 1-inch pieces, reserving the green tops for another use. You will need 1 large or 2 small skewers per person. Alternate the scallops and green onions.

2. Let the fire on your grill burn down to medium heat. Season the scallops with salt and pepper. Dredge in oil and place the skewers on the grill. Brush the scallops generously with melted curry butter. After 2 minutes turn and brush with more of the butter. In 1 or 2 minutes the scallops will be cooked. Transfer to plates, garnish with pancakes and spoon any remaining curry butter over the scallops.

Curry Butter

This flavored butter can be used for many dishes. It is especially good with poultry.

MAKES ABOUT ONE CUP

9 tablespoons unsalted butter
2 tablespoons finely chopped red
    onion
2 tablespoons finely chopped red
    or green bell pepper
2 tablespoons Madras curry
    powder
2 tablespoons finely chopped
    cilantro
1 tablespoon chopped scallion
1 tablespoon finely chopped
    raisins
¼ teaspoon cayenne pepper
juice of ½ lemon
salt and freshly ground black
    pepper

1. Soften 8 tablespoons butter (¼ pound). Place the remaining tablespoon of butter in a small sauté pan and heat up slowly. Add the onion and pepper and cook slowly for 2 minutes. Add the curry powder and cook 1 minute more. Remove from the heat. (The cooking expands the flavor of the curry.)

2. When the curry mixture has cooled, blend with the softened butter. Add the cilantro, scallion, raisins, cayenne pepper and lemon juice. Mix well and season to taste with salt and pepper. Store, tightly covered, in the refrigerator.

These tiny ocean snails have an interesting taste and texture, but they are not for people with a short attention span. They require quite a bit of time to prepare and some work to get at. This is messy finger food best for casual eating. Periwinkles are very abundant and are easier to find on a rocky beach than at the fish market. If you pick your own, wait for low tide and take them from the deeper waters, where the size will be about that of a marble. Anything smaller is almost impossible to deal with.

Periwinkles Poached in a Spicy Saffron Broth

Bradford Cole was my sous-chef for many years before striking out on his own. Shortly after leaving to become chef of what would be one of Boston's hot new restaurants, Brad had a final bout with the cancer he had been courageously fighting for years. He had an incredible mind for food and I am sure he would have made his mark if time had allowed. Brad had a fondness for the esoteric. He created this dish for the new restaurant's first menu. I may have been the only one to order it, but I thought it was great.

SERVES FOUR AS AN APPETIZER

1 tablespoon chopped garlic
1/2 medium onion, chopped
1 tablespoon finely chopped hot
    chili peppers
3 tablespoons olive oil
1 cup tomatoes, peeled, seeded
    and chopped
1 1/2 cups Fish Stock (page 327)
1/2 teaspoon Spanish string
    saffron
1 tablespoon chopped fresh basil
2 teaspoons grated orange rind
salt and freshly ground pepper
2 pounds Blanched Periwinkles
    (page 31)

For Serving
1 cup Aïoli (page 332)
French or Italian bread, plain or
    toasted, for serving

1. Sauté the garlic, onion and chilies in olive oil. Add the tomatoes, fish stock, saffron, basil and orange rind and simmer, uncovered, for 20 minutes. Season with salt and pepper. Place the periwinkles in a wire mesh basket and submerge in the simmering broth for 5 minutes.

2. Divide periwinkles among 4 bowls with a little broth to keep them hot. Serve with individual bowls of broth and small dishes of aïoli; set out extra bowls for the empty shells. Eat the periwinkles like steamers, pulling them out of the shell with a snail fork, toothpick or bamboo skewer and dipping them in the broth, then the aïoli. Serve the bread on the side.

Periwinkles with Escargot Butter

SERVES FOUR AS AN APPETIZER

8 tablespoons (1 stick) unsalted
  butter, softened
2 tablespoons finely chopped
  garlic
2 tablespoons finely chopped
  chervil
2 tablespoons finely chopped
  parsley
2 tablespoons finely chopped
  chives
juice of ½ lemon
salt and freshly ground black
  pepper
2 pounds Blanched Periwinkles
  (recipe follows)
French or Italian bread for
  serving

1. Combine the softened butter with the garlic, chervil, parsley, chives and lemon juice. Season to taste with salt and pepper and mix well.

2. Combine the periwinkles and butter in a 10-inch sauté pan. Slowly bring to a bubble, stirring gently but frequently. Continue cooking for about 5 minutes until the periwinkles are heated through and the butter begins to brown.

3. Divide among 4 soup bowls. You will need snail forks or toothpicks to remove the periwinkles from their shells. Serve bread on the side for sopping up extra sauce.

Blanched Periwinkles

Periwinkles need a preliminary cooking before being used as a garnish or as part of a more complicated dish. You can store them in the refrigerator until ready to use.

MAKES ENOUGH FOR TWO
POUNDS OF PERIWINKLES

2 pounds periwinkles
½ cup distilled white vinegar
2 tablespoons salt

Court Bouillon
1 cup white wine
1 teaspoon whole black
  peppercorns
2 bay leaves
3 cloves of garlic, chopped
½ medium onion, chopped
6 sprigs fresh thyme
6 parsley stems

1. Check the periwinkles one by one for life, making sure that each shell is inhabited. Like snails they will retreat into their shells when poked.

2. Bring the vinegar and salt with 2 cups water to a boil. Cook the periwinkles in this solution for 1 minute. Remove and rinse in clean water.

3. Combine 1 cup water, the wine, peppercorns, bay leaves, garlic, onion, thyme and parsley stems and bring to a boil. Simmer for 10 minutes, then add the periwinkles and simmer 5 minutes more. Remove from heat and allow periwinkles to cool in the bouillon.

4. Remove from the liquid and drain. With a pair of tweezers or clamps remove the little disk-shaped lid from the opening in each shell.

SEA URCHINS

Urchins are a true delicacy, less appreciated in the United States than in Japan, Europe, the Caribbean and South America. The green urchin is extremely abundant along the New England coast, especially in Maine; in good weather divers can easily gather bushels of them. Our green urchins look like spiny pincushions and are greenish brown in color. The part that is eaten is usually referred to as urchin roe, but it is really the gonads. Getting to this creamy roelike substance is simpler than it looks.

Cut around the mouth (bottom) of the urchin, using a pair of wire cutters or scissors. Rinse gently in cold water and remove the viscera that surround the golden substance attached to the top of the urchin. Invert and place on crushed ice. Serve with toast and lemon or lime wedges. Use a demitasse spoon to scoop out the roe; spread on the toast and squeeze a bit of lemon or lime over it. The roe can also be removed and used to flavor and garnish sauces.

SQUID

As few as eight years ago, I remember watching fishermen throwing squid on the dock to rot in Little Compton, Rhode Island, as they unloaded their catch of cod and bass. At the time it was almost impossible to buy fresh squid in New England. Not that there were no squid, there was no demand. Most squid was shipped directly to Mediterranean countries and if you wanted to buy squid in Boston, you usually had to settle for a frozen product from California.

Fortunately that has changed. Fresh squid is readily available, and although the price has quadrupled in the last few years, it is still affordable. Many purveyors sell squid already cleaned, and that alone, I think, has helped to increase its popularity. It really isn't much work, however, to clean squid for a small dinner.

Separate the tentacles from the body. Clean out the body and remove the long thin bone. The skin will peel off easily. The body can be sliced into rings, cut into triangles (Chinese style) or left whole for stuffing. The tentacles can be chopped for stuffing or divided into smaller pieces for other uses. Be sure to remove the ball located where the tentacles meet the body.

Squid and Olive Salad

This salad can serve as part of an antipasto or as an appetizer or as a light luncheon main course. It is also nice for a summer cold buffet. For best results, make this a day in advance.

SERVES EIGHT AS AN APPETIZER

2 pounds squid
6 cloves garlic, finely chopped
1 small red onion, thinly sliced
1 red or green bell pepper, thinly
 sliced
1½ cups spicy Italian olives,
 green and black, pitted
½ cup Italian parsley, coarsely
 chopped
1 hot chili pepper, split
⅔ cup olive oil
juice of 2 lemons
salt and freshly ground black
 pepper

1. Clean the squid as described above and cut the body into rings about ⅜ inch thick. Cut the tentacles into small pieces. Steam the squid for 2 to 3 minutes until tender. Allow to cool.

2. Place the cooled squid in a bowl with the garlic, onion, pepper, olives, parsley, chili pepper, olive oil and lemon juice. Season to taste with salt and pepper. Keep chilled.

3. Before serving, remove the chili pepper and check the seasoning. Let stand at room temperature for 20 to 30 minutes before serving.

Fried Squid, North-End Style

Summer is street festival time in Boston's Italian North End. The name of the saint being honored changes from week to week as the festivals move from one street to another. But the food—and the vendors—are pretty much the same: sausage and pepper sandwiches, pizza, calzone, fried dough and fried squid. Here's how to fry squid in this popular fashion.

SERVES FOUR TO SIX
AS AN APPETIZER

2 pounds squid
1 cup yellow cornmeal
1 cup all-purpose flour
salt and freshly ground black
 pepper
cayenne pepper
olive oil for frying
lemon wedges
1 cup Basic Tomato Sauce, page
 338 (optional)

1. Clean the squid as described on page 32 and cut the bodies into rings about ⅜ inch thick. Separate the tentacles into manageable pieces.

2. Mix the cornmeal and flour and season with salt, pepper and cayenne pepper. Dip the pieces of squid in this mixture so that they are completely coated.

3. Fill a deep pot with at least 3 inches of olive oil and heat to 360 degrees. Drop in the squid a little at a time so that there is ample room for circulation and so that the oil doesn't cool off. Fry for about 1 minute until golden brown. Remove and drain on paper towels.

4. When all the squid is cooked, serve on a platter with lemon wedges. Serve a bowl or two small bowls of warm tomato sauce on the side for dipping, if desired.

MAINE SHRIMP

Boreal red shrimp, a relative of the northern European prawn, inhabit our waters from the Bay of Fundy to Connecticut. It is only from Maine north, however, that they are found in any really significant abundance. During the cold winter months when lobsters are harder to trap, many Maine lobstermen convert their trawlers for netting shrimp, which provide a more dependable income. Maine shrimp are only available from November to March for this reason.

They are small, usually averaging 50 to 60 shrimp per pound, tasty and incredibly sweet. They cook fast and are perfect for quick sautés, stir-fries or flash frying. I have made great "Cajun popcorn" substituting these shrimp for crayfish. I also put them in rarebit (page 214). They make fabulous soup and are also excellent poached and served cold. Be very careful not to overcook them or they will turn to mush.

Maine shrimp is not widely known outside of New England, although many people have probably had it canned or frozen without knowing it. In fact, outside of Maine, many New Englanders are not all that familiar with it. I find it contemptible that some restaurants use frozen jumbo shrimp (from Central and South America) during the height of the local fresh shrimp season. The irony is that the fresh shrimp are relatively inexpensive compared with the frozen. In Maine they can sell for as little as a dollar a pound. In other New England markets, they may sell for three or four times more, but that still represents good value.

Maine shrimp are often sold whole with the head on, but they can also be found headless and sometimes peeled. The recipes that follow are for head-off shrimp. Figure on using about a quarter of a pound per person for an appetizer and half a pound for a main course dish. The shells account for about a fourth of the weight: one pound of shrimp yields about twelve ounces of meat after peeling. The shrimp that are sold already peeled are not very useful because for most preparations the shells are needed for flavoring. Even if the shrimp are to be served cold, they should be poached in the shell. If you find some bluish roe attached to the bottom of the shrimp, remove the roe and discard it.

Shrimp Bisque with Shrimp Toasts

This recipe is very classical in its use of veal stock and burnt brandy. In addition to giving the bisque great body, the veal stock enriches and mellows the flavor. When this soup is made perfectly it is savory without being too spicy; the texture is rich and smooth without being heavy; the flavor is complex without losing the predominant flavor of shrimp. It has a deep reddish brown color and it is heart-warming and suave at the same time. This is the perfect starter for an elegant dinner on a cold winter night.

SERVES EIGHT TO TEN
AS A STARTER

3 pounds Maine shrimp
4 tablespoons clarified butter
    (page 329)
2 tablespoons chopped garlic
    (6 to 8 cloves)
1 large onion, cut in small
    (¼ inch) dice (about 2 cups)
2 large carrots, peeled and finely
    chopped
4 tablespoons all-purpose flour
1 cup white wine
1 cup Reduced Veal Stock
    (page 328)
1 can (6 ounces) tomato paste
5 cups Fish Stock (page 327) or
    water
2 bay leaves
2 teaspoons chopped fresh
    thyme
1 tablespoon chopped fresh
    tarragon
1 tablespoon whole black
    peppercorns
½ teaspoon cayenne pepper
2 tablespoons unsalted butter
¼ cup brandy
¼ cup amontillado sherry
1 cup heavy cream
salt and freshly ground black
    pepper
Shrimp Toasts (page 36) for
    serving

1. Peel 2 pounds of the shrimp; refrigerate the shrimp until later. Roughly chop the shells with the remaining shrimp and their shells. Drain the shrimp and shells of any moisture.

2. Heat a very large sauté pan to smoking hot. Add the clarified butter, chopped shrimp and shrimp shells. Cook for 1 minute, tossing or stirring occasionally. Add the garlic, onion and carrots. Turn the heat down and cook for 5 minutes. Sprinkle with flour and cook 3 minutes more, stirring almost constantly.

3. At this point, transfer everything from the sauté pan to a soup pot. Deglaze the empty sauté pan with white wine and pour into the soup pot; make sure you transfer every drop, leaving nothing stuck to the pan.

4. Put the soup pot on medium heat. Add the veal stock and tomato paste. When this thickens, add the fish stock a little at a time, allowing the bisque to thicken each time before adding more. Bring to a boil and skim. Reduce to a simmer and add the bay leaves, thyme, tarragon, peppercorns and cayenne pepper. Simmer for 1 hour 30 minutes. About halfway through the cooking, add 1 to 2 cups of water, enough to keep the soup simmering freely. Stir the soup once in a while, to keep it from sticking to the bottom.

5. When the bisque is cooked out (the consistency will be just a little thicker than heavy cream), strain through a coarse strainer, mashing and pushing as much through as possible. Then pass the bisque through a fine strainer, again pushing through as much as possible. At this point the bisque can be set aside until ready to serve (chilled if not to be served for a while).

6. A few minutes before serving, melt the butter in a pot large enough to reheat the bisque. Add the shrimp and cook for 30 seconds. Add the brandy and flame the shrimp. When the flames die down, add the sherry, the strained bisque and the heavy cream. Bring to a boil; skim. Season to taste with salt and pepper. Serve piping hot in small bowls that have been warmed in the oven with shrimp toasts on small side plates.

Shrimp Toasts

MAKES TWENTY SLICES

1 pound Maine shrimp
8 tablespoons unsalted butter
2 tablespoons finely chopped
    onion
1 tablespoon finely chopped
    garlic (3 cloves)
2 tablespoons finely chopped red
    bell pepper
2 tablespoons finely chopped
    Italian parsley
salt and freshly ground pepper
cayenne pepper
1 baguette (long French bread)

1. Peel the shrimp; you should have about 2 cups. Chop half of the shrimp very fine; set aside. Put the other half in the workbowl of a food processor together with 7 tablespoons butter and process until very fine. Transfer to a small mixing bowl.

2. Cook the onion, garlic and bell pepper with the remaining butter in a small frying pan until the vegetables are tender (4 to 5 minutes); let cool. Combine the vegetables, chopped shrimp and parsley with the pureed mixture. Season to taste with salt, pepper and cayenne pepper. Refrigerate, covered, until ready to use.

3. About 20 minutes before serving, preheat the oven to 350 degrees. Slice the baguette into 20 rounds about ⅓ inch thick. Toast lightly on both sides. Spread each evenly with the shrimp mixture. Bake in the preheated oven for 8 to 10 minutes. Serve immediately.

Saffron Noodles with Maine Shrimp, Country Bacon and Pine Nuts

There is a lot going on in this lively dish. The flavors of saffron, shrimp and bacon bounce around, making each bite taste a little different, while the chewy noodles are juxtaposed to the crunchy pine nuts. If you wish to omit the bacon, substitute olive oil for the fat and add a few pieces of olive for garnish. Another alternative that can be used is to make this dish a dry-fry, omitting the stock and butter.

SERVES SIX TO EIGHT
AS AN APPETIZER

1½ pounds Maine shrimp
½ cup Shrimp Stock, made from
    the shells (page 38)
1 pound Saffron Pasta (page
    278) or 10 ounces dry noodles
¼ pound slab smoked bacon, cut
    in small (¼ inch) dice (see
    Note)
1 teaspoon finely chopped garlic
½ cup sundried tomatoes, cut in
    strips
4 tablespoons unsalted butter or
    Shrimp Butter (page 38)
1 tablespoon finely chopped
    Italian parsley
salt and freshly ground pepper
¼ cup toasted pine nuts

1. Peel the shrimp and set aside. Use the shells to make stock as directed on page 38.

2. Bring a large pot of salted water to a boil. Heat up a sauté pan to medium hot. Right before you start the bacon in the pan, drop the noodles in the boiling water; homemade noodles need to cook for only 4 to 5 minutes.

3. Render the bacon until it begins to crisp; pour off half the fat. Add the shrimp and garlic, toss or stir occasionally for 1 minute. Add the tomatoes and ½ cup of stock. Bring to a boil. Drain noodles well and transfer to the sauté pan; add the butter and parsley.

4. Remove from heat and keep tossing or stirring so that the butter combines with the other liquids in the pan. Season to taste with salt and pepper. Divide among plates or bowls and sprinkle with toasted pine nuts.

Nam Tran's Shrimp and Cabbage Salad

Nam Van Tran somehow made his way halfway around the world from Vietnam to Boston, miraculously surviving a journey that began in a small boat with a score of other people fleeing their homeland. He has been the bartender at my restaurant since we opened in 1983. Nam usually comes in about two or three o'clock in the afternoon; more often than not he is carrying lunch. He always brings extra, especially if it is Vietnamese food, which I am quite fond of. The first time I tasted this salad, I knew it would be perfect for Maine shrimp. With Nam's guidance, it soon made it onto our menu as an appetizer. While the dish is true to its Vietnamese roots, the amount of shrimp is greater than in the original.

SERVES SIX TO EIGHT
AS AN APPETIZER

½ cup white rice wine vinegar
1 small onion, sliced
cilantro stems
1 tablespoon salt
1 tablespoon black peppercorns
2 pounds Maine shrimp

Cabbage Salad
1 Chinese or Napa cabbage,
    finely shredded (5 cups)
1 large carrot, cut in paper-thin
    julienne (½ cup)
¼ pound Chinese ham or
    cappicola, cut in thin
    (¼ × 1 inch) julienne
1 cup cilantro leaves
½ cup white rice wine vinegar
⅓ cup peanut oil
2 tablespoons Chinese hot-chili
    oil
2 tablespoons sugar
salt and freshly ground black
    pepper

½ cup roasted peanuts, chopped
fried white shrimp chips for
    garnish (optional)

1. Combine 3 cups water with ½ cup vinegar in a saucepan with the onion, cilantro stems, salt and peppercorns. Simmer for 5 minutes, then bring to a rolling boil. Add the unpeeled shrimp. After exactly 1 minute, scoop out the shrimp with a wire basket or slotted spoon and spread out on a sheetpan. Peel the shrimp and set aside.

2. Prepare the salad ingredients, but do not mix the salad until about 20 minutes before it is to be served. Then combine the shrimp, cabbage, carrot, ham, cilantro leaves, vinegar, peanut oil, hot-chili oil and sugar; season to taste with salt and pepper. Chill.

3. Right before serving, add the peanuts, check the seasoning and toss once more. Serve on small plates or in shallow glass bowls. Garnish with shrimp chips, if using.

Shrimp Stock with Tomato

This stock, which you need for the Saffron Noodles with Maine Shrimp, Country Bacon and Pine Nuts, will also come in handy for shrimp sautés or shrimp and pasta combinations that you yourself create. The recipe is designed for the shells from one pound of shrimp (the heads and roe are not good for stock), but you may multiply or divide it to suit your needs. Extra stock may be frozen.

MAKES ONE AND A HALF
TO TWO CUPS

1 pound of shrimp
1 tablespoon olive oil
¼ cup white wine
2 medium tomatoes, coarsely
  chopped, or 2 tablespoons
  tomato paste
½ medium onion, chopped
  coarsely (½ cup)
1 clove garlic
½ bay leaf
4 sprigs of thyme
6 parsley stems
1 teaspoon whole black
  peppercorns
pinch of saffron strings
  (optional)

1. Remove the heads and any roe attached to the shrimp and discard. Peel the shrimp, separating the shells and meat. Refrigerate the shrimp until ready to use.

2. Heat the olive oil in a saucepan. Add the shells; they should sizzle. Stir the shells about twice a minute for 3 or 4 minutes. Add the wine and water to cover (about 2 cups); bring to a boil. Skim the top and add the tomatoes or tomato paste, onion, garlic, bay leaf, thyme, parsley stems, peppercorns and saffron, if using. Simmer for 1 hour. Strain through a fine strainer and chill if not using right away.

Shrimp Butter

Here is a quick and easy preparation that can be used to flavor a soup or light sauce, whether for a shrimp dish or for another seafood. It is a good way to use up leftover cooked shrimp. This recipe is for the cooked meat from half a pound of shrimp, but it can be adjusted according to how much shrimp you have on hand.

MAKES ABOUT ONE CUP

cooked shrimp from ½ pound
  shrimp (about 6 ounces)
6 tablespoons butter
1 teaspoon lemon juice
salt and freshly ground pepper
Worcestershire sauce

1. Combine the shrimp, butter and lemon juice in the workbowl of a food processor. Season with salt and pepper and a few drops of Worcestershire sauce.

2. Puree as fine as possible. Check seasoning. Refrigerate or freeze if not to be used right away.

MAINE CRAB (ROCK CRAB)

For the most part, rock crab is *the* crab found in New England waters; the blue crab is rarely found north of Cape Cod. The rock crab (cousin to the West Coast Dungeness crab) does not venture into fresh or brackish water, like the common blue crab; these crabs prefer cold salty water. They do range as far south as the Carolinas, but they prefer deeper waters in the South. Only from Maine north will you find rock crabs in shallow coastal waters, and Maine is the major source for crabs in New England. Because of this rock crab is called Maine crab. You will never hear a New Englander ask for rock crabmeat. Like lobster, Maine crab is available year-round, alive or as cooked picked meat. Maine crabmeat can be distinguished from the lump or backfin lump of the blue crab by its red pigmentation and its super-sweet flavor.

As great as these crabs are, they have always gotten the second-class treatment in New England cookery compared to the highly esteemed lobster. Maine crabs are delicious simply boiled or steamed, but for this ritual, 90 out of 100 New Englanders would choose lobster over crab. I have noticed, curiously enough, that the local Chinese community prefers crab.

The following recipes pay homage to our delicious Maine crab, which I hope you will try sometime, but any good fresh crabmeat can be substituted. Cooked Maine crabmeat from reputable distributors can be very good, but the surest way to have the best is to cook and pick the crabs yourself.

How to Cook Crabs

Submerge the live crabs in boiling sea or salted water and cook for 6 minutes per pound. Remove the crabs from the water. Allow to cool, then pick every morsel of meat from the legs and body.

Antipasto with Maine Crab and Prosciutto

Eating whole crabs is messy and should be reserved for informal occasions. Cold crabmeat, on the other hand, is useful for even the most formal occasions. It can be served simply with just a little lettuce, lemon and mustard sauce made with Mayonnaise (page 333), crème fraîche (page 220) or sour cream, or as part of a more complex composed salad. This antipasto is one of my favorites.

SERVES FOUR TO SIX
AS AN APPETIZER

2 large artichoke bottoms,
  cooked and sliced
2 roasted peppers (page 247),
  red or green, quartered
2 cloves garlic
¼ cup olive oil
2 tablespoons balsamic vinegar
1 small head Boston or Bibb
  lettuce
8 to 10 scallions
1 pound fresh Maine crabmeat,
  drained and well chilled
¼ pound prosciutto, sliced
  paper-thin
½ cup imported oil-cured or
  spiced olives
lemon wedges

1. Mix the sliced artichoke bottoms with the roasted peppers, chopped garlic, olive oil and vinegar earlier in the day. Wash and dry the lettuce leaves. Trim off some of the green part of the scallions, and discard. Rinse the whole scallions.

2. Shortly before serving, assemble the antipasto on a large platter or on individual plates. Pour a little of the sauce from the artichokes on the lettuce leaves; toss and line the bottom of the platter or plates. Put the chilled crabmeat in the center. Circle the crabmeat with individual piles of loosely folded slices of prosciutto, artichokes and peppers, scallions and olives and lemon wedges.

Garden Tomatoes with Maine Crab

SERVES FOUR AS AN APPETIZER

4 small ripe tomatoes, cored, cut
  in half and then cut in ½-inch
  wedges
1 cucumber, peeled and sliced
  into ½-inch rounds
½ red onion, thinly sliced
½ cup crème fraîche (page 220)
3 tablespoons balsamic vinegar
1 cup (loosely packed) basil
  leaves
salt and freshly ground black
  pepper
lettuce for garnish
1 pound fresh Maine crabmeat,
  drained and well chilled

1. Mix the tomatoes, cucumber and onion with the crème fraîche, vinegar and basil. Season to taste with salt and pepper. Chill for 30 minutes.

2. Line plates with lettuce leaves and spoon the tomato mixture into the center, making a nest for the crabmeat. Reserve some of the dressing. Put the crabmeat in the center of each salad and spoon the remaining dressing over it.

Maine Crabmeat Turnovers

Each spring I serve these little turnovers with a salad of fresh asparagus with a light mustard dressing (page 226). You could also serve an assortment of turnovers with other fillings like cheese, sausage, shrimp and so on. For extra-crisp turnovers, double the amount of phyllo. Butter a sheet of phyllo, then lay a second sheet on top of it. Butter the second sheet, then continue as directed.

MAKES THIRTY-TWO
SMALL TURNOVERS

Crabmeat Filling
2 tablespoons finely diced red
  bell pepper
2 tablespoons finely diced carrot
2 tablespoons finely diced celery
1 small chili pepper (optional)
1 tablespoon unsalted butter
1 pound fresh Maine crabmeat,
  drained
2 scallions, finely chopped
1 tablespoon Dijon mustard
1 tablespoon Mayonnaise
  (page 333)
¼ cup dry white breadcrumbs
juice of ½ lemon
salt and freshly ground black
  pepper

8 sheets phyllo dough, 12 × 17
  inches (about ½ pound)
8 tablespoons (1 stick) unsalted
  butter, melted

1. Sauté the pepper, carrot, celery and chili pepper, if using, in 1 tablespoon butter. Allow to cool, then chill. Mix with crabmeat, scallions, mustard, mayonnaise, breadcrumbs and lemon juice. Season to taste with salt and pepper. Try to mix gently so that the crabmeat is not completely shredded.

2. If you work fast you will not need to bother with the damp cloth that is sometimes recommended when working with phyllo dough. Brush each sheet generously with the melted butter. Cut lengthwise into 4 even strips (2 inches wide). Put a heaping teaspoonful of the filling in the bottom corner of a strip and fold over into a triangle. Continue folding until you reach the end of the strip. Place on a sheetpan and brush with butter. Continue until all the turnovers are done.

3. About 25 minutes before serving, preheat the oven to 350 degrees. Bake for 12 to 15 minutes or until very crisp and golden brown.

Crab Cakes

Just about any place you find crabs, you will find crab cakes, even in New England, where the crab plays second fiddle to lobster and the crab cake is overshadowed by the venerable cod cake (see Old-Fashioned Salt-Cod Cakes, page 102). Assuming that the freshest and tastiest crabmeat is being used, the best crab cakes are the ones with the most crabmeat. Sounds obvious, yet many people stretch the crabmeat too far with breadcrumbs or, in New England especially, cracker crumbs.

In summer I like to serve crab cakes with tomato concassée (page 337) cooked in sweet butter with fresh chives from the garden. I also like the contrast of crab cakes with salad greens warmed with a little mustard vinaigrette or even with heartier greens, like collards or beet or mustard greens, cooked with onions and bacon. Sauces that work well with crab cakes include Rémoulade and Tartare Sauce (page 333) and a simple mustard-cream sauce made with Coleman's dry mustard.

MAKES EIGHT CRAB CAKES

1 egg
2 tablespoons Mayonnaise
    (page 333)
1 tablespoon Dijon mustard
2 teaspoons Coleman's dry
    mustard
2 tablespoons finely chopped
    Italian parsley
2 tablespoons chopped chives or
    scallions
juice of 1 lemon
1½ pounds crabmeat, drained
1 cup white breadcrumbs or
    common cracker crumbs
salt and freshly ground black
    pepper
hot-pepper sauce (optional)
clarifed butter (page 329)

1. Combine the egg, mayonnaise, Dijon mustard, dry mustard, parsley and chives in a mixing bowl. Blend thoroughly and season to taste with lemon juice. Add the crabmeat and crumbs and mix together. Be careful not to overmix or cause the crab to become too shredded; it is nice to leave big chunks of crabmeat. Season with salt, pepper and hot-pepper sauce. Form into 8 patties.

2. Heat a large sauté pan to medium heat. Panfry the crabcakes in clarified butter until golden brown. This will take about 2 to 3 minutes on each side. Drain on paper towels to absorb any excess butter and serve at once.

Crab or Lobster Salad

This is the basic recipe for mayonnaise-based crab or lobster salad. I do not use raw onion because it can turn the salad bitter, but if you like onion, add it at the last minute or use scallions. Crab or lobster salad has many uses—cold hors d'oeuvres, salad plates, sandwiches. My favorite is to spread it on toast and cover it with aged Cheddar cheese. Then I melt the cheese slowly so the salad warms through.

SERVES FOUR

1 pound fresh Maine crabmeat,
    drained, or lobster meat
2 medium celery stalks, peeled
    and cut in small (¼ inch) dice
½ red bell pepper, cut in small
    (¼ inch) dice
3 tablespoons Mayonnaise
    (page 333)
1 tablespoon Dijon mustard
2 tablespoons chopped Italian
    parsley or cilantro
lemon juice
salt and freshly ground pepper
2 scallions, thinly sliced
    (optional)

1. Mix the crab or lobster meat with the celery, pepper, mayonnaise, mustard and parsley or cilantro. Season with lemon juice and salt and pepper to taste. Refrigerate for at least 30 minutes.

2. Add the scallions, if using, and check the seasoning before serving.

NOTE. Dice the lobster meat according to the way you are going to use the salad, finer for sandwiches, chunkier for hors d'oeuvres. The crabmeat, of course, does not have to be diced.

LOBSTER

In New England lobster is very important, important enough to be the subject of the first *appellation controllée*-style legislation in the United States. According to chapter 598 of the General Laws of the Commonwealth of Massachusetts:

> No person shall sell, or represent for the purpose of sale, any lobster as a native lobster unless the same shall have been originally caught or taken in the coastal waters; nor shall any person sell, or represent for the purpose of sale, any crustacean as a lobster unless the same is of the species known as *Homarus Americanus;* nor shall any person sell, or represent for the purpose of sale, any meat as lobster meat unless such meat is wholly from crustaceans of such species.

Since I moved here ten years ago, I have not once cooked with a rock lobster or any other type. Furthermore, I do not care to. It is almost an insult that any other creature should bear this name. I have eaten lobsterlike crustaceans while traveling in the Caribbean and elsewhere, and they are not in the same league, not even close to the New England lobster. Only in France have I tasted anything that resembles it. The lobster of northern Europe, *Homarus vulgaris,* is closely related. When this book refers to lobster, it is *Homarus americanus.*

The lobster has two large claws, two sets of antennae (one short, one long), four pairs of walking legs with little claws and seven tail segments, each having its own pair of appendages. You can determine the sex of the lobster from the first pair of tail appendages, those closest to the body: the female has small, softer appendages; the male, larger and harder ones. The hard shell of the lobster can range in color from a blackish or even greenish blue to a reddish brown. There is a very rare genetic defect that causes one out of a million lobsters to be bright aquamarine or blue. The New England aquarium usually has one on display: it is like a piece of living turquoise, truly spectacular.

All of the lobster is edible except the spongy lung or gills, the head sac (which is not the brain, but the stomach) and the intestinal tract in the tail. Any meat you can pull, squeeze or suck from a lobster will taste good. The pale green tomalley or liver is especially good; the dark gray, almost black roe, which turns reddish orange when cooked, can also be quite nice.

There exists a myth that smaller lobsters are superior to larger ones, but this is only partly true and largely because larger lobsters are often poorly handled. You wouldn't grill a leg of beef as you would a twelve-ounce sirloin, but many people boil a large lobster the same way as a small one. Larger lobsters should be poached at a lower heat, enabling the meat to cook evenly. The cut-off point is at about seven pounds; then the flavor of the meat begins to lose intensity because there is less contact with the shell. For a boiled lobster, I am very fond of three- to four-pounders, which are perfect for two people.

Lobsters are sold by weight and have names that correspond to those weights. The smallest legally allowed lobsters are called chickens (¾ to 1 pound); next are quarters (1 to 1¼ pounds). Selects (1½ to 2 pounds) are the most expensive. Jumbos (over 2 pounds) are most often referred to by weight. Culls are lobsters with one or both claws missing. If priced significantly lower, culls can represent a good deal; all too often the yield-price relationship is about the same as for other lobsters. Lobsters have been known to weigh upward of 40 pounds, although the largest I have ever seen was 25 pounds.

Lobsters are available year-round, but since they go into virtual hibernation when the ocean waters reach about 35 degrees, they can be scarce and quite expensive in the deep winter months. One lobsterman told me last January that one day he landed only 30 pounds of lobsters from 300 traps. During the summer months lobsters molt, shedding the old shells and forming a new larger one. They fill the roomy new shell with water until they grow into it. For this reason soft-shell lobsters are not a very good deal, pound for pound, nor are they especially flavorful. These lobsters are easy to spot because their shells are still soft, they feel lighter and if shaken, they rattle. Their color is often more red than usual. If you happen to be one of those people who are afraid to touch lobsters (like Woody Allen in *Annie Hall*), you stand a pretty good chance of getting a little lobster in a big shell, come summer.

A good lobster has a hard dark shell and a very lively disposition. Newly trapped lobsters can be quite ferocious and will swing their claws at you like a prizefighter. After a few days in captivity, they slow down considerably. If a lobster cannot hold its own arms in the air, it is not a good buy: it will die shortly. These are called sleepers and are usually cooked off for meat by lobster vendors. (I do not recommend buying cooked lobster meat. It is very expensive and can vary greatly in quality. It is easy to learn how to shuck your own.)

Be smart when you purchase lobsters. If you like the roe, insist on a female; if you want to make soup or salad, check the price for culls. If the lobsters are for a clambake or a buffet, buy chickens (one per person). Buy selects for special occasions. Although I call for specific sizes in the recipes that follow, it is easy to adjust them for different size lobsters, as long as you adjust the cooking times as well.

After cooking thousands of lobsters—and eating a lot of them—I can honestly say that no two lobsters taste exactly alike. This may be the reason that I still look forward to eating lobster, whenever the occasion arises. It is one of the foods that deserve to be eaten with gusto; every bite should be savored.

How to Boil or Steam Lobster

Boiled or steamed lobster is the essence of simplicity. It is also most people's favorite. The best liquid for boiling or steaming is fresh unpolluted sea water; if not available, use salted water (one tablespoon salt per quart of water). Whether steaming or boiling, always use a pot that

COOKING WHOLE LOBSTERS
Time in Minutes

Name	Chickens	Quarters	Selects	Jumbos
Size (pounds)	*¾ to 1*	*1 to 1¼*	*1½ to 2*	*3 to 5*
Parboil (for sautéed lobster)	3 to 4	4 to 5	6 to 7	10 —
Boil	5 to 6	7 to 8	9 to 10	15 to 20
Steam	6 to 8	9 to 10	10 to 12	18 to 25

is larger than the volume of lobster to be cooked: a quick return to boiling is essential, as is room for the steam to circulate. For boiling, fill the pot three-quarters full. For steaming, fill the pot with two inches of water and put a steaming rack in place so that the lobsters are not touching the water. For either preparation, some seaweed can be added to the pot for flavoring; other flavorings are not important. Make sure you are at a rolling boil before you begin either method. Start counting the time once the pot has come back to a boil or after it has filled with steam. Consult the table for approximate times for different sizes of lobster and different cooking methods. Simmer lobsters that weigh four or more pounds; do not boil.

After cooking, I always punch a little hole with a knife behind the lobster's eyes to allow the water to drain from the body. This keeps the tomalley nice and firm and prevents a flood on the plate. I also crack the claws in the kitchen before serving the lobster, and I give each person a cracker to help remove the meat from the arms and claws.

How to Shell Lobster Claws

This is the only part of the lobster that is tricky to shuck. Shucking the tail is an easy matter of splitting the shell and removing the meat, and the body meat is removed simply by ripping the body open and picking out the meat. The claws and arms are also easy if you know how.

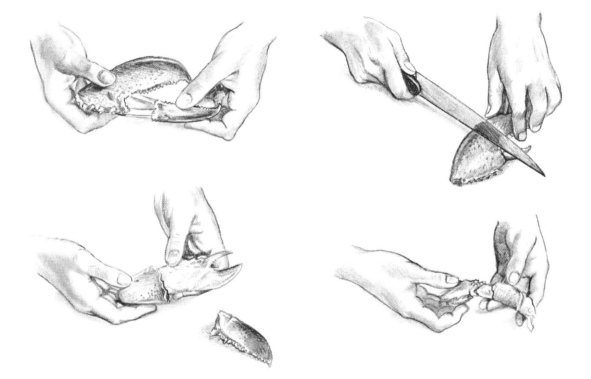

1. Break the arm from the claw.
2. Loosen the movable part of the claw by twisting it slowly from side to side until it snaps off. The meat should still be attached, but the shell removed.
3. With one swift and precise motion, crack the claw with your knife. Hit the claw across the shell right below the joint. Do not cut into the lobster meat.
4. Break open the shell with your hands. The piece should pop out whole.
5. With the back of your knife, tap on the arm until the shell is cracked completely around the joint. Peel back the shell with your hands. Remove the meat.

Lobster and Corn Chowder

This chowder epitomizes the summer foods of New England and our down-to-earth style of good cooking, and for the past seven summers I have featured this soup, first at the Bostonian Hotel and then in my restaurant. I use native butter and sugar corn, Vermont corncob-smoked bacon, the first new potatoes and onions of the year, Maine lobsters and unprocessed sweet cream from Guilford, Vermont.

In the true spirit of chowder this is a hearty soup. It is most suitable for serving as a main course, but in smaller portions it could make a good starter too. If you are serving this as a main course, I recommend Corn Fritters (page 267) as a side dish. If not, serve with Cream Biscuits (page 269) or toasted common crackers.

SERVES FOUR AS A MAIN COURSE
OR EIGHT TO TEN AS A STARTER

4 chicken (1 pound) lobsters
6 ears corn on the cob (3½ cups kernels)
½ pound slab smoked bacon, with rind
8 sprigs fresh thyme
1 teaspoon whole black peppercorns
4 bay leaves
1 onion, peeled, for stock
3 medium onions, cut in large (¾ inch) dice (3 cups)
4 tablespoons unsalted butter
8 small new potatoes (1 pound), red or white, cut in ⅓-inch slices
1½ cups heavy cream
salt and freshly ground black pepper
chopped chives or parsley for garnish

1. Bring a generous amount of fresh sea water or salted water to a boil, enough to cover the lobsters completely when they are added. When water is at a rolling boil, add the lobsters. When the water comes back to a boil, cook the lobsters 3 minutes exactly. Drain. When the lobsters have cooled down enough, break off the tail and claws.

2. Crack the claws and arms and carefully remove all the meat. Cut the tails in half lengthwise and remove the intestinal tracts. Cut the meat into large bite-size pieces; set aside in the refrigerator. Put all the shells and the bodies in a large kettle and cover with 12 cups of water. Bring to a simmer.

3. Cut the corn kernels off the cobs; set aside. Cut the cobs across and add to the kettle. Do not add the kernels. Cut the rind off the bacon and add to the kettle. Pick the leaves off the fresh thyme and set aside; put the stems of thyme in the kettle. Add the peppercorns, bay leaves and whole onion to the kettle. Simmer for 1 hour and 15 minutes. Strain the stock (you should have 6 to 7 cups).

4. Cut the bacon into small (¼ inch) dice and render in a soup pot until crisp. Add the diced onions, thyme leaves and butter and cook until the onions are wilted and tender (about 6 minutes); do not brown. Add the corn, potatoes and stock. Simmer about 20 minutes or until potatoes are cooked through. Add the cream and lobster meat. Season to taste with salt and pepper and simmer 2 minutes more. Serve in soup plates with the chunks of ingredients sticking out above the broth. Sprinkle each bowl with chopped chives or parsley.

Chunky Lobster Stew

Lobster stew is a very traditional dish made with lobster, milk, butter, salt and pepper. You will find this in many restaurants in Maine, the best being the ones with the most lobster. I have embellished on the original dish but have left intact the strong and rich lobster flavor. When Craig Claiborne asked me to put together a New England Thanksgiving dinner, this was the soup I served. It is also great as a hearty main course soup.

SERVES FIVE AS A MAIN COURSE
OR TEN AS A STARTER

5 chicken (1 pound) lobsters
1 medium onion, roughly
    chopped
4 bay leaves
2 large tomatoes
20 sprigs of fresh chervil
1 pint heavy cream
2 large leeks, white and yellow
    parts only, cut in medium
    (½ inch) dice
2 medium carrots, peeled and
    sliced very thin
8 tablespoons (1 stick) unsalted
    sweet butter
salt and freshly ground black
    pepper
cayenne pepper
Tomalley Croutons (recipe
    follows)

1. Blanch the lobsters for 4 minutes in a large pot of boiling fresh sea water or salted water. Remove from water, punch a little hole in the top of each head and allow to drain. Break off the claws and the tail. Remove the tomalley from the body and set aside in the refrigerator. Shuck the meat, chop into large bite-size pieces and set aside in the refrigerator. Be sure to remove intestinal tracts from the tails.

2. Place all the shell and bodies in a large saucepan and barely cover with water (about 2½ quarts). Add the onion and bay leaves. Bring to a boil, skim and reduce to simmer.

3. Peel and seed the tomatoes. Put the seeds and juice into the lobster stock and cut the tomato into medium dice; set aside. Pick the chervil off the stems. Add the stems to the stock and coarsely chop the chervil leaves; set aside.

4. After the stock has simmered for about 1 hour, add the heavy cream; simmer about 20 minutes more.

5. Simmer the leeks and carrots in butter in a soup pot until they begin to get tender (about 5 minutes). Now add the tomatoes and lobster meat and simmer 2 or 3 minutes more. Strain the creamy lobster stock into the soup pot (you should have about 6 cups of liquid). Season to taste with salt, pepper and cayenne pepper and sprinkle with chervil. Serve with tomalley croutons.

Tomalley Croutons

Besides garnishing lobster stew, tomalley croutons can be served as an hors d'oeuvre or if you wish to elaborate, as a topping for crostini or pizza. Lobster tomalley can be purchased separately from most lobster dealers. It is inexpensive and tasty.

MAKES TWENTY CROUTONS

1 teaspoon chopped garlic
2 tablespoons chopped onion
4 tablespoons unsalted butter,
    softened
1 tablespoon chopped parsley
½ cup cooked lobster tomalley
salt and freshly ground pepper
1 baguette (long French bread)

1. Sauté the garlic and onion in 1 tablespoon butter. Let cool somewhat, then mix with the remaining butter and parsley. Whip in the tomalley and season to taste with salt and pepper.

2. Preheat the oven to 400 degrees. Slice the French bread ⅜ inch thick and toast on both sides. Spread each piece with the tomalley-butter mixture. Place on a sheetpan and put in the preheated oven or under a broiler until croutons are crispy and hot. Serve immediately.

Warm Salad with Lobster, Foie Gras and Papaya

With this salad, portions have to be kept small. It is very festive and complex as salads go; it is also very rich. The most important part of the recipe is warming the lobster in oil. The lobster imparts its flavor to the oil, which, in turn, imparts the flavor to the salad, thus tying all the ingredients together. Adding papaya at the end helps cut the richness.

I get fresh Moulard duck foie gras from the Catskill region of New York (see List of Sources, page 356), and I quickly sauté the raw foie gras for this salad. If it is not available in your area, substitute prepared goose or duck foie gras, cut in strips, at room temperature.

SERVES FOUR AS AN APPETIZER

2 chicken (1 pound) lobsters or
 1 select (2 pound) lobster
4 tablespoons peanut oil
1 tablespoon chopped shallots
2 tablespoons sherry vinegar
2 tablespoons chopped chives
1 tablespoon finely sliced or
 grated lemon rind
4 cups mixed hearty salad greens
lemon juice
salt and freshly ground black
 pepper
4 ounces fresh Moulard duck
 foie gras, cut in 4 slices
all-purpose flour for dusting
1 large papaya, peeled and cut in
 large (1 inch) chunks

1. Partially cook the lobster as described on page 44 and shuck the meat.

2. Warm the peanut oil in a 12-inch sauté pan on medium heat. Add the lobster meat and shallots and begin to cook. Do not stir the lobster meat for 1 minute. You will see the meat underneath begin to redden. Turn the lobster and cook 1 minute more. Add the vinegar, chives and lemon rind. When the vinegar begins to boil, add the salad greens. Keep the pan on the fire and toss the greens until they begin to warm through, but not wilt. Season the greens with lemon juice, salt and pepper to taste. Quickly transfer to plates, putting the greens underneath and the chunks of lobster on top, where they are visible.

3. Season and lightly dust the foie gras with flour. Sauté quickly (30 seconds on each side) in a hot nonstick pan, using no fat for the cooking. Garnish the salad with the foie gras and papaya.

NOTE. Choose among frisée (tender curly endive), chicory, escarole, radicchio, arugula, romaine, watercress and spinach with Italian parsley leaves, depending on what is available and looks good.

Lobster Sausage with Savoy Cabbage

When I first created this dish for the opening of the Bostonian Hotel in 1982, it was the talk of the town. I found myself making it daily and sometimes twice a day. Within a year it started to appear on different menus around town, much to my dismay. Some people told me that they had tried them in other places and that mine were the best. But it wasn't until I was accused of stealing the idea that I decided to retire the dish. Testing the recipe for this book was the first time in four years that I made these sausages, and if I do say so myself, they are still the best.

This dish may sound like a culinary affectation, which I try to avoid as much as possible, but it is really a very practical way to use large lobsters or culls. In this recipe I call for two five-pound culls, but you can use any combination of lobsters with a total weight of ten pounds. The recipe can be cut in half if desired. The important equation is one-third raw lobster meat to two-thirds cooked. The amount of butter may seem like too much, but it is the only fat for the sausage, so it is important not to skimp.

Ten pounds of lobster makes about three pounds of sausage, enough to serve about eight as an entree or sixteen as an appetizer. The forcemeat could also be stuffed into lamb casings to make miniature sausages or it could be used to stuff cabbage leaves or leeks.

MAKES ABOUT THREE POUNDS

pig casings (about 4 feet)
2 five-pound culls (lobsters with one claw)
2 egg whites
1 red bell pepper, roasted and peeled (page 247)
2 celery stalks, peeled and cut in small (¼ inch) dice (½ cup)
1 large carrot, peeled and cut in small (¼ inch) dice (½ cup)
12 tablespoons (1½ sticks) unsalted butter
1 cup fresh white breadcrumbs (page 67)
1 tablespoon finely chopped Italian parsley
1 tablespoon finely chopped fresh chervil (see Note)
2 tablespoons chopped chives
salt and freshly ground black pepper
Court Bouillon (page 79) or Fish Stock (page 327) for poaching (optional)

For Serving
Warm Savoy Slaw (recipe follows)
Boiled or Steamed New Potatoes (page 249)

1. The day before making the sausages, rinse the casings well and put to soak in papaya or pineapple juice for 24 hours. (For more details on sausage-making, see pages 178–179.)

2. Break off the tail of 1 lobster. Remove the meat and set aside. Boil the rest of the body and the claw with the other lobster, following the directions on page 44. Pick every piece of meat from the cooked lobsters, including the body and even the walking legs. Large lobsters have meat everywhere. Chop into small (¼- to ½-inch) pieces. Set aside.

3. Puree the raw lobster with the egg whites and roasted pepper in a food processor until very fine and pink in color. Cook the celery and carrot in butter until the butter boils; remove from heat. When the butter-vegetable mixture is at room temperature, fold into the pureed lobster. Add the breadcrumbs, cooked lobster, parsley, chervil and chives. Season lightly with salt and pepper.

4. Stuff the forcemeat into casings. For small batches of sausage like this, the easiest way is to put the sausage nozzle (pig stuffer) into a pastry bag rather than a mechanical device. Chill the sausages a few hours before using.

5. Poach the sausages in simmering court bouillon, fish stock or water for about 4 minutes. Finish them by grilling or panfrying.

NOTE. If chervil is not available, increase the amount of Italian parsley to 2 tablespoons.

Warm Savoy Slaw

SERVES EIGHT AS A SIDE DISH

½ head Savoy cabbage, finely shredded
1 carrot, cut in very fine julienne (⅛ × 1½ inches)
1 red pepper, cut in very fine julienne (⅛ × 1½ inches)
4 tablespoons unsalted butter
salt and freshly ground black pepper

1. Blanch the cabbage for 1 minute in a large pot of boiling salted water. (Blanching gives the slaw a milder flavor.)

2. Sauté the carrot and pepper in butter until tender. Add the cabbage and cook until the mixture is hot. Season to taste with salt and pepper.

Lobster Sautéed with Spring Vegetables

The ingredients of a lobster sauté can change with the seasons as long as the flavors go with lobster. In autumn you might use wild chanterelles; in winter, cabbage. Some people sauté raw lobster meat, but I think partially cooked meat works better. I have chosen to include a few noodles in this sauté, but a puff pastry garnish could be used instead. The recipe is for four appetizers portions, but it can easily be doubled for four main courses.

SERVES FOUR AS AN APPETIZER

2 chicken (1 pound) lobsters
8 ounces fresh wide egg noodles,
    such as pappardelle (page 277)
2 tablespoons clarified butter
    (page 329)
1 tablespoon chopped shallots
1 cup fresh morels, sliced into
    ³⁄₈-inch rings
1 small carrot, peeled and thinly
    sliced, blanched
½ cup fiddlehead ferns, blanched
    (page 236)
2 tablespoons amontillado
    sherry
2 tablespoons unsalted butter
salt and freshly ground black
    pepper
chopped chives and chive
    flowers, broken up, for
    garnish

1. Partially cook the lobster as described on page 44 and shuck the meat.

2. Bring a pot of salted water to a boil. Drop the noodles into the water.

3. Heat a 12-inch sauté pan to medium-high heat. Add the clarified butter, lobster meat, shallots and morels to the pan. Do not move or stir for 1 minute. The butter should start to color slightly from the lobster.

4. Add the carrot and fiddlehead ferns and cook 2 minutes more, stirring or tossing occasionally. Add the sherry and the noodles. Also add the butter; toss. Season to taste with salt and pepper.

4. Put the noodles toward the back of the plates. Arrange the lobster and sautéed vegetables loosely around the front. Spoon any extra sauce over the lobster and sprinkle with the chopped chives and chive flowers. Serve at once.

Panroasted Lobster with Chervil and Chives

Of all the lobster dishes I have served in my restaurant, this has been by far the most popular. Since the day we introduced it, it has never been off the menu. Actually it is an adaptation of *Homard grillé simple* from the repertoire of Fernand Point, the brilliant French restaurateur and chef who so greatly influenced twentieth-century French—and American—cooking. Taking just a few simple ingredients and an easy cooking method, he knew how to create a perfect balance of flavors. I think that my version of this dish, in which I panroast the lobster instead of grilling it and substitute our own bourbon for French cognac, proves that inspiration that builds upon the past outlives most of our more fanciful creations.

This recipe is for two lobsters, which is the most you can fit into a twelve-inch sauté pan. Before you attempt to increase the recipe, be sure you have two large pans and enough room on your range and in the broiler.

SERVES TWO AS AN ENTREE
OR FOUR AS AN APPETIZER

2 select (1½ to 2 pound) lobsters
2 tablespoons peanut oil
¼ cup bourbon
¼ cup white wine
4 tablespoons unsalted butter
2 teaspoons finely chopped fresh chervil or parsley
2 teaspoons finely chopped chives
salt and freshly ground black pepper

For Serving
grilled shiitake or Roman mushrooms or batter-fried vegetables

1. Break off the arms and claws of the lobsters. The lobsters will remain alive. Boil the arms and claws in salted water for 3 minutes; drain. When cool enough to handle, carefully remove all the meat as described on page 45; set aside. The claws should remain in one piece. This can be done up to 1 hour in advance. If you wish to omit this step and serve the claws in the shell, simply break them off and crack them when you cut up the lobsters. (Precooking and shelling the claws makes this an elegant dish requiring minimal use of the hands at the table.)

2. Preheat the broiler as hot as possible. Preheat a 12-inch sauté pan.

3. With a sharp cleaver chop off the top third of the lobster body (the head) and discard. Most of the body and the walking legs should remain intact. Split the lobster in half lengthwise. Remove the intestinal tract from the tail. Split the pieces in half again. You will have 4 pieces per lobster.

4. Add the peanut oil to the hot sauté pan and place the pieces, shell side down, in the pan. Cook for 1 minute, turn the pieces over and place under the broiler until the shells begin to char a bit (1 minute 30 seconds). Return to the stove, add the cooked lobster (claws) and the bourbon. Ignite. When the flames burn off, add the wine and cook 1 minute more, stirring frequently. Most of the liquid should have evaporated by now. Add the butter and herbs, swirling the pan so the butter blends with the pan drippings and juices. Season with salt and pepper and arrange the lobster on plates so that it begins to resemble itself again. Pile the claws on top of the shells and spoon any excess butter over the pieces. Garnish with mushrooms or other vegetables.

Grilled Lobster

If I had to choose only one way to eat lobster, this would be it. Since the meat never really touches the grill, the charred shells flavor the lobster, not the wood or charcoal. The meat has a wonderful, intense aroma. And you need no utensils for shucking the lobster: grilling makes the shells very brittle and easy to crack open. Last week I did a mixed grill for some friends, starting with lobster, followed by quail and then steak. We took our time and ate slowly but steadily for the better part of the evening, enjoying each food as it was cooked.

SERVES TWO AS AN ENTREE
OR FOUR AS AN APPETIZER

2 select (2 pound) lobsters
vegetable oil for brushing
salt and freshly ground pepper
4 to 5 tablespoons Garlic Butter
(page 330), melted (see Note)
lemon wedges

1. Let the fire on your grill burn down to medium heat.
2. Take a sharp knife and put the tip where the body meets the tail, with the blade facing the head. Split the body, then turn the knife around and split the tail. Remove the head sac and intestinal tract. If the lobster has roe, remove some of it and place it in the head so that it cooks faster. (The meat of the lobster cooks faster than the roe.)
3. Crack the claws on the side facing up. Lightly brush the shell and tail meat with oil, sprinkle with salt and pepper and place the lobster, shell side down, over the coals. Brush the body and tail meat with melted garlic butter. Try to work some into the cracked claws. Repeat after 2 minutes. Cover the grill with a lid or loosely with aluminum foil. Cook 5 minutes more or until the lobster meat is firm and white. Serve with lemon wedges and the remaining butter or garlic butter.

NOTE. Substitute plain butter if you wish or baste with oil and serve with drawn butter.

Fish

The Cod Family
New England Fish Chowder

New England Boiled Dinner with Fish

Haddock Stew with Saffron, Fennel, Tomatoes and Mussels

Boston Scrod

Fisherman's-Style Whiting

Plaice, Flounder, Fluke, Dabs and Sole
Flounder or Fluke *à l'Anglaise*

Sand-Dabs *Doré*

Atlantic Halibut
Halibut Braised in White Wine with Shallots and Wild Mushrooms

Halibut with Lobster Bordelaise, Pearl Onions, Mushrooms and Periwinkles

Baked Halibut

Lobster Bordelaise Sauce

Bluefish
Bluefish with Clams and Sweet Garlic Pasta

Barbecued Bluefish with Smoked-Shrimp Butter

Striped Bass

Salmon
Steamed Salmon with Egg Sauce and Peas

Salad of Cold Poached Salmon, Fresh Peas, Red Onions and New Potatotes

Poached Salmon

Grilled Salmon Steaks with Aïoli and Parsley Salad

Trout and Char
Panfried Trout

Shad and Shad Roe
Shad Roe Slowly Roasted in Butter

Shad Roe Wrapped in Bacon and Grilled with Wilted Spinach, Red Onions and Oranges

Monkfish
Roasted Monkfish

Swordfish and Shark
Grilled Swordfish or Shark with Basil Butter and Tomato Sauce

Bluefin Tuna
Tuna Carpaccio

Medaillons of Tuna Wrapped in Bacon with Red Wine Sauce

Grilled Tuna Steaks with Caramelized Onion Sauce

Tautog, Tilefish and Wolffish
Fish and Chips

Black Sea Bass and Ocean Perch
Jasper's Half-Crispy Fish with Scallion Puree

Steamed Whole Fish, Chinese Style

Mackerel
Tinkers and Bacon for Breakfast

Grilled Mackerel in a Quick Soy Marinade

Porgies and Butterfish

Smelts, Silversides (Spearing), Alewife, Menhadin and Other Small Fish

"Where are you going and what do you wish?"
the old man asked the three.
"We've come to fish for the herring fish
that swim in the beautiful sea.
Nets of silver and gold have we,"
said Wynken, Blynken and Nod.
—EUGENE FIELD

Since the birth of my son, J.P., I have become familiar with several lullabies. This one touches a melancholy chord for me with its romantic references to the sea. I wonder will he enjoy the fish that swim in the "beautiful sea" the way I have? The sea with all its fury and might seems so much greater than man that it is hard to imagine that we could destroy it. Yet that is exactly the course we seem to be intent on.

In my lifetime I have watched what as a child seemed to be God's greatest creation, abundant beyond belief, turn fragile and threatened.

Even so, New England is still one of the world's greatest fishing regions. On any given day, I can go fishing on my little (twenty-foot) Bertram, out near the Cuckolds at the mouth of the Sheepscott River, where I keep a summer cottage on Sawyer's Island, and bring home mackerel, bluefish, and haddock. Unfortunately, however, I can do this only in Maine; it would be futile to keep a boat here in Boston, where we are surrounded by waters that once were but no longer are rich and beautiful fishing grounds.

I am chauvinistic about the fish and shellfish that I serve in my restaurant, using New England and Atlantic Canadian seafood exclusively. Besides the obvious fact that local seafood is very fresh, many people visit New England hoping to taste our delicious seafood; it seems ridiculous to me to offer them foreign fish. I know where each type of fish that I serve comes from, and how it is handled. I buy fish from the most reputable purveyors and in many cases direct from the sources. And I have a lot of seafood shipped from Maine, not far from where I myself fish in the summer.

Fishing and fish are intimately intertwined with the life-style and history of the people of coastal New England. From the earliest times the incredible abundance of cod and other fish made survival in the New World easier than it might otherwise have been. And at the present time a good number of people, including myself, make their living, in one way or the other, from the bounty of icy North Atlantic waters. It wasn't long after this region was settled that the first fisheries came into existence and the first fortunes were made from exporting cod. The codfish aristocracy of Boston was the basis of the new wealthy class of New Englanders, who provided the capital for the further development of this region. In relation to the rest of the economy, fishing as an industry peaked prior to the Revolutionary War; though other industries, like textiles, have come and gone, fishing still employs a significant number of New Englanders.

The most important and richest fishing ground in New England, and possibly the world, is Georges Bank, which is a 24-hour boat ride from Gloucester, Boston or New Bedford, due east. Georges Bank is divided between the United States and Canada, with the United States controlling the largest portion, but Canada controlling the most productive. Every day astronomical amounts of cod, haddock, pollock, hake, wolffish, cusk, tilefish, monkfish and many other species are landed at Georges Bank by American and Canadian vessels. Every now and then, a New England fishing trawler is seized by the Canadian government for fishing illegally in their waters. Canadian fishermen are subsidized by their government, which has been extremely aggressive about building the Canadian fishing fleet and the industry in general. Canadian fishermen are generally better equipped than the American entrepreneurial fishermen, who at times can barely make a living. These inequalities have led to some bitterness and animosity between the competing fishing fleets.

Another important fishing grounds in New England is the Channel, a body of deep water that stretches from the easternmost tip of Boston harbor south around Cape Cod and down to Long Island. Flounder and sea scallops are the biggest part of the catch for the boats from Cape Cod and New Bedford that fish the Channel.

The Gulf of Maine is also a rich fishing region, although the commercial fleets of this region have been depleted over the years in the wake of competition from the fishermen from Georges Bank. The once-thriving sardine industry is all but defunct and many fisheries have shut down. Lobstering and other shellfishing predominate in this region, but the fish are still there in abundance. The Gulf of Maine is especially rich in smaller fish like mackerel, porgies, butterfish, silversides, alewife and smelts; it is also home to some very fine halibut, monkfish and many of the groundfish that are common at Georges Bank. Bluefish, striped bass, tuna, and swordfish also migrate, although not in great numbers, into the Gulf of Maine.

Anyone who makes a living from the sea must go to the most fertile fishing grounds, but for the sport fisherman New England offers a variety of species and pretty good fishing along most of its coast, with the exception of the polluted harbors. Summer offers the sport fisherman the chance to catch not only groundfish but also the great migratory fish like swordfish, tuna and bluefish. I usually confine myself to fishing the smaller species, like bluefish, mackerel and cod.

Groundfish. Stationary ocean fish that can be caught year-round in the fertile fishing grounds of New England. The most famous of these is cod and its cousins, haddock, pollock and silver hake or whiting. Next in popularity are the flatfish, halibut, the most sought-after, and then flounder, fluke and dabs, which are all usually sold as sole. Another groundfish, which is becoming more popular, is monkfish or lotte. Other less utilized but readily available groundfish are eels, wolffish, sea trout, tautog, perch and sea bass, to name a few. With today's exorbitant fish prices, readers would be wise to acquaint themselves with these lesser-known fish.

Small Ocean Fish. Fish like mackerel, porgies, butterfish, smelts and other miniature fish that are most often caught in the bays and river mouths of New England. These fish are an abundant supply of delicious food available at reasonable prices. Most of these are brought to market by small-scale day fishermen.

Migratory and Anadromous Fish. Species which come north in the late spring and leave as winter approaches, such as swordfish, shark, tuna and bluefish, as well as fish like salmon, striped bass and shad that are usually caught in river mouths as they head upstream to spawn in spring. They can all be found here at different times of year, to varying degrees. Most knowledgeable people agree that both these types of fish reach their peak of flavor in our cold New England and Canadian waters.

Freshwater Fish. Less important in our region than ocean fish. The fame and sheer abundance of New England's ocean fish probably accounts for the absence of lore concerning its freshwater fish. Although it cannot be compared with the Rockies, Great Lakes, and other renowned freshwater fishing regions, New England does have some good river and lake fishing. Vermont, New Hampshire and Maine have very fine rivers that are home to rainbow and brook trout. And some lakes have excellent bass and trout fishing. Another popular freshwater fish is the landlocked salmon, a leftover from the Ice Age that can be found in some of the lakes of eastern Maine. I know of a few people who have caught twenty-pound fish in such lakes. In addition to the wild freshwater fish of this region, there are several reputable fish farms, which produce fairly good-tasting trout (see List of Sources, pages 356–357).

Fish cookery is to the advanced cook what jazz or other improvisational music is to the virtuoso. With the basics of fish cookery in mind, one can wander, explore and create. Almost every day I create a new variation for my fish special of the day. Some, of course, are more successful than others, but all are good. In this chapter you will find a few of my favorites as well as some elementary dishes that capture the essence of each particular kind of fish. Fish cookery can be mastered only through experience, experience based on a sound knowledge of the fundamentals and a healthy respect for the true flavor and texture of the fish involved. If that flavor is compromised or if the fish is improperly cooked, all else is lost.

When approaching fish, gastronomically speaking, you find as many differences as there are similarities. One fish may be suitable to almost all preparations, another to only one or two. Conversely, one preparation may be suitable to many different types of fish, another to only one or two. Another factor to take into account is the size of the fish. In many cases different size fish of the same species must be treated as different fish. I will limit the rest of this introduction to the purchasing, care and handling of fish in general and cover the specifics of each fish as I go along. I will give the different cooking methods in the form of individual recipes and, where appropriate, note other types of fish that can be treated the same way.

THE PURCHASING, CARE
AND HANDLING OF FRESH FISH

It takes a lot of knowledge to understand what distinguishes truly great fish. Location, time of year, species, the fishing method, the boat itself, and the fishermen are all factors. As with shellfish, freshness and quality are synonymous, but fish, unlike shellfish, die quickly out of water (and even in the water).

The very finest fish are caught in small nets or traps and brought onto the boat alive. For large species like swordfish, harpooning is the most desirable method, yielding fish of the highest quality. The next best method is known as jig-fishing, where lines usually hold about eight baited hooks, which obviously need frequent tending. What is important is that the fish are not dragged around dead underwater. In long-lining and tug-trawling miles of baited hooks are put out; when the lines are carefully tended, fish of fairly good quality can be harvested, but when they are not, the fish can be watery and mushy. Absolutely the worst method of commercial fishing is gill-netting, which entails dragging a wire net designed to hook fish in the gills. This method often mutilates the fish, hooking them in the tail and sides as well as the gills. Since gill-netting kills the fish quickly, they are waterlogged as well. The reputation of pollock, which is frequently gill-netted, has suffered not because of the fish, but because of this inferior fishing method.

On-board storage of the caught fish is also important. Does the boat carry ice to chill the freshly caught fish? If it does not, a fish may be only 10 hours old and yet inferior to a 30-hour-old fish that has been properly iced. Is the fish gutted on board? Heaven help you if not. There is more to freshness and quality than how many hours the fish has been out of the water. People will tell you they only buy "the top of the trip," by which they mean the freshest fish, the ones that were caught last. But top can mean everything that isn't on the very bottom. It's an imaginary line.

This information may not be directly helpful to you as a consumer, but it is what your purveyors must know to obtain the best quality of fish. A good fishmonger knows the different boats and captains, and he supports the good ones. And that is how you as the consumer should treat the mongers: support the good ones and don't shop for bargains. There is no such thing. (See the List of Sources, pages 356–357, for a few of the best seafood distributors in New England.)

How to Buy Fish

I once saw Paul Prudhomme interviewed on TV, and he said, "In New Orleans when a fishmonger dies, they don't bury him. They screw him into the ground." The fish business has the terrible burden of dealing in the most perishable commodity there is, and a totally honest fishmonger is just as rare in Boston as in New Orleans. I have met a few. As with all purveyors, it helps if you keep them honest, and in order to do this, you must know what to look for. There is no way for the average consumer to know the different boats and the ins and outs of the commercial market, but anyone can learn to recognize the difference between good and bad fish.

Let me say first, frozen fish doesn't count. It can never be anything but second-rate. The very nature of fish, its delicate watery flesh, prohibits this method of storage from having anything but minimal success. Frozen fish has a dull appearance, lifeless flavor and flaccid texture.

When you buy fresh fish, look to see if it is kept on shaved or crushed ice in drain pans. That is standard good practice for handling fish. If a fishmonger does not follow that most basic precaution, then he is not serious about quality. Buy whole, head-on fish; it is a surefire way to tell if you are getting a truly fresh fish. Look that fish in the eye—bright, shiny, clear eyes are a definite sign of freshness. After a fish is dead for more than two days, the eyes cloud over and look very dull. Pick up the fish. Is it still stiff (rigor mortis)? If it is you have a beauty.

Is it still slimy? That thick gooey slime is a sign of freshness, not age. Fish loses its slime after two days. Smell the fish. If it has any noticeable odor other than that of the sea, it is old.

When you buy fillets, ask for them skin-on when possible. At least then you are sure you are getting the fish you are paying for. There are people out there who would pass off a pollock as a haddock if you let them. Not that there is anything wrong with pollock, but you shouldn't be paying haddock prices for it. Don't get too excited about the first native Atlantic salmon of the spring until you see the black spots near the tail. With each fish in this book is a brief description of its appearance, to help you identify it at market.

If you can't use a whole fish, you will have to determine freshness from the flesh alone. Is it clear and shiny or is it dull? Very fresh fish have beautiful clear flesh, no matter what the color. I have seen freshly caught halibut that you could literally see through. Feel the flesh. Is it firm and relatively dry or is it soft and mushy? If it is mushy and wet, it is not good. And if your purveyor will not allow you to handle the fish, then find one who will.

When you go fishing, bring along a large cooler or other container and place your fish in it, in the same water they were caught in. Keep the fish alive as long as possible. If they die, gut them and keep them in a cool place, on ice (like your beer) when possible. This will make a world of difference, especially if you are out all day and the weather is hot. Here there is no need to worry about getting the fish fresh, only about keeping it fresh.

How to Scale Fish

If you intend to cook your fish with the skin on, you must remove the scales. Even if you purchase the fish scaled, you have to go over it again. Always scale the whole fish first. Although there are tools for scaling, all you need is a knife with a substantial blade. A knife that is a bit dull is best; a sharp knife will tear the skin. Some people use the back of the knife for scaling. Holding the fish by the tail and your knife at about a 25-degree angle to the fish, scrape toward the head. You will need to change the angle of the knife as you work around the fins. Turn the fish over and repeat. Rinse and double-check to see if the job is complete.

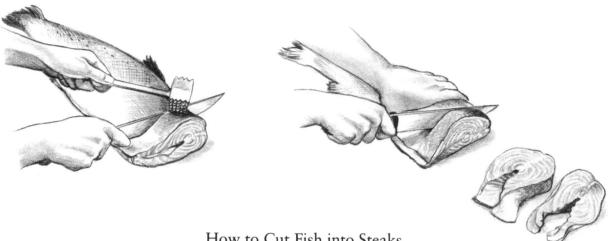

How to Cut Fish into Steaks

A true fish steak is cut across the backbone. This treatment is usually reserved for salmon, bass, cod, large eels and other fish weighing at least eight pounds. Halibut is the only flatfish that is cut into steaks, and it is done differently than for round fish. Steaks from tuna and swordfish, which I doubt you will ever find yourself cutting, are more often fillets resembling steaks than true steaks.

To cut steaks, lay the fish on its side. Using a very sharp and somewhat heavy knife, cut the steaks straight through the meat and the bone. If your knife gets stuck in the backbone, give it a tap with a cleaver or hammer and it will go right through. The size of the fish will determine the thickness of the steaks, but they should be no less than one inch thick. Start at the head and work down to the tail. When you get to where the fish starts to narrow, leave it in one piece and fillet it.

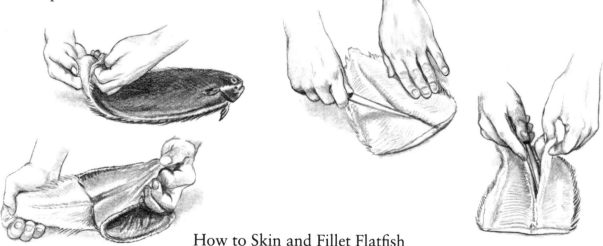

How to Skin and Fillet Flatfish

For the flounder, it is best to skin the fish before filleting; for halibut and for the various round fish, the opposite is true. To skin flounder, make an incision near the tail and loosen up the skin enough to get a firm grip on it. In one sweeping motion, pull the skin in the direction of the head. It should come off in one piece. Turn the fish over and repeat.

Although there is a way to cut flounder and halibut into two fillets, this is not easy for the novice. The method I will explain here is called the quarter fillet. Make an incision from head to tail straight down the backbone, which is almost dead center on the fish. Halibut have a light marking that indicates this line. If you are not sure, feel with your fingers for the bone after the incision is started. Using a flexible knife with a thin blade, work from the head down. Lean your knife at about a twenty-degree angle against the bone. Keep your knife in this position separating the meat from the bone as you work your way down. Fold the meat over as you cut, so you can see what you are doing. Remove the two fillets. Repeat on the other side.

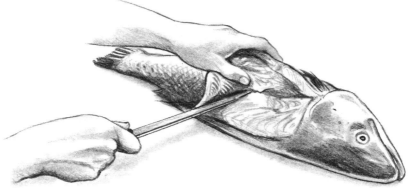

How to Fillet Round Fish

Make an incision behind the head of the fish. Find the backbone. Keep the tip of the knife pressed firmly against that bone, without letting it extend past the bone. Keep it almost flat as you cut down the side of the fish. Fold the flesh up as you go so you can see where you are. Now, starting at the head, hold the knife at a more downward angle and cut the fillet away from the rib bones. Turn the fish over and repeat. With practice you will become quite adept and will probably devise a technique of your own.

How to Debone a Fillet

The Japanese have a special type of pliers for pulling the bones out of fish. I use these exclusively, but if you cannot locate a pair, needle-nose pliers will suffice. Another tool that is excellent for this is Kelly clamps, a medical pliers. Since the bones go through the meat, you want to remove them as cleanly as possible. Pull them straight out in the same direction in which they lie.

How to Skin a Fillet

Place the fillet skin side down on the table. Make an incision near the tail, positioning your knife between the meat and the skin. Hold the skin firmly with one hand as you separate the meat from the skin in one motion, keeping your knife at a slight angle toward the table.

How to Cut Medaillons or Individual Pieces from a Fillet

First remove all bones. Starting near the head, cut through the fillet at a 45-degree angle, portioning the fish into six-ounce pieces on the average. Thicker fish like halibut may not require this cutting on an angle; it depends on the cooking method to be used. Any fish to be sautéed should be cut on a wide bias, creating larger but thinner pieces. This can be done whether the skin is on or off.

THE COD FAMILY

Commercial fishing for cod began in Gloucester, Massachusetts, in 1623, and great fortunes were built from the salt cod trade. Cod and the cod fisherman have been immortalized in works of art and literature as well as in traditional pottery, of which the most famous example is the "gurgling cod" water pitcher, which makes a gulping sound when the water is poured. Cape Cod, of course, was named for it. The "Sacred Cod" has hung in the Massachusetts House of Representatives since 1784, symbolizing the importance of cod politically and economically.

Cod and its cousins—haddock, pollock and hake or whiting—are closely associated with the history of our region as well as with the Mediterranean, which depended on salt cod as a staple food. The appeal of cod has been universal; it has been embraced in one form or another by every wave of immigrants from the Yankees of English descent, who adored their chowders, fish cakes and finnan haddie, to the Italians and Portuguese, who were well versed in cod cookery, both fresh and dried, long before their migration to America. Classic French cooking also holds both dry and fresh cod in high esteem. Fish from the cod family are tasty and versatile, and can almost always be found in excellent quality in New England. They have similar cooking qualities. I have tried to give examples of how each one is best utilized, but you should feel free to use any member of the cod family in the recipes that follow.

Because even an experienced shopper may be confused by the different members of the cod family, it is best always to ask for skin-on fillets or whole fish. Prices vary greatly, haddock and cod being much more expensive than pollock and hake. You should know what you are paying for.

Atlantic Cod. Brown and spotted with a light lateral line running down its side. It also has a large barbel under its chin, resembling a big whisker. Cod varies in size from small, 1½ pounds, to very large, over 25 pounds, but it is most commonly marketed between 2½ and 10 pounds.

Haddock. A smaller fish than the cod and a bit rounder in shape. It has grayish blue skin with a black lateral line running down its side. Haddock also has a black patch of skin above its pectoral fin. It is usually marketed at two to five pounds. This excellent fish commands the highest price in the cod family. Split and smoked, it is known as finnan haddie (see pages 102–104).

Pollock. A very abundant member of the cod family. It is greenish gray with a light lateral line running down its side. It is generally marketed at four to six pounds, and it is relatively inexpensive. Its reputation has been marred by the practice of gill-netting, which damages the fish (see page 58). Because of its lower price, pollock is often handled with less respect than cod and haddock, but at its best it is excellent, especially in fish chowder.

Hake. The only true cod, with a rounded tail and only two dorsal fins (the others have three). It has a different, coarser texture than the other members of the cod family, but it is full-flavored and is excellent when matched with other full-flavored foods, like tomatoes. Most of the hake marketed in New England is silver hake, which is sold as whiting; it is usually marketed at three to five pounds, though it can be quite a bit larger.

New England Fish Chowder

By rights any fish can be used for chowder, and often is. But the very best fish chowder is made with cod or one of its relatives. Salmon, monkfish, tautog, tilefish and wolffish also make very good chowder. Finely textured fish like flounder, mackerel and sea bass are not good for chowder; they fall apart too easily. After very fresh fish, the most important ingredient is a good, strong Fish Stock (page 327). To keep the fish from breaking up too much, I have learned to add the fillets whole or in as large pieces as possible. They will break up by themselves as the chowder is stirred. The exception to this is tautog and tilefish, which are very firm; you should cut them into one-inch pieces. Like all chowders, this one is best served as a main course for lunch or as a light supper. Common crackers or Cream Biscuits (page 269) make an excellent accompaniment.

SERVES EIGHT TO TEN
AS A MAIN COURSE

3½ pounds fresh fillets, skinless
   and boneless
¼ pound meaty salt pork, cut in
   ¼- to ½-inch dice
4 tablespoons unsalted butter
2 medium to large onions, cut in
   large (¾ inch) dice (3 cups)
3 bay leaves
1 tablespoon chopped fresh
   thyme leaves
3 or 4 large Maine or other
   boiling potatoes, peeled and
   cut lengthwise in half, then
   into ¼-inch slices
3 cups strong Fish Stock
   (page 327)
2 cups heavy cream
salt and freshly ground black
   pepper
2 tablespoons chopped fresh
   parsley and/or chervil
8 tablespoons (1 stick) unsalted
   butter

1. Prepare the fish by removing any excess skin and picking out any bones with a pair of tweezers. If you use a knife to cut out bones, be sure to leave the fillets in as large pieces as possible.

2. Render the salt pork in a large soup pot until it begins to crisp. Add the butter, onions, bay leaves and thyme. Cook for 5 minutes or until the onions become soft. Add the potatoes and fish stock and simmer for 20 minutes or until the potatoes are tender.

3. Remove the bay leaves and add the cod fillets and heavy cream. Simmer slowly until the fish is cooked through and begins to flake (about 8 to 10 minutes). Season to taste with salt and pepper. Stir in the chopped parsley and/or chervil. Remove from heat.

4. Using a slotted spoon, transfer the chunks of fish, the onions and potatoes to soup plates; then ladle over the piping hot broth. Put a dollop of butter into each plate of soup and serve with crackers or biscuits.

New England Boiled Dinner with Fish

I created this dish while working on this book. I had been testing the recipe for New England Boiled Dinner (page 166) the previous day, and being housebound due to a snowstorm, I scraped together a dinner with the extra ingredients from the boiled dinner and some cod that I had bought earlier in the day. In a boiling frame of mind, I paired the cod (since then I have tried salmon and haddock with equal success) with spices, bacon, potatoes, carrots, turnips, onions and cabbage. We sat watching the snow fall, and as I brought this heart-warming pot of food to the table, I remember thinking how perfect it seemed. And then we tasted it. It was right the very first time. A rare occurrence, indeed!

SERVES FOUR AS AN ENTREE

¼ pound of slab country bacon, cut into 4 thick slices
3 bay leaves
3 cloves garlic
4 sprigs fresh thyme
¼ teaspoon crushed red pepper
2 tablespoons kosher salt
freshly ground black pepper
2 large or 4 medium carrots, peeled and cut in 1-inch chunks
8 new potatoes, peeled and cut in half
6 to 8 medium-size, white boiling onions, peeled
2 turnips, peeled and cut in half
½ head Savoy cabbage, cut into 4 wedges
4 pieces of cod, haddock or salmon fillet, 6 ounces each
2 tablespoons chopped fresh parsley

Condiments
butter
prepared mustard
freshly grated horseradish (optional)

1. Bring 8 cups water to a boil in a large flat pot with the bacon slices, bay leaves, garlic, thyme, crushed red pepper, salt and a little black pepper.

2. Turn down to a simmer and add the carrots, potatoes, onions and turnips. Slowly simmer for 15 to 20 minutes until the carrots are tender. (Vegetables in this dish are not supposed to be al dente.) Now add the cabbage wedges and simmer 8 minutes more. Add the fish fillets and simmer 3 minutes. Remove from heat and allow to stand 3 or 4 minutes.

3. Using a slotted spoon, carefully remove the fish to the center of a large platter. Arrange all the vegetables and the bacon around the platter and spoon a little of the broth over everything. Sprinkle with chopped parsley and serve at once. Pass the butter (for the potatoes and turnips) and your favorite mustard or even a little horseradish.

Haddock Stew with Saffron, Fennel, Tomatoes and Mussels

For this robustly flavored fish stew it is essential that you first prepare a very good fish stock with white wine (page 327). The stock is further enriched as the fish, mussels and vegetables slowly simmer in it. This is best served in large soup plates with ample room for the broth. Serve with garlic bread and set out spoons as well as forks and fish knives.

SERVES FOUR TO SIX
AS A MAIN COURSE

2 pounds haddock fillets, skin
    on, bones removed
salt and freshly ground black
    pepper
24 to 30 mussels, scrubbed and
    debearded
3 tablespoons olive oil
2 cloves garlic, finely chopped
1 small onion, thinly sliced
    (½ cup)
1 carrot, cut into thin (⅛ inch)
    julienne (¼ cup)
1 large bulb fennel, tops
    reserved, bottom stalks peeled
    if stringy and cut into thin
    (⅛ inch) julienne (1½ to 2
    cups)
2 medium tomatoes, peeled and
    seeded, cut into ¼-inch strips
1 tablespoon finely grated
    orange peel
½ teaspoon Spanish string
    saffron
1½ cups Fish Stock (page 327)
4 tablespoons unsalted butter
garlic bread for serving

1. Cut the fillets into small pieces and season lightly with salt and pepper. Place the pieces of fish in a large earthenware or glass baking dish and place the mussels around and between them.

2. Preheat the oven to 350 degrees. Heat a large sauté pan. Add olive oil, garlic, onion, carrot and fennel. Cook for about 5 minutes or until the vegetables begin to get limp. Add the tomatoes, grated orange peel, saffron and fish stock and bring to a boil. Pour this over the fish and mussels and cover with a lid or aluminum foil. Place in the preheated oven for about 20 minutes or until the fish is cooked and the mussels have opened.

3. Using a slotted spoon, lift the fish out of the pan and place in the middle of a large platter. Place the mussels around the fish. Scatter the vegetables around the platter and over the fish.

4. Stir the butter into the remaining broth and season with a bit more pepper. (You will most likely not need additional salt, as the mussels add salt to the broth.) Garnish with sprigs of fennel and serve a big basket of garlic bread alongside.

Boston Scrod

If you want the absolute definition of scrod, or schrod as it is sometimes spelled, you will be disappointed to learn there is none. Although most people say it is baby cod (under two pounds), others will tell you that young haddock and pollock are acceptable as scrod. Some tourist-oriented restaurants along the waterfront in Boston pass off almost any fish as scrod, claiming that scrod means "fish of the day." Another point in question is how it is cooked: if it is not broiled with breadcrumbs, most New Englanders would not consider it to be scrod; it would just be baby cod.

The Parker House, Boston's oldest and most famous hotel, claims to have invented the term and the dish of scrod. When I was chef at Parker's, the main dining room of the hotel, I subscribed to their official version of Boston scrod: baby cod, split, bones removed, skin-on, oiled, covered with breadcrumbs and broiled. Of course you can cook any member of the cod family this way, but if you call it scrod, you may create some controversy.

Do not assume anything when buying scrod at the market or ordering it in a restaurant. In a restaurant, ask what fish they use for scrod. At the market, ask for baby cod, also called scrod cod; it should have a light brown skin, just like larger cod. If the fillet weighs more than ten ounces, it should not be considered scrod.

SERVES FOUR AS AN ENTREE

4 baby cod fillets, skin on, bones removed, about 8 ounces each
salt and freshly ground black pepper
1 tablespoon chopped fresh parsley
2 cups white breadcrumbs (see Note)
vegetable oil
4 tablespoons unsalted butter, melted

For Serving
lemon wedges
boiled potatoes
seasonal vegetables

1. Preheat the broiler. Season the scrod with salt and pepper on both sides. Mix the parsley and breadcrumbs.

2. Dip the scrod into the oil. Remove the fish from the oil, allowing it to drain and then quickly dredge it in the breadcrumbs. Place on the broiling pan skin side up.

3. Place the pan on a lower shelf of the broiler so that the crumbs don't burn before the fish is cooked. After about 5 minutes of cooking the fish should be more than half cooked and the skin side should be crisp and brown. Remove the pan from the broiler and quickly turn the fish. Sprinkle the top of the fish with a little more breadcrumbs and drizzle with melted butter. Return to the broiler for about 2 to 3 minutes or until the fish is golden brown. Serve with lemon wedges, boiled potatoes and seasonal vegetables.

NOTE. Bake or buy a loaf of unsliced white bread the day before. Trim off the crust and allow the bread to become a bit stale by leaving it out overnight. Make the breadcrumbs the next morning in a food processor or by rubbing the bread through a colander or sieve.

Fisherman's-Style Whiting

This easy-to-prepare summer dish is inspired by the fishermen from the Azores, who are among the best in the world and who now dominate much of the fishing in New England. Whiting, which is the market name for hake in New England, is very popular in Portugal. Bay leaves, olive oil, peppers, tomatoes and olives are all typical of Portuguese cooking. The cornmeal coating, however, seems to be unique to the Azores. Start the sauce a few minutes before the fish to give the flavors time to mingle. This method of dredging in cornmeal and panfrying is excellent for many fish, with or without sauce.

SERVES FOUR AS AN ENTREE

4 whiting fillets, 6 to 8 ounces each (see Note)
6 tablespoons olive oil
2 bay leaves
4 cloves garlic, finely chopped
1 large green pepper, thinly sliced
1 medium onion, thinly sliced
2 large ripe tomatoes, peeled, seeded and sliced ¼ inch thick
¼ cup dry white wine
½ cup small black Portuguese or niçoise olives, pitted
salt and freshly ground pepper
yellow cornmeal for dredging

1. Trim, debone and skin the fillets; set aside.

2. Heat 3 tablespoons of the olive oil in a saucepan until quite hot. Add the bay leaves. When they begin to color, add the garlic, pepper and onion. Cook for 5 minutes, then add the tomatoes and wine. Rinse the olives in cold water and add to the pan. Turn the heat down so the sauce simmers gently.

3. Heat a large sauté pan with the remaining olive oil. Season the whiting with salt and pepper and dredge in cornmeal; shake off any excess and place in the pan. Cook on one side until golden brown, about 3 minutes. Turn the fish and allow to finish cooking (2 to 3 minutes more).

4. While the fish is cooking, remove the bay leaves from the sauce and season to taste with salt and pepper. Spread the sauce on a platter or divide evenly among 4 plates. Lift the fish out of the pan, allowing it to drain a bit, and place in the center on top of the sauce. Serve at once.

NOTE. Substitute cod, haddock, pollock, tilefish or tautog, if desired.

PLAICE, FLOUNDER, FLUKE, DABS AND SOLE

The nomenclature of flatfish can be very confusing. The term *sole*, for example, is borrowed from a family of European flatfish that do not inhabit our part of the Atlantic in substantial quantities. There are a few varieties, but they are scarce and not commercially available, since few exceed eight ounces. The European or Dover sole, of which there are several types, has a firm texture and a distinct flavor. Classical French cuisine has hundreds of variations on cooking this fish, but few of them are appropriate to our softer textured and milder flavored lemon sole, which is not sole at all, but flounder marketed under that name.

Winter flounder, summer flounder (fluke) and American plaice are all members of the flounder family. Plaice—more commonly marketed as dabs, sand-dabs and even sole—are scooped up in enormous quantities out on Georges Bank. Summer flounder, which moves into shallower waters in the summer, making it seem more plentiful then, are widely known as fluke but often sold as sole. Winter flounder, which is generally known in the fishing industry as flounder, yellowtail flounder or blackbacks, is most often marketed as lemon sole.

These mild and pleasant, though uninspiring, flatfish have always enjoyed a high level of popularity. For the unadventurous palate, flounder or lemon sole is considered safe territory.

I do not dislike flounder, but I do find it somewhat limited; its mildness and softness cannot hold up to the kind of assertive flavors I am fond of. It can be very good when prepared simply —breaded *à l'anglaise*, batter-fried, sautéed *à la meunière* or panfried *doré*.

Flounder or Fluke à l'Anglaise

When perfectly executed, the method of breading and frying food that is called *à l'anglaise* (English style) by the French and standard breading procedure by most American cooking professionals forms a case that keeps the grease out and lets the food inside it steam. The breading separates from the food—fish in this instance—creating a puffy bubble. The proper format is: season lightly, dredge in flour, dip in egg wash, drain and cover with breadcrumbs. The food must be completely sealed. For best results the breadcrumbs should be fresh and the fish breaded seconds prior to cooking.

The fish can be deep-fried in hot oil or panfried in clarified butter, which is what I prefer. Besides flounder, many other kinds of fish, such as wolffish, tautog, ocean perch, tilefish, hake and pollock, can be prepared *à l'anglaise*. Very small fish, like smelts and alewife, are ideal (see page 96). Firm fish (swordfish, tuna, shark) and fatty fish like salmon and bluefish are not suitable.

SERVES FOUR TO SIX
AS AN ENTREE

2½ to 3 pounds skinless and boneless flounder or fluke fillets, 4 to 6 ounces each
4 eggs
½ cup milk
1 tablespoon peanut or other vegetable oil
2 cups breadcrumbs, preferably fresh white (page 67)
2 tablespoons chopped fresh parsley and/or chervil
salt and freshly ground black pepper
cayenne pepper (optional)
1 cup all-purpose or bread flour
peanut or other vegetable oil or clarified butter (page 329) for frying

For Serving
flat anchovies (optional)
parsley
lemon wedges
Tartare Sauce (page 333)

1. Check the fillets for bones. Mix the eggs with the milk and oil to make a wash. Mix the breadcrumbs with the herbs.

2. If you are deep-frying, preheat the oil to 350 degrees. Season the fillets with salt and pepper and cayenne pepper, if using. Dredge in flour, shaking off any excess, then submerge in the egg wash. Drain lightly and place in the breadcrumbs. Cover the fillets quickly with the crumbs to form an airtight seal.

3. If you are panfrying, heat the clarified butter to very hot but not smoking. Place the fillets in the pan, cook for 3 minutes on each side. You may need to turn down the heat a bit if they begin to color too quickly. For deep-frying, place the fillets in the oil and cook for 4 to 5 minutes or until golden brown.

4. Drain on paper towels. For family-style dining it is nice to place the fillets on a large platter lined with white napkins. Place an anchovy fillet on each fillet, if using. Sprinkle the parsley over the fillets and place the lemon wedges around the platter. Serve with tartare sauce.

Sand-Dabs Doré

In the *doré* method of cooking, the food is dusted with flour, then dipped in a seasoned egg wash and cooked quickly in clarified butter until golden, like its name (*doré* refers to a golden glaze in French). It is ideal for thin delicate fillets of fish like dabs or sand-dabs (plaice), but it can also be used for small thin scaloppine of monkfish or bass. When I was cooking in San Francisco in 1975, this was a popular way to prepare pounded slices of abalone. The eggs enrich a dish and make it look like there's more food than there really is. Of more practical significance, the egg wash helps prevent the delicate fillets from breaking apart.

SERVES FOUR AS AN ENTREE

1½ to 2 pounds skinless and
    boneless sand-dab fillets,
    about 3 to 4 ounces each
4 eggs
½ cup milk
1 tablespoon vegetable oil
1 tablespoon chopped fresh
    parsley
salt and freshly ground black
    pepper
hot-pepper sauce or cayenne
    pepper (optional)
clarified butter (page 329) for
    panfrying
1 cup all-purpose flour
lemon wedges
lime wedges

For Serving

White Wine Butter Sauce or
    brown butter (pages 329–330)
    or drawn butter (page 330),
    flavored with herbs, tomato
    concassée (page 337), chopped
    anchovies or diced lemon or
    lime

1. Trim the fillets and remove any bone that may still be attached.

2. Mix together the eggs, milk, oil and parsley; season the wash with salt and pepper and hot-pepper sauce or cayenne pepper, if using.

3. Heat a large skillet with just a little more clarified butter than necessary to cover the bottom of the pan to medium-high heat. Dust the fillets lightly in flour. Dip the fillets in the egg wash, then drain each one quickly before placing in the pan. Work very fast. As soon as one side is colored golden brown, turn the fillet and cook it on the other side. Remove to individual plates or to a platter and garnish with wedges of lemon and lime.

Although halibut is a member of the flounder family, the largest of the flatfish in fact, I decided to treat it separately because its firm white flesh makes it suitable for a variety of cooking methods that our flounder, flukes and dabs just cannot hold up to. Halibut fillets can be poached, steamed, baked, braised, sautéed, grilled or broiled. Bone-in steaks are excellent grilled, broiled or poached. The flavor is delicate, but not so delicate that it cannot be combined with interesting flavors like wild mushrooms, leeks, saffron, wine and various herbs.

Halibut are most commonly sold at weights between 15 and 80 pounds, but they are often found weighing more than 200 pounds. Smaller halibut, from 5 to 10 pounds, are sold as chicken halibut. The halibut lives on the sandy ocean bottom in very deep waters, from 200 to 3,000 feet deep, and therefore is not frequently caught by sports fishermen. Halibut used to be fairly abundant along the Maine coast and especially in the Penobscot Bay area, but recently they seem to be much more scarce. This shortage has driven up the price of halibut very high, but I think it is still worth it for what to my mind is the finest of our native flatfish.

Halibut Braised in White Wine with Shallots and Wild Mushrooms

Here is a beautiful and fairly simple autumn dish that pays tribute to my early training in French kitchens. This classic combination of white wine, shallots, mushrooms and fish is as timeless as it is flawless. Chanterelles are my preference here, but any combination of wild or cultivated mushrooms will work. In keeping with the French style of this dish, I would serve it with small steamed *tourné* (shaped) potatoes.

SERVES FOUR AS AN ENTREE

4 pieces of skinless and boneless halibut fillet, about 6 ounces each
salt and freshly ground black pepper
2 tablespoons unsalted butter
2 tablespoons diced shallots
1 pound chanterelles or other mushrooms, sliced about ¼ inch thick
¼ cup white wine
¼ cup Fish Stock (page 327) or water
½ cup heavy cream
juice of ½ lemon
fresh chervil sprigs for garnish
Boiled or Steamed New Potatoes (page 249) for serving

1. Trim the fillets if necessary. Lightly season with salt and pepper.
2. Preheat the oven to 375 degrees. Melt the butter in a large sauté pan (at least 12 inches) on medium heat. Add the shallots and mushrooms and cook for about 5 minutes. Pour the wine and fish stock into the pan and bring to a slow simmer. Add the halibut fillets and cover the pan with a lid or aluminum foil.
3. Place the pan in the oven. After 8 minutes, check to see if the halibut is cooked through. It should be firm to the touch, but not hard. When perfectly cooked, remove from the oven. Place the fillets on a platter. Cover and keep warm.
4. Put the pan on high heat. Add the cream and reduce until it has good body and can coat a spoon. The sauce should develop a tan color from the mushrooms. Uncover the fish and pour any juices from the platter into the pan. Season the sauce to taste with lemon juice, salt and pepper; spoon the mushrooms and sauce over each fillet, coating each completely. Garnish with chervil sprigs and serve with potatoes.

Halibut with Lobster Bordelaise, Pearl Onions, Mushrooms and Periwinkles

This is one of those fish dishes that you just had to be there for. Let me describe the occasion, and then follow through with recipes for the key components.

Last spring, William Hill Winery from Napa Valley, California, sponsored a dinner at my restaurant, reuniting me with Lydia Shire, my cooking partner for more than five years. It was several years since we had cooked together and we were thrilled; we really wanted this to be an exciting dinner. We wanted to push our guests' taste limits to the edge—and we did.

We started with a selection of six different fish and shellfish in various stages of raw, cured and cooked, sort of a New England sashimi plate. This was served with Chardonnay. (The remaining courses were accompanied by a vertical selection of William Hill's Cabernet Sauvignons; there were three or four with each course.) The next course was whole quail marinated with star anise and cinnamon, then deep-fried. The quail were served with a puree of spring-dug parsnips (page 241) and stir-fried hon tsai tai (oriental spinach).

For the third course, which was to accompany the oldest and most serious of the red wines, we cooked halibut with lobster bordelaise. Square chunks cut from a beautifully fresh 30-pound halibut were browned on one side and then baked in the oven with just a tiny bit of butter on top and a little shallots and some Cabernet Sauvignon from the dinner. The sauce was also made with wines that were being served that night: a rich bordelaise made with red wine, veal stock, lobster bodies, vegetables and the slightest whisper of fresh tarragon. The halibut was placed in the center of the plate with the bordelaise surrounding it. Thick slices of beef marrow poached in wine were set askew to the halibut. Surrounding it were little piles of morels sautéed with shallots, periwinkles picked out of the shell and sautéed with garlic, small pearl onions glazed with butter and the tiniest amount of sugar, and crispy fried potatoes. It was smashing, a bit farfetched but it worked well and certainly held its own with the wines, even the enormous and delicious 1978 reserve.

We followed the fish with a vintners' salad—a James Beard recipe—that we adorned with a thin slice of savory cheesecake and single thick slice from a grilled double rib of beef. This was served with some tasty and light barrel samples from recent vintages. Dessert was a wine glass filled with sliced fresh fruits with a dollop of sabayon, also made with the host's wines.

It was truly memorable.

Baked Halibut

Baking is one of the best ways to cook very large pieces of fish because at slower heats the outside of the fish does not become dry. If the halibut fillet is from a fish weighing more than 30 pounds, you can cut pieces that are almost square: split the fillet lengthwise, then cut it into six- to eight-ounce portions. I brown the top of the fish quickly before baking to add dimension in flavor, texture and color. This method can also be used to cook large pieces of cod, monkfish, wolffish or bass or even jumbo sea scallops (at least three and one-half ounces each—somewhat rare). Do not use this method on any fillet that is less than one and one-half inches thick.

SERVES FOUR AS AN ENTREE

4 thick pieces skinless and
    boneless halibut fillet, 6 to 8
    ounces each
salt and freshly ground pepper
clarified butter (page 329) or
    vegetable oil for searing
all-purpose flour for dusting
4 tablespoons unsalted butter
2 shallots, finely chopped
½ cup red wine

For Serving
Lobster Bordelaise Sauce (recipe
    follows) or Red Wine Butter
    Sauce (page 331)

1. Preheat the oven to 350 degrees. Season the halibut with salt and pepper. Heat a skillet to fairly high heat with clarified butter or oil. Lightly flour the side of the halibut that was next to the skin. (It will have the more pronounced markings.) Try not to get flour on other parts of the fish. Place the floured side of the fish down in the hot pan and sear until nicely browned.

2. Generously butter the bottom of a baking dish that is large enough to hold the fish with a little space between the pieces. Sprinkle the bottom of the dish with the chopped shallots. Place the pieces of fish in the dish with the browned side on top. Divide the remaining butter into 4 pieces and put 1 on top of each piece of halibut. Pour the wine into the dish and place, uncovered, in the oven. Allow about 20 minutes for the fish to cook through but still be moist and tender. Remove to a platter and keep warm.

3. Pour the juices from the pan into whatever sauce you wish to serve.

Lobster Bordelaise Sauce

I included this sauce with fish rather than shellfish because with the exception of scallops, it does not complement shellfish very well. For a rich main course of fish, however, it is superb and ties in well with red table wines. Garnish the fish with poached beef marrow or sliced lobster.

MAKES TWO CUPS

2 or 3 lobster bodies, about
    1 pound
2 cloves garlic, peeled
1 small onion, coarsely chopped
1 small carrot, peeled and sliced
2 tablespoons olive oil
2 cups red wine
1 cup Reduced Veal Stock
    (page 328)
1 cup Fish Stock (page 327)
4 sprigs fresh thyme
4 sprigs fresh tarragon
1 small fresh chili, split
1 teaspoon black peppercorns
2 bay leaves
salt and freshly ground black
    pepper
unsalted butter (optional)

1. Preheat the oven to 400 degrees. Split the lobster bodies in half; and remove and discard the head sacs. Place the lobsters in a small roasting pan, shell side up, along with the garlic, onion and carrot. Sprinkle with olive oil and place in the preheated oven. After about 15 minutes, stir then continue roasting until the shells begin to char. A wonderful smell will permeate the air.

2. Remove the roasted bodies and vegetables to a saucepan. Deglaze the roasting pan with a little water and add that to the saucepan. Add the red wine, veal stock and fish stock. Bring to a boil; skim off the foam and reduce to a gentle simmer. Add the thyme, tarragon, chili, peppercorns and bay leaves. Simmer slowly for 2 hours, adding a little water if needed.

3. Strain the sauce twice, once through a coarse strainer and once through a fine one, pushing through as much as possible. If you get more than 2 cups of sauce or if it is not flavorful with good body, reduce until it is. Chill if not using within the hour.

4. Reheat 1 cup of sauce by boiling, skimming and then simmering for 1 or 2 minutes. Season to taste with salt and pepper and finish with 2 tablespoons butter if desired.

NOTE. You have to make 2 cups of sauce for it to come out right in my judgment, but you need only 1 cup for 4 portions. You can freeze the second cup for another occasion.

BLUEFISH

There is no surer sign that New England's summer is in full swing than the first appearance of the bluefish. This migratory fish, which ranges the entire eastern coast of North and South America, as well as parts of the Mediterranean, Africa and Australia, is legendary for its fierceness and voracity. Bluefish are always hungry and almost always feeding, even when their bellies are full. Traveling in large schools, they devastate almost anything that gets in their way; they will even attack fish of near equal size. No other fish lives in this constant feeding frenzy; no other fish is known to kill, seemingly for the sake of killing. For the sport fisherman, there is nothing quite like the "blue." They are, pound for pound, as powerful as any fish and they have a mean and wild temperament. "Blues strike like blacksmiths' hammers," says John Hersey, who eloquently describes the mystery, beauty, strength and complexities of the fish in *Blues,* his tribute to bluefish.

Bluefish is also a very fine eating fish. Since I like to fish, we almost always eat it the day it is caught, often only a few hours later. The smaller blues, weighing less than two pounds and called snappers or snapper blues, are quite versatile but are best for panfrying or quick grilling. Their meat is very light in color and turns white when cooked. Bluefish three to five pounds in size are excellent grilled or broiled and can be very good baked. This size bluefish is also ideal for curing (see page 107). The larger fish, five to fifteen pounds (I have never encountered one larger, although there are many twenty pounds and over), are best grilled over a slow fire. They are also excellent smoked.

Because the bluefish has a high content of oil, which increases in relation to its size, it has sometimes been maligned as a poor eating fish, too strong or too fishy. Fresh snapper bluefish have a unique but mild flavor; the larger ones are more distinctive but are certainly not strong by any means. The so-called strong flavor results from improper handling and/or aging; it is not a normal characteristic of this fish.

The grayish-blue color of the skin of bluefish makes it unmistakable at market. Bluefish is almost always sold skin-on, as indeed it should. The skin is good for eating, as well as for holding this flaky fish together. The flesh color can vary from white to grayish blue with some dark meat. Look for clear and shiny flesh, no matter what the hue.

The distinct flavor of bluefish pairs especially well with acids like lemon, lime, tomato, white wine and vinegar. It also stands up well to numerous other seasonings, like mustard, garlic, basil and other herbs. In addition to the following recipes, try baking bluefish with the Portuguese-style tomato sauce for whiting on page 68.

Bluefish with Clams and Sweet Garlic Pasta

This dish has made believers out of people who claim not to like bluefish. Fillets cut from larger bluefish work best as they are thicker and take up less room on the plate. Buy one large piece of fish and cut it yourself. If you prefer not to make the homemade garlic pasta, substitute dried linguine or spaghetti; be sure to allow for the difference in cooking time. Proper timing of the clam sauce, pasta and bluefish is essential. Have all ingredients ready to go and follow these instructions carefully.

SERVES FOUR AS AN ENTREE

4 bluefish fillets, skin-on, 4 to 6
  ounces each
vegetable oil for rubbing
salt and freshly ground pepper
24 littleneck clams
3 tablespoons olive oil
2 bay leaves
6 cloves garlic, finely chopped
1 medium onion, finely diced
¼ cup white wine
¼ cup Fish Stock (page 327) or
  water
2 teaspoons finely chopped fresh
  basil
¼ cup finely chopped Italian
  parsley
6 tablespoons unsalted butter
1 pound Sweet Garlic Pasta
  (page 278)

1. Preheat the broiler. Have a large pot of salted water boiling for pasta. Heat a large sauté pan (at least 10 inches).

2. Trim the bluefish and remove any scales or bones. Rub with oil and season with salt and pepper. Place in a pan suitable for broiling. Scrub clams well and set aside.

3. Add the olive oil and bay leaves to the sauté pan. When the leaves begin to brown, add the garlic and onion. Cook until light brown. At this point place the bluefish under the broiler. (If you are using dried pasta, add that to the pot of water now.) Turn up the heat under the sauté pan to high and add the white wine and fish stock. When the sauce begins to boil, add the clams and cover with a lid or pie tin.

4. After 1 minute, drop the homemade pasta, if using, into the boiling water. Stir occasionally. In a few minutes the pasta will be cooked, the bluefish done and the clams open. Since this is happening all at once, you need to work fast.

5. Drain the pasta and place in a bowl; spoon a little of the liquid from the clams over the pasta and toss. Divide the pasta evenly among 4 plates, leaving a little opening in the center of each plate. Place the bluefish fillets in the middle of the pasta. Quickly remove the clams and place them around the outside of each plate (6 each). Return the pan to the stove. Remove the bay leaves and add the basil and parsley. Swirl in the butter and season to taste with pepper. (The clams provide enough salt.) Spoon this sauce over the bluefish, clams and pasta and serve at once.

Barbecued Bluefish with Smoked-Shrimp Butter

This fabulous recipe comes from Hamersley's Bistro in the South End of Boston. Operated by Gordon Hamersley, one of Boston's finest chefs, and his charming wife Fiona, this restaurant gained an instant reputation for full-flavored and exciting, yet earthy food. This dish, created by Gordon and his talented sous-chef, Jody Adams, uses a rub in the tradition of southern barbecue. The flavor of the smoked-shrimp butter adds even more depth to this dish. It really is quite ingenious and delicious.

SERVES FOUR AS AN ENTREE

Smoked-Shrimp Butter

6 tablespoons unsalted butter, softened
3 medium smoked shrimp, finely chopped
1 teaspoon minced shallot
1/2 teaspoon minced garlic
1 teaspoon chopped fresh parsley
2 teaspoons lemon juice
salt and freshly ground black pepper

4 bluefish fillets, skin-on, 6 to 8 ounces each
olive oil

Spice Rub

1/2 teaspoon cayenne pepper
1/4 teaspoon paprika
1/4 teaspoon onion powder or 1 teaspoon finely chopped onion
1/4 teaspoon garlic powder or 1 teaspoon finely chopped garlic
1/4 teaspoon herbes de Provence
1/4 teaspoon sugar
1/2 teaspoon ground black pepper
1/2 teaspoon salt

Cole Slaw (page 231) for serving

1. Beat the butter until smooth. Add the chopped shrimp, shallot, garlic and parsley. Season to taste with lemon juice, salt and pepper. Using a piece of plastic wrap, roll the butter into a cylinder. Secure tightly at both ends. Refrigerate until firm.

2. Build a fire with wood or charcoal and allow to cook down. Trim the bluefish fillets and remove any scales that may still be attached. Coat each fillet with olive oil. Blend together the cayenne pepper, paprika, onion powder or onion, garlic powder or garlic, herbes de Provence, sugar, pepper and salt and rub the fillets gently with the mixture. Marinate for 10 minutes.

3. When the fire is ready, place the fillets on the grill, skin side down, and cook until the skin is very crisp and the sides of the fish begin to turn white (6 to 8 minutes). Turn the fillets and cook for 2 or 3 minutes more until done. Place the fillets, skin side up, on plates or a platter and top immediately with slices of the smoked-shrimp butter. Spoon the cole slaw on the plates or platter and serve at once.

STRIPED BASS

Because I have been boycotting the commercial use of striped bass for more than five years now, I will not include any recipes for it. Perhaps some time in the future this once-abundant fish will grace our tables again. For that happy day, you ought to know that large striped bass can be cut into steaks or filleted, then baked, broiled, grilled, poached, steamed, sautéed or braised. Smaller fish are best filleted, then broiled, sautéed or grilled. The flavor and texture of striped bass are second to none.

Like salmon, striped bass has to return to still fresh waters in order to spawn. The polluted and logjammed condition of many East Coast rivers has made that a problem. In addition, by about six years ago intensive sport and commercial fishing had reduced the population of striped bass to the point of endangering the species. Some states have passed laws to protect it to a certain extent: some fishing is still allowed, but limits have been imposed on the size of the catch. I urge you to do what you can to help save the striped bass. Do not be tempted to buy it if by chance you see it on the market, and if you catch one, return it to the sea.

SALMON

For the most part, the wild Atlantic salmon has become an oddity in New England. In earlier times most New England rivers, like the Connecticut, Merrimack, Kennebec and Penobscot, were rich with salmon. Unfortunately, the population has declined, largely because of pollution, to a mere token. In spring and early summer there are small landings of Atlantic salmon in the rivers of northeastern Maine, but these are commercially insignificant. The Atlantic salmon has fared better in Quebec, Iceland, Scotland and Ireland. This year, however, the Atlantic salmon did appear in more abundant numbers in Maine than it has in the past. Let's hope this trend continues.

Most of the salmon available on the market, even New England markets, is Pacific king (Chinook) and coho salmon; farmed Norwegian salmon has also become common at our markets. When Atlantic salmon is not available, my preference is for Pacific king salmon. The Norwegian farmed salmon is very fatty; it has a nice appearance but is lacking in flavor. There are some salmon of very high quality being farmed in Maine. These are a hybrid of farmed Atlantic and wild salmon (see List of Sources, pages 356–357). Landlocked Atlantic salmon, which is a freshwater fish, is available only to the sports fisherman. It is very flavorful and well worth pursuing.

Both the wild Atlantic and the landlocked Atlantic salmon have a medium oil content, neither too fat nor too lean, which makes them quite versatile in the kitchen. Poached, baked, steamed, sautéed, broiled or grilled, these fish make good eating. Pacific salmon is fattier and lends itself especially to grilling, but it can also be treated in the other manners. Whether filleted, cut in steaks or left whole, whether served hot or cold, salmon always proves to be tasty and fun to cook.

The color of salmon can vary from white to deep red, depending on what the fish was feeding on; pinkish orange is most common. Look for clear firm flesh and all the other signs that indicate freshness. The wild Atlantic salmon is most easily identified by its spotted tail. It is best when caught at sea, since they stop feeding and begin to deteriorate as they head upstream to spawn.

Steamed Salmon with Egg Sauce and Peas

It is a real Yankee tradition to eat "boiled" whole salmon (really steamed or poached) with fresh peas for the Fourth of July. Although my family and friends usually cook steamers, burgers and hot dogs for the holiday, I do use this combination frequently in late spring and early summer, when the season for both salmon and peas is at its height. You will need a pound of peas in the pod for each cup of shelled peas.

SERVES FOUR AS AN ENTREE

4 skinless salmon fillets, 6 or 7
  ounces each
salt and freshly ground black
  pepper
¾ cup white wine
1 small onion, sliced
several sprigs fresh thyme and
  parsley
¼ cup Fish Stock (page 327)
2 leeks, cut in fine julienne
  (about 1 cup)
¼ cup heavy cream
1 cup freshly shelled peas
4 tablespoons unsalted butter
3 hard-boiled eggs, coarsely
  chopped
2 tablespoons chopped chives
juice of ¼ lemon
Boiled or Steamed New Potatoes
  (page 249) for serving

1. Trim the salmon fillets and remove any pieces of bone. Season lightly with salt and pepper. Combine ½ cup wine with the onion, thyme and parsley and 1 inch water in the bottom of a steamer suitable for holding the fillets. While the steamer is heating up, combine the remaining ¼ cup wine and the fish stock in a 9-inch sauté pan. Although the pan may seem large, it will be needed later.

2. Place the salmon in the steamer and cover with leeks.

3. On fairly high heat, reduce the liquid in the sauté pan to half its original volume. Add the heavy cream and reduce again by half. Turn down the heat and add the peas. Cook the peas gently, until they are tender but not soft. Cut the butter into chunks and stir into the pan. When the butter is almost completely incorporated, add the chopped eggs and remove from the heat. Stir gently so that the egg yolks do not break up too much. Add the chopped chives and season to taste with salt and pepper and lemon juice.

4. By now the salmon has steamed about 8 minutes and that is about right. Check to make sure it is cooked properly. Remove the salmon and leeks from the steamer and place on plates or a platter. After they have sat for 30 seconds, pour the juices from the plates or platter into the sauce. Stir the sauce one last time and spoon on top of the salmon and leeks. Serve with potatoes.

Salad of Cold Poached Salmon, Fresh Peas, Red Onions and New Potatoes

This may just suit the bill for your next Fourth of July buffet. It is also excellent as a luncheon main course or in small portions as an appetizer. You could also use thin slices of gravlax or smoked salmon instead of poached salmon. In that case, cut the quantity of salmon in half.

SERVES EIGHT TO TEN
AS AN APPETIZER

2 pounds salmon fillets
1 pound red new potatoes
2 cups freshly shelled peas
1 cup sour cream
juice of 1 lemon
2 tablespoons chopped fresh dill
1 tablespoon freshly grated
  horseradish
salt and freshly ground black
  pepper
1 medium red onion, thinly sliced
1 head Boston lettuce

1. Poach the salmon as described on page 79. Allow to cool at room temperature. Peel off the skin, then break into larger flakes (approximately 1 inch); chill in the refrigerator.

2. Scrub the new potatoes and boil them in the skin until cooked but still firm. Shock in cold water and chill thoroughly. Cut into ⅜-inch slices.

3. Blanch the peas in boiling salted water until tender (1 to 2 minutes). Shock in cold water. Drain and chill.

4. Combine the sour cream, lemon juice, dill and horseradish in a large bowl. Season to taste with salt and pepper. Add the potatoes, onion rings and peas and toss well. Add the salmon and toss gently. Allow to chill at least 20 minutes before serving.

5. When ready to serve, line individual plates or a platter or bowl with the tender leaves of Boston lettuce. Check the seasoning of the salad and place on top of the lettuce.

Poached Salmon

Although salmon is the most commonly poached fish, others including trout, halibut, sole, cod, bass, tilefish, shad and many more, can be poached. Any fish that is to be served cold will benefit from the gentle cooking that is the essence of poaching. It can be done in salted water, vinegar and water, milk or fish stock; but the best and most universally accepted medium is court bouillon. Court bouillon is basically an acidic blend of wine or vinegar, water, vegetables, herbs and spices; it is cooked to allow the flavors to marry and then strained. Which court bouillon you use depends on the desired effect: for example, if you are planning a white wine-based sauce, make a white wine court bouillon and use it in the sauce. The same principle applies to red wine. If the poaching liquid is not to be used in sauce, flavor it more assertively with vinegar and spices. As always in cooking, let common sense be your guide.

Sauces made with a little cream or butter are particularly good with poached fish. Often some of the poaching liquid can be incorporated into the sauce. A good example of this is Finnan Haddie with Egg Sauce (page 104). Cold poached fish goes best with mayonnaise-based sauces (page 333), crème fraîche (page 220) or sour cream.

MAKES ENOUGH FOR FOUR SERVINGS

White Wine Court Bouillon
1½ cups dry white wine
1 small onion, coarsely chopped
1 small carrot, coarsely chopped
2 celery stalks, coarsely chopped
1 teaspoon black peppercorns
4 sprigs fresh thyme or
  ½ teaspoon dried thyme
2 bay leaves
several stems or sprigs parsley
  and/or chervil

fish steaks or fillets or whole fish

1. Combine the wine, 3 cups water, onion, carrot, celery, peppercorns, thyme, bay leaves and parsley or chervil in a saucepan and bring to a slow boil. Simmer for 20 minutes. Cool in the saucepan, then strain. Set aside until needed.

2. When ready to poach the fish, select a pot that is wide enough to hold the fish comfortably and deep enough for it to be submerged in liquid. Pour in the court bouillon and heat until vapors rise from the surface, but there is no boil. Slip the fish into the court bouillon. A slotted spatula or similar tool is good for handling fish when poaching.

3. Cook until done. Cooking times vary greatly according to the type and size of the fish. Check doneness by using the finger test: if the fish feels firm and has little spring to it, it is most likely ready. A white substance may form on the surface of the fish. This is a sign that the fish is done, but if there is too much, it may indicate that the fish was cooked at too high a temperature or that it was overcooked. Check the fish constantly to prevent this. To give a rough idea of timing, a salmon fillet weighing 8 ounces will take from 8 to 10 minutes; a halibut fillet of the same size will take 10 to 12 minutes; a whole trout, weighing close to 1 pound, will take about 15 minutes.

4. Remove fish carefully from liquid. Serve hot with sauce or let cool and refrigerate to serve cold.

Grilled Salmon Steaks with Aïoli and Parsley Salad

This method is good not only for salmon but also for bluefish, striped bass, sea trout, swordfish and numerous other fish. Coating the salmon with aïoli keeps it from sticking to the grill and adds a garlicky flavor as well. No sauce is necessary, just some extra aïoli on the side. (You may substitute plain Mayonnaise, page 333, for the aïoli if garlic flavor is not desired.)

Grilled fish steaks are more interesting than fillets. You get both a crispy fatty bit (the thin belly part of the steak) and juicy meat from the thick center part. After the steak is cooked through, you may remove the bones by holding the meaty part of the steak with two fingers and pulling the round backbone down with the other hand. When this is carefully done, all the smaller bones come out with the back bone. I like to serve grilled salmon steaks with Parsley Salad. The clean, light but pronounced flavor of the salad offsets the richness of the fish.

SERVES FOUR AS AN ENTREE

4 center cut salmon steaks, at
    least 1 inch thick, 8 to 10
    ounces each
1½ cups Aïoli (page 332)
salt and freshly ground black
    pepper

For Serving
lemon wedges
Parsley Salad (page 253)

1. Make a fire with wood or charcoal and allow it to burn down to glowing embers.

2. Season the salmon fillets with salt and pepper and coat generously with aïoli. Place on the grill and cook for about 5 minutes, searing fish to create a crust that will hold the juices. Do not move the steaks until this is accomplished. The skin should begin to char and become crisp.

3. Turn over the steaks and cook about 5 minutes more. The exact timing depends on the thickness of the steaks and the heat of the grill. Serve at once with remaining aïoli, lemon wedges and parsley salad.

TROUT AND CHAR

Trout and char are very closely related to salmon, but an analysis of this complicated family serves little culinary purpose since the factors that affect flavor are as much or even more due to environment than to genetic makeup. The flesh of salmon, trout and char, for example, varies in color from white to deep red, reflecting the elements of the fish's diet—whether it ate shrimp, crayfish or other foods. Size, on the other hand, is important; cooking properties are similar among fish of the same size.

The single most striking difference in trout is between wild fish and farmed fish. Although some decent farmed trout is available, there is simply no comparing it to a fish caught in the wild. I learned about trout fishing in the mountains of Montana and Idaho when I was working as chef at a dude ranch near Yellowstone Park. I became spoiled for life by the delicious rainbows, browns, cutthroats and Dolly Vardens that come out of the crystal-clear icy waters of the Rockies. In New England the preponderant species of trout for the angler are brook trout, lake trout and rainbow trout, which was brought in from the West over a hundred years ago.

For the fisherman, the size of trout is important, but for the consumer buying farmed fish, all are of standard pan size, from twelve to sixteen ounces. Trout weighing over one pound are more versatile than pan-size fish and are suitable for many of the same preparations as salmon. Oceangoing brook brout, commonly marketed as sea trout, can also be handled like salmon, but they are inferior in taste and texture. Pan-size trout can be poached, broiled or grilled whole, but the single most popular method is panfrying. This size trout is also excellent smoked. Au bleu trout (poached in a vinegary court bouillon) is as strikingly beautiful as it is delicious, but it can only be done with very, very fresh trout. Any trout more than a couple of hours out of the water will not turn blue.

The best rule for cooking trout is to keep it simple. If you are using pan-size fish, stay away from recipes that call for boneless trout, especially for stuffing them. These are affectations that do not do justice to this little fish, which needs the extra flavor that cooking on the bone gives. Keep sauces and garnishes light. A little brown butter and lemon is all it really needs; if you wish to incorporate herbs, stick to parsley, chervil and chives. A small amount of fresh tomato works well, but never a rich tomato sauce. Other flavorings like mustard, saffron and garlic are simply too much.

Always buy head-on, bone-in trout. The eyes should be clear. The best sign of freshness is rigor mortis, which guarantees the fish is less than 24 hours old. A light coating of slime is also a good sign. Brilliant coloring, be that the rainbow's reddish band or the brook trout's multicolored spots, is a good omen. If you catch your own trout, gut the fish as soon as you catch it.

Cook trout with the head on: as with most fish, there is a delicious little morsel of meat behind the cheek, and the bones are simple to remove after cooking. And remember, trout is like champagne: it is good at any time of day. A breakfast of panfried trout is hard to beat, especially if the fish was just caught that morning.

How to Bone a Cooked Trout

Too many people have a phobia about bones. It is another sad example of how we have become distant from the food we eat, preferring it in its least natural state and willing to sacrifice flavor for convenience. It is also a failing of modern etiquette, which disdains the use of our hands at the table. I always try to encourage customers at the restaurant and guests in my home to use their hands when appropriate. Then I offer hot towels for them to wipe their hands afterward.

Be that as it may, here is the best and quickest way to bone a trout. First remove the head and tail. Take a sharp knife and cut the skin along the length of the backbone. Slip your knife between the backbone and upper fillet and loosen the fish away from the bone. In one motion lift the fillet up off the bone. It should come off easily in one piece. Now hold the fingers of one hand gently on the lower fillet as you lift the backbone off, starting from the head, with the other hand. Discard the bones and put the fish back together on a plate with the head and tail. With a little practice, this entire procedure will take you less than 30 seconds.

Panfried Trout

I feel panfrying extracts the maximum flavor from trout. In addition, the skin becomes very crisp, adding another dimension of flavor as well as texture. You can use either flour or cornmeal for dredging: flour gives more of a pure trout flavor; cornmeal gives crisper results as well as contributing another flavor. Since I like both ways, I can only suggest that you try them both and decide for yourself which you prefer.

To accompany floured fish, I recommend brown butter (page 329), lemon and parsley; for cornmeal-dipped fish, butter sauce (page 330) flavored with fresh herbs and even a little tomato concassée (page 337). Almost any kind of potatoes are good with trout; for a special treat, serve Corn Fritters (page 267).

SERVES TWO AS AN ENTREE

2 pan-size trout, about 1 pound each, scaled and gutted
milk
salt and freshly ground black pepper
all-purpose flour or yellow cornmeal for dredging
clarified butter (page 329) for frying

1. Wash the fish inside and out; using a pair of kitchen shears, trim off the fins. Dip the trout in milk, remove and season with salt and pepper. Dredge in flour or cornmeal.

2. Heat a pan large enough to hold the fish to medium-high heat. Add enough clarified butter so that there is about ¼ inch in the pan. Heat to close to the smoking point, add the fish for 2 to 3 minutes, tilting the pan occasionally so all parts of the trout, including the tail, become crisp. Gently turn the fish, being careful not to spatter any hot butter on yourself. Continue cooking until done (about 3 minutes more). Check inside the cavity along the backbone. You will see a little red as the heat pushes the blood away from the flesh; when these spots turn white, the fish is cooked through. It is important to cook trout perfectly: undercooking makes it impossible to separate the meat from the bones; overcooking destroys the texture and flavor.

3. Remove the fish from the pan, letting the excess butter drip off before transferring it to a plate or a work surface to debone.

SHAD AND SHAD ROE

"When the shadbush is in bloom and the roe is fresh, the swamp Yankees like to fix it with a plate of johnnycakes." So says Tim the Miller of Gray's Mill in Adamsville, Rhode Island, and he is right. The shad has made a considerable comeback, not only in numbers but also in acceptance and popularity. This bony member of the herring family is an ocean fish that like salmon spawns in the small estuaries of the rivers it enters each spring. In the Connecticut shad cookout, an old New England tradition, a firebox with applewood is used to slow-cook the shad and its roe, imbuing them with a fine smoky flavor.

Although fillet of shad is quite good when properly boned (almost impossible to find) and prepared, I will concentrate on shad roe, which is one of North America's truly great delicacies. Shad roe is usually sold in sets or pairs that already have the outer membrane removed. If you catch your own shad, remove this outer membrane carefully, so as not to damage the thin inner membrane that protects the delicate eggs. Always handle the roe sacs with the utmost care. Trim off the excess membrane that holds the pair together and also remove any blood clots or veins. Wash the roe very gently. When purchasing shad roe, look for lobes that are in perfect condition, with no torn membrane or other damage. The color of the roe will vary from yellowish red to deep red. Color is not a quality factor, unless the roe is extremely under- or over-ripened, and you will rarely see that at market. The key factor is odor—there should be none—which is a sign of aging. As with all fish and fish eggs, the fresher the better.

Shad roe does not take well to any type of intense heat. It requires gentle cooking. If you wish to sauté shad roe, you must gently poach it first. It is too delicate to sauté from the raw state. You can use the directions for poaching shad roe on page 84 and then season and dust the roe with flour before slowly browning it in butter or bacon fat. Be careful of popping, which can throw hot fat far enough to burn the cook.

Shad Roe Slowly Roasted in Butter

Over the years, I have tried just about every known method for cooking shad roe. Still not completely happy, I invented my own method, which pays heed to the most important elements in cooking shad roe: slow cooking and basting. The trick is to find a sauté pan that is just barely big enough to hold the roe. For one pair weighing about six ounces a six-inch pan with one-inch sides is perfect; for two pairs of that size, a nine-inch pan is about right. The roe is roasted slowly in this pan with enough sweet butter to almost cover the lobes. This eliminates basting, and since the dish is started from the cold state and uses a very gentle cooking, it also eliminates poaching. When the roe is perfectly cooked, it is transferred to a warm plate to rest for just a minute, while you prepare a brown butter from the butter in the pan. I like a bit of chopped bacon, anchovies and capers, but if you wish to enjoy the lovely nutty flavor of shad roe unadulterated, simply omit these ingredients. Serve one piece of lobe as an appetizer or two as a main course. I think the richness of this dish, however, makes it more suitable as a starter.

SERVES FOUR AS AN APPETIZER
OR TWO AS AN ENTREE

2 pairs shad roe, about 6 ounces
  each
salt and freshly ground black
  pepper
6 to 8 tablespoons unsalted
  butter
1 tablespoon finely chopped
  capers
2 tablespoons chopped fresh
  parsley
2 anchovies, finely chopped
1 tablespoon finely chopped
  cooked bacon or ham
juice of ½ lemon
8 slices of baguette (long French
  bread), cut on the diagonal,
  toasted or grilled, or 8
  Traditional Johnnycakes
  (page 262)

1. Preheat the oven to 350 degrees. Trim and clean the shad roe as described on page 82. Wash gently and pat dry. Season with salt and pepper.

2. Place a 9-inch sauté pan on low to medium heat and melt 6 tablespoons of the butter. Place the shad roe in the pan; if the butter is not nearly covering the lobes, add a little more.

3. Place the pan in the preheated oven. The cooking should take about 15 minutes, but you should check in 10 or 12 minutes to be on the safe side. Squeeze the roe in the thickest part to feel for firmness. If it is still soft, cook a little longer.

4. When the roe is done, place on warm plates. Pour off about half of the butter and place the pan back on the burner. On medium heat, cook the butter until it begins to brown and develop a nutty aroma. Watch out for the popping of a few eggs that may have fallen into the butter. When the butter is well browned, quickly add the chopped capers, parsley, anchovies, bacon or ham and lemon juice. Spoon the foamy butter over the roe. Garnish with toast or johnnycakes and serve immediately.

Shad Roe Wrapped in Bacon and Grilled with Wilted Spinach, Red Onions and Oranges

This beautiful salad takes the traditional combination of shad roe and bacon and presents it in a tasty new way. In order to grill the roe successfully, you first have to poach it. Then wrap it in partially cooked bacon and reheat it over a very slow fire. The excess fat from the bacon is used to flavor the dressing for the warm spinach salad.

SERVES FOUR AS AN APPETIZER

2 pairs shad roe, about 6 ounces each

Court Bouillon

1 medium leek, roughly chopped and rinsed well

1 small onion, roughly chopped

1 large stalk celery, roughly chopped

1 teaspoon whole black peppercorns

4 sprigs fresh thyme

2 bay leaves

1 cup white wine

juice of ½ lemon

12 strips sliced lean bacon

2 navel oranges

2 tablespoons peanut oil

2 tablespoons sherry or other wine vinegar

salt and freshly ground black pepper

1 small red onion, peeled and sliced into thin rings

1 pound spinach, picked and washed

1. Trim and clean the shad roe as described on page 82. Leave at room temperature while you prepare the court bouillon.

2. Combine the leek, onion, celery, peppercorns, thyme, bay leaves, wine, 2 to 3 cups water and the lemon juice in a saucepan and boil for 10 to 15 minutes. Strain liquid into a shallow pan that is suitable for poaching the roe. You should have enough liquid to cover the roe.

3. With the poaching liquid below the boiling point, gently slide the roe in. Cook on low heat for 1 minute, then remove the pan from the fire. Allow the roe to cool completely in the liquid.

4. Cook the bacon strips until they are partially rendered yet limp and pliable enough to wrap around the shad. Reserve the bacon fat. Cut each lobe of roe into thirds and wrap in bacon, covering most of the sac and especially the part that was cut. Use toothpicks to hold the bacon in place. Keep refrigerated while you prepare a fire and the other ingredients.

5. Peel half of 1 orange, removing any white, and make an extremely fine julienne with the peel. Peel the skin and white off the rest of the oranges and cut them in segments. Squeeze what remains and set the juice aside.

6. When the fire has cooked down to a low heat, place the pieces of shad roe on the grill away from the heat, so they cook slowly. They will take about 8 to 10 minutes to cook through.

7. About 5 minutes before the roe is cooked, heat a very large sauté pan on medium heat. Add the bacon fat that was rendered earlier, along with the peanut oil, vinegar, orange julienned zest and the juice from the orange. Allow this mixture to simmer for 1 minute. Taste and season with salt and pepper. Add the onion rings and cook for 30 seconds. Add the spinach and toss until it is warm and has begun to wilt but is not cooked.

8. Lift the spinach out of the pan and place on plates so that at least a few of the onion rings are showing. Place 3 pieces of grilled roe on each salad and arrange the orange segments loosely over the salad. Spoon any dressing that remains in the pan over the roe and salad. Serve at once.

Nature was not overly generous in the looks department when it came to the monkfish (also sold as goosefish or lotte). The face may be ugly, but the meat from the tail (the only edible part) is firm and sweet. It is sometimes called "poor man's lobster" for that reason, but this is an exaggeration. With an excellent supply at a fair price coming year-round from the grounds at Georges Bank, the monkfish has become more popular in recent years. The texture and character of monkfish requires very careful cooking. It especially takes a little experience to perfect the roasting of this fish.

Monkfish tails are sold whole or filleted. Even if you buy the fillets, you will need to trim off quite a bit of the heavy sinewlike cartilage that surrounds the fillets on the exposed part. Where the meat is trimmed from the bone, you will need to check and perhaps trim small pieces of cartilage from the backbone; there are no other bones running through the meat of the tail.

Look at the part of the filet that was cut off the bone. It is hard to tell the quality looking elsewhere because of the pinkish covering. If you are buying whole tails, look at the eye of the fillet. The fish should be a shiny clear white and there should be absolutely no detectable odor. I prefer medium-size monkfish, with whole tails weighing from three to four pounds. The fillets from this size fish would weigh from one to one and a half pounds. With fish any smaller, there is too much loss in trimming; larger fish can sometimes, though not always, be spongy.

Monkfish can be cut into medaillons and sautéed, or cut into fingers and batter-fried (page 9), or thinly sliced and cooked *doré* style (page 70) or be poached and served cold in salad. Large monkfish tails can also be grilled with very good results. The best method I have found by far is roasting and slicing the whole tail. Although this method does not allow much room for error, it is worth mastering if you like the sweet white meat of the monkfish.

Roasted Monkfish

This is the best way I know to cook monkfish. The trick here is to undercook the fish just enough to allow for the carry-over cooking that occurs while it is resting after being removed from the oven. Use a very sharp knife to cut the fish into neat and uniform slices. The sweet flesh of monkfish lends itself to a wide variety of sauces and garnishes. The sauté pan the fish was cooked in can be used to make or rewarm the accompanying sauce. The sauces can range from a simple brown butter with lemon (page 329) to a rich Lobster Bordelaise Sauce (page 73). Relishes made with olives, roast peppers, artichokes and other similar ingredients can be ad-libbed to accompany the sliced fish. Use your imagination with this method. If you cook the fish right, your chances of success are excellent.

SERVES FOUR TO SIX
AS AN ENTREE

*2 medium monkfish tails, about
    1 pound each*
*salt and freshly ground black
    pepper*
*several sprigs fresh thyme,
    picked and finely chopped*
all-purpose flour for dredging
*clarified butter (page 329) or
    vegetable oil for searing*

1. Trim the monkfish tails of the heavy sinewy coating surrounding the fillet. Preheat the oven to 350 degrees.

2. Season the fish with salt, pepper and chopped thyme. Rub the seasonings in a bit so they adhere. Dredge the monkfish tails in flour, shaking off any excess.

3. Heat a large sauté pan with the butter or oil. When it has reached medium-high heat, place the 2 pieces of fish in the pan. Allow them to brown before turning. After the fish is browned on all sides, place the pan in the oven. Turn the fish over after 5 minutes, cook for 5 minutes more, then check for doneness. It will take no more than 12 minutes; it is better if it is slightly undercooked.

4. Remove the fish to a warm platter to rest. Prepare the desired sauce to accompany the fish while it is resting. It should rest for at least 5 minutes. Pour any juices from the platter into the sauce. Slice the tails into uniform pieces about ⅜ inch thick. Arrange on plates or on a platter, fanning the slices to dramatize this technique. Pour the sauce or relish around the slices and serve at once.

SWORDFISH AND SHARK

My mother used to tell me, "If you don't have anything nice to say, you shouldn't say anything at all." For that reason, I nearly left swordfish out of this book completely. On second thought, I did think of a few nice things to say. At its best, a thick swordfish steak, properly grilled, is one of the juiciest, full flavored and delicious tasting fish going. I haven't given up completely yet. But I have one serious problem with swordfish, and that is parasites. In my experience no other kind of fish is so infested with worms as swordfish. The swordfish likes warm waters and can only be caught, never in great abundance, during the summer months in New England. This may be a partial explanation for the amount of parasites. Although they are harmless, I find them disgusting, and I have for the most part lost interest in this fish that I once was very fond of.

Swordfish, named fittingly enough for the large sword that protrudes from its head, can be enormous, often weighing hundreds of pounds and it is known to exceed a thousand pounds. My preference is for the smaller "pups" that weigh 60 to 100 pounds. I find these to be more free of worms and of lighter character in texture and flavor. The meat of the swordfish is very dense and ranges in color from white to pink. It has a strong resemblance to mako shark. Recipes for shark and swordfish can be used interchangeably. When purchasing swordfish, whether in a large piece or cut into steaks, look first for clear flesh that is firm and dry. Also check for small white dots, especially around the belly section—those are worms; if you see them, don't buy the fish. If the fish is spongy or wet looking, it was most likely long-lined (see page 58); don't buy this fish either. The only really proper way to catch swordfish commercially is by harpoon.

Mako Shark

This, the most flavorful of the sharks caught in New England, has long been passed off as swordfish by fishmongers, who know the aversion most Americans have to shark. The mere mention of the word conjures up the kind of thoughts that swiftly drive down prices. And yet, it is a very good fish. In my mind mako shark is not an inferior substitute for swordfish, it is equal or even better.

Another shark used for cooking is the blue or bull shark, which is called harbor halibut in Maine because of its flaky white flesh. Dogfish is the market name for the small gray shark, which is also of some culinary value. The recipe that follows, however, is specifically intended for swordfish or mako shark.

Grilled Swordfish or Shark with Basil Butter and Tomato Sauce

The use of two assertively flavored sauces demonstrates the ability of these fish to hold their own with other pronounced flavors. This recipe can also be used with bluefin tuna. The grilled fish is placed on top of a thin layer of rich tomato sauce and is then topped with a softened basil compound butter. The flavors complement each other as well as the fish. Garlic-flavored or plain noodles tossed in a little butter or extra tomato sauce will go well with this substantial summer meal.

SERVES FOUR AS AN ENTREE

Basil Butter
1 cup picked fresh basil leaves,
  washed
2 cloves garlic
6 tablespoons unsalted butter,
  softened
1 tablespoon lemon juice
salt and freshly ground black
  pepper

4 swordfish or mako shark
  steaks, at least 1 inch thick,
  about 8 ounces each
olive oil for brushing
2½ cups Basic Tomato Sauce
  (page 338)
whole basil leaves for garnish
  (optional)

1. Make the basil butter by combining the basil, garlic and butter in a food processor. Puree until smooth and season to taste with lemon juice, salt and pepper. Keep at room temperature.

2. Build a charcoal or wood fire and allow it to cook down to glowing embers. Season the fish with salt and pepper and brush with oil before putting on the grill. Heat up the tomato sauce.

3. Brush the fish occasionally with oil as it cooks. After the first side is seared, turn the fish to allow the second side to sear. Move the steaks to a cooler spot on the grill and let them finish slowly for a few minutes more. Figure about 5 minutes on each side and maybe a few more in the cooler spot, if necessary. The cooking time will depend on the thickness of the steaks.

4. Spread a layer of sauce on the bottom of each plate and place the fish on top. Top each piece with a dollop of basil butter. Garnish with basil leaves, if you have them.

NOTE. To make the basil butter by hand, chop the basil and garlic as fine as possible and combine with the softened butter; mix well. Season to taste with lemon juice, salt and pepper.

For years the Japanese fished our North Atlantic waters for the most revered of all sushi and sashimi fish, the bluefin tuna. We virtually ignored this giant fish, which can weigh as much as 1500 pounds, while the Japanese fleet scooped them up as fast as they could catch them. Since the revision of U.S. and Canadian territorial limits, the bluefin, which is the only tuna that is abundant in New England waters, has come under the control of Americans and Canadians for the first time in history. Now Japanese factory boats wait outside our 250-mile limit to buy the prized bluefin; in perfect fattened condition (late summer and fall) it can fetch as much as thirty dollars a pound, wholesale, for the prime sushi and sashimi cuts.

The bluefin is a migratory fish, which comes to New England in summer after spawning in the Caribbean; some migrate as far as Norway. Bluefins attain their peak of quality in New England after feeding on mackerel and other small fish, including squid. The bulk of the bluefin tuna that reaches market here is called school bluefin; individual fish weigh in the neighborhood of 50 to 60 pounds, though 200,- 300- and 400-pound bluefins are not that uncommon.

Bluefin tuna is sold in chunks or steaks. Look for clear shiny flesh. The lighter and fattier red meat is better. Since all tuna has some dark meat, pick the pieces with less of it. If there is too much, you are not getting the best cut.

Americans for many years knew little about tuna other than canned tuna, which is not made from the dark red bluefin tuna. In many other parts of the world fresh tuna is highly esteemed, and it gets special treatment in butchering as well as cooking. The brining of tuna prior to cooking it well done was and still is a common practice among the Portuguese and some Mediterranean peoples. I cannot comment on this method since I am not sure which of the six types of tuna is typically used. But knowing what we have learned from the Japanese about our bluefin tuna, I, like most modern American chefs, now usually cook tuna rare, preserving its mild flavor (it gets stronger as it cooks) and soft texture. Another way is to serve it raw, like the Japanese.

During the first half of my cooking career, I never dealt with fresh tuna. Only in the last seven or eight years has it become common to our market. It is mind-boggling that this marvelous fish was ignored for so long, especially considering the sometimes passionate following it has recently found in New England. I think it is a great addition to our culinary repertoire. The following are a few of my favorite preparations for bluefin tuna. I also recommend the soy marinade on page 95 for tuna steaks.

Tuna Carpaccio

Like tuna medaillons, this dish is inspired by a well-known beef dish. Salmon can also be used. The fish must be sliced very thin, and it must be very well chilled. Be sure to cut against the grain, otherwise the slices will get mushy when pounded.

SERVES FOUR AS AN APPETIZER

1 chunk of bluefin tuna, about 12 ounces

1. Slice the tuna against the grain into the thinnest slices possible. Place them between 2 pieces of plastic wrap and pound very lightly. Place on dinner plates, cover with wrap and chill.

2 tablespoons finely diced red
   onion
2 tablespoons coarsely chopped
   Italian parsley
1 tablespoon small capers
coarse sea salt
freshly ground black pepper
4 tablespoons first-press olive oil

For Serving
lemon wedges (optional)
thinly sliced bread, grilled or
   toasted

2. Remove the plates just before serving, unwrap and sprinkle the tuna with red onions, chopped parsley and capers. Salt and pepper them to taste and drizzle with olive oil. Serve immediately with lemon wedges and grilled or toasted bread, if desired.

Medaillons of Tuna Wrapped in Bacon
with Red Wine Sauce

The similarities between beef and tuna led me to this dish, which was inspired by beef tournedos cut from the tenderloin. Both are cooked rare to medium rare, and both are good with red wine. If a rich main course of fish to accompany red wines is what you are looking for, this will certainly fill the bill. Serve it with french fries or panfried potatoes and a vegetable side dish.

SERVES FOUR AS AN ENTREE

1½ to 1¾ pounds bluefish tuna,
   at least 1½ inches thick
8 strips bacon
salt and freshly ground black
   pepper or cracked black
   pepper
1 cup Red Wine Butter Sauce
   (page 331)

1. Divide the tuna into 8 pieces, each weighing about 3 ounces with a diameter of about 2 inches. Wrap and keep chilled to help prevent overcooking later.

2. Partially cook the bacon until slightly rendered, yet limp enough to wrap the tuna medaillons. Reserve the bacon fat. Wrap each medaillon in a piece of bacon and use a toothpick to hold the bacon in place. Keep chilled.

2. Build a charcoal or wood fire and let it cook down to glowing embers.

3. Season the medaillons lightly with salt and heavily with ground or even cracked black pepper. Brush the sides with a little bacon fat and place over the coals. Sear for about 1½ to 2 minutes on each side. After searing, turn the pieces so the bacon crisps a little.

4. Ladle a little red wine sauce on each plate. Remove the toothpicks and place 2 medaillons on each plate.

Grilled Tuna Steaks with Caramelized Onion Sauce

In this dish the tuna is grilled rare to medium rare and paired with a naturally sweet onion sauce. The onions have to be browned slowly, but completely, to accentuate their natural sweetness. A splash of vinegar cuts the richness of the sauce and creates a sweet-and-sour effect that works well with most seafood. This sauce is also good with swordfish, shark, bass and ocean perch.

SERVES FOUR AS AN ENTREE

Caramelized Onion Sauce
2 tablespoons vegetable oil
2 medium onions, cut in fine
  (¼ inch) dice (2 cups)
¼ cup white wine
2 tablespoons heavy cream
4 tablespoons unsalted butter
2 tablespoons sherry vinegar
salt and freshly ground black
  pepper

4 tuna steaks, cut 1 inch thick,
  6 to 8 ounces each
vegetable oil for brushing

1. Build a fire with wood or charcoal and let it cook down to glowing embers. Start the sauce about 30 minutes before you cook the fish.

2. Put a large sauté pan on medium-high heat. Add the oil and onions. Let the onions sit in the pan; do not stir them. After 5 minutes or so, stir the onions once; let them sit again. Stirring is counter-productive when you want to brown onions. Stir only enough to keep them from burning. After about 20 minutes the onions should be dark brown and substantially reduced in volume.

3. Add the wine and cream and cook for about 5 minutes. Cut the butter into chunks and stir into the pan. Remove from the heat and season to taste with vinegar, salt and pepper. If the sauce seems too thick (it should run freely, like cream or just slightly thicker), add a few drops of water.

4. Brush the tuna with oil and season with salt and pepper. Place on the grill, close to the heat, so it sears quickly. Allow 1½ to 2 minutes for each side. Keep it rare to medium rare. Transfer the tuna to plates and spoon the sauce over part of each steak and around it.

TAUTOG, TILEFISH AND WOLFFISH

Here are three lesser known but tasty and inexpensive fish, which are brought back daily by fishing trawlers who catch them while pursuing cod and haddock. Though unrelated, they have some similar qualities and are good for chowder, stew, broiling and deep-frying. For all three of these fish look for firm white fillets.

Tautog is also known as blackfish. Its flesh is very firm and white and does not shred. For chowders it should be cut into bite-size pieces; For frying, it is good to cut it into strips. It can be identified by its grayish black skin.

Tilefish is a beautifully colored fish, yellow and red, which is often marketed as golden bass. Tilefish has a fine sweet flavor and firm white meat. In addition to the cooking methods already mentioned, tilefish can be poached and chilled for an excellent fish salad.

The wolffish is a peculiar looking beast, with a large head and huge front teeth, which it uses to open its favorite foods—clams, oysters and other crustaceans. This feed gives wolffish a delicious flavor and firm white flesh. I especially like it batter-fried. Wolffish is sometimes marketed as ocean catfish.

Fish and Chips

Any fish fillet can be used for fish and chips (french fries in British parlance). At the highly commercial level, the cheapest is generally the rule. I too prefer to use less expensive fish; I would choose among tautog, tilefish, wolffish, hake or pollock, not because they are cheap but because this is a very good way to cook them. For the home cook, a meal of fish and chips properly done is neither easy nor cheap. It takes quite a bit of peanut oil, which is my choice for deep-frying fish because of its clean flavor.

You may cook the chips first and let them sit, but ideally you should have one pot for the fish and one for the french fries and do both at the same time. Place the fish and chips on platters lined with napkins or paper. Serve with cole slaw or salad and condiments.

SERVES FOUR AS AN ENTREE

peanut oil for frying
2 pounds firm-fleshed fish fillets

Beer Batter
1 egg
1½ cups (12-ounce can or bottle) beer
1½ cups all-purpose or bread flour
3 tablespoons peanut oil
2 scallions, finely chopped
salt and freshly ground black pepper
cayenne pepper

French Fried Potatoes (page 250)

For Serving
Cole Slaw (page 231) or green salad
cider vinegar
lemon wedges
Tartare Sauce or other mayonnaise-based sauces (page 333)

1. Heat at least 3 inches peanut oil in a deep pot to 360 degrees. Cut the fillets into serving-size pieces, allowing 2 pieces per portion.

2. Mix together the egg, beer and 3 tablespoons oil in a bowl. Stir in the flour and chopped scallions and season to taste with salt, pepper and cayenne. Allow to sit at least 10 minutes.

3. Dip the fillets, one at a time, into the batter and then drop into the hot oil. Do not crowd the pot; cook only as many as will fit, allowing for floating and turning. Turn the fillets so they cook evenly on both sides. Remove when they reach a golden brown. Drain on paper towels before placing on a platter. Serve with french fries, cole slaw or salad and assorted condiments.

VARIATION

Fish Fingers Cut fillets of tautog, wolffish or tilefish into strips about ¾ inch wide and 2½ inches long. Use the batter and procedure for fish and chips, but increase the heat of the cooking oil to 375 degrees. Serve as an hors d'oeuvre with Tartare Sauce or any of the other mayonnaise-based sauces (page 333).

Although these two fish are unrelated, I have grouped them together because of their similar size and cooking qualities. These fish are common, but not inexpensive, at our New England fish markets. The recipes that follow are suitable for both these fish or for red snapper and yellowtail, if you are not from New England.

Black sea bass is especially loved by the Chinese, who usually cook it whole, either steamed or crispy-fried. In recent years, black sea bass have become scarcer and extremely expensive. If you can afford it, however, you will not be disappointed. The white flesh of the black sea bass is among the finest in flavor and texture of any fish.

The true perch is a freshwater fish. Ocean perch or red perch is the market name for this species of rockfish that is commonly found in New England's great fishing grounds. It has beautiful red and white skin, resembling red snapper. On the West Coast this fish is often marketed (falsely) as snapper.

Both black sea bass and ocean perch are sold whole or filleted. It is always best to buy whole fish, but if you buy fillets, look for shiny white flesh. Always buy fillets with the skin on. Fillets can range in weight from a few ounces to two pounds. Be sure to remove any scales that may still be attached.

Jasper's Half-Crispy Fish with Scallion Puree

I invented this method of cooking small skin-on fillets of fish, which resembles the Chinese way of crispy-frying a whole fish. When a fish is fried whole, the skin is crisp and the inside is soft and tender. By cooking fillets on the skin side only, with a lid over the pan, you can achieve the results of frying a whole fish, with remarkable success. I like to serve the fish with sautéed garden vegetables. This method can also be used to cook snapper blues, small haddock, red snapper, yellowtail and other similar fish.

SERVES FOUR AS AN ENTREE

Scallion Puree
12 scallions
6 tablespoons unsalted butter
1 tablespoon white rice wine
   vinegar
salt and freshly ground black
   pepper
Fish Stock, page 327 (optional)

4 fillets black sea bass or ocean
   perch, 6 to 8 ounces each
1 cup milk
1 cup flour, seasoned to taste
   with salt, black pepper and
   cayenne
about ¼ cup peanut oil for
   frying

1. Start making the scallion puree about 30 minutes before it is time to cook the fish. Cut the scallions across in half. Cut off and discard the roots. Cut half of the green part of the scallion into thin diagonal slices for garnish. Set aside both the sliced and unsliced green parts of the scallions. Place the white parts in a small saucepan with 3 tablespoons butter and 2 tablespoons water. Simmer very slowly until tender (about 10 minutes). Add the unsliced green parts and cook for 1 minute. Remove from the heat and puree in a food processor or blender. Pass through a coarse strainer into a clean small saucepan. Rewarm gently as the fish is cooking; stir in the remaining butter. Season to taste with vinegar, salt and pepper. Adjust consistency with a little water or even fish stock so that it will spread on a plate. Keep warm.

2. Remove any scales or bones from the fillets; do not remove the skin. Score the skin of each fillet about ¾ inch apart, cutting into the meat as little as possible. Carefully dip the skin side of a fillet in the milk, then in the seasoned flour. Repeat. Continue with the remaining fillets. Do not get any flour on the flesh of the fish.

3. Heat the sauté pan with ¼ inch peanut oil to medium heat. Put the fillets in the pan skin side down. Cover the pan loosely with a lid or pie tin. The fish should be sizzling. Check periodically. While the skin side is crisping, the other side is steaming. Total cooking time is about 5 to 7 minutes, depending on the size of the fillets.

4. Spread the scallion puree on each plate and place the fish, skin side up, on the puree.

Steamed Whole Fish, Chinese Style

There are times when the use of cream, butter, oil or other rich ingredients is just not appropriate. The Chinese method of steaming whole fish offers a light and low-calorie alternative that sacrifices no flavor in the process; in fact, it delivers the essence of the fish. You have to be sure the fish you choose is very fresh. Black sea bass is my first choice, but ocean perch, snapper bluefish, trout or any other small fish that weighs between one and two pounds can be cooked this way. If you are serving a Chinese-style meal with lots of other foods, one fish may be enough for four or five, but if it is to stand as the main dish, you should figure a two-pound fish will serve three at most. In China the head, being considered the best part, is usually offered to the most honored guest.

FOR ONE FISH

2 dried Chinese black
    mushrooms
1 black sea bass or other whole
    fish, about 1½ pounds
1 tablespoon fresh ginger,
    cut in very fine julienne
    (⅛ inch × 1½ inches)
2 scallions, cut in very fine
    julienne (⅛ inch × 1½ inches)

Soy-Sesame Sauce
2 tablespoons rich Fish or
    Chicken Stock (page 327)
2 tablespoons soy sauce
1 teaspoon sesame oil
freshly ground black pepper
hot-chili oil (optional)

1. Soak the mushrooms in warm water to cover for 30 minutes.

2. If the fish is not scaled, do so; make it as scale-free as possible. Do not trim off any fins. Cut a slit through the thickest part of the fish along the backbone. This will allow the fish to cook more evenly and will prevent the skin from tearing.

3. Drain the mushrooms and set up a steamer using the water the mushrooms soaked in as well as any scraps of ginger and scallion left over from making the julienne.

4. Cut the mushrooms in fine (⅛ inch) julienne and mix with the ginger and scallions. Cover the top of the fish with this mixture and place in the steamer. Cook until the fish is firm, yet still very tender; a whole fish will take about 20 minutes.

5. Heat the stock, soy sauce and sesame oil in a small saucepan. Season to taste with pepper and hot-chili oil, if using.

6. Remove the fish from the steamer and place on a platter. Pour the sauce over the fish and serve at once.

MACKEREL

One of the prettiest fish in the sea, the greenish-blue striped mackerel is abundant in the bays of northern Maine. This is a school fish and very easy to catch in quantity, provided you find a school and have a boat and fishing gear. Tinker is the name given to small Atlantic mackerel, less than 12 inches long; larger fish are referred to simply as mackerel. Other types of mackerel, like the king, cero and wahoo, do not range in New England waters. The flavor of Atlantic mackerel is pronounced and delicious. Tinkers are slightly milder in flavor. I favor these at breakfast, filleted and panfried in butter or bacon fat, but they are also good grilled, and they stand up well to assertive flavors like soy sauce, tomatoes, wine, mustard or ginger. The mackerel is a favorite of the Japanese for sushi or sashimi and is also quite good pickled like herring. In addition to the recipes in this section, the recipes for bluefish also suit mackerel.

To preserve the true flavor of mackerel it must be properly handled, which means being iced as soon after they are caught as possible. I fish for these at the mouth of the Sheepscott River in Maine, and seldom come back without a meal. Having them so fresh has spoiled me for market fish, but if you can find a good purveyor, preferably one who is handling the fish for consumption in Japanese restaurants, I urge you to try them.

Tinkers and Bacon for Breakfast

Like a lot of fishermen, I often prefer to eat my catch for breakfast rather than supper. My two favorite breakfast fish, with the exception of smoked fish, are fresh trout and tinker mackerel. Unlike trout, which I cook whole, on the bone (the best way), I like to fillet mackerel, no matter how small, and remove the little bones using tweezers. For quick panfrying, I also recommend skinning the fillets, but that is not a must.

Once you have started your home fries cooking in one pan, cook bacon to your liking in another. Keep the bacon warm while you cook the fish in the same pan. Pour off the excess bacon fat, leaving just enough to panfry the fish. Season the tinker fillets with salt, freshly ground black pepper and a sprinkling of cayenne, if you like. Dredge them in flour or cornmeal and place in the hot fat. Cook for about a minute on each side and remove to a platter. Pour off the bacon fat and deglaze the pan with lemon juice and swirl in a bit of butter. Add some chopped parsley and spoon over the fish. Place the strips of bacon around the platter. Serve with potatoes, eggs, toast and jam.

Grilled Mackerel in a Quick Soy Marinade

The trick to this preparation is not to overmarinate the fish. I leave the fillets in the marinade for only five minutes and then grill them immediately. This preparation is good for large mackerel as well as tinkers. The sweet Japanese wine, mirin, complements the already sweet flavor of fresh mackerel. Serve this with rice and stir-fried greens or green vegetables. Batter-fried (tempura-style) vegetables are also nice.

SERVES FOUR AS AN ENTREE

4 to 6 tinker mackerel, filleted
   and bones removed, or
4 pieces of mackerel fillet,
   about 8 ounces each

Quick Soy Marinade
⅓ cup soy sauce
⅓ cup mirin
1 tablespoon sesame oil
1 thumb-size piece of fresh
   ginger, cut in very fine julienne
   (⅛ inch × 1½ inches)
4 scallions, cut on the bias in
   ¼-inch slices

freshly ground black pepper
peanut oil

1. Trim the mackerel fillets; keep refrigerated. Build a fire with wood or charcoal and allow to cook down to glowing embers.
2. Combine the soy, mirin, sesame oil, ginger and scallions. Allow to sit for at least 1 hour.
3. Just 5 minutes prior to cooking, place the mackerel fillets in the soy marinade. Remove after 5 minutes and season with pepper. Lightly brush with peanut oil and place on the grill, skin side down. After 2 minutes turn the fillets and cook until done (about 2 minutes more). Serve at once.

PORGIES AND BUTTERFISH

The porgy and the butterfish are both very small fish that are quite abundant in New England during the summer months. Although they are quite inexpensive, they are not popular, because they are too large to eat whole (bones and all) and too small to fillet. The best way to fix these fish is to grill them whole over wood or charcoal and then lift the fillets off the bone.

Porgies are also known as scup in New England. In Maine they are called pogies. All three names are derived from the Narraganset Indian's name for this fish: mishcuppauog. Pauog means fertilizer, which was a common use for this fish at one time. Although quite a lot of porgies and most butterfish are sold as food, it is still a common sight in Maine to see pogies being packed in barrels of salt to be sold as bait for lobstering.

Butterfish are generally smaller than porgies, rarely exceeding eight inches but most commonly sold at about four or five inches long. Much of the butterfish caught commercially in New England skirts our markets and is shipped directly to Japan, where they are quite popular.

Both of these species have a good shelf life for their size, but freshness is still an important factor in retaining the original sweetness of these fish. Since they are always sold whole, it is easy to check for quality by following the general rules that apply to all fish. If the fish are not gutted, avoid them unless they are extremely fresh. The scales of both these fish are very fine and come off easily.

How to Cook Porgies or Butterfish

Brush the whole gutted and scaled fish with butter or oil and grill just a few minutes on each side. Serve whole with a compound butter (page 330) melted over the fish. The recipe for Grilled Mackerel in a Quick Soy Marinade (page 95) can also be adapted to these fish by simply scoring the skin to allow the marinade to penetrate. Follow the rest of the recipe as given.

SMELTS, SILVERSIDES (SPEARING), ALEWIFE, MENHADIN AND OTHER SMALL FISH

All of these small fish, less than six inches long, are quite abundant and inexpensive. I have seen the little cove in front of my house in Sawyer's Island, Maine, so full of menhadin and other small fish that it looked as if the water was boiling and bubbling over with tiny fish. Since schools of the different small fish often intermingle, it is sometimes hard to differentiate one from the other. But it doesn't matter anyway because they are all delicious and all cook up about the same.

Whitebait—a dish, not a fish—is a highly esteemed culinary preparation, a mixture of these little fish breaded and fried. A whitebait dinner can be scooped out of almost any major estuary, bay or inlet in New England. If you catch your own and eat them the same day, you will have one of the finest meals the sea can provide.

The only preparation required is to gut the fish. Keep them on ice after they are gutted. They can be floured and panfried, rolled in cornmeal and panfried or deep-fried or breaded *à l'anglaise* (see page 69) and deep-fried. I like the *anglaise* treatment for all whitebait and particularly for smelts, which are sometimes a bit larger than the other species. Serve the fish with lemon wedges and parsley as an appetizer or main course. If you wish, make a little Tartare Sauce (page 333) to accompany them. The entire fish, including head, tail and bones, is edible.

3

Dried, Smoked and Cured Fish

Salt Cod
My Grandmother's Baccalà Salad

Brandade de Morue

Old-Fashioned Salt-Cod Cakes

Finnan Haddie
Fresh and Smoked Haddock Chowder

Poached Finnan Haddie with Butter

Other Smoked and Cured Fish
Smoked Trout with Red Onion Vinaigrette

Potato and Smoked Bluefish Salad

Penne with Smoked Cape Scallops and Smoked
Maine Shrimp

Gravlax-Style Bluefish with Mustard–Dill Sauce

Curing, smoking and drying fish are age-old methods for preserving fish for future use. They also change the texture and flavor of seafood, and what was once a necessity is now done to accommodate taste preferences.

There are many ways to preserve fish. I will only cover seafood and fish cured by the three most common methods of preserving:

- Drying. The fish or seafood is heavily salted with pure sodium chloride, then it is layered in airtight barrels. The method used today is hundreds of years old. In China shrimp and squid are often dried this way; in New England it is cod. Salt cod, sometimes referred to as Cape Cod turkey, has been a staple in parts of New England since colonial times. New England has been the world's largest producers of salt cod for centuries. Most of it is exported to Mediterranean countries.

- Smoking. The fish is first cured, to varying degrees, in a salt brine or by dry salting; then it can be either cold- or hot-smoked with many different kinds of wood. This is also a very common way to cure shrimp and other shellfish. The variations are incredible; almost any kind of seafood or fresh-water fish can be smoked. It can be served as is, warm or cold, in salads, soups, ragouts and many other dishes. The most common smoked fish in this region is finnan haddie (haddock), but Atlantic salmon, bluefish, tuna, shark, lake trout, Maine shrimp, scallops and mussels are also popular.

- Sugar and salt curing (gravlax). Fish fillets, usually salmon, are rubbed with a mixture of sugar, salt, pepper and dill. The fillets are then weighted slightly and turned daily. In two to three days, as the mixture penetrates the flesh liquid is released. The fish is then ready to slice and eat without cooking. This type of curing can be done to various stages, but it is meant as a slight preserving method for fish that will be eaten within two weeks. It is at its best the first week after being removed from the cure. On page 107 I offer a variation on this method, using bluefish instead of salmon.

With the exception of the gravlax-style bluefish, it is not my intention to tell how to make various kinds of cured and smoked fish. There are many nuances to the art. It takes time and experience to make a product as good as some that are readily available from the finer smokehouses in New England, Scotland, the Pacific Northwest and other regions famous for smoking seafood. I do not mean to discourage readers from smoking their own fish; I only wish to point out that it is not something that can easily be done right the first time, especially from an oversimplified recipe.

SALT COD

The salting of the abundant cod was one of the first industries in New England and the New World. By the mid-1600s hundreds of thousands of pounds of salt cod were being exported from Gloucester, Massachusetts, each year. Salt cod was so important in colonial times that it was used as currency. It became an integral means of exchange in the slave-trade triangle: slaves to the Caribbean, molasses to New England and salt cod and rum to southern Europe and Africa.

As well as being an important export item, salt cod was a mainstay in inland areas away from the coast. In old cookbooks from landlocked states like Vermont, it is sometimes the only fish mentioned. It was not until the advent of refrigeration that some New Englanders began to lose interest in salt cod. New waves of immigrants, like the Italians and Portuguese who still appreciate it (it's called *baccalà* in Italian, *bacalhau* in Portuguese), are the main reason salt cod has retained its place of importance in our local New England markets.

Two types of salt cod are available. The first, whole split-open, bone-in fish, is sold in most ethnic markets but is hard to find elsewhere. It is considered by most cooks to be the best. The second type is boneless and skinless, and it is readily available in most supermarkets; it is usually packed in small boxes. The recipes that follow call for this type of salt-cod fillets.

Quality varies with both kinds of salt cod. Factors that affect it are the purity of the salt used for curing as well as the original quality of the fish. Handling and storing are also important factors. Avoid salt cod that is yellow or is beginning to yellow; it is a sign of old age (over two years old). If you wish to use bone-in salt cod, double the quantity of fish (about half of the weight is skin and bones).

How to Soak Salt Cod

Salt cod must be soaked in water before cooking. How long is a matter of taste. Many people prefer to leave some of the strong flavor by using a short soaking period. The size and type of salt cod are also factors to consider. For fillets 5 or 6 hours is the minimum, 36 hours, the maximum. For bone-in cod 12 hours is the minimum, 60 hours, the maximum. I always start by rinsing the fish under cold running water for 10 or 15 minutes. Then I soak the fillets for about 16 to 24 hours, depending on the thickness of the fish. For whole fish I recommend between 36 and 48 hours for soaking. For either type, it is important to change the water at least four times during this process. For more ethnic types of preparations, like baccalà salad (page 101), you may wish to shorten the soaking period.

My Grandmother's Baccalà Salad

My paternal grandmother, Ida Padagrosi, emigrated from Rome in the first decade of this century. Like many other Italians, she brought with her a love for her native foods, baccalà or salt cod among them. Most holiday and special-occasion meals at her house started with a large array of antipasti, which might include oil-cured olives, roast peppers, crudités and small salads. This was one of my favorites.

MAKES TEN SMALL PORTIONS

1 pound boneless salt cod
6 to 8 cloves garlic, thinly sliced
    lengthwise
1 small onion, thinly sliced
    (1 cup)
½ bunch coarsely chopped
    Italian parsley leaves
2 bay leaves
juice of 2 lemons
1½ cups olive oil
freshly ground black pepper
¼ teaspoon crushed red pepper

1. Soak the salt cod as described on page 100.
2. Remove salt cod from soaking liquid and place in a flat pot with enough cold water to cover; cut the fish in half if necessary. Bring to a near boil and simmer for about 5 minutes. It is important to cook the fish through without overcooking. Remove and allow to cool before breaking into big flakes.
3. Combine the sliced garlic and onion with the parsley, bay leaves, lemon juice and oil. Fold in the flaked fish. Season to taste with pepper and red pepper. Wrap airtight and refrigerate for at least 24 hours to allow the flavors to marry. Bring back to room temperature before serving.

NOTE. This salad can be served by itself with salad greens and toasted bread, but it is best as one of many components of an antipasto.

Brandade de Morue

I cannot resist including this delicious salt cod puree from the Provence region of France. My dear friend and colleague, Lydia Shire, serves it each year at her Christmas party on slices of boiled new potatoes with a dollop of good caviar. It also makes a great pass-around warm canapé, spread on slices of toasted baguette.

MAKES TWO AND A HALF CUPS

½ pound boneless salt cod
2 cloves garlic, mashed
½ cup heavy cream
½ cup olive oil
2 tablespoons finely chopped
    onion
freshly ground black pepper
lemon juice
1 baguette (long French bread),
    sliced and toasted

1. Soak the salt cod as described on page 100.
2. Remove from soaking liquid, place in a flat pot and cover with cold water. Bring to a simmer. Simmer for 5 minutes, then drain and transfer to a mixing bowl. Add mashed garlic.
3. Warm the cream in a small pot. With an electric mixer, food processor or by hand (it is harder, but it can be done using a wire whisk), slowly add all the warm cream, then the olive oil. The puree will be white and fluffy. Add the chopped onion and season to taste with pepper and a few drops of lemon juice. No salt should be needed. Keep warm. Spread on slices of toast.

Old-Fashioned Salt-Cod Cakes

The simple fish cake, made with potatoes and salt cod, has been a staple for New Englanders for the last 300 years. It is quite traditional to serve fish cakes at breakfast or brunch with slices of panfried bacon.

MAKES SIX TO EIGHT BREAKFAST
PORTIONS

1 pound boneless salt cod
2 pounds russet or Maine
    potatoes, peeled and cut in
    half
½ small onion, finely chopped
    (¼ cup)
4 tablespoons unsalted butter
1 teaspoon Coleman's dry
    mustard
Worcestershire sauce
1 egg
3 egg yolks
freshly ground black pepper
all-purpose flour for dusting

For Serving
½ pound slab smoked bacon, cut
    in strips, ¼ to ⅜ inch thick
parsley
lemon wedges
Tartare Sauce, page 333
    (optional)

1. Soak the salt cod as described on page 100.
2. Remove from soaking liquid, place in a flat pot and cover with cold water. Bring to a simmer. Simmer 5 minutes and remove. Drain well. Break the salt cod into flakes and keep warm.
3. Boil the peeled potatoes in salted water until done (about 30 minutes). Drain thoroughly in a colander. It is important for the potatoes to be as dry as possible. Cook the onion in the butter until limp.
4. Puree or mash the potatoes while still warm. Add the melted butter and onion, flaked fish, dry mustard and a few dashes of Worcestershire sauce. Add the egg and egg yolks. Mix very thoroughly with a fork. Season with pepper. Form into small cakes and chill in the refrigerator. This may all be done as much as 4 hours in advance.
4. When ready to serve, dust the fish cakes with flour. Panfry the bacon until browned but not too crisp; remove from pan and keep warm. Fry the fish cakes in the bacon fat in the same pan, about 2 minutes on each side. Serve with the small slices of bacon, parsley and lemon wedges. Tartare sauce can be served on the side, if desired.

VARIATION

Fish Balls   Roll the fish and potato mixture into little balls, roll in flour and deep-fry at 360 degrees. Serve with parsley and lemon wedges.

FINNAN HADDIE

Haddock until just recently was the favorite fish of New Englanders. It is not surprising then that smoked haddock, better known as finnan haddie, is also quite popular, especially in the larger towns and cities, where New Englanders sometimes still try to emulate British (in this case, Scottish) customs. You will find finnan haddie on the breakfast menu of most of the grand hotels of Boston. For breakfast, the fish is usually poached in milk and served with melted butter and lemon or egg sauce; it is accompanied by so-called rashers of bacon and toast with jam and marmalade. I think it is one of the finest breakfasts going.

Finnan haddie is said to have originated in Findon, Scotland, around the year 1840, when a bit of sawdust caught fire in a shed where the haddock was hanging to dry. The "ruined" fish was given away to the neighbors, who instantly took a liking to it, and thus Findon haddock, later finnan haddie, was born.

True finnan haddie is haddock that is split with the bones left in, then lightly salted and smoked. Smoked boneless cod is often passed off as finnan haddie, but it is an inferior substitute. The bones add flavor to the fish and to the poaching liquid. Several New England smokehouses make excellent finnan haddie (see List of Sources, page 356–357). It is also available from Scotland. Finnan haddie is a semifresh fish and should be consumed as close to the time it is made as possible. It will lose its quality after just one week.

Different producers use different amounts of salt; all use some. I find that a quick soak (twenty minutes) in cold water is desirable: it removes some of the salt while it plumps the fish slightly.

Fresh and Smoked Haddock Chowder

This recipe is dedicated to my original editor, Pat Brown, who has suggested that there must be a way I could fly this soup down from Boston to her office in New York for her lunch once or twice a week.

SERVES EIGHT TO TEN
AS A MAIN COURSE

1 large or 2 small whole finnan haddie (2½ to 3 pounds)
1 medium onion, coarsely chopped
2 celery stalks, coarsely chopped
2 bay leaves
several parsley stems
¼ pound meaty salt pork, cut in ¼- to ½-inch dice
4 tablespoons unsalted butter
2 medium onions, cut in medium (½ inch) dice (2 cups)
1 tablespoon chopped fresh thyme leaves
10 small new potatoes, sliced ¼ inch thick
2 cups heavy cream
2½ pounds whole boneless and skinless haddock fillets
salt and freshly ground black pepper

For Garnish
4 hard-boiled eggs, coarsely chopped
2 tablespoons chopped fresh parsley and/or chives
common crackers, split, brushed with butter and toasted

1. Soak the finnan haddie in cold water for 20 minutes. Bring 4 cups water to a boil in a large frying or roasting pan with the chopped onion, celery, bay leaves and parsley stems. Let simmer 5 minutes, then add the finnan haddie. If it won't fit, cut it across in half. It should be just barely covered with the court bouillon. Slowly poach the finnan haddie for about 10 minutes. Remove and allow to cool.

2. Carefully pick the meat from the finnan haddie, leaving it in as large pieces as possible; set aside. Put the bones back in the pan with the poaching liquid and simmer 10 minutes more. Strain the liquid and set aside.

3. Render the salt pork in a large soup pot until it begins to crisp. Add the butter, diced onions and thyme. Cook for 5 minutes until the onions are translucent. Add 4 cups of the poaching liquid and the sliced potatoes; simmer about 12 minutes or until the potatoes are cooked. Stir in the cream.

4. Gently slip the whole haddock fillets into the soup. After 2 minutes add the finnan haddie. Simmer about 3 minutes and season to taste with salt (you will not need much) and pepper (I like a lot). Be careful when stirring so as not to break up the fish too much. Ladle some fish, potato and onion into each soup plate, then fill with piping hot broth.

5. Sprinkle the hard-boiled eggs, parsley and chives over the chowder. Put 4 toasted common cracker halves around each soup plate and serve.

Poached Finnan Haddie with Butter

This is a very simple and delicious breakfast dish of poached fish with *beurre fondu*. Because it is intended to be only a part of the meal and because the meal, in accordance with our modern lifestyle, calls for small portions, I have allowed for four portions out of one small finnan haddie. You may wish to increase the portion by as much as double if you are feeding hearty eaters or are serving this later in the day for brunch or a light supper.

MAKES FOUR BREAKFAST PORTIONS

1 small finnan haddie (1¼ to 1½ pounds)
freshly ground black pepper
3 cups milk
1 small onion, thinly sliced
2 whole cloves
2 bay leaves
4 sprigs fresh thyme
6 tablespoons unsalted butter
1 tablespoon chopped fresh parsley and/or chives

For Serving
rashers of country bacon
fried, poached or shirred eggs (pages 207–210)
boiled small red new potatoes
Boston Brown Bread (page 270) and toasted breads
butter
marmalade and preserves

1. Soak the fish in cold water for 20 to 30 minutes. Divide the fish into portions by cutting across the bone. Season with freshly ground black pepper; set aside. Trim off the tail, fins and any bones that are easy to remove without breaking up the fish.

2. Slowly warm the milk with the onion, cloves, bay leaves and thyme in a 10-inch sauté pan. Simmer for 5 minutes, but do not boil. Submerge the pieces of fish in the poaching liquid and simmer slowly for about 10 minutes. Remove the poached fish to a platter or individual plates.

3. Carefully remove 6 tablespoons of the poaching liquid to a small saucepan without incorporating any of the bits of onion, cloves, etc.; strain if necessary. Put the saucepan on medium heat and add the butter, 1 tablespoon at a time, until it is all incorporated. Add the parsley and/or chives and season to taste with pepper. Spoon over the fish. Serve with any or all of the suggested accompaniments.

VARIATION

Finnan Haddie with Egg Sauce

This is a lighter version of the very traditional New England egg sauce, which goes well with almost any poached fish but is most typically used with fresh salmon, salt cod and finnan haddie. Prepare the fish as for Poached Finnan Haddie with Butter. After the fish is poached, remove to a platter or individual plates and keep warm. Strain 1 cup of the poaching liquid into a small saucepan and put on medium heat. Combine 1½ tablespoons softened butter with 1 tablespoon flour and knead by hand to make *beurre manié*. Whisk this into the hot liquid bit by bit until it is lightly thickened. Add ¼ cup heavy cream and 4 coarsely chopped hard-boiled eggs; bring to a near boil. Add 1 tablespoon chopped chives and/or parsley and season to taste with lemon juice, salt and pepper. Spoon over the finnan haddie.

The following recipes use smoked and cured fish and smoked shellfish that differ from finnan haddie in that they do not require any further cooking; warming them can enhance their flavor but it is strictly optional. I would like to encourage you to take these recipes as guidelines and experiment on your own, using different types or combinations of different types of smoked seafood. Match them with different garnishes as well as different herbs and spices.

Smoked Trout with Red Onion Vinaigrette

After a short brining, trout is usually hot-smoked. You start by cold-smoking and then gradually increase the temperature until the fish is cooked through. Since it is so easy to overcook trout, the temperature must be controlled very carefully. When prepared perfectly, smoked trout are smoky, but not overly so, and very moist. Des Fitzgerald, of Ducktrap River Fish Farm in Lincolnville, Maine, raises and smokes his own rainbow trout. They are, in my opinion, among the finest produced anywhere (see List of Sources, page 356).

SERVES FOUR AS AN APPETIZER

2 smoked trout, at least 12 ounces each

Red Onion Vinaigrette
1 large red onion, very thinly sliced
1 small carrot, cut in very fine julienne (1/8 × 1 1/2 inches)
1/2 cup champagne vinegar
1/4 cup vegetable oil
salt and freshly ground black pepper

For Serving
1 small head Boston or Bibb lettuce
6 to 8 slices pumpernickel bread, toasted
4 tablespoons unsalted butter

1. Using a very sharp paring knife, carefully cut the skin of each trout along the back, from head to tail. Place a chef's knife along the backbone and lift the fillet off the bone by keeping the blade of the knife pressed against the rib bones as you use the flat side of the knife for lifting. This sounds harder than it actually is: because the fish is cooked, the fillet is very easy to remove in one piece. Lay the other fillet skin side down and simply pull out the backbone (and rib bones) with one motion. Use a pair of tweezers to pull out any small bones that may be in the fillets. You can serve the fillet with the skin on or off. For a very unusual presentation, with half of the skin and half of the meat showing, use the paring knife to slit the skin lengthwise down the center of each fillet. Be very careful not to cut into the flesh. Fold the bottom portion of the skin up and cut it away. Set aside the fillets.

2. To make the vinaigrette, combine the onion, carrot, vinegar and oil. Season with salt and pepper and refrigerate for at least 1 hour. Toss the mixture occasionally to allow all the onion rings to come in contact with the vinaigrette. Eventually the onions will wilt; at the same time they will impart their color and flavor to the mixture.

3. When ready to serve, make long beds for the trout on 4 dinner plates with the tender inner leaves of the lettuce. Place the fillets, skin side up, on the lettuce. Lift the onions and carrots out of the vinaigrette and arrange over the fish. Stir the vinaigrette and spoon over the fish and lettuce. Serve lightly buttered pumpernickel toast, cut into rectangles, on the side.

Potato and Smoked Bluefish Salad

The beginning of summer in New England is marked by the homecoming of the migratory bluefish. Bluefish are loved by sportsmen because they are such scrappy fighters and because they are so abundant. On a good day of bluefishing you will usually catch much more than you can eat. One great way to preserve the fish is by hot-smoking them. This is done by curing the fish in brine (the exact time determined by the size of the fish), then cold-smoking it to start and gradually increasing the temperature until it is done. Unlike trout, hearty-flavored bluefish can take a fairly heavy dose of smoke.

Large bluefish is an oily fish, perfect for smoking. It is almost always moist, even if slightly overcooked. Fish oil, like the fat on meat, is very flavorful, but it changes flavor quickly. Because of this, bluefish should be as fresh as possible, especially if you want to preserve it. Smoking will add two weeks of shelf life to bluefish, but it is best when eaten within a week.

Many different things can be done with smoked bluefish. It can be served as is with some dark bread and onions, made into canapés or small sandwiches, pureed for mousse or warmed in a soup. It is wonderful served with the red onion vinaigrette on page 105. The season for bluefish being summer, it is only logical that it be used in different salads. This recipe is for a composed salad that can be added to or improvised upon. Use fresh greens from the garden along with vegetables that can stand up to the robust flavor of smoked bluefish. The following recipe will make four large salads, perfect for a main course at lunch or dinner.

SERVES FOUR TO SIX
AS AN ENTREE

1½ pounds smoked bluefish
6 to 8 small new potatoes
½ pound green beans
8 cups assorted garden lettuce
1 medium red onion, sliced
1 cup thinly sliced cucumber
2 medium tomatoes, cut in thin
   wedges
3 branches fresh mint, leaves
   removed and chopped
   (4 tablespoons)
juice of 1 lemon
4 tablespoons white wine
   vinegar
¼ cup vegetable oil
¼ cup olive oil
salt and freshly ground pepper
crusty whole-grain bread for
   serving

1. To divide the bluefish into portions, use a very sharp knife to slice very gently lengthwise down the center of the fillet. Then cut across into rectangles. You should have about 4 pieces for each person.

2. Scrub the potatoes and cook in salted water until done, but still very firm. Set aside in the refrigerator.

3. Snap off the stems of the green beans, leaving the tip attached. Blanch in boiling salted water until al dente, then shock in cold water to stop the cooking.

4. Wash and dry the lettuce. Combine the onion, cucumber and tomatoes in a mixing bowl with the chopped mint, lemon juice, vinegar and vegetable and olive oil. Add the potatoes and green beans. Season to taste with salt and pepper and chill in the refrigerator for about 20 minutes.

5. Just before serving, put the lettuce in a large bowl and toss with enough of the dressing from the vegetables to coat it lightly. Divide among 4 dinner plates. Arrange the vegetables and smoked bluefish around the plate. (I like to put the different vegetables in separate piles.) Serve with warm (or grilled or toasted) crusty whole-grain bread.

Penne with Smoked Cape Scallops and Smoked Maine Shrimp

This recipe combines two of New England's finest smoked shellfish with pasta. The scallops are usually cold-smoked, the shrimp hot-smoked. In this recipe, they have the same cooking time because they are being warmed, not cooked. I chose penne for this dish because I like the contrast of shapes: the barrel-shaped scallops, the half-moon shrimp and the bias-cut tubes of penne. When cutting the vegetables for this dish, keep them small. Nothing should be cut larger than the penne.

SERVES FOUR AS AN APPETIZER

½ pound smoked cape scallops
½ pound smoked Maine shrimp
1 carrot, cut in 1-inch bâtonnets
    (like matchsticks)
8 ounces imported penne or
    other top-quality dry pasta
4 to 6 shiitake mushrooms,
    sliced ¼ inch thick
2 tablespoons peanut oil
4 scallions, cut diagonally into
    1-inch pieces
¼ cup Fish Stock (page 327) or
    2 tablespoons water
4 tablespoons unsalted butter
1 tablespoon finely chopped
    Italian parsley
salt and freshly ground black
    pepper

1. Pick over the scallops and remove the strap if necessary. Remove the shells from the shrimp.

2. Blanch the carrot in boiling salted water for about 1 minute. Shock in cold water. The carrots should be crisp.

3. Bring a large pot of salted water to a boil and add the penne. Cook the mushrooms in the peanut oil in a sauté pan on medium heat for 1 minute. Add the carrots, scallions, scallops, shrimp and fish stock. Simmer for about 2 minutes to warm the ingredients, stirring or tossing occasionally. When the pasta is al dente, drain it very well in a colander and add to the pan. Cut butter into small pieces and add a bit at a time while stirring or tossing vigorously. The butter will combine with the liquid to form enough sauce to coat the other ingredients. Add the chopped parsley and season to taste with salt and pepper. Divide among 4 soup plates or pasta bowls and serve at once.

Gravlax-Style Bluefish with Mustard–Dill Sauce

Gravlax is the famous Scandinavian preparation of salmon cured with sugar, salt, pepper and dill. It is usually served in thin slices with a sauce made of mustard and dill and garnished with little strips of skin that have been crisped in butter; it can also be lightly grilled.

When dealing with any traditional foods, my tendency is usually to leave well enough alone, but an experiment I undertook many summers ago in my never-ending pursuit of ways to utilize the abundant and inexpensive bluefish produced the most delicately flavored bluefish preparation you will probably ever encounter. Once you have learned the technique, you can go on to experiment with other types of fish and other herbs and spices. The ratio of salt to sugar is not a scientific formula; the proportions can be adjusted to suit your taste. Both ingredients are preservatives.

The oils in bluefish are what gives it a pronounced flavor, but improper handling is what makes people think it is "too strong." Bluefish is a very clean fish providing it is taken from clean waters, and it is therefore quite safe to eat uncooked.

In my restaurant, this dish is prepared by filleting two whole medium-size bluefish (six to eight pounds), which fit perfectly into a "hotel pan." I have adapted the technique for the home kitchen by using two center-cut fillets. You will need a rectangular dish or pan approximately ten by five inches, at least one inch deep. A nine-inch pie plate will also work.

Cucumber and onion salad is a very good accompaniment for this dish.

SERVES EIGHT AS AN APPETIZER

For Curing the Bluefish
2 center-cut bluefish fillets
    (1 pound each), skin on
¼ cup kosher salt
½ cup sugar
2 tablespoons cracked black
    peppercorns
about 12 sprigs fresh dill

Mustard–Dill Sauce
1 egg yolk
2 tablespoons Pommery or other
    whole-grain mustard
1 tablespoon honey
⅓ cup vegetable oil
1½ tablespoons cider vinegar
2 tablespoons chopped fresh dill
salt and freshly ground pepper
lettuce leaves for garnish

1. Prepare the bluefish fillets by carefully removing any bones or scales that may still be attached.

2. Mix together the salt, sugar and cracked pepper.

3. Sprinkle a little of the sugar mixture in the bottom of the pan and cover with a thin layer of dill. Place one of the fillets, skin side down, on the dill. Sprinkle the fillet with more of the sugar mixture, rubbing it in and being sure to cover every part of the fillet. Top with a thick layer of dill. Holding the other fillet over the pan, rub the flesh with the sugar mixture, then place this fillet on top of the other, with the thick part of one against the thin part of the other. Top this with the remaining sugar mixture and remaining dill.

4. Put a piece of plastic wrap over the fish and place a light weight on top. The weight could be another pan of the same size with some added weight, like a jar of mustard. A small cutting board or a couple plates could also work. Be inventive.

5. After you have weighted the fish, place it in the refrigerator for 12 hours. Then turn the fish over, replace the weight and refrigerate for another 12 hours. You will notice that the bluefish has given off quite a bit of liquid. Pour off the liquid and return the bluefish, covered with plastic wrap but not weighted, to the refrigerator. Keep refrigerated for another 48 hours, turning the fish over 3 or 4 times during that period. The fish is now ready to be used or the fillets can be rewrapped individually for future use.

6. To make the sauce, combine the egg yolk, mustard and honey in a small mixing bowl. Whisk in the oil, a few drops at a time. When half of the oil has been incorporated, add a few drops of vinegar; alternate oil and vinegar until both are used up. Add the chopped dill and season to taste with salt and pepper.

7. When ready to serve, slice the bluefish as thin as possible on the diagonal. Present it as is on a decorative plate, with a bit of the sauce drizzled over. A few lettuce leaves could be used as garnish.

Poultry

Chicken

Indian Summer Chowder with Smoked Chicken
or Poussin, Sweet Potatoes and Corn

Chicken Broth

Chicken Livers with Madeira Sauce and
Johnnycake Polenta

Chicken Pot Pie

Grilled Chicken

Spatchcocked and Grilled Poussin or Cornish Hen
with Maple and Lemon Glaze

Five-Spice Roast Chicken for Two

Roast Capon with Oyster Stuffing

Duck

Salad of Grilled Duck with Cranberries and
Spiced Nuts

Duck with Ginger and Scallions

Duck Sausages

Duck Cracklings

Roast Breast of Duck Wrapped in Smoked Bacon,
with Cider Vinegar Sauce

Goose

Lydia's "Chinese" Christmas Goose

Turkey

Roast Vermont Turkey with Giblet Gravy and
Sausage and Sage Dressing, for Thanksgiving

Country Sausage and Sage Dressing

Chicken Pot Pie, Roast Capon with Oyster Stuffing and Roast Vermont Turkey are just a few of New England's traditional poultry dishes. There are more, but the list is surprisingly short considering the large role that New England has played in the development of different types of chicken, not to mention ducks and geese. The Rhode Island Red, Plymouth Rock and New Hampshire chickens, named for their places of origin, were all developed in this region. Even the Rock Cornish game hen, whose name has been shortened to Cornish hen, has New England ancestry, being half Plymouth Rock. With the exception of Cornish hens, most of these New England chickens are more highly prized for their eggs than their meat. This emphasis on egg production, along with the abundance of feathered game, may explain why there are so few traditional New England poultry dishes.

Because poultry is so versatile, nutritious and reasonably priced—and because it tastes good —it has become almost a staple. In this chapter, I have concentrated on basic techniques and cooking methods that I hope will expand your understanding of this important food. Limits of time and space prohibit the inclusion of esoteric recipes for parts like the hearts or feet, but I have included a recipe for chicken livers and another for the fattened liver of Moulard duck. A newcomer in American cooking, Moulard duck foie gras is a sublime treat. It is very rich and quite expensive. In contrast, chicken livers, which can also be very delicious, are one of the best food bargains to be had.

When purchasing any type of poultry, look for nice shiny skin and clean, white-looking fat. Yellow fat is a sign of poor fattening methods and I find yellow skin, which is often created purposely through diet, just plain obnoxious. Real poultry has white skin. In addition to the color, good fresh poultry should have no noticeable odor. The best source for poultry is usually a small ethnic or kosher butcher, not a large supermarket. (See the chapter on Meat and Venison for more information on purchasing from butchers.) I recommend that you always buy whole birds and cut them up yourself.

BONING AND CARVING POULTRY

It is very difficult to judge the quality of a bird that is already cut to pieces. For this reason alone, I always recommend buying whole birds, not parts. Expense is another good reason: for a few cents more than the price of two chicken breasts, you can usually take home a whole bird, and if you need only the breasts, you can save the rest for a good soup or for the next day's lunch or snack. Cutting up your own poultry is easy. Just be sure to use a very sharp knife. The pressure needed to cut with a dull knife causes most problems and bad accidents.

The bone structure of all birds is similar. The techniques used for boning and carving are also basically the same, although some of those used for small birds are not used for large, and vice versa. And certain dishes require special ways of cutting up the bird. Certain subtle factors, like the amount of fat and the thickness of the skin, can make boning some birds a little different than others. Experience will teach you about these better than words. In the chapter on meat, I describe from start to finish how to break down the meat into primary and smaller cuts. There is, however, no set way to break down poultry; it is cut according to the specific cooking treatment it will receive.

How to Split for Grilling (Spatchcocking)

Small birds like quail, poussin and Cornish hens are excellent simply split, marinated and grilled. In old English cookbooks, such split and grilled birds are referred to as spatchcocked.

To split the bird, put it on the table on its side with the neck facing away from you. To prevent an accident, tuck your left thumb under the wing of the bird. Place the tip of your knife on the left side of the backbone at the neck. Starting up at the top, firmly cut down the back, keeping your knife pointed slightly toward the backbone (that way if you slip, it will not cut into the meat). Cut straight through and the bird will be split. Now turn the bird over, this time with the neck pointing toward you, and tuck your left thumb under the leg to the left of the backbone. Cut straight down, as before, to remove the backbone. (This removal of

the backbone is also the first step in cutting up a chicken for stewing.) Open up the bird and place it skin side down on a work surface. Push down around the center of the breastbone to flatten the bird. The soft, translucent breastbone should pop out a bit; remove it by pulling up on the bone with one hand as you use the other to hold the meat down. A little cutting will be needed to remove this bone totally. Depending on the occasion the grilled birds are to be served at, you may wish to remove the rib bones to facilitate eating with a fork and knife. The rib bones can be easily removed after cooking by simply pulling them off, using your fingers. Trim the wingtips as well as any excess fat or skin. The bird is now ready to be marinated.

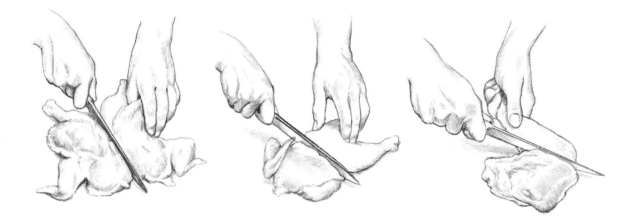

How to Cut up for Stewing, Frying or Barbecuing (Bone-in)

The first step here is to remove the backbone as described in the directions for splitting (above). After removing the backbone, cut between the two breasts, splitting the bird in two pieces. For some dishes, you may stop here. Otherwise, separate the legs from the breasts by cutting the skin where the breast and legs join. You now have four pieces. If you want big pieces, particularly for grilling or barbecuing, stop here. If you want smaller pieces, keep cutting. Split the breast with one chopping motion, right below the wing. To split the leg, place it, skin side down, on the cutting board. You will see a line of fat between the thigh and the drumstick; if you cut right on that line of fat, you will not hit a single bone while cutting this piece in half. You now have eight pieces. Reserve the backbone, wingtips and excess skin for Chicken Stock (page 327).

The Statler Breast

For those who especially favor the breast (I am a wing and thigh man myself), here is a cut that is well known to professionals but rarely used by the home cook. The Statler breast (also called a hotel-style breast) is a whole breast (both sides) left completely on the bone but separated from the legs. It is an excellent way to roast game birds, wild duck for example, whose legs are better for other uses. I personally would rather roast a chicken whole, but if I had to eat chicken breast only, I would prefer to have it roasted on the bone and then removed.

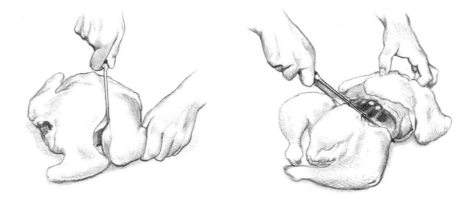

To prepare a Statler breast, first cut off the wingtips. Loosen the legs and carefully cut the skin between the leg and breast on both sides, meeting on the backbone just below the breast. Press down and lightly crack the backbone. Now cut away the legs from the breast.

The Statler breast is roasted with the wings up and the large cavity created by removing the legs facing down. To remove the breast after cooking, cut the skin between the two breasts. For chicken, remove the breast by sticking your thumb under the wing bone, cracking it and then quickly peeling off the breast. (If the bird is too hot, dip your fingers in ice water first.) For birds that are cooked rare or medium rare, like wild duck or goose, you will need to use a knife. Carve out the breast by making a long incision along the breastbone, Now slowly cut down, always keeping your knife tilted toward the rib cage. Cut behind the wing bone to separate it completely from the carcass.

Boneless Breasts (with or without the Wing)

I find the simplest way to make a boneless breast is to start by cutting a Statler breast as described above. Then, keeping your knife pointed slightly toward the breast bone, make a long incision down both sides of the breastbone. Now carefully carve down along the rib cage with your knife slightly pointed toward the ribs, separating the meat from the carcass. Complete the separation by cutting behind the wing bone.

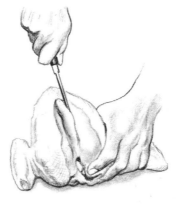
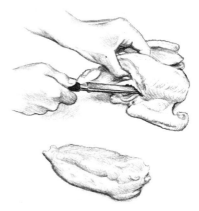

How to Truss a Bird

Trussing or tying up a bird before roasting enhances its appearance by holding its shape; it also helps the bird cook more evenly. There are several ways to do this. Here is a simple and easy way that I use for all birds.

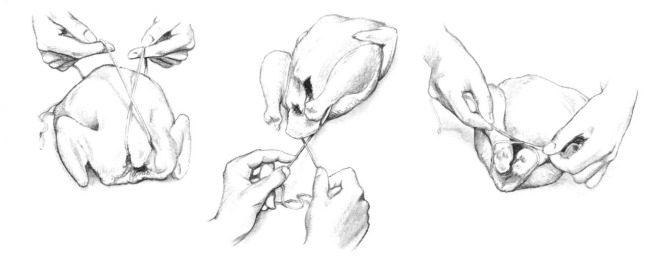

Cut a piece of butcher's twine four times the length of the bird that you will be trussing. Holding the bird with the breast side down and the neck away from you, place the twine (folded in half) under the neck. Turn the bird over and, pulling from both ends of the string, pull along the breast, pinning the wings to the side of the bird. Let the string go in between the legs and the breast and pull until you reach the tail (sometimes called the Pope's nose). Go under the tail, crossing the twine; then lift up, wrap the legs and tie them securely to the tail. Make a tight double knot. That's it.

How to Carve a Roasted Bird

Few dishes are as heart-warming and appealing as a whole roasted pheasant, chicken, capon, goose or turkey. Large roasts of any kind are meant to be shared and thus by their presence alone stand for what good food is all about. Unfortunately, the once glorious sight is all too often turned into an abomination at the hands of an inexperienced or sloppy carver, and even worse if the carver is using that ridiculous tool known as the electric knife.

Carving is very simple. Most people are surprised and pleased to find how easy it is. First and foremost, you must start with a very sharp carving knife. Dull knives are far more dangerous than sharp knives. Every kitchen should have a steel, a fluted round rod which removes the burrs that dull a knife, and an oilstone for sharpening. If you knife is hopelessly dull, take it to a cutlery shop and have them put a new edge on it. The carving knife is designed so that the long blade can make a slice with one sweeping motion. If you keep this principle in mind, you are halfway there. Sawing is good for wood, not for food.

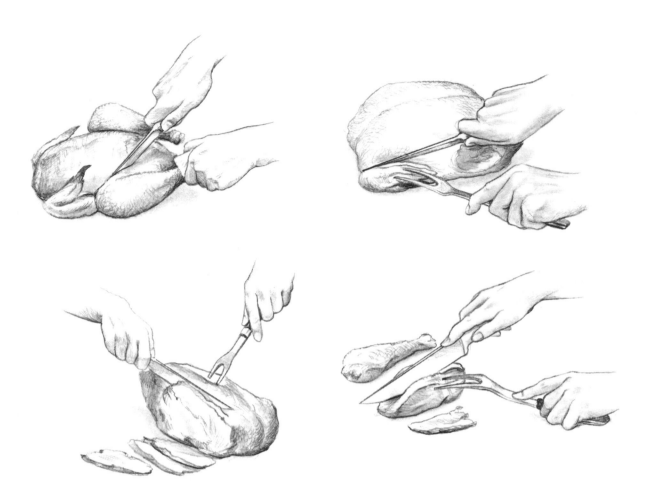

To carve a whole bird, start by removing the legs. Cut the drumstick away from the thigh and carve slices from the thigh, parallel to the bone. Reach under the carcass and pull off the two oysters from either side of the backbone. (These prize morsels should be given to the most honored guest.) Next cut off the wings. You now have an obstacle-free breast to carve. Starting toward the front of the breast, carve down with one sweeping motion, to make beautiful thin slices. This will become a little more difficult as you approach the carcass, but the last few slices need not be perfect. An easier way to carve the breast is to remove the whole breast and then slice it on a cutting board. This does not make for a good show, however.

CHICKEN

Like all animals, the chicken was also once a wild creature. History teaches that the many types of chicken we know today are all descendants of the wild red *Gallus gallus,* which was first domesticated in India about four thousand years ago. The popularity of the chicken in very early times varied from place to place: in some cultures it was more highly prized for eggs than for meat; in others, it had already become a staple food. By the time of Christ, the chicken had become an extremely important domesticated food source, prized for both meat and eggs in almost every corner of the world. Today, the earth's population of chicken is far greater than that of man.

Man's love for chicken is universal. With its almost limitless versatility, the chicken is a recurring theme in almost all of mankind's great cuisines. I cannot think of any cooking method that is not suitable for chicken: roasting, grilling, broiling, poaching, steaming, sautéing, panfrying, stir-frying, deep-frying, etc. Whether cooked whole or in parts, stuffed or unstuffed, served hot or cold, chicken dishes range from very simple to very complex. The flavor of chicken can reach heights of perfection all on its own, or it can be combined with seafood, meats, fruits, vegetables, herbs and spices of every description.

The chicken is so common, such an integral part of everyday life that we often take its greatness for granted. But make no mistake about it, a perfectly cooked farm-raised chicken is second to none. I remember a meal in Hong Kong (at the Golden Unicorn Restaurant) where I was served a chicken that had been air-dried and roasted like Peking duck. Ridiculous as this may sound, I literally had to get a grip on myself, because the texture and flavor of that chicken was so beautiful I was on the verge of crying. Other vivid memories include a *poularde de Bresse,* perhaps the world's most famous kind of chicken, stuffed with truffles and foie gras and poached *en vessie* (in a pig's bladder) that my wife and I shared at Paul Bocuse in Collonges-au-Mont-d'Or outside of Lyons, France, during our honeymoon in 1981. These dishes, which to me epitomize poultry cookery, had one thing in common: they began with finest quality chickens.

Although there are very good chickens to be had in America, we have yet to commercially produce a chicken of the caliber of the free-range chickens of Bresse. Free-ranging chickens is not new, of course: prior to the industrialized farming of this century, all chickens were allowed to roam around the farm, eating a diet of insects and plant life combined with feed, like corn. Although man has always played a part in the evolution of this creature, breeding used to be done more naturally, with motives that were quality oriented. The super-commercial, artificial breeding of chickens today is mostly profit oriented, and it has caused major setbacks in quality. The free-range style of farming chickens is making a reappearance and with it new hope for easy availability of delicious chickens, which until recently have been available only to people in farming communities.

In New England, especially in Maine, there are several medium-size producers who, although they do not free-range their chickens, are providing the birds with a sanitary and decent environment, free of synthetic stimulus. They are raising very tasty birds that are a little more expensive, but not completely out of line. You should be able to locate good chickens almost everywhere in the United States. A properly raised local chicken will have a more pronounced flavor, one that should be noticeably better than the national brand name chickens.

Chicken spoils faster than other types of poultry and meat, so freshness is a vital factor. In Boston's Chinatown chickens are sold live, their necks snapped when the price is finally negotiated. The Chinese use every edible part of the chicken, so the freshness of the bird is crucial. For Americans, who are somewhat squeamish about parts like the feet, the comb and the heart, requirements are different. As with other poultry and meat, some aging (how much depends on the size) is beneficial. A chicken that is cooked on the day of slaughter has too much blood and will appear rare, even after being fully cooked; it will also not be as tender. Chickens are perfect for eating on the second or third day after slaughter and are rarely good after a week.

Types and Sizes of Chickens

A simple generalization, true for all poultry and meat, is that it is good to eat during any stage of growth; that is, while the animal is growing and is "on the gain." When the weight stabilizes, the quality of the meat begins to decline. The different names for chickens refer to different stages of growth and, sometimes, to the cooking method they are most commonly used for.

Poussin. A baby chicken weighing about fourteen to eighteen ounces. It is a wonderful treat, just about the right size for one person. Poussins are good for grilling or roasting and can be used interchangeably (in most recipes) with Cornish hens.

Hen. An egg-laying female not used for cooking until the egg-production period has ended. At this point, hens are referred to as fowl. Fowl is generally sold for use in broths, stock and soup.

Pullet. A young female used for meat. Pullets, along with their young male counterparts, are sold as *broilers* (weighing from 1¼ to 2½ pounds) or as *fryers* (from 2½ to 3½ pounds). Pullets seldom weigh more than 3½ pounds.

Roasters. Young males not sold as broilers and fryers are often raised to be roasters (four to six pounds). These larger chickens are better suited to roasting than other cooking methods, but that does not mean that smaller birds are not equally good roasted.

Capons. Males that have been castrated. They are particularly plump and juicy. These chickens can reach enormous sizes. Capons usually weigh between seven and twelve pounds; most are sold at around ten pounds.

Roosters or cocks. Males that are used primarily for breeding. They are also renowned for their prowess as fighters. Roosters can be used for broths, stocks and soups.

Indian Summer Chowder with Smoked Chicken or Poussin, Sweet Potatoes and Corn

This seafoodless chowder was created by Stan Frankenthaler, my right-hand man in the kitchen of my restaurant. It is intended to be served as a main course. It is a great way to savor the last of the year's corn on an Indian summer evening or cool autumn night.

The smoking of chicken requires liquid brining followed by warm smoking, which partially cooks the chicken while infusing it with smoke. Smoking has many subtleties and requires practice as well as know-how, and I feel recipes and written instructions cannot do justice to this art. I recommend that you find someone who can demonstrate the techniques if you are interested in doing your own smoking. In most places, though, you should be able to purchase good smoked chicken or poussin. See the List of Sources (page 356) for New England purveyors of smoked poultry.

SERVES EIGHT TO TEN
AS A MAIN COURSE

1 small smoked chicken, 2½
  pounds, or 2 smoked poussins
2½ cups Chicken Stock (page
  327) or Chicken Broth (recipe
  follows) and 2½ cups water or
  5 cups water
2 bay leaves
1 tablespoon whole black
  peppercorns
6 to 8 sprigs fresh thyme
6 ears fresh corn on the cob
2 medium to large onions, cut in
  large (¾ inch) dice (3 cups)
2 medium red bell peppers, cut
  in large (¾ inch) dice (1 cup)
2 pounds sweet potatoes, peeled
  and cut in large (¾ inch) dice
½ pound salt pork, rind
  removed, cut in small
  (¼ inch) dice
4 tablespoons unsalted butter
1½ cups heavy cream
salt and freshly ground black
  pepper
2 tablespoons freshly chopped
  Italian parsley and/or chives

For Serving
Cream Biscuits (page 269) or
  Cheddar Cheese Biscuits (page
  269) or common crackers

1. Pick the meat from the smoked bird. Dice the meat into ¾-inch pieces and set aside. Place the carcass in a saucepan and cover with stock and water. Bring to a boil and skim; then reduce heat to a gentle simmer. Add the bay leaves and peppercorns. Pick the leaves from the thyme and set aside; add the stems to the stock. Shave the corn off the cobs and set aside; add the cobs to the stock. Simmer for 1 hour, adding more liquid during that time if it cooks down too far. Strain through a medium strainer. You should have 4 cups.

2. Meanwhile, prepare the onions, peppers and sweet potatoes. Blanch the sweet potatoes for 5 minutes in boiling salted water, then run under cold water to stop the cooking.

3. Render the salt pork in a heated stock or soup pot until it is lightly browned and most of the fat extracted. Add the butter, onions and thyme leaves and cook until tender, 3 to 4 minutes.

4. Add the stock, as well as the corn and sweet potatoes. Bring to a boil and simmer for 5 minutes. Add the cream and pieces of smoked chicken and heat through for a few more minutes. Season to taste with salt and pepper.

5. Ladle into soup plates and sprinkle with chopped parsley and/or chives.

Chicken Broth

There is probably no ingredient in soup-making that is used more frequently than chicken stock or broth. Soup-making in both Eastern and Western cultures is largely based on this one single ingredient. Chicken Stock (page 327) is made with bones—necks, backs and any and all other bones—not meat. Broth is made with whole fowl or other stewing chickens. Stock and broth can be used interchangeably, but for a really great clear soup, chicken broth is better. Following the basic recipe are suggestions for making different kinds of soups based on chicken broth. Try these combinations; then when you feel ready, make up your own.

Once you have a good broth you are almost guaranteed a good soup. It is simply a matter of adding complementary ingredients and allowing them to simmer in the broth. There are basically four categories of garnishes to add to a broth: vegetables, starches, meat, and herbs and spices. They can be combined in various ways to create hundreds of different soups.

Following are more specific recommendations for making different types of soup based on clear chicken broth. Quantities will vary according to how many servings of soup you want to prepare.

MAKES THREE QUARTS

1 fowl, about 5 pounds
2 medium onions, peeled and cut
  in half
2 or 3 leeks, split and washed
3 large carrots, peeled and cut in
  large pieces
4 or 5 stalks celery, cut in large
  pieces
2 cloves garlic
1 tablespoon whole black
  peppercorns
12 sprigs fresh thyme
4 bay leaves
salt

1. Rinse the fowl, inside and out. Place in a stockpot, cover with water and bring to a boil. Skim and reduce to a simmer. Add all the other ingredients, *except* salt, and continue to simmer for about 2 hours.

2. Remove the fowl from the pot. As soon as it is cool enough to handle, pick all the meat from the carcass. Set aside the meat and return the bones to the pot. Continue to cook for 1 hour more. Strain and season lightly with salt. The broth is now ready to drink as is or to be made into soup.

VARIATIONS

Vegetables Vegetables can be used in many combinations and can be either the featured garnish or one of many garnishes. Vegetables like leeks, onions, carrots, celery or celery root, peppers, green beans, fiddlehead ferns, mushrooms, peas and corn, cut to uniform size if necessary, should be cooked in a little butter or chicken fat before adding the broth; it should then be simmered briefly to allow the flavors to expand. Other root vegetables (potatoes, turnips, parsnips and sweet potatoes) should also be cooked in the broth. Leafy vegetables like spinach, watercress, escarole and sorrel should be added right before the soup is to be served. Fresh tomatoes are always good in soups. When to add the tomatoes depends on the depth of tomato flavor you wish to obtain. For instance, a fresh mixed vegetable soup may require only a short cooking time, while a soup with tomatoes, garlic, beans and escarole would take longer.

Starches	Beans, noodles, stuffed pasta and dumplings add substance to soups. These types of garnishes usually need to be partially pre-cooked separately. Add them to the soup at the end.
Meat	Chicken is most often used with chicken broth. Sausages and bacon can also be added to enhance the flavor of the soup.
Herbs and Spices	Fennel, chervil, thyme, marjoram, basil, chives, parsley and dill add depth and complexity to the broth. Add them toward the end in order to preserve their fresh taste. Pepper, chilies, cloves, bay leaf and other strong seasonings like garlic or ginger need to be cooked longer in order to extract their full flavor.
Mixed Vegetable Soup with Chicken	Combine 10 or more fresh vegetables of the season cut into uniform shapes. Cook these in a little butter or chicken fat in a soup pot. Pour the broth over, add diced chicken meat and simmer 10 minutes. Add freshly chopped parsley, chives and chervil. Season to taste with salt and pepper.
Mixed Vegetable Soup with Chicken and Pasta	Make Mixed Vegetable Soup with Chicken, adding cooked pasta about 1 minute before the soup is finished. Use a pasta with a shape that goes with the vegetables in the soup. Small shapes like shells, alphabets, elbow macaroni and orzo are best.
Chicken-Noodle Soup	The pasta is featured in this soup. Sauté some finely diced onion and/or leeks with diced celery and carrot in butter or chicken fat. Pour the broth over and simmer for 10 minutes. Add any shape or type of noodle, precooked, along with some diced chicken meat; simmer for a few minutes more. Season to taste with salt and pepper. Finish with lots of chopped parsley.
Ravioli en Brodo	Brodo means broth in Italian, and ravioli en brodo is a very Italian soup. Heat a little olive oil, sauté finely diced onion, celery, carrot and mushrooms along with a "fingertip" of chopped garlic (½ teaspoon). Pour the broth over and simmer for a few minutes. Add small ricotta cheese ravioli, partially cooked, and some diced chicken meat; simmer a few more minutes. Or, instead of the cheese ravioli make ravioli stuffed with very finely chopped chicken meat. Finish the soup with chopped herbs and a few slices of truffle, if available. Season to taste with salt and pepper. (See page 277 for ravioli directions.)
Chicken Broth with White Beans, Pasta, Tomatoes and Spinach	Soak the beans overnight and cook in salted water. Sauté chopped garlic and onions in olive oil. Pour the broth over and add the beans and tomato concassé (page 337). Simmer for 30 minutes. Add cooked pasta (like macaroni or shells), chopped spinach and a little chopped basil. Simmer for 10 more minutes. Season to taste and serve with grated parmesan or romano cheese.

Chicken Livers with Madeira Sauce and Johnnycake Polenta

Madeira is a small island in the Atlantic, off the coast of Morocco, famous for its sweet wine. Madeira wine has long been a favorite of Bostonians. The famous Boston Tea Party was the act of angry men who were fed up with increased taxes that raised the price of Madeira and other imported items, like the tea they threw overboard. I doubt that any of those men would have thrown their beloved Madeira to the fish; the tea, however, was not considered quite as important.

Here the wine enhances the natural sweet flavor of chicken livers. Not everyone likes chicken livers, but for those who do, they make for a tasty and enjoyable dish that is also very easy on the wallet. Chicken liver is one of the least expensive meats on the market. Look for plump, lightly colored livers that have no dark spots, which are a sign of age. The livers should have no detectable odor. A preliminary soaking in milk extracts some of the blood and removes any bitterness.

SERVES FOUR AS AN APPETIZER

¾ pound chicken livers, trimmed and soaked in milk for up to 24 hours
salt and freshly ground black pepper
¼ cup clarified butter (page 329)
4 portions Johnnycake Polenta (page 263), cut in triangles
all-purpose flour for dredging (about 1 cup)
4 shallots, finely chopped (4 tablespoons)
½ cup Madeira wine
½ cup Reduced Veal Stock (page 328) or Chicken Stock (page 327) or Chicken Broth (page 120)
2 tablespoons unsalted butter
1 tablespoon freshly chopped parsley

1. Drain the livers and separate the large and the small pieces. Season with salt and pepper.

2. Heat 2 large 10-inch sauté pans. Add a bit of clarified butter to one pan, dredge the polenta in flour and place in the pan. Use enough heat to make the polenta crisp, but do not burn it or cook it too fast. When the polenta is well colored and very crisp, flip it over and continue to cook.

3. As soon as you turn the polenta, begin to cook the livers. Add some clarified butter to the other pan. Dredge the livers in flour. Shake off any excess flour before putting livers in the pan. Add the big pieces of liver first and give them a 30-second head start before adding the smaller ones. Do not shake the pan. Allow the livers to sear and become crisp before turning them. The edges will curl a bit and a few drops of blood will surface. When you turn the livers, allow them to cook as on the first side—until seared and crisp. The cooking should take 3 to 4 minutes in all. Check the polenta. When it is ready, drain on paper towels before placing one piece in the center of each plate. Remove the livers and arrange them around the polenta; you should have 3 or 4 nice pieces per plate.

4. Pour off any excess fat, leaving only a few drops. Add the shallots and cook until lightly browned. Add the Madeira and stock and turn up the heat. Quickly reduce the liquid by half. Remove from the heat and whip in the butter and parsley. Check the seasoning and spoon the sauce around the livers. Serve at once.

Chicken Pot Pie

Traditionally this familiar dish is made with a fowl that is boiled for hours, but in this recipe tender young chickens are gently poached. The meat is then removed and the bones thrown back to make a rich stock. Chicken pot pie is a meal in itself and requires no accompanying dishes, except possibly a small salad. It is best on the cold nights of autumn, winter and early spring.

SERVES FOUR TO SIX
AS AN ENTREE

½ recipe for Lard Crust (page 285)
2 small chickens, 2 to 2½ pounds each
1 medium onion, coarsely chopped
2 stalks celery, coarsely chopped
1 carrot, peeled and coarsely chopped
2 bay leaves
several sprigs fresh thyme
10 whole black peppercorns
4 tablespoons chicken fat, vegetable oil or butter
4 tablespoons all-purpose flour
½ cup heavy cream
salt and freshly ground black pepper
juice of ½ lemon
2 medium carrots, peeled and cut into 1-inch sticks (1 cup)
1 sweet potato, peeled and cut into 1-inch sticks (1 cup)
½ pound mushrooms (buttons, shiitakes, etc.), thickly sliced
1 small celery root or 3 stalks celery, peeled and cut into 1-inch sticks (1 cup)
1 pint basket pearl onions, parboiled and peeled (about ¾ pound)
butter
sugar
3 tablespoons coarsely chopped Italian parsley leaves

1. Make the dough for the lard crust and allow it to rest in the refrigerator.

2. Rinse the chickens inside and out and put into a pot just large enough to hold them. Cover with water and bring to a simmer. As soon as the pot begins to simmer, skim off the foam and reduce heat to a very gentle simmer. Add the onion, celery, carrots, bay leaves, thyme and peppercorns. Simmer for about 20 minutes and remove the chickens. As soon as the chicken is cool enough to handle, tear off all the meat, leaving it in as large pieces as possible; set aside the meat. Put all the bones and skin back into the pot and allow to simmer for at least 1 hour.

3. Roll out the lard crust to fit a 9-inch deep-dish-pie dish, preferably glass.

4. When the stock is quite reduced and strong in flavor, strain it through a fine strainer. You should have 3 cups or more. In a heavy saucepan, slowly heat the chicken fat, oil or butter. Make a roux by adding the flour and stirring frequently, until a nutty smell develops (about 2 minutes). Slowly add the stock, little by little, stirring constantly and allowing the sauce to thicken before adding more. When all the stock has been added, slowly add the cream. Allow to simmer a few minutes and season to taste with salt, pepper and lemon juice. Now add the carrot and sweet potato sticks and mushrooms. Simmer for 10 minutes. Add the celery and remove from heat.

5. While you are making the sauce, lightly brown the pearl onions in a separate pan with a bit of butter and a pinch of sugar. Combine the chicken, parsley, onions and vegetable-sauce mixture. Check the seasoning.

6. Preheat the oven to 375 degrees. Put the mixture into the pie dish and quickly cover with the dough. Bake until golden brown, 50 to 60 minutes. Allow to cool a few minutes before serving.

Grilled Chicken

One of the easiest and tastiest ways to cook chicken is outdoors on the grill, and at any summer cookout grilled chicken is almost everyone's favorite. The combination of grilled chicken and sausage is my absolute favorite (I particularly like Italian Sausages, page 181, but Veal Sausages, page 177, are also good).

The chicken can be marinated with oil, lemon, garlic and provençale-type herbs, like basil, marjoram, oregano, thyme and mint, as in this recipe. It can also be marinated in a soy-based, teriyaki-style sauce like the one for grilled duck on page 129. If the chicken is not marinated or is in a soy-based marinade, brush it with a little oil before placing it on the grill. No salt is needed for soy-marinated chicken, but all others should be seasoned with kosher salt and black pepper as well. If quick preparation is the order of the day, the chicken can be cooked plain and basted with a garlic-herb oil, Barbecue Sauce (page 339) or a sweet glaze made from honey or maple sugar (use the one on page 125).

The size of the chickens you wish to grill will determine the way that the chicken is cut for grilling. If the chicken is fairly small (2 pounds or less), you may simply split it in half. For slightly larger birds (2 to 2½ pounds), you may want to quarter them into breast and leg pieces. If you are using even larger birds (2½ to 3½ pounds), you may want to cut each one into 8 pieces.

SERVES FOUR TO TEN
AS AN ENTREE
DEPENDING ON CHICKEN SIZE

2 or 3 chickens

Oil, Lemon and Herb Marinade
1 cup olive oil
1 cup corn or other vegetable oil
3 lemons, thinly sliced
6 cloves (or more) garlic, chopped
2 tablespoons cracked black pepper
1 cup roughly chopped mixed fresh herbs, such as basil, oregano, marjoram, Italian parsley, cilantro, thyme, rosemary or tarragon (see Note)

kosher salt

1. Cut up the chickens as described on page 113.

2. Mix the marinade ingredients in a pan or dish large enough to hold all the chicken pieces and add the chicken. (The marinade will cover the chicken completely.) Allow to marinate 24 hours or more, turning the chicken once or twice.

3. Build a fire of wood or charcoal and allow it to burn down to glowing embers. Brush, clean and lightly oil the grill. Drain the chicken pieces, sprinkle with a little kosher salt and place them, skin side down, on the grill. Sear the pieces on both sides, moving and turning them as little as possible. Once the meat is well seared, it can be moved to a cooler spot on the grill to finish cooking. The size of the chicken pieces will determine the cooking time.

NOTE. Use less of the stronger herbs (thyme, rosemary, tarragon) than of the others.

Spatchcocked and Grilled Poussin or Cornish Hen with Maple and Lemon Glaze

I buy delicious free-range baby chickens from Green Acres Farm, close by in Wrentham, Massachusetts. (See List of Sources, page 357.) Even at only three weeks of age, the poussin has already developed full flavor. Although the flavor of poussin is different from that of Cornish hen, their size (from fourteen to eighteen ounces) makes them interchangeable for many preparations.

If you wish, marinate the birds after they are split, using a little vegetable oil with a bit of onion, lemon, light herbs and spices. It is not necessary, but it certainly doesn't hurt. It will tenderize the meat and impart additional flavors. As the birds cook on the grill, the maple-lemon glaze caramelizes, resulting in crisp and shiny skin with spots of black.

SERVES FOUR TO SIX
AS AN ENTREE

4 poussins or Cornish hens,
  approximately 14 ounces
  each, spatchcocked (page 112)
½ recipe Oil, Lemon and Herb
  Marinade (page 124), if
  desired

Maple and Lemon Glaze
⅔ cup maple sugar
⅓ cup lemon juice (4 or 5
  lemons)
½ cup Chicken Stock (page 327)
  or Chicken Broth (page 120)
  or water
vegetable oil
kosher salt and freshly ground
  black pepper

1. Put the spatchcocked birds in the marinade, if desired.

2. Make a glaze by combining the sugar and lemon juice in a small heavy saucepan. Bring to a boil and continue to boil for 4 or 5 minutes. The color should darken. Add the stock or water and continue to cook for about 15 minutes. The liquid should be reduced by about half, leaving about ¾ cup glaze.

3. Build a fire with wood or charcoal and let it burn down to glowing embers. Brush, clean and lightly oil the grill. If the birds have been marinated, simply season lightly with kosher salt and ground pepper. Otherwise, rub them in oil before seasoning. Place the birds, skin side down, on the grill and baste the meat side with the glaze several times. After the skin side is seared lightly (2 to 3 minutes), turn the birds over and baste the skin with the glaze a few times. In another 2 to 3 minutes turn again, basting right before turning. Allow the skin to get very crisp and caramelized. Turn one more time to finish cooking, giving the birds a last glazing. The total cooking time should be from 8 to 10 minutes.

Five-Spice Roast Chicken for Two

During the years I spent as a hotel chef, I was often constrained by the opinions (or should I say prejudices?) of "experts," namely, my superiors. It seemed like every time I tried to put roast chicken on the menu, it was railroaded. Comments like "Too down market!" or "Why don't you do something fancier?" were the typical reaction. It drove me crazy and, eventually, out of the hotel business. One of the first dishes I did when I opened my own restaurant was this roast chicken, which I served for two.

As bold as I thought I was being at the time, I was still sufficiently intimidated to stretch far for a unique way to flavor the chicken. After many experiments, I stumbled upon the combination of traditional flavors like rosemary and garlic mixed with a little Chinese five-spice powder, with its pronounced flavor of cinnamon. The chicken was very tasty, and it became popular immediately. Although it is no longer on the menu, I do still make it on request for some of my original customers.

SERVES TWO AS AN ENTREE

1 small chicken, 2 to 2½ pounds
4 cloves garlic, finely chopped
    (2 tablespoons)
4 sprigs fresh thyme, leaves
    chopped (1 teaspoon)
2 branches fresh rosemary,
    leaves chopped (1 teaspoon)
3 branches fresh tarragon, leaves
    chopped (1 teaspoon)
2 tablespoons Chinese five-spice
    powder
1 tablespoon cracked black
    pepper
4 tablespoons peanut or other
    vegetable oil
1 small onion, cut in small
    (¼ inch) dice (1 cup)
2 stalks celery, cut in small
    (¼ inch) dice (½ cup)
additional vegetable oil
kosher salt
1 cup Chicken Stock (page 327)
    or Chicken Broth (page 120)
freshly ground black pepper

1. Remove and discard excess fat from the chicken. Trim the wingtips and neck and use to make stock.

2. Preheat the oven to 400 degrees. Combine the garlic, thyme, rosemary, tarragon, five-spice powder and cracked pepper with the oil to make a paste. Rub the bird all over, inside and out, with the herb mixture. Combine any remaining mixture with the diced onion and celery and stuff inside the cavity. Truss the chicken.

3. Place the chicken in a small roasting pan or sauté pan and rub one last time with a little oil. Sprinkle with kosher salt and place in the hot oven. After 10 minutes, remove from oven and baste chicken with the drippings in the pan. Reduce oven temperature to 350 degrees and return to the oven. Cook for 10 minutes more and baste again. After another 10 minutes baste again and return to the oven for the last time. Cook for about 10 minutes more and remove. The skin should be nice and crisp and the chicken should be just cooked through. To check, stick a skewer into the thickest part of the thigh: the juices should run clear.

4. Untie the chicken and scoop the vegetables from the cavity and put in the roasting pan. Allow the chicken to rest while you prepare the sauce.

5. Place the roasting pan with the vegetables over medium heat. Cook for about 5 minutes, then add the stock. Simmer for 10 minutes more and strain. Degrease and adjust seasoning.

6. To serve, cut off the legs first and then the breasts. Slice if desired or serve whole pieces. Moisten the platter with the sauce; do not pour it over the pieces or the crisp skin will be ruined.

Roast Capon with Oyster Stuffing

The combination of chicken with oysters dates back to colonial New England, when oysters were used as much as an extender as for their own great flavor. Scalloped chicken and oysters and roast chicken with oyster sauce are two other popular dishes from that period.

Capon with oyster stuffing makes a great Sunday dinner for a large gathering. Capon is a wonderful bird for roasting. It is big and plump, grand to look at, and it cooks up quite juicy. In fact, this is the only bird, in my opinion, that is moist enough to cook with a bread stuffing. To prevent the stuffing from drying out the bird, be sure it is quite moist, without being soggy. It should also have a reasonably high content of fat, like the butter and bacon in this recipe. This recipe makes a little extra stuffing, which you may need for a large group. Bake the extra stuffing in a buttered pan for 45 minutes, along with the capon, at 325 degrees.

Serve the capon with mashed potatoes or Parsnip Puree (page 243) and fresh vegetables in season. Glazed pearl onions are especially good with roast capon. So are mushrooms.

SERVES EIGHT AS AN ENTREE

1 fresh capon, about 10 pounds

1. This recipe calls for chicken stock in both the stuffing and gravy. If you do not have any on hand, you will need to make some well ahead of time. Trim off the wingtips of the capon and combine

Oyster Stuffing

2 baguettes (long French bread),
  stale, cut into ¾-inch cubes
  (6 cups)

30 medium oysters in the shell or
  shucked in their juices

2 cups Chicken Stock (page 327)
  or Chicken Broth (page 120)

1 bag (10 ounces) fresh spinach

½ pound slab country bacon, cut
  in medium (½ inch) dice

2 medium onions, cut in large
  (½ inch) dice (2 cups)

6 stalks celery, peeled and cut in
  large (¾ inch) dice (1½ cups)

12 sprigs fresh thyme, leaves
  picked

1 tablespoon Bell's Seasoning

leaves from tops and heart of
  celery, coarsely chopped

2 tablespoons coarsely chopped
  Italian parsley leaves

3 eggs

6 tablespoons unsalted butter

salt and freshly ground black
  pepper

For Roasting

3 tablespoons vegetable oil or
  melted butter

½ onion, roughly chopped

1 carrot, roughly chopped

Pan Gravy

4 tablespoons all-purpose flour

3 cups Chicken Stock (page 327)
  or Chicken Broth (page 120)

with the neck and any trimmings in a saucepan. Cover with water and bring to a boil. Skim and reduce the heat. Add any scraps of onion, celery and carrot, parsley and thyme stems you may have on hand; simmer 2 to 3 hours. Strain and reserve.

2. The bread for the stuffing should be completely stale. If your bread is not stale, put it in a low oven (250 degrees) to dry it out. This will take from 1 hour to 1 hour 30 minutes. (I actually think the light golden color the bread picks up in the oven gives the stuffing a better flavor.)

3. Trim up the capon if you have not already done so and allow it to come to room temperature as you prepare the stuffing. Shuck the oysters and keep them in their juices, if necessary. Heat 2 cups of chicken stock and put the oysters and their juices in until the oysters "plump" or just barely cook. Remove the oysters from the liquid. Reserve both oysters and liquid separately.

4. Wash the spinach and cook it briefly in a small amount of boiling salted water. Shock, drain and chop coarsely.

5. Render the bacon in a sauté pan until it begins to get crisp. Add the onions, and celery and cook for 3 or 4 minutes. Stir in most of the thyme leaves, setting some aside to rub on capon (step 7), and poultry seasoning and remove from the heat. Now add the chopped celery leaves and parsley.

6. When the vegetables have cooled a bit, break the eggs into a bowl large enough to hold the bread and oysters and add about half of the stock that the oysters were cooked in. Mix well. Melt the butter and keep warm. Fold the bread cubes and oysters into the wet mixture. Add the rest of the chicken-oyster stock and the melted butter. Toss gently and season to taste with salt and pepper. Do not overmix the stuffing; overmixing will result in heaviness.

7. Preheat oven to 400 degrees. Lightly season the cavity of the capon with salt and pepper. Fill the cavity with the oyster stuffing and truss the capon (see page 116). Rub with oil or melted butter, salt, pepper and the reserved thyme leaves. Spread the chopped onion and carrot on the bottom of a roasting pan and put the capon on top and place in the oven. After 30 minutes, or when the capon is beginning to brown, baste it and turn the oven down to 325 degrees. Cook for 1 hour 40 minutes more, basting about every 20 minutes. Remove from oven. Place the capon on a platter and allow to rest for at least 30 minutes, while you prepare the pan gravy.

8. Pour off about two-thirds of the fat in the pan. Place the roasting pan over medium heat and cook until most of the excess liquids have evaporated, about 5 minutes. Sprinkle with flour and cook for another 4 to 5 minutes. Scrape the pan to loosen up any drippings that may be stuck. Slowly add the 3 cups of chicken stock, allowing the gravy to thicken lightly before adding more. At this point you may transfer the gravy to a small saucepan if you wish. Be sure to transfer every drop. Simmer for 15 or 20 minutes. Strain and serve on the side.

9. Scoop out the stuffing and put in a serving bowl. Carve the capon (see page 116 for directions) and pass the gravy.

DUCK

Domestic ducks were first brought to Europe from China, by Marco Polo. The first domestic ducks in America were also brought from China, during the China Trade era, when clipper ships were constantly on the go between New England and Shanghai. The industry, which started in Connecticut, soon took firmer roots in Long Island, New York, and Long Island is still the largest duck-producing region in the United States. The so-called Long Island duck is descended from the original Chinese ducks. It is extremely fatty and quite tasty, although much milder in flavor than wild ducks. Not too long ago almost all of these ducks were sold frozen. Today, in the Northeast at least, fresh Long Island ducks are readily available. Wild ducks, which are much leaner and smaller, are covered in the following chapter.

Most Americans used to roast ducks until well done. In recent years it was discovered that the duck breast is best when cooked medium rare. The only problem with the medium rare breast is that the fat is usually not rendered from the skin, and nobody likes undercooked fat. In the following recipes I propose two ways to resolve this. The first is the most obvious—the boneless, skinless breast. The second is a small innovation of mine, which calls for scoring the skin and rendering the fat in a hot pan. Duck legs should be reserved and used for stews, sausages, *confits* and other dishes. Excess skin should be saved and used to make cracklings.

Foie Gras

West of the Berkshires in the Catskill mountains of New York lies the birthplace of America's first French-style foie gras. There, at Commonwealth Enterprises in Mongaup Valley, they raise the Moulard duck, which has been especially bred for its liver. In France foie gras (literally, fat liver) comes from both geese and ducks; cooked foie gras from France has been available for years, but not the fresh. To date, this Moulard duck foie gras is the only one of its kind in America. It is so good and so exciting that no treatise on modern cookery would be complete without mentioning it. If you have never had fresh foie gras, you are really missing something sensational; you must try it. It would be like tasting chocolate for the first time. I tasted my first fresh foie gras in France years ago and have been addicted ever since.

Sautéing small slices of foie gras is a very easy way to bring out its pure, delicious flavor. I often serve foie gras cooked in this manner with a little warm salad tossed with a tangy mustard dressing and sprinkled with Duck Cracklings (page 130). Grilled country bread with port wine sauce or jelly is also good. On occasion, I have served foie gras with a warm cabbage slaw (page 231) or with Brussels sprouts (page 233), both of which were great. Sautéed foie gras can also be combined with lobster, as in my Warm Salad with Lobster, Foie Gras and Papaya (page 48). Generally speaking, warm foie gras is best complemented by something acidic, cold foie gras by something sweet and sour, like Cumberland sauce, brandied peaches, grape conserve, and the like. To sauté fresh foie gras:

- Heat the knife blade in boiling water and cut 1 small slice of foie gras, about ½ to ¾ inch thick, per person. Each piece should weigh about 1½ to 2 ounces.

- Heat a nonstick pan on medium-high heat. Salt and pepper the pieces and dredge lightly in flour. Put the pieces in the pan with no added fat. They should sizzle as soon as they hit the pan and some fat will be released immediately.

- Do not move or shake the pan. Sear for 30 to 45 seconds, depending on the size of the pieces, then turn over and cook on the other side for the same length of time. Serve at once.

Salad of Grilled Duck with Cranberries and Spiced Nuts

This recipe is dedicated to all of my regular customers, who have eaten a good many of the 30,000 orders of this dish sold at my restaurant in the last five years. At first I was tempted not to include the recipe, but New Englanders have taken a liking to this modern classic, just like sophisticated Americans everywhere. Warm duck salad made its way from France in the late sixties and has been done so many times, in so many restaurants that it has almost become trite. This is my rendition, and if I do say so myself, it is much livelier than what you will find in most restaurants. This salad is always on my menu; my customers insist on it. When you make it, be sure to let the meat sit in the marinade for *exactly* two hours: an extended marinade will almost cook the meat and make it very salty.

The recipe calls for starting the duck breasts in a pan to render the fat, then finishing them on the grill. The duck can be finished all the way in the pan if you do not wish to bother with a fire. The honey caramelizes in the pan, giving the duck a black crust. Results are similar to grilling, but with less of a smoky flavor.

SERVES FOUR AS AN APPETIZER

1 fresh Long Island duck, 5 to 6
    pounds

Soy Marinade
½ cup soy sauce
¼ cup honey
¼ cup dry sherry
3 tablespoons sesame oil
8 cloves garlic, finely chopped
1 small piece (2 inches) ginger,
    finely chopped

Salad Dressing
⅓ cup balsamic vinegar
⅓ cup peanut oil
salt and freshly ground black
    pepper

½ cup whole cranberries
1 ripe papaya, cut into 1-inch
    chunks, or 2 oranges,
    sectioned
6 to 8 cups mixed salad greens
1 cup spiced pecans (page 344)

1. Bone out the duck breasts as described on page 114, making 2 boneless breasts; do not skin. Trim the breasts and carefully score the skin at about ½-inch intervals, cutting into the fat without cutting into the meat. Reserve the legs: wrap and freeze them for later use in broth and forcemeat. Wrap and freeze any trimmings for broth.

2. Combine the soy sauce, honey, sherry, sesame oil, garlic and ginger and mix well. Place the breasts in this marinade and let sit for *exactly* 2 hours. The marinade should cover the breasts; if not, turn them from time to time. Remove from the marinade and drain.

3. Prepare the dressing by combining the vinegar and oil and seasoning lightly with salt and pepper.

4. Wash and pick over the cranberries; blanch them in boiling water for about 30 seconds and drain. They will split slightly. Cut up the papaya or oranges. Wash and dry the greens.

5. If you are going to grill the duck, make a nice wood or charcoal fire about 1 hour beforehand. Allow it to burn down to glowing embers. Have all ingredients ready to assemble. Heat a sauté pan on high heat and place the duck breasts in it, skin side down. Keep the heat on high (there will be quite a bit of smoke), allowing most of the fat to be rendered. This will take 3 to 4 minutes. At this point the duck can be turned and finished in the pan (pour off the fat first) or transferred to the grill to finish the searing on the meat side. When the meat side is seared, turn the duck again to finish crisping the skin. Remove from the fire and allow to rest 5 minutes while assembling the salad.

6. Toss the greens and cranberries with half of the dressing, coating the greens lightly. Divide among individual plates.

7. Carve the duck breasts into thin slices (12 per breast) and fan 6 slices around each salad. Top with the chunks of papaya or orange sections and the spiced nuts. Drizzle the remaining dressing over the duck and salad. Serve at once.

Duck with Ginger and Scallions

Bone, trim and score the breasts of a duck as described in the recipe for Salad of Grilled Duck (page 129). Marinate the breasts and the legs for 2 hours and roast the legs on a rack set in a roasting pan for 2 hours at 300 degrees. Make stock with the carcass and combine it with some of the marinade into a light sauce. Cook the breast as instructed in the recipe. Put a leg or a piece of the leg on each plate. Slice the breasts and fan the slices around the leg. Moisten the plate with a little sauce and sprinkle with chopped scallions. Serve with Chinese noodles or scallion pancakes.

Duck Sausages

In the chapter on Feathered Game there is a recipe for Pheasant Sausages (page 144) that you can use to make sausages with extra duck legs as well. Wrap the duck legs tightly in plastic wrap and store in the freezer until you have enough to make a batch of sausage. Pull them out the day before you are going to use them, to allow them to defrost slowly in the refrigerator. This slow defrosting reduces the loss of blood and juices. The duck could be mixed with other poultry or game birds.

Grill or panfry the sausages and serve with warm lentils finished with a splash of vinegar. Or, brown the sausages and place in a crock of homemade Boston Baked Beans (page 229) for their last 20 minutes of cooking. The sausages are also good with mustard or collard greens or with a warm salad.

Duck Cracklings

Many recipes, like the Roast Breast of Duck Wrapped in Smoked Bacon, with Cider Vinegar Sauce (page 131), will leave you with excess fatty skin. Even when the duck is not skinned, the large flappy piece of skin at the tail of the bird has to be removed. These pieces of skin make wonderful cracklings. Save them, wrapped tightly in plastic wrap and frozen, until you have enough to use in a dish. Cracklings can be used as garnish for salads, entrees, fritters, pancakes, and even in omelets.

To make duck cracklings, preheat the oven to 350 degrees and roast the whole pieces of skin on a rack set in a rimmed pan until golden brown and very crisp; then cut into strips. For smaller cracklings, cut the skin into medium (½ inch) dice and roast the pieces on a rimmed sheetpan at 350 degrees until crisp. Drain on paper towels. Discard the fat.

Roast Breast of Duck Wrapped in Smoked Bacon, with Cider Vinegar Sauce

This modern preparation of sliced rare duck fanned around a mound of pureed parsnips or potatoes is like a farm boy in a three-piece suit—the heart is country but the presentation is downtown.

SERVES FOUR TO SIX
AS AN ENTREE

2 fresh Long Island ducks, about
    5 pounds each

Cider Vinegar Sauce
1 medium onion, roughly
    chopped
2 medium carrots, roughly
    chopped
1 cup Reduced Veal Stock (page
    328) and 4 cups water or
    5 cups water
4 sprigs fresh thyme
1 branch fresh sage
2 whole cloves
2 bay leaves
10 whole black peppercorns

For Finishing
salt and freshly ground black
    pepper
4 sprigs fresh thyme, leaves
    picked
about ½ pound smoked bacon,
    thinly sliced (10 to 12 slices)
1 tablespoon plus 1 teaspoon
    cider vinegar (4 teaspoons)
2 level tablespoons brown sugar

For Serving
Parsnip Puree (page 243) or
    mashed potatoes (page 249)

1. Bone out the duck breasts as described on page 114; set aside. Remove the skin and reserve it for cracklings (page 130). Set aside a few pieces of duck fat for the duck stock; discard the rest. Chop the carcass and neck of one of the ducks into 1-inch pieces for making stock; set aside. Wrap and freeze the other carcass and neck for later use in broth. Wrap and freeze the legs for later use in broth and forcemeat.

2. Heat a large sauté pan and render a few pieces (about ¼ cup) of the excess duck fat. When the fat is rendered, discard the crisp brown pieces of fat that remain. You should have 2 to 3 tablespoons of hot fat. Add the pieces of chopped carcass and cook until they begin to brown. Now add the onion and carrots and continue browning (total cooking time: 10 to 15 minutes).

3. Add the stock and water and bring to a boil. Skim. Reduce heat and add the thyme, sage, cloves, bay leaves and peppercorns. Transfer this sauce to a saucepan, if desired. Simmer for 2 hours. Strain through a fine sieve and put back on the heat and let simmer. Degrease the sauce as much as possible.

4. Meanwhile rub the duck breasts with salt, pepper and thyme leaves. Wrap each breast in bacon, using toothpicks to hold it together. It will take about 2½ slices of bacon to wrap each breast. Keep refrigerated.

5. Preheat oven to 400 degrees. Add the vinegar and brown sugar to the simmering sauce; keep at a slow simmer until needed. Season lightly with salt, pepper and a splash more of vinegar, if you like. You may also want to add a few drops of water to the sauce. You should have 1 cup of rich brown sauce, the duck flavor predominating with nuances of sweet and sour.

6. Heat a large sauté pan and add the duck breasts. Lightly brown the bacon on both sides. Pour off any excess bacon fat and place entire pan in the oven. After 5 minutes, turn the breasts over and cook for 5 minutes on the other side. Remove from the oven and allow to rest at least 5 minutes before carving.

7. Remove the toothpicks from the duck breasts and with the bacon intact, make 4 or 5 thick slices per breast. Fan the breast pieces around some parsnip puree or mashed potatoes and spoon the cider vinegar sauce over the duck.

The exact origin of the domestic American goose is hard to pinpoint. Geese have been domesticated in Europe since the time of the Romans and date back even further in China. We do know that the domestic goose is not related to the wild geese of North America. They were probably introduced by the Europeans or, even more likely, by the New England traders during the China Trade era of our history. Watertown, Massachusetts, which is now a suburb of Boston, was once famous for its high-quality geese. Geese have never been a big commercial success anywhere in health-conscious America. "Too much fat" is the most common complaint. But gastronomically speaking, the fat is what makes goose a great roast. In fact, the fat is the best part of the domestic goose. It has a pure, clean flavor and can be heated to very high temperatures. I think it is the finest of all animal fats (directions for rendering fat are on page 331). Be sure not to miss the recipe for Boston's most famous potatoes, Freddie's Famous Roast Potatoes (page 251), which are roasted in goose fat with whole cloves of garlic.

Like wild goose, domestic goose is best when young, weighing no more than eight or nine pounds.

Lydia's "Chinese" Christmas Goose

In 1986 my friend and colleague, Lydia Shire, who was then living in California, came to spend Christmas in Boston with us, the thought of Christmas in Los Angeles being too bizarre to consider. Both our families met at my house for a marathon day of eating, with a bit of drinking and gift-giving thrown in. We talked about the menu weeks before, making sure that we didn't forget a thing.

We spent the afternoon drinking champagne with smoked Scottish salmon, beluga caviar, Brandade de Morue (page 101), and scores of delicious tiny littleneck clams on the halfshell. Later we drank magnums of 1955 Pommard and 1964 Clos de la Roche with our very traditional Christmas dinner of goose and roasted ribs of beef, au jus. We also cooked Yorkshire pudding, Brussels sprouts, glazed onions (page 240), mashed parsnips (page 243) and potatoes roasted in goose fat (page 251). We had plum pudding, shortbread (page 303) and Mincemeat Tartelets (page 290) with our coffee and brandy.

When it was all over, Lydia and I opened another bottle of champagne and finished off what was left of the goose. It was the best domestic goose I had ever tasted. The presence of the goose was traditional, but that was the only thing about this goose that was. Lydia steamed it for two hours with star anise and ginger and then glazed it with Hoisin sauce and blasted it for about ten minutes at 500 degrees to make it very crispy. It was fabulous and, surprisingly, great together with all the other, more traditional food on the table.

This recipe may seem overwhelming at first glance, but it is not really that difficult. I have broken down the ingredients and instructions into five steps, each of which is fairly simple. First you prepare an aromatic stuffing to flavor the goose. This is best done a day in advance, but is not completely necessary. Then you season the outside of the goose and prepare a steamer. Start this about four to five hours before you plan to eat. The steaming will take close to two hours, followed by a thorough resting of over one hour, during which time you prepare the sauce. The last step is glazing and cooking in a very hot oven.

Lydia is chef and proprietor of the fabulous restaurant Biba, which overlooks the Boston Public Gardens.

1 large fresh goose, about 12 to
   14 pounds

Aromatic Stuffing

2 tablespoons Hoisin sauce
1 piece (1 inch) ginger, unpeeled
   and cut in 1/4-inch slices
8 scallions, coarsely chopped
12 cloves garlic, crushed
1 tablespoon five-spice powder
1 tablespoon crushed Szechwan
   peppercorns

2 tablespoons Hoisin sauce
2 tablespoons kosher salt
1 tablespoon five-spice powder

For Steaming

1 small onion, coarsely chopped
2 celery stalks, coarsely chopped
10 cilantro stems
6 whole star anise
1 cup white wine
4 cups Chicken Stock (page 327)
   or water

Sauce

1 small onion, cut in medium
   (1/2 inch) dice
1 carrot, peeled and cut in
   medium (1/2 inch) dice
5 cloves garlic, finely chopped
1 cup white wine
peel of 1 lemon (no white pith)
5 or 6 cilantro stems
salt and freshly ground black
   pepper

Glaze

2 tablespoons granulated sugar
grated rind and juice of 1 lemon
2 tablespoons soy sauce
2 teaspoons Hoisin sauce
1 tablespoon honey
1/4 teaspoon five-spice powder

cilantro leaves for garnish

1. If possible, prepare and stuff the goose 1 day in advance. Trim off the wingtips and reserve them, along with the neck and giblets. Rub the inside of the goose with Hoisin sauce. Mix together the ginger, scallions, garlic cloves, five-spice powder and Szechwan peppercorns and stuff into the goose. Truss the goose (as explained on page 115), cover and refrigerate overnight.

2. At least 5 hours before serving, remove the goose from the refrigerator and bring to room temperature. Rub the outside of the goose all over with Hoisin sauce, then sprinkle with salt and five-spice powder. Sprinkle the bottom of a roasting pan large enough to hold the goose with onion, celery, cilantro stems and star anise. Add the white wine and chicken stock or water. Put the goose giblets into this mixture. Set a sufficiently high rack into the pan; you may need to use 2 racks. Place the goose on the rack and cover loosely with heavy aluminum foil, making an airtight tent. Place the pan over two burners (front and back) and turn on to high heat. When the foil on top feels warm (about 10 minutes), turn the heat down to low. Since stoves vary, check the goose after 1 hour 30 minutes, but most will take 2 hours to be done. To check, remove the tent in one piece (you may need to put it back). Poke a metal skewer into the thickest part of the leg. If the juices are red or if the meat feels very tense, continue steaming for 30 minutes more. When the steaming is finished, remove the goose and allow it to rest and cool completely. This will take a minimum of 1 hour, but it is best to allow for 2 hours resting because if the bird is not completely cooled, it will overcook during the final phase.

3. For the sauce, remove the giblets from the steaming liquid, finely chop and set aside. Roughly chop the neck and wingtips into 1-inch pieces. Skim about 2 tablespoons goose fat from the steaming pan and place into a 3-quart saucepan on medium-high heat. Add the chopped neck and wingtips along with the diced onion, carrot and chopped garlic and brown. Add the white wine, 3 cups of the steaming liquid, cilantro stems and lemon peel. Simmer slowly for about 1 hour. Strain and season to taste with salt and pepper. You should have about 2 1/2 cups of sauce. Add the chopped giblets and keep hot until ready to serve.

4. Preheat the oven to 500 degrees. Untie the goose and place on a rack in a roasting pan. If you are using the same pan, clean it out (no liquid this time). Make a glaze by combining the sugar, lemon rind and juice, soy sauce, Hoisin sauce, honey and five-spice powder. Brush the goose all over with about half the glaze and place in the oven. After 10 minutes brush or pour over the remaining glaze and return to the oven for 10 or 15 minutes more. The goose will be crispy; it will have a few black spots.

5. Carve the goose as you would any fowl (page 116) and sprinkle the slices with cilantro leaves. Serve the sauce on the side.

Turkey, a native American wild bird, is finally making a big comeback. It is reported that wild turkeys can be found in all 50 states, a range more vast than the original, which did not include Hawaii. Not too long ago this creature, which Benjamin Franklin proposed to be our national bird, was the victim of a serious population decline. Careful and thoughtful conservation has brought the population back to the point where it can, once again, be hunted in most places. I have seen huge flocks of wild turkeys in West Texas, but not yet in New England, though I am told that Vermont and New Hampshire have greatly increased their wild turkey population.

American turkeys, both wild and domestic, are still considered to be the best in the world. (Turkey has become very popular in Italy and other parts of Europe.) Turkeys can reach enormous weights of up to 50 pounds, but American breeders have very little use for the giant turkeys of yesteryear and have concentrated their efforts on raising smaller birds that are more suitable to the smaller families of our times.

Roast Vermont Turkey with Giblet Gravy and Sausage and Sage Dressing, for Thanksgiving

Turkey may not have played as big a part in the first Thanksgiving, held back in 1621, as it does in our contemporary celebration. If turkey was served at all, it was probably one of many game birds that were served along with venison, oysters, clams, lobsters and eels, as well as succotash, beach plums, sweet potatoes, leeks and cornbread. My own Thanksgiving menu (page 351) is intended to pay homage to the foods of the first Thanksgiving, as well as to the foods that have become associated with this holiday. I believe that holidays by their very nature demand that traditional foods be served. In America there is no stronger correlation between the food and the day than that of the venerable Thanksgiving Day turkey.

Roasting a whole turkey perfectly is difficult if not near to impossible. Because the legs take longer to cook than the breast, many professional chefs separate the breasts from the legs and roast them separately. This, of course, would look pretty silly on the family's finest platter. When Craig Claiborne asked me to cook Thanksgiving dinner for a feature in the *New York Times Sunday Magazine,* I experimented with different size birds as well as cooking techniques. I found that the smaller birds (about ten pounds) were the easiest to cook properly. I also think that a smaller bird is more appropriate when serving more than one main course, and in the true spirit of Thanksgiving, I like to offer a second main dish, such as a venison roast (page 193), as well.

I adapted this recipe from the original (1896) edition of Fannie Merritt Farmer's *The Boston Cooking-School Cook Book.* Although most of my recipe is different from Miss Farmer's, the most intriguing part of her recipe, a paste made of butter and flour which forms a crust around the turkey, is still there. This recipe, if followed carefully, will yield a very juicy turkey that is neither undercooked nor overcooked. The skin will not be as crackling crisp as when dry roasted, but that is a small price to pay for a near perfect bird.

To make this recipe easier to follow, I have broken down the ingredients for each step of the recipe. Many of them repeat, making the recipe appear more complicated than it is. For your convenience, I have drawn up a shopping list (page 136) that gives a total of all that is needed for this very special recipe and the dressing that goes with it.

SERVES ABOUT TEN AS AN ENTREE

1 Vermont or other fresh turkey,
    about 10 pounds, fattened on
    corn and walnuts, killed 3
    days earlier
kosher salt and freshly ground
    black pepper

Vegetable Stuffing

1 lemon
½ apple
½ medium onion
10 sprigs fresh thyme
4 branches fresh rosemary
2 branches fresh sage
10 sprigs Italian parsley
4 bay leaves
¼ cup vegetable oil

Turkey Stock

trimmings from the turkey
½ medium onion
2 stalks celery
1 carrot
2 bay leaves
10 black peppercorns
5 Italian parsley stems

Flour Paste

6 tablespoons unsalted butter
¼ cup all-purpose flour

For the Pan

4 tablespoons all-purpose flour

For Basting

8 tablespoons unsalted butter
1 teaspoon water

Giblet Gravy

1 large leek, white part only, cut
    in ¼-inch dice
3 cups turkey stock
giblets from turkey, finely diced
1 hard-boiled egg, finely diced
salt and freshly ground pepper

For Serving

Country Sausage and Sage
    Dressing (recipe follows)
Cranberry Relish (page 341)

1. Prepare the turkey. Remove all extra parts; reserve giblets. Cut off wingtips and any excess neck, etc. Season turkey inside and out with kosher salt and freshly ground black pepper; be generous. Loosen up leg joints without tearing skin.

2. Make the stuffing by roughly chopping the lemon, apple, onion, thyme, rosemary, sage, parsley and bay leaves into ½-inch pieces. Mix with oil. Put stuffing into cavity and truss the bird (page 115). Do not tie too tight.

3. Start the stock at least 30 minutes before roasting the turkey. Place the wingtips and neck in a saucepan; add 6 cups of water. Bring to a boil. Skim off any foam. Reduce heat to a slow simmer. Add onion, celery, carrot, bay leaves, peppercorns and parsley stems. Allow to simmer about 2½ hours. Strain stock and reserve. You should have about 3 cups.

4. Make a paste by kneading 6 tablespoons unsalted butter with ¼ cup flour. Rub this vigorously and thoroughly into the skin of the bird.

5. Preheat the oven to 450 degrees. Sprinkle 4 tablespoons flour evenly on the bottom of a roasting pan. Place turkey on a rack in the pan. Allow time for turkey to come to room temperature if it is still cold to the touch.

6. Place turkey in oven. Leave in oven for 40 minutes or until the bird is browned all over. Combine 8 tablespoons butter with 1 teaspoon of water and bring to a boil. Turn the oven down to 350 degrees and baste the turkey generously with the butter mixture. Repeat this process twice, once every 10 minutes, until basting liquid is used up. At this point the turkey should be in the oven about 1 hour. Now baste 2 more times at intervals of 15 minutes, using the pan drippings. At this point, the turkey has been in about 1 hour 30 minutes. Cook 20 minutes more without basting, to allow the skin to crisp. Remove from oven. Allow to rest at least 30 minutes before carving. Make the gravy during this resting period.

7. To make the gravy, remove turkey to a serving platter. Place roasting pan directly on top of a burner on medium heat. Cook for about 5 minutes, allowing excess liquid to evaporate. Stir constantly. Now, carefully remove any excess fat that has not combined with the flour to make a roux. Add the diced leek and cook for 1 minute. Slowly add 3 cups turkey stock, allowing the gravy to thicken as it comes to a boil. At this point it may be switched to a saucepan. Make sure that every bit of the pan drippings has been incorporated into the gravy. Add the giblets and simmer for about 15 minutes. Stir in the hard-boiled egg and remove from heat. Season to taste with freshly ground pepper and salt, if necessary.

8. Carve the turkey and pass the gravy. Serve with country sausage and sage dressing and cranberry relish.

Country Sausage and Sage Dressing

This recipe is intended as a baked dressing to accompany the Thanksgiving turkey. It can be used as stuffing (a practice I do not recommend for turkey) if you desire. It also makes a good stuffing for capon or pork.

SERVES TEN TO TWELVE
AS A SIDE DISH

2 baguettes (long French bread),
    stale, cut into 1-inch cubes
1 tablespoon vegetable oil
1 pound Breakfast Sausages,
    preferably homemade (page
    180)
1 large onion, cut in large (³/₄ to
    1 inch) dice (2 cups)
5 stalks celery, peeled, split
    lengthwise and cut in large
    (³/₄ to 1 inch) dice
2 medium apples, peeled, cored
    and cut in large (³/₄ to 1 inch)
    dice
15 sprigs Italian parsley, leaves
    picked and very coarsely
    chopped (¹/₂ cup)
6 to 8 branches fresh sage, leaves
    picked and coarsely chopped
    (¹/₄ cup)
4 eggs
2 cups Turkey Stock (page 135),
    Chicken Stock (page 327) or
    Chicken Broth (page 120)
1 teaspoon salt
1 teaspoon freshly ground black
    pepper
6 tablespoons unsalted butter

1. The bread should be completely stale. If not, spread the cubes on a baking sheet and put in a low oven (250 degrees) for about 1 hour to dry them out. (I think this light toasting gives the dressing a better flavor.)

2. Heat the vegetable oil in a large skillet. Add the sausage meat and brown it, breaking up meat into pieces about the size of a quarter. This need not be precise. Transfer meat from skillet to large bowl, using a slotted spoon. Add onion and celery to the skillet. After 1 minute, add the apples and cook 2 more minutes. Place in bowl with the sausage.

3. Add bread cubes, parsley and sage to the bowl.

4. In a separate bowl, mix the eggs and stock with the salt and pepper. Pour this over the sausage mixture and gently toss all the ingredients. They should combine without mushing.

5. Generously butter a 16-inch baking pan (2 tablespoons). Spread the mixture in the pan and dot with more butter (4 table-spoons).

6. Preheat oven to 350 degrees and bake for 50 minutes to 1 hour. The top should have a nice golden brown crust.

THANKSGIVING DINNER SHOPPING LIST

1 fresh turkey, about 10 pounds	fresh sage
1 lemon	Italian parsley
3 apples	vegetable oil
2 medium onions	unsalted butter (use 10 ounces)
1 carrot	5 eggs
1 bunch celery	all-purpose flour
1 large leek	bay leaves
fresh thyme	whole black peppercorns
fresh rosemary	kosher salt
	2 baguettes (long French bread)

5 Feathered Game

Pheasant

Pheasant Broth with Wild Mushrooms and Quenelles

Pheasant Ravioli en Brodo

Pheasant Broth with Escarole, Beans and Pheasant Meatballs

Pheasant Broth

Pheasant Sausage Forcemeat

Pheasant Mousse

Breast of Pheasant, Hunter Style

Roast Pheasant

English Bread Sauce

Guinea Hen (Pintade)

Partridge

Roast Partridge with Tarragon and Green Peppercorns

Quail

Grilled Nantucket Quail

Wild Duck and Goose

Wild Duck or Goose Broth with Stuffed Cabbages

Breast of Wild Duck with Bitter Greens and Turnips

Roast Breast of Wild Goose

The New World had an incredible abundance of game birds. Since the time of the Pilgrims, snipe, woodcock, partridge, grouse, duck, geese—and turkey, of course—have all occupied an important place on the American table. The turkey, which has become a symbol of the first Thanksgiving, was probably only one of many birds served at the famous feast back in 1621. Although the population of feathered game has dwindled to a mere fraction of what it once was, it continues to provide New Englanders, and other Americans, with a wonderful source of free food. Once a taste for real game is awakened, though, the desire for it becomes a matter of preference, not economy.

My father was, and still is, a great hunter. As children growing up in New Jersey, my brothers and I were taught how to spot, flush and shoot quail, pheasant and woodcock. Our English setter, Patches, was usually the real star of the show, but we always took the credit. We were taught that a good sportsman would never shoot a bird that wasn't flying. To this day I can remember pheasants in the cornfield that were so fat you practically had to kick them to get them in the air.

In this chapter, I will deal not only with wild game birds, but also with domesticated birds of wild origin. Farm-raised game birds represent most of what is consumed in our time. Good hunting grounds are becoming harder to find, and the sport has become nonexistent in many areas. Another factor is that restaurants are not allowed to serve meat that is not government inspected. It is ironic that many of the finest professional cooks are prohibited by law from using real game.

Demand for pheasant, quail, Guinea hen, and other feathered game is increasing rapidly, and New England is fast becoming one of the nation's finest and largest producers. In my travels around the United States, I have often cooked with quail from Nantucket Island raised by my friend, Stephen Swift, and have heard repeatedly that "they are the best I ever tasted." Stephen free-ranges the birds, and he tells me that the biggest problem is keeping wild birds from mixing with the flock that he breeds so carefully.

I have excluded several game birds from this chapter for various reasons. The wild turkey, for example, is still uncommon at the table. (I have included a recipe for the domestic variety on page 134.) There are still a few ruffed grouse around, but they too are quite scarce. If you have the chance to try grouse, however, you will find it to be one of the finest of the wild birds. Pigeon and dove have adapted all too well to urban civilization; unfortunately they carry disease. Where these birds range freely, far away from cities, it is quite safe to eat them, but in New England it is not advisable. (Squab, a cousin of the pigeon, is farm-raised.) Also omitted is the woodcock, a relative of the snipe. I have enjoyed these tiny red-meat birds many times, especially in my youth, but, alas, they are very scarce in New England, probably because of the development of our marshlands. This tiny bird, with its incredibly big eyes and long beak, migrates 1,500 miles each year, from Nova Scotia and other Canadian provinces to southern states as far away as Louisiana. Each year, they congregate in Cape May, New Jersey, awaiting a wind strong enough to carry them across the Chesapeake. Woodcock are best panfried to prevent overcooking. For a dramatic presentation, carefully split the entire bird, including the head and beak.

The hunting season for game birds is October through January; laws vary from state to state. The exception to this rule is turkey, which in addition to the usual fall hunting season has a short hunting season in spring for males (toms or gobblers) in some states. After the New Year, game birds become more scarce because of deep nesting and death from harsh weather conditions and starvation. Those that survive are less desirable due to weight loss. Most farmed birds follow the same seasonal cycle, but some, especially quail, are now available year-round. Fall and winter weather seems to enhance the eating of game birds, perhaps because our appetites are more in tune with the richer preparations that work so well with them.

Wild birds should be eviscerated immediately after the hunt and hung for at least two days, with the feathers on, in a cold place or the refrigerator; then they should be plucked and aged further in the refrigerator. At this point they are ready for marinating or cooking or smoking. Farmed birds also should be aged in the refrigerator for at least two or three days after they are killed. They are best when marinated for a few more days after aging. I prefer to use an oil-based marinade rather than a dry or wine-based marinade.

The cooking methods most commonly used for wild birds are roasting, grilling, braising, and sautéing. It is also common to cure and hot-smoke wild birds, pheasant in particular. The size of the bird and the type of meat, red or white, determine the best cooking method. (Because migratory birds need to pump so much blood through their bodies on their long journeys, their flesh is red. Stationary birds, like pheasant and partridge, do very little flying in comparison, hence their lighter-colored flesh.) Red-meat birds—duck, geese, squab, dove, woodcock and some species of quail—are best cooked rare to medium rare. The lighter-meat birds—turkey, pheasant, grouse, partridge and Guinea hen—should be cooked medium to just barely cooked through, according to preference. Game birds, and particularly wild game birds, should *never* be overcooked. They are naturally lean and will dry out completely if overcooked. Marinating in oil, larding with fat or barding (wrapping in fat) will help keep the bird juicy, but nothing can cure overcooking.

There is a truism that applies to game birds as well as to other meat and fish: The place of origin or habitation is as important as the species or breed. Harvested fields of grain or areas rich in wild berries produce the finest game birds. When good feed runs low and the birds are forced to eat less desirable food, pinecones for example, or when birds migrate to less desirable regions, they will pick up the flavor of the new feed. A good example is the duck or goose that has been feeding in the rich interior of Canada. This fabulous-tasting meat becomes tainted during migration once the birds reach the coastal areas where they begin to feed on bay cabbage or skunk cabbage. Birds that eat fish, like some species of duck, are not palatable on account of their strong fishy flavor. Game birds also fare better in certain years than in others.

All birds have similar bone structure. The basic methods of boning and carving described on pages 113–116 in the chapter on poultry also apply to feathered game. Specific information concerning the various birds is included in individual recipes. The recipes for Pheasant Broth and Forcemeat (pages 143–145) can serve as a guideline for other game.

Pheasant has been held in high esteem since the time of ancient Rome and feudal Europe, most species coming originally from the East and Far East. To this day it is the most popular of all feathered game.

Food historians have never been able to say exactly when pheasant was introduced to the United States. Some make reference to the late 1800s; others date it to the earlier part of that century. And whether American pheasants came from Europe or the Far East is also uncertain.

Today there are several species and hybrids living in the wild. The single most common type is the ringed-neck pheasant, of Chinese extraction, noted for the beautiful plumage of the male bird. In certain parts of New England, particularly on the coastal islands, the ringed-neck pheasant is very abundant in the wild. There are also many pheasantries that sell birds either live as stock for sportsmen or dressed for consumption.

There is something of a disagreement about how long a pheasant should be aged. The classical gourmands insisted on five days minimum; some modern chefs claim that no aging is necessary. My experience has taught me that two to three days hanging in the cold outdoors or in a refrigerator, with the plumage left intact, improves the bird. After plucking, further time spent in a marinade will also enhance the flavor and texture of pheasant. Domesticated birds are best kept refrigerated at least two days before cooking; they can then be held longer in a marinade, if desired.

Hens are very pretty but of a dull brown color, which affords camouflage, so important to the species during the nesting season. Hens tend to run a bit smaller than cocks; most people consider them to be slightly tastier. There are fewer hens than cocks available because the legal hunting season is shorter for females. The pheasant is a close relative of the Guinea hen (page 149), another fabulous-looking bird.

Pheasant Broth with Wild Mushrooms and Quenelles

This and the next two soups combine the recipes for Pheasant Broth and Pheasant Sausage Forcemeats (pages 143–144). Use what you have on hand and improvise the rest. You may find that your own variations are nothing short of excellent. Many of the world's great dishes were created in this manner.

SERVES SIX TO EIGHT

1½ pounds Pheasant Mousse
   (page 145)
1 onion, finely diced
2 cups finely sliced chanterelles
   or other wild mushrooms
2 tablespoons butter
4 cups Pheasant Broth (page
   143)
salt and freshly ground black
   pepper
Italian parsley leaves and chervil
   leaves for garnish

1. Make 12 to 18 quenelles as directed on page 145 and set aside.

2. Sauté the onion and mushrooms in butter for 5 minutes. Heat the broth and pour it over. Simmer for 10 minutes.

3. Slip the quenelles into the broth and simmer briefly. Season the broth to taste with salt and pepper and divide among soup cups. Garnish each cup with some parsley and chervil leaves and serve.

Pheasant Ravioli en Brodo

SERVES SIX

about 1 pound Pasta (page 277)
1½ pounds Pheasant Sausage Forcemeat (page 144)
2 cups finely diced onion, celery, carrot, turnips and truffle (the last is optional), combined
2 tablespoons unsalted butter
4 cups Pheasant Broth (page 143)
salt and freshly ground black pepper
1 tablespoon chopped Italian parsley for garnish

1. Prepare the pasta and make about 36 ravioli with the forcemeat, as directed on page 277; set aside.
2. Sauté the vegetables in butter for 5 minutes. Heat the broth and pour it over. Simmer for 10 minutes.
3. Add the ravioli and cook 5 minutes more. Season to taste with salt and pepper and divide among soup bowls. Garnish with chopped parsley and serve.

NOTE. Tortellini may be substituted for ravioli.

Pheasant Broth with Escarole, Beans and Pheasant Meatballs

SERVES SIX

1½ pounds Pheasant Sausage Forcemeat (page 144)
3 tablespoons olive oil
1 onion, thinly sliced
2 carrots, thinly sliced
4 cups Pheasant Broth (page 143)
1 cup cooked beans (see Note)
2 cups chopped escarole
grated parmesan or romano cheese

1. Form 24 to 30 meatballs, about the size of a quarter. Fry in olive oil, remove from pan and set aside.
2. Cook the onion and carrots in the same pan for 6 minutes. Transfer to a soup pot and add the broth, beans and escarole. Simmer for 20 minutes.
3. Add the meatballs and cook 5 minutes more. Divide among soup bowls and sprinkle with grated cheese. Serve with extra grated cheese on the side.

NOTE. Any kind of beans may be used: white, kidney, shell, fava and so on.

Pheasant Broth

If you like to cook feathered game, you will inevitably accumulate all kinds of leftover bones, carcasses, legs, livers, wingtips and the like. Although the leftovers from one meal will hardly provide enough material to make a soup, if you freeze the leftovers from a few meals you will soon have the ingredients for a good strong broth and some interesting and tasty garnishes for it. The drumsticks from many game birds are very stringy and full of tendons and sinews, but they are perfect for making a flavorful broth. (A broth by definition is made with some meat; if only bones are used, it is a stock.)

The meat from the thighs can be coarsely ground or finely processed to make quenelles, sausages, meatballs or a forcemeat for wrapping in pasta, cabbage leaves or other things. These garnishes can transform a simple broth into an elegant soup. There are infinite variations based on this concept, and I will list a few after the directions for making the broth. First, a couple of pointers:

- A fine game broth should be golden brown, never dark brown. To obtain the desired color, you must first examine the bones and carcasses that you have collected. If you have some carcasses left from roasted birds, it will not be necessary to brown the bones. If all the parts you are using are raw, you will need to roast them lightly to add color to the broth. Another way to color it is to blacken some onion halves and add them to the broth. (To blacken an onion, cut it in half, leaving the skin on. Place the onion, skin side down, under the broiler and cook until black.)

- Carcasses and trimmings from different types of game birds may be mixed together; in fact, the broth will gain in complexity if you do so. The same principle applies to forcemeat.

- The following recipe is based on two pounds of leftover bones, carcasses, drumsticks and so on. Use it as a guide, adjusting the amounts of vegetables, herbs and spices to the quantity of bones and meat you have on hand.

MAKES ABOUT ONE QUART

*2 pounds carcasses and
   trimmings from pheasants and
   other game birds*
*Chicken Stock (page 327), as
   needed (optional)*
*1 medium onion, roughly
   chopped*
1 carrot, roughly chopped
1 stalk celery, roughly chopped
1 bay leaf
2 whole cloves
10 whole black peppercorns
6 Italian parsley stems
6 sprigs fresh thyme

1. Place all the bones, carcasses, drumsticks and so on in a stock pot large enough to allow for movement when simmering. Cover with equal amounts of chicken stock and water or all water if no stock is available. Bring to a boil, skim and reduce to a slow simmer. Add the vegetables, herbs and spices.

2. Simmer the broth slowly for 3 hours, until rich color and flavor have developed. Strain, first through a coarse strainer and then through a fine one. The broth is now ready to be cooled and refrigerated (frozen if not to be used within 3 days) or transformed into a wonderful soup.

These two recipes are designed to utilize the leftover thigh meat from recipes for pheasant, Guinea hen, goose and duck that call for the breasts only. It would be a shame to grind up the fine breast meat from any of these birds, but the recipes will work with any meat you choose. These are not complete dishes but components that will be useful in the game broth soups that follow. For your convenience, both recipes are based on one pound of thigh meat from any of the above-mentioned birds. (Use the drumsticks for broth.)

Pheasant Sausage Forcemeat

This is a coarse forcemeat for sausages, meatballs and some of the more rustic dishes. The seasonings are straightforward and compatible with Pheasant Broth (page 143), but many other seasonings could be used, such as hot chilies, garlic, cilantro, fennel seed, tarragon, oregano, paprika, etc., depending on the desired final outcome. As with all cooking, the variations are almost infinite. The forcemeat is best if made a day ahead to allow time for the flavors to marry.

MAKES ONE AND A HALF POUNDS

1 pound pheasant (or other)
    thigh meat
4 ounces fatback
3 shallots, finely chopped
    (4 tablespoons)
1 clove garlic, finely chopped
    (1 teaspoon)
1 tablespoon vegetable oil
3 tablespoons finely chopped
    Italian parsley
1 teaspoon finely chopped fresh
    sage
1 teaspoon fresh thyme leaves
¼ cup water
1 cup white breadcrumbs (page
    67)
about 2 teaspoons salt
coarsely ground black pepper

1. Trim the meat, being sure to remove any sinews and the outer membrane (the silver-skin), and cut it in ¼-inch dice. Cut the fatback also in ¼-inch dice. Combine the two and chill thoroughly. Chill the meat-grinder parts as well. When the meat and fatback are very cold, grind once through the medium blade of the grinder.

2. Meanwhile, sauté the shallots and garlic in the oil. Work quickly, so that they are just barely cooked. Cool and combine with the ground meat. Mix in the parsley, sage and thyme. Add the water and breadcrumbs. Season the mixture with salt and pepper. Mix well. Make a small patty and fry until cooked through. Taste it for salt and pepper. It is important that the seasoning be perfect, especially for sausage, because this is the last chance to correct it. The salt should be noticeable but the mixture should not be over-salted. Pepper is a matter of personal preference; I like mine quite peppery.

3. Now the meat should be ground again. Be sure that both the mixture and all the parts of the grinder are thoroughly chilled. For meatballs, stuffing or other preparations, pass the mixture straight through the medium blade of the grinder. Wrap meat tightly in plastic wrap and refrigerate for at least 1 day. For sausages, attach the sausage nozzle (pig stuffer) to the grinder and grind the meat directly into the casings; wrap tightly in plastic wrap and refrigerate. (For details on sausage-stuffing, see page 179). Poach the sausages lightly, then finish them on the grill or in a frying pan. Serve with garnishes appropriate for the particular bird, for instance, pheasant sausages with wild mushrooms or goose sausages with braised red cabbage.

Pheasant Mousse

This mousse is intended for quenelles or as a fine, elegant stuffing. I have long believed that using perfectly good meat or fish to make mousse is one of the silliest acts in our repertoire. The classic *mousse de brochet* (pike mousse) was created to utilize a delicious but extremely bony fish. This mousse is offered in the same spirit, a way to use the delicious but tough thigh meat of game birds. I implore you, don't waste the breast of any bird for this recipe!

MAKES ONE AND A HALF POUNDS

1 pound pheasant (or other)
  thigh meat
2 shallots, finely chopped
  (3 tablespoons)
2 egg whites
1½ cups heavy cream
cognac or other fine brandy
pinch of nutmeg
pinch of cayenne pepper
1 tablespoon finely chopped
  Italian parsley
1 tablespoon finely chopped
  chives
salt and freshly ground black
  pepper

1. Trim the pheasant meat, being sure to remove any sinews and outer membrane (silver-skin), and cut it in ¼-inch dice. Mix with the shallots and egg whites. Chill well. Puree to a completely smooth paste in a food processor. Remove to a stainless steel mixing bowl.

2. Place the mixing bowl over a bowl of ice. Add the cream a few drops at a time, whipping with a whisk so that the mixture emulsifies. The consistency should remain about the same through the entire process. After incorporating all of the cream, add the cognac, nutmeg, cayenne pepper, parsley and chives. Season lightly with salt and pepper. Drop a spoonful into a little simmering broth and cook. Taste and adjust the seasoning. Chill well until ready to form and cook the quenelles.

3. Quenelles should be cooked shortly before serving; they may be made up to half a day in advance. You will need a pot of broth for poaching, as well as a bowl of hot water and 2 tablespoons to form the oval shape. Bring the broth to a slow simmer. Take a spoonful of mousse and use the other spoon to help shape the quenelle and slip it off into the broth. Dip the spoons in hot water each time for easy handling. Form the quenelles as you go, cooking them a few at a time. Poach until just firm (about 8 to 10 minutes). Remove from the broth with a slotted spoon and drain briefly. Store in a container covered with a damp cloth.

Breast of Pheasant, Hunter Style

The pairing of wild game and wild mushrooms epitomizes the hunting season. This is a hearty dish and you will need to prepare a good veal stock at least a day in advance. If you are lucky enough to have some of the last ripe tomatoes of summer on hand, be sure to use them; they will further enhance this already excellent combination. Serve the pheasant with panfried polenta or Johnnycake Polenta (page 263); johnnycakes (page 262); Corn Fritters (page 267) or noodles (page 277) or Potato Pancakes (page 251).

The recipe calls for skinless boneless breasts from two pheasants, wild or farmed. If the pheasants weigh less than four pounds altogether, the meat from the thighs will be needed to round out the portions. (See the Variation at the end of the recipe.) In any event, be sure that the birds have been properly hung and aged. For the very best results, get your pheasants two or three days ahead of time and marinate the breasts in an oil-based marinade.

SERVES FOUR AS AN ENTREE

2 pheasants, 2½ to 3 pounds each

Oil-based Marinade, page 152 (optional)

Rich Pheasant Stock

vegetable oil

1 medium onion, coarsely chopped

1 medium carrot, coarsely chopped

1 cup Reduced Veal Stock (page 328)

2 bay leaves

4 sprigs fresh thyme

1 tablespoon whole black peppercorns

clarified butter (page 329) for searing

salt and freshly ground black pepper

4 medium shallots, finely chopped (4 tablespoons)

2 cups thickly sliced chanterelles or other wild mushrooms

1. Bone out the pheasant breasts, leaving the wing, but not the tip, attached, as described on page 113; discard the skin. Chop the carcass and neck of one of the pheasants into small pieces for making stock; set aside. Wrap and freeze the other carcass and neck for later use in broth. Reserve the legs: either set the thighs aside for the variation at the end of this recipe or wrap and freeze the legs for later use in broth and forcemeat.

2. Prepare the marinade, if using, and marinate the breasts for 2 to 3 days. The marinade should cover the breasts; if not, turn them from time to time.

3. Heat up a small amount of oil in a large sauté pan. Add the chopped carcass, the wingtips, onion and carrot. When these are browned, add the veal stock, 2 cups water, bay leaves, thyme and peppercorns. Simmer slowly for 2 hours, skimming any foam that may come to the top. If stock becomes too thick, add more water. Strain and set aside. You should have 1 cup of rich pheasant stock.

4. About 30 minutes before serving, heat a sauté pan large enough to hold all 4 breast pieces to medium-high heat. Add about 2 tablespoons clarified butter to the pan. Season the breasts with salt and pepper and brown them in the pan, about 5 minutes on each side. Remove the breasts and add the shallots and mushrooms to the pan. At this point you may need to add a little more clarified butter.

¼ cup white wine
*2 large tomatoes, peeled, seeded
and diced (2 cups)*
*2 teaspoons finely chopped fresh
tarragon*
*2 tablespoons roughly chopped
Italian parsley*
2 tablespoons unsalted butter

5. Cook for 5 minutes and add the wine. Cook 5 minutes more. Now add the tomatoes, tarragon and rich pheasant stock. Bring to a simmer and add the seared pheasant breasts. Simmer 8 to 10 minutes.

6. Remove the breasts to 4 warm plates, leaving the sauce on the heat. Each pheasant breast can be sliced and fanned or left whole. Add the parsley to the sauce and season to taste with salt and pepper. Whip in the butter and spoon the sauce over the pheasant.

V A R I A T I O N

With pheasants weighing 2 pounds or less, the portions can be stretched by boning out the thighs and cutting the meat into ½-inch dice. Brown the meat and add it to the sauce with the breasts (Step 4). The thigh meat should be left in the sauce when the breasts are removed (Step 5), making it like a fricassee. Spoon the sauce with meat in it around the breast, not over it.

Roast Pheasant

Roasting pheasant, or any large game bird for that matter, is an imperfect art, the problem being that if you cook the legs through, you risk overcooking the breasts. The legs of pheasant, and especially wild pheasant, are very tasty, but usually dry and somewhat stringy. In this recipe I offer one solution; while not the last word on the subject, it will bring about the most desirable results. Browning and partially cooking the legs prior to roasting the whole bird produces a roasted bird that has perfectly cooked breast meat and is only slightly rare around the joints. It can be eaten that way, or the legs can be returned to the oven for a few minutes after the carving ceremony. If you want perfectly cooked pheasant breasts, it is best to cook them separately from the legs, as in the recipe for Breast of Pheasant, Hunter Style (page 146). Though flawless, the dish is not as dramatic as the presentation of a whole roasted bird.

The pheasant could be served with any number of side dishes, such as sautéed cabbage, Ladies' Cabbage with Potatoes (page 232) or Braised Sweet-and-Sour Red Cabbage (page 232); Old-fashioned Glazed Onions (page 240); sautéed wild mushrooms; baked squash; roasted carrots, turnips or potatoes (try Freddie's Famous Roast Potatoes, page 251); Potato Pancakes (page 251) or wild rice.

Traditional English Bread Sauce, a recipe for which follows this one, is an excellent accompaniment to roast pheasant. It is intended as an optional condiment and should not replace the bird's own natural sauce.

SERVES FOUR AS AN ENTREE

2 pheasants, approximately 2½
    pounds each, properly hung
    and aged (page 141)
2 cups Chicken Stock (page 327)
    or water
4 tablespoons unsalted butter
1 medium onion, cut in small
    (¼ inch) dice
2 stalks celery, cut in small
    (¼ inch) dice
8 sprigs fresh thyme
4 branches fresh sage
½ lemon, thinly sliced
salt and freshly ground black
    pepper
vegetable oil for frying
2 tablespoons all-purpose flour
¼ pound fatback, thinly sliced

1. Trim up the pheasant, removing the wingtips, neck and feet (if applicable). Put all these in a saucepan and simmer with the chicken stock and 1 cup water (or 3 cups water). Simmer for about 1 hour 30 minutes and strain. You should have about 1 cup of rich pheasant stock.

2. Heat the butter in a sauté pan and add the onion, celery, thyme and sage. Cook briefly (1 minute). Allow to cool. Add the sliced lemon.

3. Preheat the oven to 375 degrees. Season the pheasant inside and out with salt and pepper. Place the vegetable mix in the cavities of the birds and truss. Film the bottom of a large sauté pan with oil and heat on medium heat. Place the leg and thigh portion of one of the pheasants in the hot oil. Cook 5 minutes on each side, then quickly brown the rest of the bird. Repeat with the other bird.

4. Sprinkle the flour on the bottom of a roasting pan large enough for the 2 birds. Put the birds on a rack in the pan and cover each completely with fatback. Place the pheasants in the preheated oven. After 15 minutes, remove and baste, being sure to baste the legs very well. Cook 15 to 20 minutes more and remove from the oven. Transfer the pheasants to a nice platter and allow them to rest while you prepare the sauce.

5. Carefully pour off half the fat from the roasting pan, making sure not to remove any of the cooked flour. Place the roasting pan on medium heat and add the pheasant stock bit by bit, allowing it to thicken slightly each time before adding more. Loosen all the drippings that have stuck to the bottom of the pan so that they can add maximum flavor to the sauce.

6. Remove the fatback from the pheasants and discard. Untie the birds and add the vegetables from the cavity to the sauce. At this point the sauce can be switched to a saucepan, if desired. Simmer for 10 to 15 minutes and strain. Degrease and season the sauce to taste with salt and pepper.

7. Garnish the platter with any number of side dishes. Carve the pheasant as you would a roast chicken (see page 116 for directions). Serve the sauce on the side.

English Bread Sauce

Made properly, this traditional sauce is velvety and rich, and the flavor of the cognac or brandy predominates, without tasting harsh or raw. I like to serve the sauce as a condiment, allowing my guests to help themselves. It is good with other roasted game birds, too, not just pheasant. To have it come out right, you will need to use a very small heavy saucepan.

MAKES ONE AND A HALF CUPS

1 bay leaf
½ small onion
2 cloves
¾ cup milk
½ cup heavy cream
2 tablespoons cognac or brandy
  of superior quality
¾ slice fresh white bread, crust
  removed, cut in ½-inch cubes
  (¼ cup)
1 teaspoon lemon juice
salt and freshly ground black
  pepper

1. Make an *oignon piqué* by nailing the bay leaf to the onion with the cloves. Put it in a very small heavy saucepan and cover with the milk, cream and brandy.

2. Heat up very slowly until the mixture reaches a slow simmer. Add the bread cubes and continue to simmer, very slowly, for about 30 minutes. Stir frequently. Strain through a fine strainer, allowing whatever goes through to be and not forcing the rest. Season to taste with a few drops of lemon juice, salt and pepper.

GUINEA HEN (PINTADE)

Named after its place of origin in West Africa, the Guinea fowl (or as I was brought up to call it, regardless of sex, Guinea hen) is among the most flavorful of the barnyard birds. Despite an odd shaped head, the birds are very beautiful, with identical brilliant plumage on both the male and female.

In America, the supply is very limited because of their resistance to domestication. They do not breed easily in captivity, and they remain fiercely independent, rarely ever allowing a person to get close to them. They accept feed, but they also seek out every other edible thing in sight. This constant foraging is the reason for their slightly dark meat and pronounced flavor.

If you are lucky enough to have a source (as I do) or if you have a farm, you will find Guinea hen a fabulous taste treat. It is a close relative of the pheasant, though usually larger, especially in the breasts, and it should be treated like pheasant. Guinea hen requires a little extra cooking time.

In New England there is a bit of confusion surrounding the partridge. The ruffed grouse, which is fast becoming a rarity, has long been called by the name partridge. Waverley Root, in his excellent dictionary entitled *Food*, confesses, "As a New Englander, when I learned that the bird which I had trustingly called a partridge. . . was the 'ruffed grouse,' the disillusionment was comparable to that of a child when he discovers that there is no Santa Claus." This regional misnomer adds even more to the confusion in determining which species, if any, were native to our region. Whether they were native or whether they were introduced for hunting and then they adapted to the environment, there are several species found in the United States, none of them plentiful in New England. Even though partridge seems to be more glamorous than grouse, I am of the opinion that the grouse, which is becoming scarcer every year, is a more flavorful bird than the true partridge.

The most common partridge found today is the chukar, originally imported from Asia for American hunters and now being raised for domestic consumption by a few producers I know. It is a mild-tasting white-meat bird that roasts very evenly and has unusually tender leg meat for a bird of this kind. The chukar is one of many types of partridge from around the world; different types have different flavors.

The best way I have found to cook partridge is to stuff a bit of herb butter between the skin and the flesh, and then roast and baste the bird. I cook the bird to the point where it is just three-quarters done, then I take it out of the oven and allow it to rest. As it rests it finishes cooking to that perfect point where the meat is set.

Roast Partridge with Tarragon and Green Peppercorns

The crucial part of this recipe is the way you stuff flavored butter between the skin and the meat of the bird. Here herb butter is made with shallots, tarragon, green peppercorns and lemon, but other compound butters (page 330) can be used to create different effects. Whatever the flavor, the extra fat from the butter helps keep the partridge moist and tender.

This dish goes well with a multitude of accompaniments: Apple or Corn Fritters (pages 266–267), johnnycakes (page 262) or ground sweet corn cakes (page 265); sautéed greens, Ladies' Cabbage with Potatoes (page 232) and fried potatoes (page 250), to name just a few.

SERVES FOUR AS AN ENTREE

4 chukar partridges, 14 to 16 ounces each

Herb Butter
2 tablespoons chopped fresh tarragon
2 tablespoons green peppercorns, very finely chopped

1. Trim the wingtips and necks of the birds. If you like, make a little stock from these parts for deglazing the roasting pan at the end of the cooking. Put them in a saucepan with 2 cups water (or water and chicken stock) and simmer while preparing and roasting the birds (about 1 hour). Strain. You should have about 1 cup rich partridge stock.

2. Massage the outside skin of each bird to loosen it up. With your index finger, loosen the skin from the flesh by gently working your finger from a small opening in the front all the way to the back. Also loosen up some of the skin around the leg.

2 shallots, finely chopped
  (2 tablespoons)
2 lemons
8 tablespoons unsalted butter,
  softened

1 small onion, cut in small
  (¼ inch) dice (½ cup)
½ cup roughly chopped Italian
  parsley
¼ cup vegetable oil
kosher salt
1 cup partridge stock (Step 1),
  Pheasant Broth (page 143) or
  Chicken Stock (page 327)

3. Make an herb butter by mixing the tarragon, green peppercorns and shallots with the juice from half a lemon and the softened butter. Rub a quarter of the compound butter between the flesh and the skin of each bird. Try to distribute it as evenly as possible.

4. Thinly slice the rest of the lemons and mix with the onion, parsley and all but 2 tablespoons of the oil. Stuff this mixture into the cavity of each bird. Truss each bird, rub with the remaining oil and sprinkle with salt.

5. Preheat the oven to 400 degrees. Place the partridges in a roasting pan just large enough to leave a little space between each. After 10 minutes pull the birds out and baste thoroughly. Return to the oven and cook 10 minutes more. Remove from oven. Place the birds on a platter and allow to rest for 10 minutes before serving.

6. Put the roasting pan directly on a burner on medium heat and add the stock all at once; scrape the bottom of the pan to loosen up any drippings. Simmer 5 minutes and strain.

7. Present the birds whole before carving. Spoon the sauce over the pieces of meat.

VARIATIONS

Roast Partridge with Garlic and Sage

Make a garlic and sage butter by substituting 2 tablespoons finely chopped garlic and 2 tablespoons finely chopped fresh sage leaves for the tarragon, peppercorns and shallots in Step 3. Proceed as for Roast Partridge with Tarragon and Green Peppercorns. Serve with polenta (page 263) or pasta (page 277).

Roast Partridge with Curry

Make a curry butter as described on page 29. Proceed with the recipe. Serve with rice and spinach, kale or chard.

Quail are small in size, but not in flavor. I am very fond of all game birds, but if I had to pick just one, it would be quail. I love the flavor and I also enjoy eating with my fingers, a requirement for truly enjoying these delicious birds.

Out on Nantucket Island, Stephen Swift raises a migratory species from Africa; they are the tastiest birds I have ever had. Otherwise the most common type of quail found both in the wild and commercially is the bobwhite. The bobwhite is lighter in color than the Nantucket quail, but a little darker than pheasant or partridge. It is also full-flavored.

Many restaurants are now using sleeve-boned quail for stuffing or grilling, but I advise you to buy whole quail. If you wish to bone them, split them down the backbone and remove the back and breast bones. This method is best for quail to be eaten with fork and knife.

Quail are delicious covered with bacon and roasted whole. They can be excellent if sautéed perfectly, and I have had deep-fried quail that were very good. They can also be smoked. My favorite way, by far, is grilling. The birds are spatchcocked and flattened, then marinated for at least 36 hours, or up to three days. They are cooked swiftly over glowing embers.

Grilled Nantucket Quail

SERVES FOUR AS AN ENTREE OR EIGHT AS AN APPETIZER

8 Nantucket (or other) quail
4 tablespoons Dijon mustard

Oil-based Marinade
1 small onion, thinly sliced
1 lemon, thinly sliced
8 to 10 cloves garlic, thinly sliced
6 bay leaves, broken
12 sprigs fresh thyme
4 tablespoons cracked black pepper
1 cup vegetable oil

Natural Sauce
1 small onion, coarsely chopped
1 carrot, coarsely chopped
1 tablespoon vegetable oil or clarified butter (page 329)
thyme stems
1 cup Reduced Veal Stock (page 328) and 1 cup Chicken Stock (page 327) or 2 cups Chicken Stock
kosher salt and freshly ground black pepper

1. Trim the wingtips and neck of each quail and reserve for the sauce. Spatchcock the birds as described on page 112, reserving the backbones for the natural sauce. Smear each quail lightly with mustard.

2. Prepare the marinade by combining the onion, lemon, garlic, bay leaves, chopped thyme leaves, cracked pepper and oil. Place the quail in the marinade; it should be covered completely. Marinate for at least 36 hours or up to 3 days.

3. To make the natural sauce, sauté the quail wingtips, backbones and necks, along with the onion and carrot, in a little oil or clarified butter. When the quail trimmings and vegetables have browned, add the thyme stems and stock. Simmer slowly for 2 hours; add a little water during the cooking if the sauce begins to get too thick. Strain and season to taste with salt and pepper. Reserve the liquid until ready to serve. You should have about 1½ cups.

4. Make a fire with charcoal, grapevines, mesquite or other woods, and let it burn down to glowing embers. Brush, clean and lightly oil the grill. Remove the quail from the marinade, sprinkle lightly with kosher salt and grill for about 2 to 3 minutes on each side. Warm the natural sauce and spoon over the grilled quail.

WILD DUCK AND GOOSE

Wild duck and wild goose are substantially different from their domestic counterparts. Wild duck and goose are much leaner and are generally smaller than the domestic version and require different handling in the kitchen.

More than 30 species of wild duck are found along the Atlantic coast. Many are fish eaters and are not of any culinary worth. The wild ducks most commonly found in New England are the mallard, black and canvasback. The mallard is renowned for the male's beautiful green plumage, the canvasback for its excellent flavor. All three ducks are about the same size (2½ to 3 pounds). Another species of wild duck that is fairly common is the wood duck. It is much smaller (1¼ to 1½ pounds) and could possibly be the tastiest of all. The recipe on page 155 calls for the larger ducks, but it can easily be adapted for wood ducks. Allow one duck per person if serving the small wood ducks.

By far the most common goose hunted in our region is the Canada goose, also known as the cackling goose. The birds usually weigh between seven and ten pounds, but they can reach weights up to eighteen pounds. Another goose, less abundant, is from Canada, the snow goose. Both are excellent game birds, providing that they are from the interior, not the coastal regions.

Both duck and geese are of Canadian origin, although over time many have settled farther south in the United States. All are migratory, leaving each fall for their second home in the southern states. Florida, especially, is a winter haven for duck and geese. The legal hunting season varies from state to state, but basically it is October and November. Duck and goose hunting takes a great deal of patience. Geese, especially, fly so high that the only real shot you ever get is when they are landing. Sometimes you must wait hours for a few good shots.

Although both duck and goose have a layer of fat to protect them in cold waters, the meat is very lean. Flavors vary depending on what the birds have been feeding on during their journey. I recently had some Canada geese that were wonderfully plump with rich meat that resembled venison in appearance and taste. The last food a wild bird eats determines its flavor. Ducks and geese are at their best when they've just arrived from the interior regions of Canada and the United States. Once the birds reach the coast, it is only a matter of a few days before their flavor is ruined from feeding on bay cabbage. There is no danger of preparing a bird and finding out later that it tastes bad. As my father points out, you will know the minute you gut it.

Roasting wild duck and goose is popular, but it is not the best way to handle these birds. In my opinion, the very best treatment is to bone out the breasts and sauté, grill or roast them. Reserve the legs for soup or sausages, as described on pages 143–145.

season varies from state to state, but basically it is October and November. Duck and goose hunting takes a great deal of patience. Geese, especially, fly so high that the only real shot you ever get is when they are landing. Sometimes you must wait hours for a few good shots.

Although both duck and goose have a layer of fat to protect them in cold waters, the meat is very lean. Flavors vary depending on what the birds have been feeding on during their journey. I recently had some Canada geese that were wonderfully plump with rich meat that resembled venison in appearance and taste. The last food a wild bird eats determines its flavor. Ducks and geese are at their best when they've just arrived from the interior regions of Canada and the United States. Once the birds reach the coast, it is only a matter of a few days before their flavor is ruined from feeding on bay cabbage. There is no danger of preparing a bird and finding out later that it tastes bad. As my father points out, you will know the minute you gut it.

Roasting wild duck and goose is popular, but it is not the best way to handle these birds. In my opinion, the very best treatment is to bone out the breasts and sauté, grill or roast them. Reserve the legs for soup or sausages, as described on pages 143–145.

Wild Duck or Goose Broth with Stuffed Cabbages

SERVES SIX

about 24 small cabbage leaves
1½ pounds Pheasant Sausage Forcemeat (page 144), made with duck or goose meat
2 cups thinly sliced onion, carrot and potato, combined
2 tablespoons unsalted butter or bacon fat
4 cups Pheasant Broth (page 143), made mostly with wild duck or goose
salt and freshly ground black pepper
chopped Italian parsley for garnish

1. Blanch the cabbage leaves and make miniature stuffed-cabbage packages with the forcemeat. Use toothpicks to hold them together.

2. Sauté the onion, carrot and potato slices in butter or bacon fat for 6 to 8 minutes. Pour the broth over and simmer for 20 minutes.

3. Add the stuffed cabbage and simmer 10 minutes more. Remove the cabbage packages from the broth. Take out the toothpicks and place the cabbage packages in the bottom of soup plates.

4. Season the broth to taste with salt and pepper. Ladle it over the stuffed cabbages. Sprinkle with chopped parsley and serve.

Breast of Wild Duck with Bitter Greens and Turnips

SERVES FOUR AS AN ENTREE

*2 wild ducks, 2½ to 3 pounds
    each (see Note)*
*3 branches fresh sage, leaves
    removed and chopped*
*1 tablespoon cracked black
    peppercorns*
2 tablespoons vegetable oil

Natural Sauce
*1 tablespoon rendered duck fat
    or clarified butter (page 329)*
*1 onion, cut in medium
    (½ inch) dice*
*1 carrot, cut in medium
    (½ inch) dice*
2 tablespoons all-purpose flour
1 cup white wine
*1 cup Reduced Veal Stock
    (page 328)*
3 stems fresh sage
2 bay leaves
2 tablespoons red wine vinegar
*salt and freshly ground black
    pepper*

1 pound turnip or beet greens
kosher salt
4 thin slices pancetta (2 ounces)
*1 recipe Maple-Glazed Turnips
    (page 343), made with purple-
    top turnips or rutabaga*
*1 small onion cut in small
    (¼ inch) dice (½ cup)*
*salt and freshly ground black
    pepper*

1. Bone out the duck breasts, leaving the skin attached, as described on page 113. Score the skin at ½-inch intervals, being careful not to cut into the meat. Chop the carcass and neck of one of the ducks into small pieces for stock; set aside. Wrap and freeze the other carcass and neck (or carcasses and necks) for later use in broth. Wrap and freeze the legs for later use in broth and forcemeat.

2. Rub the breasts with the chopped sage leaves, cracked pepper and oil. Set aside or refrigerate. If refrigerated, remove from the refrigerator 30 minutes before cooking.

3. To make the sauce, heat the duck fat or clarified butter in a sauté pan and brown the carcass with the onion and carrot. When nice and brown, reduce the heat, sprinkle with flour and stir. Cook 3 to 4 minutes. Slowly add the white wine, stock and 2 cups water, bit by bit, allowing the broth to thicken slightly before adding more. When all the liquid is incorporated and has come to a boil, skim and reduce to a simmer. Add sage stems and bay leaves. Simmer 2 hours. Strain through a fine strainer. Add vinegar and season to taste with salt and pepper. Set aside.

4. Wash the greens well. Blanch them for about 1 minute in a large pot of boiling salted water. Drain and shock with cold water to cool down quickly. Drain well and set aside.

5. Season the duck breasts with kosher salt. Using a heavy cast-iron or aluminum frying pan on medium heat, cook the slices of pancetta until crisp. Remove from the pan and chop into small pieces. Turn up the heat and add the duck breasts, skin side down. Cook about 3½ minutes on each side. Remove from the pan and allow to rest. (At this time you should begin glazing the turnips or rutabaga.)

6. Add the onion and chopped pancetta to the pan the duck breasts were cooked in. When the onion is cooked, add the greens and cook for about 5 minutes. Season to taste with salt and pepper.

7. Reheat the sauce. Make a bed of greens in the center of each plate. Slice each breast on the bias and place over the bed of greens. Spoon the sauce on top and surround with the glazed turnips.

NOTE. Wild ducks vary in size. If they weigh more than 2½ pounds, one duck will suffice for two people. If they are smaller, you may have to use an extra duck to be on the safe side. Cooking times will, of course, need to be adjusted according to the size of the birds. The times I refer to in this recipe are for breasts from 2½- to 3-pound ducks. Cook smaller ducks a little less.

Roast Breast of Wild Goose

This dish of roast goose breast with a natural sauce enhanced with red wine is just right together with braised red cabbage (page 232) and potatoes fried in goose fat (page 250). The tart and sweet flavor of the cabbage is a perfect foil for the goose, and the crisp potatoes round it out to perfection. Prepare the red cabbage in advance, using stock made from the goose carcass or other bones in place of the chicken stock called for in the recipe. Allow plenty of time to marinate the goose breasts—at least twelve hours, up to two days.

SERVES FOUR AS AN ENTREE

1 wild goose, about 6 to 8 pounds

Juniper Marinade
1 cup vegetable oil
1 teaspoon cracked juniper berries
3 bay leaves coarsely chopped
1 tablespoon cracked black pepper
½ onion, thinly sliced

Rich Red-wine Sauce
1 small onion, cut in medium (½ inch) dice
1 carrot, cut in medium (½ inch) dice
1 tablespoon rendered goose fat (page 331) or clarified butter (page 329)
2 tablespoons all-purpose flour
2 cups red wine
1 cup Reduced Veal Stock (page 328)
1 cup Chicken Stock (page 327) or water
4 juniper berries, cracked
1 bay leaf
3 or 4 sprigs fresh thyme
kosher salt and freshly ground black pepper

1. Bone out the goose breasts as described on page 113; discard the skin. Chop the carcass and neck into small pieces for stock; set aside. Wrap and freeze the legs for later use in broth and forcemeat.

2. Combine the oil, juniper berries, bay leaves, cracked pepper and sliced onion and mix well. Place the breasts in this marinade and marinate for at least 12 hours or up to 2 days. The marinade should cover the breasts; if not, turn from time to time.

3. To make the sauce, brown the chopped carcass, onion and carrot in goose fat or clarified butter in a sauté pan. Lower the heat and sprinkle with flour. Cook 3 or 4 minutes, then slowly add the red wine, a little at a time, allowing the sauce to thicken before adding more. Then add the veal stock and chicken stock or water. When this comes to a boil, skim and add the juniper berries, bay leaf and thyme. Simmer for 2 hours. Season lightly with salt and pepper. Strain through a fine strainer and set aside.

4. Preheat the oven to 400 degrees. Heat a little of the oil from the marinade in a heavy sauté pan that can be put into the oven. Get the pan smoking hot. Season the goose breasts with kosher salt and place in the pan. Sear for 2 minutes on each side, then put into the oven. Cook 6 to 8 minutes more. Remove and allow to rest for at least 5 minutes.

5. Heat up the red cabbage and place a mound on each plate. Slice the goose breasts and fan the slices in front of the cabbage. Reheat the sauce and pour a little over the meat. Serve with potatoes fried in goose fat.

Meat and Venison

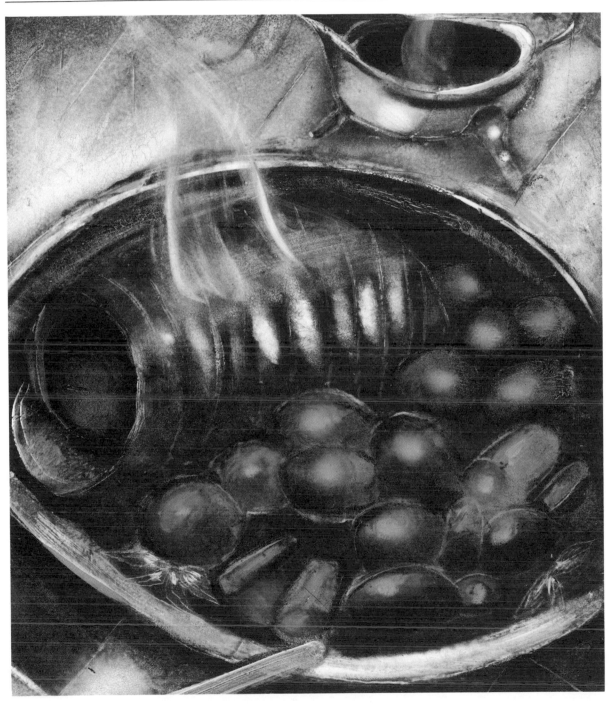

Beef

New England Boiled Dinner

Red Flannel Hash

Fresh Beef Tongue

Tuscan Green Sauce

Yankee Pot Roast

Old-Fashioned Club Steak with Oysters

Lucky's Log-Seared Skirt Steak

Veal

Grilled Sweetbreads with Bacon

Calves' Liver with Mustard Sauce and Mustard Greens

Sautéed Rib of Veal with Vermont Ham, Fresh Sage and Apples

Breaded Veal Medaillons with Green Tomatoes and Mozzarella Cheese

Veal Sausages

Pork

Breakfast Sausages

Italian Sausages

Pork Rib Chops with Clams and Garlic Sauce

Natural Pork Sauce

Roast Loin of Pork with Fennel Seeds

Mom's Fresh Ham Sunday Dinner

Vermont Smoked Ham

Lamb, Baby Lamb and Young Goat

Baby Lamb Kidneys with Morels

Roast Leg of Lamb with Garlic, Parsley and Parmesan Cheese

Grilled Rack and Braised Shanks of Lamb with Rosemary and Winter Vegetables

Barbecued Cuts of Baby Lamb or Goat

Venison

Roast Venison with Beach Plums

Marinade for Venison

Poivrade Sauce

Grand Veneur Sauce with Beach Plums

Venison Steaks

Venison Goulash

Venison Sausages with Sauerkraut

Venison Sausages

Venison Burgers

Rabbit

Warm Terrine of Rabbit with Prunes and Apples

Rabbit Stew with Red Wine, Bacon, Wild Mushrooms and Pearl Onions

Crispy Fried Rabbit

Once you leave the coastline of New England, you enter a land of gentle rolling hills and rich fertile pastures. This is old farmland, with fields that were cleared of stones by hand hundreds of years ago. Stone fences divide the land, making everything seemed scaled down, as indeed it is. Some small farmers in New England have survived the recent upheaval in farming life-style and finance. They learned long ago to concentrate on providing high-quality products for people willing to spend a little more for foods that are a lot better. This is, of course, a limited market, but then, New England is small.

New England farmers have learned to produce very fine veal and lamb, which are sold mostly to serious restaurants and hotels, and top-notch pork for ham and bacon. Some also produce ready-to-consume foods to supplement their income. They often sell ham, sausage, cider, honey, jelly, jam and cheese directly to the consumer. The absence of a middleman allows the farmer a larger profit and, in the case of meat and produce, guarantees the buyer with a fresher product. In Massachusetts, August (Gus) Schumacher, Jr., Commissioner of the Department of Food and Agriculture for the Commonwealth, has done a marvelous job of linking up farms with restaurants and other medium-size food purchasers through a newsletter called *The Fresh Connection*.

At my restaurant, a great deal of the meat we use comes directly from small high-quality producers who raise their stock in a humane, hygienic, and chemical- and hormone-free environment. Usually these animals are sold whole or, in the case of veal calves, in halves. We know the exact date of slaughter so that we can properly dry-age the meat. The quality of this fresh, aged meat is outstanding, far superior to the mass-produced meats offered at many supermarkets and other commercial outlets.

Cattle raised in New England are mostly dairy cows; Connecticut does raise some beef, but the other states have very limited production. The scaled-down landscape of our region is better suited to smaller animals, like pigs, lambs, goats and calves. Production has been increasing steadily each year, as has demand. The leaders in this kind of production are Vermont, New Hampshire and "Western Mass" (as western Massachusetts is locally known).

Most commercial meat is broken down into primal or smaller cuts shortly after it is slaughtered. Then it is usually sealed airtight in plastic to inhibit spoilage, a process known as Cryovac. Unfortunately this method also inhibits the beneficial results of dry-aging. In my opinion, it is the worst possible form of storage, resulting in meat that is mushy and reeking from the blood it is left to swim in. Cryovac is the end result of a distribution system that has become too large to perform with integrity. The large-scale style of handling meat has proven to be an overall disaster in terms of quality; change is long overdue.

If your desire is to cook with the very best quality meat, you will need to acquire some familiarity with meat-cutting, if you do not already have it. At best it will enable you to buy whole animals or primal cuts; at the very least it will enable you to specify exactly the cut of meat you want and help you decide where to buy your meat. It takes time, patience and practice, but it is a skill no serious cook should be without. Most of the good chefs I am acquainted with are excellent meat-cutters, and they take a lot of pride in being so.

There are many tricks to retail butchering, not all done for purposes of gustatory enhancement. Many butchers know very little about cooking and are therefore divorced from a real understanding of the product they are working with. There is also a kind of sloppiness, often due to the pressures of production, to be found in the work of some professional butchers. A good butcher should know as much about the preparation of meat as he does about choosing the best-quality whole animals.

When you find a good butcher, work with him and let him know what your standards are and how you like things done. Be very specific and don't be afraid to ask questions. Support the shop by buying your meat there all the time, not just on special occasions.

Most of the people I know are shameless and enthusiastic carnivores. There seems to be a primitive as well as a sensory kind of satisfaction derived from eating meat. Meat has a richness and depth of flavor with many dimensions and nuances. The down side to all this is, of course, its high cholesterol content. Worse yet are the hormones and chemical additives found in some commercial meat. I would suggest that those concerned about hormones and other additives seek out farm-raised organic meat and meat from wild animals such as deer. As for cholesterol, I would leave that up to the individual. I certainly don't think that eating meat every day is a good idea, but there are times when for me nothing can take the place of a rib of beef, a leg of lamb or a pork roast. Nothing.

Although New England's traditional repertoire of meat dishes is fairly limited, three very famous dishes appear in this chapter. All are beef: Yankee Pot Roast, New England Boiled Dinner and Red Flannel Hash, which is made from the leftovers from the boiled dinner. Then there are venison and Vermont smoked ham, which have played a vital role in New England cookery over the centuries. While I have updated some of the classic meat dishes, like the pot roast, I have chosen not to explore such regional oddities as salt pork with milk gravy and Parker House tripe. Rather, I have included dishes from more recent settlers, notably the Italians and the Portuguese, who have contributed so much to revitalizing our cuisine.

How to Choose and Handle High-Quality Meats

Very few generalizations about choosing meats can be applied to all the different kinds of meat. I will discuss my preferences as well as generally accepted standards in the introduction to each one.

USDA (U.S. Department of Agriculture) standards, which many people consider to be the absolute last word, are in serious need of reevaluation. The regulations emphasize the details of slaughtering, as well as conformation, marbling, sizes and so on, but they do not address such issues as hormone and chemical injections and types of feed—or the flavor of the meat. In addition, a wide range of quality exists within each grade. You really do need to be your own inspector.

Locally raised meat does not need to be USDA inspected; it can be inspected by the individual state authority. Basically the inspection ensures that the meat was slaughtered and handled properly. And that is all you really need to know if you already know who the farmer is or where the meat was raised.

How to Break down Meats

Breaking down meats, or butchering, is really very easy; it is mostly a matter of common sense. Once you have mastered the skill, you will be a liberated cook, no longer dependent on a butcher or supermarket meat-cutter for your meat. Since all animals used for meat have almost identical bone structure, they are all broken down the same way. There are some differences in technique, depending on the size of the animal and the end use of the cut of meat. I have used the following method for breaking down all different kinds of meat.

If you are breaking down meat for the first time, take your time; work slowly and carefully, observing everything you do and thinking ahead to the next step. For tools you will need a slightly flexible boning knife, a cleaver and hacksaw and a sharpening steel. Always use a sharp knife—it is the dull ones that cause accidents—and as you work, keep your knife facing away from you and toward a bone so that if it slips, it doesn't cut you or the meat.

The first step in breaking down an animal is to break it into primal cuts: the forequarter (neck, shoulder, breast and front leg), the rib section, often refered to as the rack, the loin section, which contains the loin and tenderloin, and the back or hind legs. With rabbits the rib and the loin are usually left in one piece. Venison is also cut this way sometimes.

Removing the Front Legs (Shoulder)

I usually start by removing the front legs. To remove the front legs, put the animal on its back with the legs sticking up in the air, the shoulder end nearest to you. Using your knife, start to loosen the meat between the leg and the body, pulling the leg away from the rib section. There will be lots of sinewy flesh: cut it through as you keep pulling the leg away. It will be obvious where to cut; allow the weight of the leg to keep opening up the separation. Soon the leg will be completely severed except at the very bottom where the shoulder meets the neck. Cut this with one clean cut. Repeat the process with the other front leg.

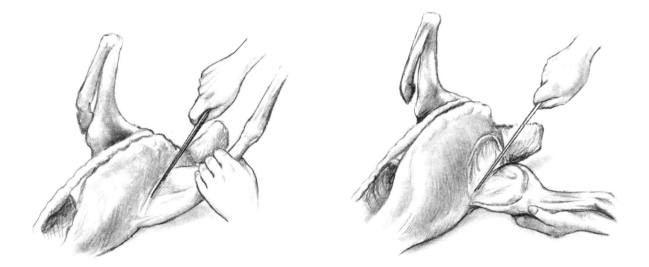

With goat and baby lamb, this shoulder meat is tender enough to marinate and grill, but in most animals it is more suitable for grinding for sausage or burgers or cutting in large or small pieces for braising. Feel the top of the front leg: a piece of cartilage runs at a 90-degree angle along the flat part of the bone. With that as a guide, remove the two large pieces on either side. They can be left whole, but the rest of the leg should be cut up for stew or ground meat. Remove all or as much of the outer membrane (silver-skin) as possible. Using a hacksaw, cut off the shanks (the lower part of the leg); if small, they can be left whole; if large, they should be cut into two-inch pieces for braising.

Removing the Back (Hind) Legs

Remove the hind legs next; it is easier to separate the ribs and the loin without them. Examine the meat closely and determine the location of the tenderloin (the underside of the loin). You want to be especially careful here: the tenderloin is in very close proximity to where you have to cut and you would not want to slip and mar it in any way. With the animal on its side and the tip of your boning knife pointed in toward the backbone, cut along the backbone and then carefully around the side where the leg is close to the loin. Now flip the carcass on its back and cut along the inside where the leg and backbone meet. When you get to the socket where the leg and the hip join, cut around the outside of the ball. Loosen it from the socket. The leg should come off very easily at this point. Repeat with the other hind leg.

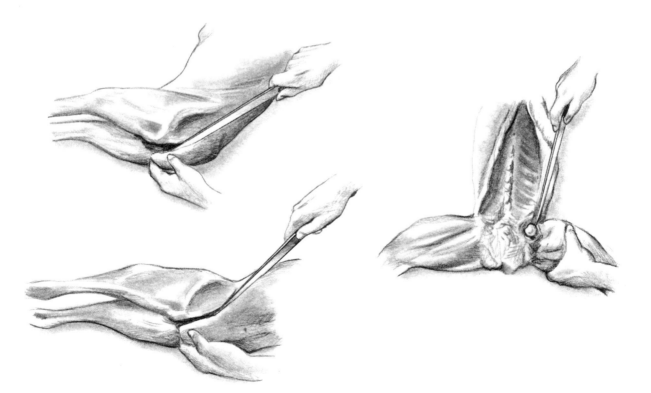

MEAT AND VENISON

For some preparations all you need to do is saw off the shank (the lower part of the leg) and trim and tie the leg for roasting. (Lamb and goat shanks can be left whole; veal and beef shanks cut in two-inch pieces with a hacksaw.) For larger animals or for other methods of preparation, you may want to break the leg down even further. Follow the sinews to cut along the seams, using your hands as well as your knife to break the top part of the leg into four pieces—the top (inside) round, the bottom (outside) round, the eye and the knuckle. These will need to be trimmed of all the outer membrane (silver-skin) and sinews.

Separating the Rib from the Loin

Locate the place where the end of the rib bone turns into cartilage. Use your knife to separate this long narrow section from the rib. When you get to the loin section, cut up to separate and remove this piece. Now carefully cut along the loin to remove the belly section (the large flap of streaky fat). On a baby lamb this is not of much use but on pork, it is the bacon. Repeat on other side.

Now insert your knife between the first and second rib. Keep you knife pressed against the first rib and cut down into the meat until you hit the backbone. Repeat this on the other side; the cuts should meet at the top of the backbone. Use a hacksaw to cut straight through the backbone, separating the rib section from the loin.

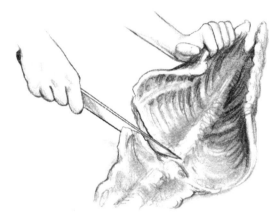

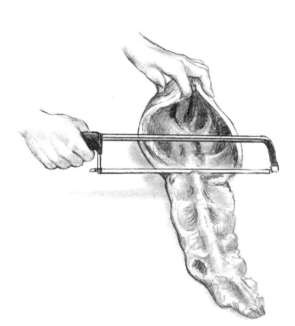

Trimming the Loin

Turn the loin over to remove the tenderloins. With your hands and knife, remove any fat covering the tenderloin. Cut straight down, along the inside of the backbone, then go back and scoop out the tenderloins, keeping your knife pressed against the bones at all times.

At this stage you have prepared a saddle, which can be used for a roast or can be boned out to create boneless loins; these can be used whole or can be broken down even farther into medaillons or steaks. To remove the loins, cut straight down the backbone and then down from front to back, always with the knife pressed close to the bones. Trim up these pieces by removing the heavy membrane (silver-skin) on top. (For more information on beefsteaks, see page 171.)

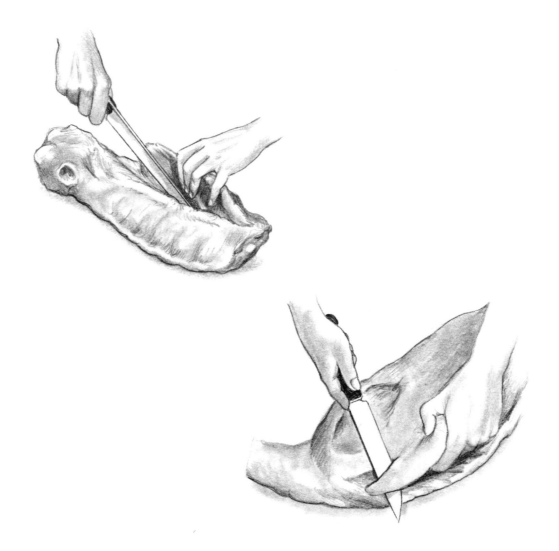

MEAT AND VENISON

Breaking down the Rib Section

With your knife, cut along the outside of the ribs, clearly marking where you intend to trim the bones down to. It will differ with each animal. For instance, for a veal chop you may want to have the bone extend three inches above the eye (rib eye), but for lamb or baby lamb you may want it to extend only one and a half inches. With the hacksaw, cut off the excess rib bones (on beef these are known as the short ribs). These bones are excellent for sauce because they are so full of flavor.

Now, count up from the loin section and place your knife between the eighth and ninth rib (actually the ninth and tenth since the first bone was left attached to the loin section). With smaller animals, you may cut even farther up, enlarging the rib section. Make a clean cut straight down to the backbone; repeat on the other side. The two cuts should meet. With the hacksaw, cut straight through the backbone. You are now left with a full rack and the remainder of the front quarter (breast and neck). Bone out the front quarter for sausage or stew meat; it is very flavorful.

Place the full rack down with the backbone facing up and make two cuts straight down, one on each side of the backbone. Very carefully—this is a little tricky—cut the bone with the hacksaw or cleaver, pulling the rib eye (with the rib bone attached) away from the backbone. You now have an untrimmed rack. If you want to leave it as a rack, make a mark across the bones where you want to French (trim) them. Cut out the meat and sinew from between the rib bones, and scrape them so they will look clean when cooked. Trim away any excess fat from the top of the rack and remove any pieces of the "strap" (the heavy yellow sinew near the chine bone) that are attached at the bottom.

If you want to cut chops, simply cut down between the bones of the untrimmed rack. As you move down the rack you may need to cut a chop with two bones, so that all the chops are of uniform size. The second bone can be removed when you trim the chops.

BEEF

Up to a few years ago New England, like the rest of America, had been a large consumer of beef, with not nearly enough local production to satisfy the needs of the market. But also like the rest of America, we are now in the midst of a love-hate relationship. We are getting mixed messages, and the current trends in American cookery show less emphasis on beef for sure. The days of our frivolous (almost reckless) consumption of beef are gone, but most Americans still do and probably always will crave a good steak.

A good steak in New England isn't always a steak. Sometimes it is an old-fashioned gray-cured brisket of beef simmered with cabbage, potatoes, parsnips and beets, sometimes a hash made from the leftovers.

Quality in beef derives from two things. First is the animal itself; second is the handling, cutting and aging of the different cuts. The first indication is one that most people never get to know: the general shape and appearance of the animal. This is known as conformation and is judged according to the structure and size of the animal in relation to its weight. A steer or heifer with good conformation, for example, would have a straight back, broad shoulders, heavy breast and a thick rump. The overall appearance would be that of a very stocky, strong, healthy animal.

As to the different cuts of meat, epecially the ri and loin section, the single most important factor is the marbling. Marbling is the fat distributed through the meat, and good marbling develops when an animal is fattened slowly and properly over time. Look for fat evenly distributed in the meat (white in the red); it should look like granite or marble, hence the name. Animals that have not been raised on rich grazing land can never acquire good marbling during a few final weeks of so-called finishing, where they are fed large amounts of grain (usually on feedlots) to fatten them for market. Poorly raised animals will often gain fat, but most of that fat remains on the outside. Sometimes it has a yellowish hue, which is a sure sign of improper feeding.

Modern standards have put less emphasis on marbling, because of cholesterol concerns. I agree that it is not necessary to have as much marbling as was required for prime grade meat in the past, but for a good steak—for flavor as well as texture—some marbling is essential. Even in the leg and parts other than the rib and loin, a small amount of marbling is a sign of good quality.

Other factors are the handling, cutting and aging of the meat. All cuts of beef need some aging to develop flavor and texture; the fancier cuts (rib and loin) need more. Look for a pinkish red rather than a blood red color and a dry texture, not wet or spongy. Steer clear of beef and any other meat Cryovac-packed (see page 159) and stay away from meat with supermarket names like London broil, pot roast and so on. These are names of dishes, not cuts of meat. Buy cuts like chuck, flank, top round, etc., that refer to a specific part of the animal. Then you know what you are cooking.

The recipes that follow include three traditional and three not-so-traditional ways to prepare beef. I have made an effort not to use only sirloin and rib steaks. They are great cuts, but there is more to beef than expensive steaks. Some of the least costly cuts can be the tastiest if properly cooked.

New England Boiled Dinner

This is a timeless and classic New England dish, perfect for an informal gathering of friends and family. It is a late fall or winter dinner: hearty, earthy and satisfying. Nearly every region of the world has a similar dish, be it France's *pot au feu*, Ireland's corned beef and cabbage, Italy's *bollito misto* or Austria's *Tafelspitz*. The ingredients and accompaniments vary, but the basic idea is the same: meat, fresh or cured, is simmered for a while, then vegetables are added. The meat flavors the vegetables, the vegetables flavor the meat and they both flavor the broth.

The New England Boiled Dinner is unique in its use of gray- or salt-cured brisket of beef as well as parsnips and beets. The gray-cured brisket, which is cured without chemical preservatives, is a regional specialty, and it may be hard to find in other parts of the country. A regular corned brisket or even a fresh brisket (which I love) make very good substitutes. Brisket is the preferred cut because of its high fat content. Leave all the fat on the brisket and trim the excess off at the end of the cooking. When you prepare this meal, be sure to make more than you need, especially the brisket, beets and potatoes; they make an excellent breakfast dish,

Red Flannel Hash, a recipe for which follows this one. The amounts of meat and vegetables in this recipe will comfortably serve six as a main course, and there will be enough left over to make some of the hash.

SERVES SIX AS AN ENTREE

1 piece gray-cured brisket of
    beef, 5 to 6 pounds

Bouquet Garni
3 bay leaves
1 tablespoon whole black
    peppercorns
5 or 6 sprigs fresh thyme
1 teaspoon mustard seeds
2 whole cloves
1 or 2 dried chilies

6 to 10 beets, depending on size
    (about 2 pounds)
20 small white boiling onions
6 or 8 medium-size carrots,
    peeled
6 to 8 medium-size Maine
    potatoes, peeled and cut in
    half
6 small purple-top turnips,
    peeled, or 1 rutabaga, peeled
    and cut in pieces
6 parsnips, peeled
1 small head Savoy cabbage, cut
    in wedges
2 tablespoons freshly chopped
    Italian parsley

Condiments
freshly grated horseradish mixed
    with a little sour cream
Dijon or Pommery mustard
mustard pickle (see Note)

1. Place the brisket in a very large pot and cover by several inches with cold water. This should take 6 to 8 quarts of water. Bring to a boil, reduce to a simmer and skim.

2. Prepare the bouquet garni by wrapping the bay leaves, peppercorns, thyme, mustard seeds, cloves and chilies in a piece of cheesecloth. Tie securely with a long string, then tie the bouquet to the handle of the pot for easy removal later. Drop the bouquet into the water.

3. Simmer slowly for about 3 hours. Start checking after 2 hours 30 minutes: stick a large two-tined fork into the meat; it should come out very easily. If not, continue simmering until it does.

4. Scrub the beets and cook them separately in salted water; when tender, peel and keep warm. When the meat is tender, add the onions, carrots, potatoes, turnips and parsnips to the pot.

5. After simmering the vegetables for 20 minutes, remove the meat and keep warm. Raise the heat under the pot and add the cabbage. In 10 to 15 minutes the boiled dinner will be ready. Remove and discard the bouquet garni.

6. Carve the meat and place in the center of a very large platter. Arrange the vegetables, including the beets, around the meat and spoon some of the broth over the platter. Sprinkle with chopped parsley. Serve with horseradish, mustard or mustard pickle.

NOTE. Mustard pickle is an old-fashioned spicy mixed vegetable pickle made with onions, cucumbers, peppers, tomatoes and cauliflower; it gets its distinctive flavor from dried mustard.

Red Flannel Hash

In Italy, the leftovers (mostly broth) from *bollito misto,* the Italian boiled dinner, are used for a soup called *stracciatella.* In the same spirit, the leftovers from a New England Boiled Dinner, which is more often than not planned with leftovers in mind, are almost religiously used to make a hash for the next morning's breakfast. The hash is colored red by the beets, hence the name Red Flannel Hash. Traditionally it is cooked slowly to form a crust, but the ingredients can also be sliced and sautéed quickly until crisp. Either way, the hash should be served with a poached egg atop each portion.

MAKES FOUR BREAKFAST
PORTIONS

*Leftovers from New England
Boiled Dinner*
2 cups boiled beef
*about 1 cup cooked vegetables,
especially onion, with some
cabbage, parsnip, turnip
and/or carrot*
2 to 3 cups cooked potatoes
1 cup cooked beets
Other Ingredients
chopped scallions or parsley
bacon or other fat for frying
*⅓ to ½ cup broth (from New
England Boiled Dinner)*
*1 poached egg per person
(page 207)*

1. Chop the leftover meat and vegetables and mix them together in a bowl; mix in the chopped scallions or parsley.
2. Heat the bacon or other fat in a skillet on medium heat, add the meat and vegetable mixture and spread it out evenly, patting it down. Pour on ⅓ cup broth. Cook until a crisp brown crust forms (20 to 30 minutes). Add a little more broth if the hash starts to get too dry.
3. Fold the hash over like an omelet. Place a poached egg on top of each portion and serve immediately.

V A R I A T I O N

Stir-Fried Red Flannel Hash

Finely slice the leftover meat and vegetables. Heat the bacon or other fat in a sauté pan, add the leftovers and the chopped scallions or parsley and cook quickly, like a stir-fry, until crisp and brown. Do not add broth. Serve immediately with a poached egg on top of each portion.

Fresh Beef Tongue

Although this dish is not, strictly speaking, a traditional Yankee dish, it is hardly a novelty to a people who pride themselves on their frugality. Tongue is very popular with Italians, who use it as part of a *bollito misto* (mixed boiled dinner). Smoked tongue, a typically Jewish dish, is also quite common in these parts; it can be cooked the same way as fresh tongue.

If you have never had fresh tongue, you are really missing something special. Cooked properly, it is juicy and moist, with a robust flavor. Boiled tongue can be served with condiments like mustard or horseradish or with a sauce—my favorite—like the Tuscan Green

Sauce, a recipe for which follows. Cold tongue makes a marvelous sandwich. You can also cook tongue as you would brisket in a boiled dinner, adding vegetables toward the end of the cooking. Or just boil some potatoes with the tongue and cook some greens, like chard or spinach, separately. Anyway you want, I'm sure you will enjoy it!

SERVES FOUR TO SIX
AS AN ENTREE

1 fresh beef tongue, about
   3 pounds
4 whole garlic cloves, peeled
1 medium onion, peeled
3 bay leaves
4 sprigs fresh thyme
1 branch rosemary
2 cloves
1 tablespoon black peppercorns
1 dried chili

Condiments
freshly grated horseradish or
   Dijon mustard or Tuscan
   Green Sauce (recipe follows)

1. Place the tongue in a large pot and cover it with cold water. Bring to a boil and skim the foam off the top. Reduce to a simmer and add the garlic, onion, bay leaves, thyme, rosemary, cloves, peppercorns and chili. Simmer for 2½ hours. Check for doneness by inserting a roasting fork into the thickest part. It should come out very easily; if not, continue to simmer until it does.

2. When the tongue is tender, remove it from the water. Peel off the skin. Most of the skin should come off easily, just with the use of your fingers. If there are any places where it is difficult to remove, carefully trim it off with a sharp knife. At the back of the tongue, you will find 2 small bones that must be removed; simply trim them out with your knife. If the tongue has cooled down too far, return it to the pot and reheat for a few minutes.

3. Slice the tongue straight down through the thick part (the back), then more on a bias as you reach the thinner (front) portion. Serve with horseradish, mustard or Tuscan green sauce.

Tuscan Green Sauce

You can prepare this savory and refreshing sauce in the food processor or the old-fashioned way, by hand. Make it at least one hour before serving time, to give the flavors time to "marry."

MAKES ONE AND A HALF CUPS

⅔ cup shelled walnuts
1½ cups Italian parsley leaves
¼ cup basil leaves
2 cloves garlic
2 hard-boiled egg yolks
⅔ cup olive oil
salt and freshly ground black
   pepper
cayenne pepper (optional)

1. Combine the walnuts, parsley, basil and garlic in the food processor and process until coarsely chopped. Add the egg yolks and process until finely chopped.

2. Add the oil a little at a time, until the mix is emulsified and creamy. Season to taste with salt and pepper and cayenne pepper, if desired.

VARIATION

To make the sauce by hand, finely chop the walnuts, parsley, basil and garlic one by one. Combine in a bowl and add the egg yolks. Mix very thoroughly until the egg yolks have dissolved. Add the oil a little at a time until the mixture is emulsified and creamy. Season to taste with salt and pepper and cayenne pepper, if desired.

Yankee Pot Roast

This dish is very special in its cooking method, with no counterpart that I know of. What makes pot-roasting different is that it combines braising and roasting. I have taken the liberty of adding a little red wine to my version of this classic dish, but the original uses none. Another break with tradition is to use the *bâtonnet* cut for the vegetables. It calls for a shorter cooking time than chunks and gives the sauce a little fresher flavor.

SERVES SIX TO EIGHT
AS AN ENTREE

1 piece of chuck, about 4
    pounds, with a thin layer of
    fat on one side
kosher salt and freshly ground
    black pepper
3 tablespoons oil
6 cloves garlic, finely chopped
1 medium onion, finely chopped
1 medium carrot, finely chopped
2 tablespoons all-purpose flour
2 cups water or 1 cup water and
    1 cup Reduced Veal Stock
    (page 328)
1 cup red wine
4 sprigs fresh thyme, leaves only
2 bay leaves
1 pint basket pearl onions
    (¾ pound)
4 carrots, cut in bâtonnets (see
    Note)
1 small or half a large rutabaga,
    cut in bâtonnets (2 cups)
4 parsnips, cut in bâtonnets
1 large celery root or 4 stalks
    celery, cut in bâtonnets
3 tablespoons freshly chopped
    Italian parsley

1. Preheat the oven to 350 degrees. Season the meat with salt and pepper. Place a deep heavy roasting pan on top of the stove over medium heat and add the oil. When the oil is hot, place the roast in the pan, fat side down. After searing the fat side, turn the meat and brown on all sides. Remove from the pan and set aside. Add the chopped garlic, onion and carrot to the pan and cook for 1 minute. Sprinkle the flour over the vegetables and cook for 1 minute more, stirring constantly. Add the water (or water and stock) and red wine, a little at a time, allowing the sauce to thicken before adding more. When all the liquid has been added and has come to a boil, add the thyme and bay leaves. Return the meat to the pan. Season the sauce lightly with salt and pepper. Place the pan, uncovered, in the oven.

2. Cook the pot roast for 2 hours, turning it every 20 to 30 minutes and checking that it is not cooking too hard. The sauce should be bubbling gently. If it seems too thick, add water.

3. Meanwhile, put the unpeeled pearl onions in a saucepan and cover with cold water. Add 1 teaspoon salt and bring the onions to a boil; simmer for 1 minute, then drain. When the onions are cool enough to handle, peel them without cutting too deeply into the root end, which holds them together. Set aside.

4. After the roast has cooked 2 hours, add the onions, carrots, rutabaga, parsnips and celery root. Simmer 20 minutes more, stirring at least once during that time. Remove from oven and put on a low heat over the stove.

5. Carve the pot roast into ½-inch slices and arrange on a platter. Skim the sauce of any excess fat. Season to taste with salt and pepper. Spoon the vegetables and sauce over the meat and sprinkle with chopped parsley.

NOTE. To make *bâtonnets*, peel the vegetable and cut into pieces 2 inches long by ⅜ inch wide (like french fries).

The Sirloin and Other Steaks

For reasons of time and space, I have not included recipes for the sirloin, tenderloin and several other popular steaks, but I do want to clarify the different steak names and cuts. The loin of beef is located between the rib and the hind leg section of the animal (see page 162). The tenderloin, called the fillet, is often removed. It can be roasted or grilled whole, or it can be cut into the following steaks: the chateaubriand, a large center cut for two; the filet mignon, cut from the thicker part; and medaillons, cut from the thin part. This thin section of the tenderloin can also be cut into so-called tenderloin tips (*émincé*). The meat from the tenderloin is very soft and lacking in flavor.

When the tenderloin is removed from the loin, the sirloin (the outside meat with the bones attached) is left. It is called a shell, and bone-in steaks cut from it are called shell steaks. When the meat is removed from the bones, a sirloin strip is left; steaks cut from it are sometimes called strip steaks, sometimes called New York steaks.

Another way to cut the loin is to leave it intact and cut straight through the meat and bone. The steaks cut through the thicker part of the tenderloin are known as Porterhouse steaks, those cut through the thinner part are known as T-bone steaks (after the appearance of the bone).

In addition to these fancy and expensive cuts of beef, there are others that provide very flavorful, though slightly chewier, steaks that are best when sliced. Both flank and skirt steaks are wonderful when cooked rare and sliced thin on the bias against the grain, as in Lucky's Log-seared Skirt Steak (page 172). These are also good when marinated and grilled. Another less expensive steak that appears commonly in supermarkets is a thick steak cut from top round. This kind of steak needs a good long marinating time and should be cooked rare to medium rare and sliced thin across the grain. Cooked in this manner, it can be just as satisfying as any of the fancier steaks.

A properly cooked steak, whether grilled, broiled or panfried, needs to be seared hard, to form an outside crust. The center should be rare or medium rare and very juicy. To accomplish this, the steak needs to be at least one inch thick. Until recent years, this has never presented a problem, but with the changing attitudes and eating habits of the eighties, I have found that the typical twelve- to sixteen-ounce sirloin steak of the past is too large. Even the smallest strip cut one inch thick yields a twelve-ounce steak. Tenderloins can be cut thick at any weight, but I do not care for them. A porterhouse or T-bone steak cut one or more inches thick is a perfect portion for two. But how do you cut a thick steak from the sirloin and have an acceptable portion size of eight to ten ounces?

I called my butcher, John Dewar (known locally as "the butcher to the stars"), and put the problem before him. After a little thought he said, "It's old-fashioned, but we used to cut club steaks from double-eye strips." (These are very large sirloin strips, sixteen pounds minimum.) The way you make a club steak is to cut an eighteen- to twenty-ounce sirloin steak from a large strip, then cut it in half crosswise. After it is trimmed and rounded off, it weighs in the neighborhood of eight ounces and resembles a filet mignon. We tried it and it worked out beautifully.

Old-Fashioned Club Steak with Oysters

This dish is my sous-chef Stan Frankenthaler's rendition of the "carpetbagger." In the original carpetbag steak, a pocket was cut into the steak, and it was stuffed with oysters. In Stan's version, the oysters are fried and served next to the steak. His third element, a mushroom ragout thickened with aïoli, is a stroke of genius. In itself the aïoli is excellent with the mushrooms, and it ties them together with the steak and oysters. The recipe may seem complicated, but it is really just three fairly simple cooking procedures combined.

SERVES FOUR AS AN ENTREE

3/4 cup Aïoli (page 332)
2 tomatoes
4 club steaks, 8 to 9 ounces each, or 2 sirloin steaks, 20 ounces each, cut from a large strip (page 171)
salt and freshly ground pepper
oil for dredging or frying the steaks
1/2 recipe Crispy Batter-Fried Oysters, using 16 medium to large oysters (page 9)

Mushroom Ragout
2 tablespoons clarified butter (page 329)
3 to 4 shallots, finely chopped (4 tablespoons)
1 pound chanterelles and/or other wild mushrooms, cleaned and sliced 1/4 inch thick
3/4 cup Reduced Veal Stock (page 328)
4 tablespoons finely chopped chives

1. Early in the day, prepare the aïoli. Measure out 1/2 cup; set aside and refrigerate. Reserve the remaining aïoli for another use. Peel, seed and dice the tomatoes. You should have 1/2 cup. Set aside and refrigerate.

2. If you are going to grill the steak, build a wood or charcoal fire about 1 hour 30 minutes before serving and let it burn down to glowing coals. Season the steaks with salt and pepper and dredge in oil. Cook the steaks on all sides; although they are somewhat round, you must think of them as six-sided. It will take at least 12 minutes, most likely closer to 15. If you are going to panfry the steaks, preheat the oven to 400 degrees. Heat 2 tablespoons oil in a large cast-iron skillet and sear the steaks on all 6 sides. Place the skillet in the oven for 10 to 12 minutes. Turn the steaks once during the cooking.

3. Meanwhile, start heating the oil for the batter-fried oysters and begin the mushroom ragout. Heat the clarified butter in a 10-inch sauté pan. Add the shallots, then the wild mushrooms. Sauté for 3 or 4 minutes until the mushrooms are lightly browned. Add the tomatoes and stock and bring to a boil. Boil down until the mixture is reduced by half. Start frying the oysters and drain on paper towels. When the mushroom mixture is reduced, remove from heat and stir in the aïoli and chives. Season to taste with salt and pepper.

4. Make small piles of the mushroom ragout at points east, west, north and south on each plate. The sauce should run enough to cover the plate. Place a piece of steak in the center of each plate and put the oysters in between the ragout. Serve at once.

Lucky's Log-Seared Skirt Steak

This unusual recipe is from Johanne Killeen and George Germon, of Lucky's and Al Forno restaurants in Providence, Rhode Island, two of the most exciting young chefs (and restaurants) in New England. The blazing fire and rustic atmosphere of Lucky's give you an idea of the soul-satisfying food that you will soon enjoy. Although New England is the source for the food here, southern France seems to be the source of inspiration. Even so, a distinctly New England feeling pervades this wonderful restaurant.

This is the ultimate "black and blue" steak, charred on the outside and rare inside. The full-flavored and reasonably priced skirt steak is Johanne and George's preference. Like the flank, the skirt steak must be cooked rare and sliced across the grain of the meat. When cooked properly, this ranks with the greatest of beef steaks. It can be done on an outdoor grill or in your fireplace. Be sure that the coals are very, very hot (red-orange) and that you shake away any ashes. Any of the traditional steak garnishes will go well, but I especially recommend the Gratin of Turnips and Potatoes (page 244) or the Garlic Mashed Potatoes (page 249).

SERVES FOUR AS AN ENTREE

4 skirt steaks, about 6 ounces each, pounded ½ inch thick

½ cup virgin olive oil, for brushing and drizzling

kosher salt and freshly ground black pepper

4 slices country bread, sliced ⅝ inch thick

1 large bunch (about 7 ounces) watercress, washed and trimmed

1. Prepare a very hot hardwood fire using wood charcoal or small logs. Cook the fire down, so that all that remains is glowing embers. With a poker, shake the coals to remove the ashes.

2. Brush the skirt steaks lightly with olive oil. Sprinkle both sides with salt and pepper. With tongs, lay the steaks directly on the burning coals. Sear for 1 minute 30 seconds. Turn the steaks and sear for only 10 to 15 seconds more. Remove the steaks from the coals, shaking them to remove any clinging embers. Let them rest on a warm plate for 5 minutes.

3. Brush the slices of country bread lightly with olive oil and toast over the coals. Cut the toasted bread into cubes and divide among 4 serving plates. Divide the watercress and place on top.

4. Slice the steaks across the grain. Hold the knife at an angle and cut thin slices (¼ inch). Place each sliced steak on the bed of watercress and drizzle a bit more olive oil on top. Serve at once.

VEAL

New England is fast becoming a leader in quality veal production. Small-scale producers in Maine, Vermont and New Hampshire (see the List of Sources, page 357) are offering veal that is a little redder, a little larger, a little chewier and a lot tastier than so-called white veal. That meat, from calves confined from birth in cages designed to restrict all movement, is tender all right, but it is also tasteless. In my opinion, the practices of factory farms—the cruel and inhumane conditions in which the animals are kept, the use of chemical and hormone substances to accelerate growth—are morally wrong. We should all, customers, chefs and home cooks alike, oppose them. Good cooking is more than just the exercise of an acquired skill; it is a way of combining good ingredients with good techniques and a good heart.

One of the producers I buy calves from is Lydia Ratcliff of Lovejoy Brook Farm in Vermont. As you approach the farm, you see cows out in the pastures with their calves; goats and sheep graze nearby. The animals look peaceful and happy. I am convinced this tranquil atmosphere makes a difference in producing an animal that is superior in every way.

The choicest cuts of veal are the loin and tenderloin, the rib section, and the top, bottom and eye rounds (from the hind quarter). The rest of the usable meat (probably about 30 percent) is quite a bit leaner and tougher and is best for braising or grinding. The meat for braising can be partially trimmed and cut into sizes ranging from one-inch cubes (for stew) to medium-size pieces (like osso buco) to even larger pieces (like the entire breast). Any meat that is left, including all the odds and ends, like the cap meat on the rib, is suitable for grinding. The ground meat can be used for sausages and meatballs, pâtés, mousses and the like.

Unlike beef, veal requires very little aging. One week is more than enough time for the meat to dry. The organ meats (brains, heart, kidneys, sweetbreads and liver) are at their best immediately after slaughter. At my restaurant, we offer these different organ meats as specials the day they arrive, which is usually the day after slaughter. The flavor is fresh and very mild. The strong flavor that people find distasteful is more often than not the result of the shortcomings of the system of food distribution. Recipes for liver and sweetbreads are in this section. For kidneys, see the recipe for baby lamb kidneys (page 188).

Grilled Sweetbreads with Bacon

Sweetbreads are extremely rich and should be served in small portions or as an appetizer. They are usually sliced and sautéed, but here they are cut into chunks, skewered with pieces of bacon and grilled. The first time I ever had sweetbreads prepared this way was at the East Coast Grill, a very popular restaurant across the river from mine in Cambridge, Massachusetts. The chef and owner, Chris Schlesinger, and his sous-chef, Robert Del Bove, offer some great barbecue as well as simple grilled dishes. The food is delicious and lively; so is the atmosphere. Their motto: "Grills just want to have fun."

SERVES FOUR AS AN ENTREE OR
SIX TO EIGHT AS AN APPETIZER

1½ pounds sweetbreads
Court Bouillon (page 79)
6 ounces slab country bacon

Balsamic Vinegar Sauce
3 shallots, finely chopped
   (3 tablespoons)
¼ cup balsamic vinegar
1 cup Reduced Veal Stock
   (page 328)
1 tablespoon beurre manié (see
   Note)
salt and freshly ground black
   pepper

vegetable oil for dredging

1. Soak the sweetbreads in cold water for at least 24 hours, changing the water frequently. If time allows, soak them for as long as 48 hours. It is important to get as much of the blood out as possible.

2. Make a court bouillon as described on page 79. Place the sweetbreads in the strained bouillon and poach very gently for about 10 minutes. Just how long depends on the size. Feel for firmness and remove the sweetbreads before they are cooked all the way through. They should be just barely set; it is important not to overcook sweetbreads. If they are not to be used right away, store them whole in the liquid for 2 to 3 days.

3. When the sweetbreads are cool, peel off all of the outer membrane and any clumps of fat. Cut the sweetbreads into 1-inch cubes. Cut the bacon into 1-inch squares, about ¼ inch thick. Alternate pieces of sweetbread and bacon on skewers.

4. Build a wood or charcoal fire and let it burn down to glowing embers. Meanwhile, start making the sauce. Put the shallots in a small pan with the vinegar. Slowly reduce this by half. Add the veal stock and bring to a boil. Skim and reduce to a simmer. After 5 minutes, whisk in small pieces of the *beurre manié*. Simmer slowly and keep whisking until the sauce is slightly thickened and silky smooth. Season to taste with salt and pepper. Keep hot.

5. When the fire is ready, dredge the skewers in oil, season with salt and pepper and place on the grill. Grill a few minutes on each side until evenly browned.

6. Put a little sauce on each plate, put the sweetbreads and bacon on top and serve the remaining sauce on the side.

NOTE. To prepare 1 tablespoon *beurre manié*, blend together ½ tablespoon unsalted butter and ½ tablespoon all-purpose flour, using a rubber spatula.

Calves' Liver with Mustard Sauce and Mustard Greens

In this dish the onions and bacon that are traditionally served with liver are cooked with mustard greens, and they are served with the liver. The mustard sauce ties together all the ingredients, making what seems at first to be a simple dish into a rather complex taste combination with a very lively exchange of flavors.

SERVES FOUR AS AN ENTREE

4 thick slices of peeled calves'
liver, 6 to 8 ounces each
milk for soaking

Mustard Sauce
1 small onion, finely chopped
(½ cup)
1 tablespoon unsalted butter
1 cup Reduced Veal Stock
(page 328)
1 tablespoon beurre manié
(page 174)
2 tablespoons whole-grain
mustard, such as Pommery
1 tablespoon cider vinegar
salt and freshly ground pepper

Mustard Greens
1½ pounds mustard greens
¼ pound slab country bacon, cut
in small (¼ inch) dice
1 medium to large onion, cut in
small (¼ inch) dice (1 to 1½
cups)

all-purpose flour for dredging
vegetable oil or clarified butter
(page 329) for frying

1. Soak the slices of liver for at least 2 hours in enough milk to cover. They can soak up to 1 day. The milk draws out any excess blood and sweetens the liver.

2. To prepare the sauce, sauté the chopped onion in butter until very brown. Add the veal stock and bring to a boil. Skim and reduce to a simmer. Whisk in small pieces of the *beurre manié* and whisk frequently until the sauce is slightly thickened and silky smooth. Add the mustard and vinegar. Season to taste with salt and pepper and keep hot until ready to serve.

3. Wash the greens well and blanch in a large pot of boiling salted water for 3 minutes. Drain and rinse under cold water to shock; drain well. Render the diced bacon in a skillet until it starts to crisp. Add the diced onion and cook until tender. Turn down the heat and add the mustard greens. Simmer, uncovered, very slowly while cooking the liver. Season to taste with salt and pepper.

4. Remove the liver from the milk and pat dry with paper towels; season lightly with salt and pepper. Heat a little oil or clarified butter in a sauté pan on medium-high heat. Dredge the liver in flour and place in the pan. Cook about 1 minute on each side for rare, a little longer for medium rare. Cooking liver past medium rare is not a good idea: the more it is cooked, the tougher the texture and the stronger the flavor.

5. Divide the mustard greens evenly on serving plates, piling them up toward the back of the plate. Spoon some sauce on each plate and place the liver on top of the sauce. Serve remaining sauce on the side.

Sautéed Rib of Veal with Vermont Ham, Fresh Sage and Apples

Vermont has a tradition of fine restaurants and inns that accommodate the skiers, leaf-peepers, fishermen and other types of flat-landers who visit this beautiful, mountainous state. One of the best is Stubb's in Stowe, run by my friends Jim Dinan and Amy Wales-Dinan. This autumn dish of theirs combines veal and cob-smoked ham, two of Vermont's finest foods, with apples and sage. It epitomizes the "haut-country" cuisine of rural New England. Serve it with roasted potatoes (page 251) or Potato Pancakes (page 251) and glazed turnips or carrots.

SERVES FOUR AS AN ENTREE

4 bone-on veal rib chops, 8 to 10 ounces each
kosher salt and freshly ground black pepper
4 tablespoons clarified butter (page 329) or vegetable oil
2 shallots, peeled and chopped (2 tablespoons)
1 green apple (Greening or Granny Smith), peeled, cored and sliced ¼ inch thick
1 cup dry white wine
1 cup Reduced Veal Stock (page 328)
¼ pound cob-smoked Vermont ham, cut in ⅜ × 1½-inch julienne (see Note)
12 sage leaves, torn in half
4 tablespoons unsalted butter, cold
4 sprigs fresh sage for garnishing

1. Preheat the oven to 200 degrees. Trim the veal chop, if necessary. Season to taste with salt and pepper. Heat a large skillet or sauté pan to medium-high heat. Add the clarified butter or vegetable oil. Place the chops in the pan and cook them about 5 minutes on each side. They should have a nice brown crust and be pink inside (medium done). Remove the chops from the pan; transfer them to a platter and place in the warm oven while you make the sauce.

2. Pour off any excess fat, leaving about 1 tablespoon in the pan. Add the shallots and apple slices to the pan and cook for about 1 minute until the apples begin to go limp.

3. Add the wine and raise heat to high. When the wine has reduced by half, add the stock and reduce by about a third. Add the ham and sage leaves and cook for 1 minute more. Pour any juices from the platter back into the sauce at this point. Remove from the heat and swirl in the butter. Season the sauce lightly with salt and pepper.

4. Place the chops on plates, arrange the apple slices around and spoon the sauce over. Garnish with sprigs of fresh sage.

NOTE. See List of Sources, page 357, for purveyors of Vermont ham.

Breaded Veal Medaillons with Green Tomatoes and Mozzarella Cheese

Here is a light, almost whimsical dinner for a warm summer night. I created it a few summers ago while fooling around with green tomatoes. The flavors are fresh and straightforward. Be sure to cut the veal, tomatoes and cheese the same size so they look similar when cooked.

SERVES FOUR AS AN ENTREE

1 pound veal loin
2 or 3 green (unripe) tomatoes
½ pound fresh mozzarella
8 cups mixed salad greens
1 cup all-purpose flour, for dredging
4 eggs
¼ cup milk
3 cups fine fresh white breadcrumbs (page 67)
2 tablespoons finely chopped Italian parsley

1. Trim the veal loin and cut into 8 medaillons about ⅓ inch thick and 3 inches in diameter. Lightly pound, if necessary. Slice the tomatoes and mozzarella cheese into 8 slices each, just as thick as the meat. Since the items being breaded should be cooked as soon as they are breaded, now would be a good time to clean the salad greens.

2. Set up a breading station. Put the flour in a pan; blend the eggs and milk and put the mixture in another pan; mix together the breadcrumbs, parsley, basil, chives, and grated cheese in a third pan. Have a flat pan ready for the breaded food.

1 tablespoon finely chopped
    fresh basil
1 tablespoon finely chopped
    chives
4 tablespoons finely grated
    romano or parmesan cheese
salt and freshly ground black
    pepper
olive oil for frying
1 small red onion, thinly sliced
¼ cup aged balsamic vinegar
¼ cup peanut oil
2 lemons, cut in wedges

3. Season each piece of meat, tomato and cheese lightly with salt and pepper. Coat thoroughly with flour, shaking off any excess. Dip in the egg wash, coat thoroughly, then let the excess drip off. Roll in the seasoned breadcrumbs. When all the pieces of veal, tomato and cheese are breaded, generously coat the bottom of a large sauté pan with olive oil. and heat until very hot but not smoking (325 degrees). Panfry all the breaded food about 1 minute on each side and remove to paper towels to absorb any grease.

4. Toss the salad greens with the red onion, balsamic vinegar, peanut oil and season to taste with salt and pepper.

5. Place a mound of salad in the center of each of 4 large plates and alternate slices of veal, tomato and cheese (2 each per person) around the salad. Serve with lemon wedges.

Veal Sausages

These sausages are coarse and rather spicy. They can be grilled for an appetizer or main course or as part of a mixed grill. They can be braised with sauerkraut (follow the recipe for Venison Sausages with Sauerkraut, page 197) or buried in a cassoulet. They can be cooked and sliced, then tossed with pasta or spread on top of a pizza. The sausage meat can be used as a stuffing for pasta or chops or as a base for various other stuffings. The possibilities are endless.

I tested this recipe with six pounds of meat, but you could cut the quantities in half if that is too much for your immediate needs. I do not recommend freezing the sausages, which I find alters the flavor and texture. In fact, I am against freezing just about everything but ice cream. Why go to all the trouble of making something good and then risk spoiling it?

MAKES ABOUT TWENTY-FOUR
FOUR-OUNCE SAUSAGES

4 pounds trimmed fresh veal, cut
    in small pieces
2 pounds fatback, without the
    rind, cut in small pieces
10 cloves garlic, sliced
6 shallots, sliced
6 branches fresh tarragon, leaves
    only, chopped
12 sprigs fresh thyme, leaves
    only
1 teaspoon fennel seeds, chopped
2 tablespoons cracked black
    pepper
1 teaspoon cayenne pepper
2 tablespoons kosher salt
3 tablespoons freshly chopped
    Italian parsley
¼ cup ice water

1. Combine all the ingredients *except* the salt, parsley and ice water. Mix well and chill. This can be done a day ahead. Also chill all the equipment that will come in contact with the meat.

2. Pass the mixture through the medium plate of a meat grinder. Keep both the meat and the machine parts chilled.

3. Add the salt, parsley and ice water. (I add the parsley with the salt so that I can see that the salt is well mixed in.) Make a small patty and fry it. Taste for proper amounts of salt and pepper; other flavorings are hard to detect properly at this point. Correct seasoning if necessary.

4. If you are going to stuff the sausages, follow the directions on page 179.

PORK

The Pilgrims brought pigs with them to the New World, and pork has held an important place on the Yankee table ever since. The early settlers and the many generations that followed stored pork in barrels of brine for the hard times of winter. By the end of January, when game birds and venison were extremely scarce, pork was the only meat available. Although it was a singular diet, I have yet to come across any complaints about it in my readings, as I have when lobster or salmon was the mainstay. One must assume that the old Yankees loved their pork. No other meat is used in New England cookery with more frequency.

New England has always been a producer of fine hams and bacon (see List of Sources, page 357), as well as fresh pork. When buying pork, look for a whitish-pink color and very fine marbling. As with beef, it is the fat in the meat, not on the meat, that is important. The finest pork I have ever tasted, other than in China, was raised by my father. For a short time, he had a deal with a local dairy to purchase ricotta cheese and sour cream that had to be returned to the dairy after the expiration date. This practice, for some odd reason, turned out to be illegal, and eventually the supply dried up. After that Dad did not bother with pigs any more, but while it lasted it was unbelievable. The meat was almost pure white, with a flavor that cannot be described.

Pork is used extensively in my kitchen and in recipes throughout this book. For the best flavor and texture, I cook the loin and tenderloin to 150 degrees (medium) and all other cuts to 160 degrees (medium well). Cooking pork to 175 degrees or more is definitely obsolete: the threat of trichinosis is a thing of the past, and it has been proven that the trichinae are killed at temperatures below 150 degrees.

Good pork has a richness, not heaviness, that no other meat, with the exception of loin of beef, can compare with. The fat has a delicate flavor that to me is surpassed only by goose fat, which is not as useful. Pork fat is most often used to enhance other meats by larding or barding or by grinding it to add to sausages. Pretty much every part of the pig is edible, and no one cut of pork can be said to be better than any other, although the chops are probably the most popular. Be it a Boston butt (shoulder), a fresh ham (leg), a loin, a rack, the ears or the feet, all the parts are equally delicious. This fact alone makes it easy for me to state that the pig is the greatest of all animals raised for meat. It is far and away my personal favorite.

Pork is also the most versatile of meats. It can be roasted whole at any stage of life from suckling pig to fully matured hog. Different cuts can be grilled, roasted, braised, boiled, sautéed, stir-fried, deep-fried, panfried—the list goes on and on. And what other single food except milk has given rise to an entire craft? I am referring, of course, to charcuterie, the art of transforming the pig into bacon, sausage, pâté and so on.

How to Make Country-Style Sausages

All country-style sausages are made the same way. First a forcemeat, a mixture of ground meat and fat, salt and spices, is prepared. Then it is forced into casings and pinched or tied into links. The sausage links are usually hung to dry; they can also be cold-smoked.

In this book you will find recipes for veal, venison, duck and pheasant sausages as well as pork. The proportion of fat added is different for each meat, and the spices also vary. After you have made a few batches, you may want to adjust the fat and seasonings to suit your own taste. In addition to various herbs and spices, vegetables and even cheese can be added.

For coarse country-style sausages, a traditional meat grinder gives best results, although you can use a food processor. Sausages that are made from pureed forcemeat, like bratwurst or the French *boudin blanc,* must be made in a food processor or similar machine, but even then the meat should be ground first.

Another piece of equipment you will need is a stuffer, either a pig stuffer or the smaller lamb stuffer. This is the nozzle the casing goes over, and it fits right onto the grinder so that the forcemeat can be ground directly into the casing on the second grinding. For small batches of sausage, though, I have found it just as easy to attach the nozzle and the casing to a pastry bag and stuff the sausages by hand.

Casings come in three sizes: most commonly used are pig casings, for Italian and other medium-size sausages, and lamb casings, for breakfast links and cocktail sausages; beef casings are used mainly for commercial preparations and are seldom found in restaurants or in the home. On the wholesale market casing is sold by the hank, which is far too much for the home cook, but you can order it by the foot. If your butcher makes his own sausages, he might be willing to sell you some casings.

The technique is the same for any kind of coarse country-style sausage. For timing remember that the casings need to be soaked 12 to 24 hours and that the forcemeat can be partially made a day ahead. And never forget the cardinal rule in sausage-making: keep everything—equipment as well as ingredients—as cold as possible at all times. The steps are as follows:

- Clean the casings. First rinse them thoroughly in cold water to remove the salt they were packed in, then tenderize them. The best natural tenderizer is papaya juice, but if that is not available, use pineapple juice. Soak overnight in papaya juice, 24 hours in pineapple juice. Rinse thoroughly in cold water to remove any traces of fruit juice.

- Prepare the forcemeat.

- Hook up the stuffer and casing. With the medium blade in place, fit the stuffer onto the grinder, using the lamb stuffer and lamb casings for breakfast links, the pig stuffer and pig casings for all the others. Slip a piece of casing all the way up over the nozzle. Start grinding and stop the machine when the meat starts coming out. Now pull the casing down over the end of the nozzle and tie it in a knot. The reason for this is to push all the air out of the machine so as to prevent air pockets in the sausage.

- Stuff the casing. Turn the machine back on and let the casing fill evenly; it should not be too tightly packed. Keep the grinder opening full at all times by stopping the machine periodically and adding more forcemeat. Continue until all the meat has been used.

- Form the links. Starting about 4 inches from the tied end of the casing, pinch the first sausage by twisting it 3 or 4 times away from you. Pinch the next sausage by twisting it toward you. Repeat until all the sausages are formed.

- Cold-smoke the sausages if desired.

- Dry the sausages. Either place the sausages on a rack or in the refrigerator for at least 1 day. This aging gives the different flavors a chance to marry.

- Cook the sausages. Sausages can be prepared an infinite variety of ways. Suggestions can be found with individual recipes.

Breakfast Sausages

Whether formed into patties or links, this kind of sausage is usually panfried and served, as I'm sure you all know, with eggs and hash browns or other traditional breakfast dishes, like pancakes. It is also excellent in stuffing or dressing for poultry or pork (see the Country Sausage and Sage Stuffing on page 136).

The predominant flavoring is sage and black pepper, but other herbs, (rosemary, marjoram and thyme) can also be used. I have made these sausages with all kinds of fresh herbs, with very good results. The best batch I made, though, was not with fresh herbs at all, but with a blend of dried herbs known as Bell's Seasoning; I have used it ever since. I tested this recipe at home with six pounds of pork and fatback; if you cannot use that much, cut all the quantities in half rather than freeze the sausages. They are best freshly made.

MAKES FORTY-EIGHT TWO-OUNCE
PATTIES OR ABOUT SIXTY LINKS

4½ pounds trimmed lean pork,
  cut in small pieces
1½ pounds fatback, without the
  rind, cut in small pieces
4 tablespoons Bell's Seasoning
2 tablespoons freshly ground
  black pepper
2 tablespoons kosher salt
3 tablespoons freshly chopped
  chives and Italian parsley or
  all parsley
¼ cup ice water

1. Combine all the ingredients *except* the salt, chives and parsley, and ice water. Mix well and chill. This can be done a day ahead. Chill all the equipment that will come in contact with the meat.

2. Pass the mixture through the medium plate of a meat grinder. Keep both the meat and the machine parts chilled.

3. Add the salt, chives and parsley, and water. (I add the fresh herbs with the salt so that I can see that the salt is well mixed in.) Make a small patty and fry it. Taste for proper amounts of salt and pepper; other flavorings are hard to detect properly at this point. Correct seasonings if necessary.

4. If you are going to make patties, just grind the meat a second time. If you are going to make links, follow the directions on page 179, using a lamb stuffer and lamb casings. Links should be about 1½ ounces each, patties about 2 ounces each.

Italian Sausages

This type of fresh pork sausage has become known in America as Italian sausage. It can be grilled or panfried and served in too many ways to count. Street vendors at the summer "Feasts" in Boston's North End put it in sandwiches with fried peppers and onions; this is a very common practice all over the Northeast. The sausage can also be used, broken up, in a Bolognese meat sauce or whole in tomato sauce for pasta. Although this kind of sausage is readily available, either hot (with crushed red pepper) or sweet, I'm sure you will find this recipe produces a sausage far superior to any you can buy. The flavorings I use are a bit more complex than you get in the commercial sausage (fennel predominates) and, of course, you know what goes into it. If the quantity is more than you can use, cut the recipe in half rather than freeze the extra sausages.

MAKES TWENTY-FOUR
FOUR-OUNCE SAUSAGES

4½ pounds trimmed lean pork,
 cut in small pieces
1½ pounds fatback, without the
 rind, cut in small pieces
6 cloves garlic, chopped
2 tablespoons fennel seeds
2 tablespoons cracked black
 pepper
1 tablespoon paprika for
 coloring
1 or 2 teaspoons crushed red
 pepper (optional)
2 tablespoons kosher salt
¼ cup ice water

1. Combine all the ingredients *except* the salt and ice water. Mix well and chill. This can be done a day ahead. Also chill all the equipment that will come in contact with the meat.

2. Pass the mixture through the medium plate of a meat grinder. Keep both the meat and the machine parts chilled.

3. Mix in the salt and water. Make a small patty and fry it. Taste for salt and pepper and correct seasoning if necessary.

4. If you are going to use the meat for Bolognese meat sauce, simply grind it a second time. If you are going to stuff the sausage meat, follow the directions on page 179.

Pork Rib Chops with Clams and Garlic Sauce

This dish, which has long been a favorite in my restaurant, was inspired by the classic Portuguese *Porco à Alentejana*. The Portuguese are an important ethnic group in New England; they are responsible for much of the commercial fishing off our coast; their cuisine is unique and very flavorful. There are several Portuguese-inspired dishes in this book, but I think this one is the most unusual and the most interesting.

Pork, be it bacon, ham or salt pork, enriches many shellfish dishes; here the roles are reversed, with clams accentuating pork chops. Combining the juice of the clams with pork sauce, garlic, onions and tomatoes turns what sounds like an odd pairing of two very different foods into a singular dish that is at once savory and exotic. Serve it with French Fried Potatoes (try the Large Fries cooked in olive oil, page 250) or panfried potatoes.

SERVES FOUR AS AN ENTREE

24 special count or small
    littleneck clams
4 pork rib chops, at least 1 inch
    thick, rib bones scraped
kosher salt and cracked black
    pepper
1 tablespoon lard or vegetable
    oil

Garlic Sauce
4 teaspoons olive oil
4 bay leaves
½ cup thinly sliced garlic
    (2 whole heads)
1 medium onion, cut in small
    (¼ inch) dice (1 cup)
2 medium tomatoes, peeled,
    seeded and diced
½ cup dry white wine
juice from the opened clams
    (about ⅔ cup)
1 cup Natural Pork Sauce (page
    183)
½ cup coarsely chopped Italian
    parsley
freshly ground black pepper

1. Open the clams, but leave each partially attached to its bottom shell. Reserve all juices and discard the top shells.

2. Season the chops with kosher salt and cracked pepper. Heat the lard or oil in a cast-iron skillet. When it is hot, add the pork chops. Brown each side well (about 5 minutes on each side) and finish by browning the fatty edge. Remove to a platter or individual plates and keep warm.

3. Start the sauce at the same time you start the chops. Put the olive oil and bay leaves in a sauté pan or skillet on medium-high heat. When the leaves brown, remove and discard them. Add the garlic and onion and cook on high heat, stirring occasionally, until they are dark brown (about 5 minutes). Now add the tomatoes, wine, clam juice and pork stock. Boil vigorously until reduced by half (about 5 minutes). The sauce should be thick enough to coat a spoon.

4. Add the clams on the halfshell and cook very briefly, just long enough to plump them and warm them through. (Extended cooking will toughen them.) Arrange the clams around the chops. Return the sauce to the stove and add the parsley. If necessary, season with additional pepper. No salt is needed; it is provided by the clams. Spoon the sauce over the chops and the clams.

Natural Pork Sauce

Pork makes excellent gravy; the same is true for sauce. You can use this sauce as is with a roast or grilled or panfried chops. You can also improvise on the theme by adding tomatoes, onions, vegetables and different herbs and spices to the finished sauce.

MAKES TWO TO THREE CUPS

Pork Stock

3 or 4 pounds meaty pork bones and scraps, cut in small pieces

1 large onion, coarsely chopped (1½ to 2 cups)

1 large carrot, coarsely chopped (1 cup)

2 stalks celery, coarsely chopped (1 cup)

½ head garlic, cloves unpeeled

vegetable oil

2 cups Reduced Veal Stock (page 328) and 3 to 4 cups water or 5 to 6 cups water

2 bay leaves

4 sprigs fresh thyme

1 teaspoon whole black peppercorns

6 to 8 stems Italian parsley

6 to 8 whole allspice (optional)

Roux

2 tablespoons clarified butter (page 329)

2 tablespoons all-purpose flour

salt and freshly ground pepper

1. Preheat the oven to 350 degrees. Combine the pork bones and scraps with the onion, carrot, celery and garlic in a roasting pan. Sprinkle with oil so that the bones and vegetables do not stick to the pan. Place in the oven and roast about 45 minutes or until the bones are a deep brown color and the vegetables have begun to caramelize.

2. Transfer the bones and vegetables to a heavy saucepan. Use a little water to deglaze the pan and add all the scrapings to the pot. Cover with stock and water (or just water) and bring to a boil. Skim the foam off the top and reduce heat to a very slow simmer. Add the bay leaves, thyme, peppercorns and parsley stems. Add allspice only if you are making the sauce for Pork Chops with Clams and Garlic Sauce (page 182). Allow to simmer for 1 hour 30 minutes.

3. Meanwhile, make a roux by combining the clarified butter and flour in a small pan. Cook this over low heat, stirring constantly, until golden brown. Remove and allow to cool.

4. After the stock has fully simmered, ladle a little liquid into the pan with the roux. Stir to a smooth paste and pour back into the large pot of pork stock. Stir until smooth and slightly thickened. It may be necessary to add a little more water. Simmer the sauce very slowly for 1 hour, stirring occasionally. Strain through a medium strainer, remove any excess fat and season to taste with salt and pepper.

Roast Loin of Pork with Fennel Seeds

This is a winter dish that goes well with purees of winter vegetables like squash or turnips. The contrast of fresh fennel, if you can find it at the market, with the fennel seeds is quite a palate teaser. (Simply cut the fennel in julienne and cook it in olive oil or butter or braise it in a little stock.) I once served this roast with cabbage strudel; that combination was extraordinary. You could also pick a warm slaw, with either regular cabbage (page 231) or Savoy cabbage (page 49), or sautéed greens (page 175). Serve mashed or roasted potatoes (pages 249–251) or Potato Pancakes (page 251) with this roast.

When you buy the meat, be sure the butcher leaves on a good layer of fat to protect it during roasting.

SERVES SIX TO EIGHT
AS AN ENTREE

1 boneless loin or rib roast of
   pork, 3½ to 4 pounds, tied
2 tablespoons fennel seeds,
   chopped
5 or 6 cloves garlic, finely
   chopped
1 tablespoon coarsely ground
   black pepper
4 tablespoons vegetable oil
kosher salt
½ cup dry white wine
2 cups Natural Pork Sauce
   (page 183)

1. Preheat the oven to 350 degrees. Mix the fennel seeds, garlic and pepper with 2 tablespoons of the oil. Rub the mixture all over the outside of the roast.

2. Heat the remaining oil in a sauté pan or skillet. Sprinkle the meat with salt and place in the pan. Allow the meat to sear. Turn only after each side is browned; too much moving around or a pan that is not hot enough will cause the seeds and garlic to fall off.

3. When all sides are browned, add the wine to the pan and place in the oven. (I have found that a little liquid is very beneficial when roasting pork.) Cook for 50 to 60 minutes, basting gently every 15 to 20 minutes.

4. While the pork is cooking, heat the natural pork sauce. When the pork is done (145 degrees on a meat thermometer), place it on a platter in a warm spot. Allow to rest at least 10 minutes. Add the wine and all other drippings from the pan to the sauce. Simmer for a few minutes, season to taste and strain if desired. Skim off any excess fat.

5. Slice the roast and spoon some sauce over each portion. Pass the remaining sauce in a sauceboat.

Mom's Fresh Ham Sunday Dinner

Up until my teenage years, Sundays were set aside as a family day. The day was usually focused around an early dinner, which would take place at either of my grandparents' homes or at our home. Because of the size of the group, never fewer than eight, the most practical meal was a roast, be it beef, lamb, pork or turkey. When it was Mom's turn she would often bake a fresh ham and serve it with red cabbage and oven-roasted potatoes. Of all the wonderful meals Mom cooked (and there were many) this dish clearly sticks out in my mind, especially the gravy. Pork does make the best gravy, you know.

Fresh ham—the expression is used to distinguish the uncured leg of pork from a cured and smoked one—seems to have gone out of style over the years. It is rarely offered at restaurants, and since I left home, no one has ever served it to me. I have had it as a special at my restaurant; people were uninterested, and it did not sell very well. But it is a fabulous roast, beautiful to look at and delicious to eat, and the gravy, as I said, is sensational. Use the leftovers for a hot open-face sandwich the next day.

Mashed or oven-roasted potatoes are a must for this dish. Use the recipe for Garlic Mashed Potatoes (page 249), omitting the garlic, or Freddie's Famous Roast Potatoes (page 251), using some of the rendered fat from the fresh ham (there is plenty to spare). Start the potatoes about one hour before the meat is going to be done. Also essential is Braised Sweet-and-Sour Red Cabbage (page 232), another of Mom's recipes.

SERVES TWELVE AS AN ENTREE
WITH LEFTOVERS

1 fresh ham, about 14 pounds
10 cloves garlic
6 sprigs fresh thyme
6 branches fresh rosemary
3 tablespoons cracked black
    pepper
2 tablespoons vegetable oil
kosher salt
1 large or 2 medium onions,
    finely chopped
2 medium carrots, finely
    chopped
3 tablespoons all-purpose flour
4 cups Reduced Veal Stock
    (page 328), Chicken Stock
    (page 327) or water
freshly ground black pepper

1. Preheat the oven to 350 degrees. Take the fresh ham out of the refrigerator about an hour before cooking, to allow it to come to room temperature. Carefully score the ham by making long slits through the skin, but not into the meat, about 1 inch apart. Turn the ham and make more long slits, creating a crisscross of 1-inch squares or diamonds. Cut only the skin: cut into the fat as little as possible and do not touch the meat.

2. Chop the garlic, thyme and rosemary and combine with the cracked pepper and oil. Rub this mostly into the meaty section of the leg, but do rub a little on the skin as well. Coat the entire leg with a very thin layer of kosher salt. Place the leg, skin side down, in a roasting pan and put into the oven.

3. After about 1 hour, turn the leg and baste with the fat that has rendered into the pan. Baste the skin every 20 to 30 minutes; the last basting should take place about 20 minutes before the ham is done. About 1 hour before the ham is done, sprinkle the onions and carrots in the bottom of the pan. (First pour off some of the fat if you are preparing oven-roasted potatoes.) A 14-pound fresh ham will take about 3 hours to cook; allow 15 minutes per pound if your roast is a different size. The little squares of crackling (skin) should be very crisp by the end of the roasting time.

4. Remove the fresh ham to a platter in a warm place and allow it to rest at least 30 minutes while you prepare the gravy. Pour off any excess fat, leaving about 3 tablespoons in the pan. Place the roasting pan on low heat on top of the stove. Sprinkle the flour over the pan and cook slowly for 3 to 4 minutes, stirring frequently. Add the stock or water, a little at a time, allowing the gravy to thicken each time before adding more. Be sure to lightly scrape the bottom of the pan to loosen up anything that is stuck there; these little particles are full of flavor. At this point, the gravy can be simmered in the roasting pan or transferred to a saucepan, with all the vegetables and other particles in it. Simmer for at least 20 minutes or, even better, 30 minutes. Strain through a coarse strainer and correct the seasoning with salt and pepper.

5. Stand up the ham so that the small end with the leg bone is sticking up. Carve the ham as thin as possible. Hold the blade of the knife in a slightly upward position, and alternate slices from each side, working in toward the bone. The bone running through the center is angled forward, so as you get toward the bottom, most of the meat will be behind, not in front of the bone. When you get to this point, simply turn the ham around. Serve with the gravy on the side.

Vermont Smoked Ham

Up in the mountains of Vermont there are a few very noteworthy producers of smoked ham and bacon, Harrington being perhaps the most famous among them (see List of Sources, page 357). The use of maple sugar for curing and corncobs for smoking is unique, and the style of curing ham yields a fresher type of ham that unlike, say, Smithfield ham from Virginia doesn't require any soaking at all. In turn, it has a relatively short shelf life. It is quite different from the hams of the South, which are saltier, and those of the Midwest, which are less smoky. The best Vermont hams come from pigs that are on the small side, with legs weighing between 12 and 15 pounds.

No scoring, glazing or studding is necessary for a Vermont ham. In fact, these embellishments only detract from the natural crispness, sweetness and smokiness of the ham. Simply place it in a pan with a little water and bake it in a slow oven (300 degrees) for 12 to 15 minutes per pound. The ham is done when the meat has shrunk and pulled down, exposing about an inch of the bone (meat thermometer reading: 170 degrees). Remove the ham from the oven and allow it to rest for at least 30 minutes before serving. Smoked ham is carved the same way as fresh ham (see page 185 for directions).

Paper-thin slices of ham can be served as an appetizer with fresh fruit (melon or figs) or fruit chutney or compote. One of my favorite combinations, which we often serve at my restaurant, is Vermont ham with Persimmon Chutney (page 342). Cranberry–Onion Jam (page 342) is also good with ham. I always serve a few Cream Biscuits (page 269) on the side.

A Vermont ham can also be the centerpiece for a sit-down dinner, with plenty of side dishes like greens and other vegetables; potatoes, mashed or otherwise; biscuits; and different condiments like mustard, chutney and horseradish. For a cocktail party or other large social gathering, serve a whole baked ham warm with small biscuits and an assortment of condiments for your guests to put together their own sandwiches. As side dishes, you could have a fresh green salad made with Sherry–Mustard Vinaigrette (page 336) and one or more of the following: All-American Potato Salad (page 248), Sweet Corn and Bread Pudding (page 235) and Gratin of Turnips and Potatoes (page 244).

Leftover ham has hundreds of uses in soups, salads and sandwiches and for egg, vegetable, potato, shellfish, fish and meat dishes. Indeed, there is nothing quite as useful as leftover ham. I would never hesitate to cook a whole ham for a small group; it never goes to waste.

LAMB, BABY LAMB AND YOUNG GOAT

The scaled-down landscape of New England is particularly appropriate for the farming of smaller animals, and lamb and goat are very well suited to the terrain. Vermont and New Hampshire are the leading producers of lamb, but Massachusetts is also noteworthy for the lamb raised in the marshes on Martha's Vineyard. It bears a striking resemblance to *pré-salé* lamb from Brittany, France, which is fattened in the meadows bordering the sea.

Farmers like Bill Tuttle of Glen Echo Farms in New Hampshire have won national acclaim for their marvelous rosy-fleshed baby lamb. Although most of their production is sold to fancy restaurants in New York and Boston, cooks everywhere are getting into the act. I hope that my explanation of how to break down meats (pages 161–163) will inspire you to buy a whole lamb. It is really not so difficult or complex to handle as it may seem.

Lamb and baby lamb are as different from one another as beef is from veal. Young goat is very similar to baby lamb. The proper weight of a whole baby lamb ranges from 15 to 30 pounds. I recommend that it be purchased at a weight of 20 to 30 pounds; those under 20 pounds are too bony and do not yield much meat. Lamb is also good at any stage of growth from 30 to 60 pounds. (A simple truism: animals (and birds) are good to eat at any stage of growth, as long as they are gaining weight. Once the weight begins to stabilize, a reversal of quality sets in.) Mutton (mature lamb) is not produced for sale in the United States.

Lamb has become very dear over the last few years; the ever popular rack and saddle of lamb are now among the most expensive of all meat. But as always there are other, less costly cuts that, cooked properly, are delicious. In fact, my single favorite lamb dish is a roast leg. Other cuts, like the shanks and shoulder, are excellent for braising. Ground lamb is also good for sausage and patties.

The liver and kidneys of baby lamb and goat are very delicious. Cook the liver as you would calves' liver (page 175); it is much smaller, so count two portions per liver. The recipe for lamb kidneys on page 188 can also be used for goat or even veal. As with all organ meats, freshness is paramount.

Baby lamb and goat do not require extensive aging; it is best to let them hang for at least three days, but no more than six. For larger lamb I recommend one week of hanging, followed by marinating or more dry-aging for certain cuts.

Baby Lamb Kidneys with Morels

To my knowledge, morels can be found in all the New England states, although they are most common in Vermont and New Hampshire. They are easy to find in the wild, and since no poisonous species resembles them, they are one of the safer mushrooms to pick. I would still recommend, however, that beginners show any mushrooms they have gathered to an experienced person. The season for morels is spring, making them an excellent match for kidneys of baby lamb. Kidneys from a mature lamb are somewhat of an acquired taste, but those of baby lamb are quite mildly flavored. You can substitute veal kidneys if you wish.

SERVES TWO AS AN APPETIZER

2 baby lamb kidneys
salt and freshly ground black
    pepper
1 tablespoon clarified butter
    (page 329)
2 medium shallots, finely
    chopped
½ cup thickly sliced morels
2 tablespoons cognac or other
    good brandy
1 teaspoon Dijon mustard
2 tablespoons Reduced Veal
    Stock (page 328)
2 tablespoons heavy cream
1 tablespoon freshly chopped
    chives
2 thick slices baguette (long
    French bread), lightly buttered
    and toasted, or 2 tartlet shells
    (pages 284–285)

1. Split the kidneys in half lengthwise and trim off any fat. Season lightly with salt and pepper. Heat the clarified butter in a small sauté pan. Add the kidneys and quickly brown on both sides; remove from the pan and put on a small plate.

2. Add the shallots and morels to the pan and sauté for 1 minute. Add the cognac or brandy and ignite. When the flame has burnt off, add the mustard, stock and heavy cream; reduce until thick enough to coat a spoon. Return the kidneys to the sauce; add the chives and cook for another 30 seconds.

3. Arrange the kidneys and morels on small appetizer plates or in tartlet shells and spoon the sauce over. If serving toast, place it on the corner of the plate; it will be needed for the extra sauce.

VARIATIONS

Baby Lamb Kidneys with Morels and Asparagus

Add four cooked asparagus tips to the sauce right before the kidneys in Step 2.

Veal Kidneys with Morels

Substitute veal kidneys for baby lamb kidneys. Trim the kidneys of fat and cut into small pieces. Proceed as for baby lamb kidneys.

Roast Leg of Lamb with Garlic, Parsley and Parmesan Cheese

An open-minded culinarian can learn something from almost everyone. Case in point: this fabulous leg of lamb. I was doing a local food talk show with my friend Dick Syatt of WRKO Radio, Boston. During the call-in part of the show, a listener asked me to recommend the proper way to roast a leg of lamb. I responded with the traditional method of studding the meat with slices of garlic and seasoning it with salt and pepper before roasting. The following caller was a woman who felt "inadequate," because she could not make a good gravy; I did my best to console her. My next caller (I do not remember her name) told me she had an even better way to roast a leg of lamb. I listened skeptically while she explained that it was a practice in her obviously Italian family to stud the leg with small slices of parmesan cheese and leaves of Italian parsley in addition to the slices of garlic. I had to admit it sounded like a good idea, but when I tried it I realized it was pure genius. This has become my favorite method for roasting leg of lamb.

If, however, you are lucky enough to obtain some of the *pré-salé* type lamb from Martha's Vineyard, I would suggest that you use only salt and black pepper for seasoning. Its unusual flavor is best appreciated at its purest state.

SERVES EIGHT OR MORE AS AN ENTREE

1 bone-in leg of lamb, 9 to 10 pounds, hip bone and shank removed and set aside
1 head garlic
8 sprigs Italian parsley, leaves only
1 ounce imported parmesan cheese, preferably Parmigiano-Reggiano
2 tablespoons olive oil
kosher salt and coarsely ground black pepper
2 medium onions, roughly chopped
1 tablespoon all-purpose flour
1 tablespoon tomato paste
2 cups Reduced Veal Stock (page 328) and 1 cup water or 3 cups water

1. Preheat the oven to 450 degrees. Carefully trim off the excess fat around the top of the leg, but leave the covering fat intact. Peel 6 cloves of garlic and cut each lengthwise in 2 or 3 thick slices. Set aside the rest of the garlic; do not peel. Puncture the meat with the tip of a sharp knife, making little pockets with very small openings. Make about 12 of these pockets, distributed evenly around the roast. Place a slice of garlic, 2 or 3 parsley leaves and a small slice of parmesan into each opening. Loosely pack any excess garlic, parsley and cheese around the exposed bone that was once attached to the hip. Fold the meat over and tie it well. Rub the entire roast with olive oil and season generously with salt and pepper.

2. Using a cleaver, break the hip bone and place it in the roasting pan with the shank, arranging them as a rack to support the leg; place the leg on top. Put the roast in the oven for about 20 minutes, or until it begins to brown. Turn the oven down to 350 degrees and add the chopped onions and unpeeled garlic to the pan. Baste the roast with any fat that has begun to render. Cook for 1 hour more, basting occasionally; the meat will be medium rare.

3. Remove the roast to a platter and keep warm. It should rest at least 20 minutes. Put the roasting pan over low heat and sprinkle the flour over the fat, onions, garlic and bones in the pan. Cook for 3 to 4 minutes, then add the tomato paste and cook another minute, stirring constantly all the while. Add the stock and water slowly, allowing the sauce to thicken before adding more. Simmer for 20 minutes or more. Skim any excess fat from the surface. Strain through a fine strainer and season to taste with salt and pepper. Carve the leg, following the directions for fresh ham on page 185. Serve with the sauce.

Grilled Rack and Braised Shanks of Lamb with Rosemary and Winter Vegetables

This knock-out dish comes from the Hanover Inn in the beautiful village of Hanover, New Hampshire. Mike Gray, a true Yankee chef, demonstrates here how the expensive rack of lamb can be stretched to serve four people by combining it with the equally tasty, but less expensive shanks. The recipe may seem long, but it is really two recipes combined at the end. If you wish, you may use either part individually. The braised shanks can be prepared the day before. It is also best to marinate the rack of lamb one day prior to serving. Large slices of potato fried in olive oil (page 250) are the perfect accompaniment to this dish.

SERVES FOUR AS AN ENTREE

Braised Lamb Shanks

2 lamb shanks, cut across into
   1- to 1½-inch-thick pieces,
   like osso buco (8 pieces)
kosher salt and freshly ground
   black pepper
4 tablespoons olive oil
4 cloves garlic, finely chopped
4 shallots, finely chopped
2 cups dry white wine
2 cups Reduced Veal Stock
   (page 328)
juice of 1 orange, zest reserved
juice of 1 lemon, zest reserved
2 tablespoons tomato paste
2 branches fresh rosemary
2 parsnips, peeled and cut into
   large (¾ to 1 inch) dice
   (1 cup)
1 small rutabaga, peeled and cut
   into large (¾ to 1 inch) dice
   (1½ cups)
1 small celery root, peeled and
   cut into large (¾ to 1 inch)
   dice (1 cup)

Grilled Rack of Lamb

1 rack of lamb, trimmed and
   frenched
2 branches fresh rosemary,
   leaves picked and chopped
2 branches fresh thyme, leaves
   picked and chopped
2 cloves of garlic, finely chopped
1 shallot, finely chopped

1. Have your butcher cut the shanks as described; otherwise carefully score the meat at intervals and cut them across with a hacksaw. Season the pieces with salt and pepper. Heat a pan suitable for braising and add the olive oil. Brown the shanks on all sides and remove from the pan.

2. Add the garlic and shallots and cook until lightly browned. Add the wine and reduce by half. Add the stock, orange juice, lemon juice, tomato paste and fresh rosemary. Stir to mix all ingredients well. Place the shanks back in the pan and bring to a boil. Reduce to a slow simmer and cover. Cook slowly on top of the stove for about 45 minutes.

3. Meanwhile, prepare a thin julienne from the zest of half an orange and half a lemon (no white pith). This would be a good time to dice the vegetables. After the shanks have cooked for 45 minutes, add the zests, along with the parsnips, rutabaga and celery root. Simmer for 20 to 30 minutes more, partially covered. The liquid will reduce a little further. Both the lamb and vegetables should be tender. Remove the rosemary and adjust the seasoning with salt and pepper. If this is not to be used immediately, you should cool it as quickly as possible and refrigerate it.

4. If the butcher has not prepared the rack for you, trim off the cap, leaving about ¼ inch of fat on top. French the rib bones and scrape clean for an extra nice appearance. Wrap the bones in aluminum foil to protect them from burning (if they burn, they will break and ruin the presentation). Combine the chopped rosemary, thyme, garlic and shallot with the cracked pepper and 1 tablespoon olive oil. Mix well and rub all over the lamb. If possible, do 1 day ahead of time; rewrap the rack in butcher's paper and refrigerate.

5. Prepare a charcoal or wood fire and allow it to burn down to glowing embers. Preheat the oven to 400 degrees.

6. About 30 minutes before serving, lightly brush the rack with a little more olive oil and sprinkle with kosher salt. Make sure the bones are well protected with foil. Place the rack fat side down on the grill and give it a hard sear until well browned. Turn the rack and repeat. Put the rack in a small pan and place in the preheated oven. Cook for 10 to 15 minutes, until medium rare (110 degrees on a meat thermometer). Let rest for 10 minutes before slicing.

1 tablespoon cracked black
  pepper
olive oil
kosher salt
4 branches fresh rosemary for
  garnishing (optional)

7. If the shanks were braised ahead of time and cooled, you should begin to reheat them at the same time you start to grill the rack.

8. When the rack is ready to be sliced, place 2 pieces of shank in the middle of each plate. Arrange the vegetables and sauce around the shanks, reserving just a little of the sauce. Carve the lamb rack between the bones into 8 chops. Lean these up against the shanks on opposite sides of the plate. Spoon a little more sauce over the lamb chops and garnish with sprigs of fresh rosemary if desired. Serve at once.

Barbecued Cuts of Baby Lamb or Goat

Last winter we had a customer who was irate because he had come back to my restaurant especially for the spring lamb and we were unable to accommodate him. "What do you mean you don't have spring lamb?" he sputtered. "That's why I came here." Our maître d', Dean Paris, politely replied, "But sir, it is the middle of January." Call it old-fashioned, but we like our lamb better after it is born. I love the seasons, if only for the way they starve you of certain foods, making their arrival each year seem even more dramatic.

If you like to start barbecuing early in the season, have a spring cookout with cuts from a whole baby lamb or goat. It will be a memorable occasion, well worth the effort. Marinate the meat for two to three days, then grill it with leeks (page 241) and other fresh vegetables such as eggplant, artichokes, peppers and so on. Serve with a green salad and rice or mashed or roasted potatoes. The meat is so juicy and flavorful that it isn't always necessary to have a natural sauce. You could serve a simple Fresh Mint Sauce (page 337) and an assortment of chutneys (mango chutney is particularly good with this) and relishes instead.

SERVES TWELVE OR MORE AS AN
ENTREE (WITH LEFTOVERS)

1 whole baby lamb or goat,
  weighing between 20 and 25
  pounds

Lemon–Oil Marinade
6 lemons, sliced
2 onions, finely chopped
10 cloves garlic, sliced
8 branches fresh mint, chopped
8 branches fresh oregano,
  chopped
6 bay leaves, broken
¼ cup cracked black pepper
2 cups vegetable oil
2 cups olive oil

kosher salt

1. Break down the lamb or goat as explained on pages 161–163; reserve the bones (see Note). Combine the lemon, onions, garlic, mint, oregano, bay leaves and pepper in a pan large enough to hold all the meat. Mix well, smashing all the lemons to release their juice. Place the pieces of meat in the pan, turn to coat all sides and cover with vegetable and olive oil. Marinate for 2 or 3 days, turning the ingredients a few times during that period.

2. Build a big fire with wood or charcoal and let it cook down to hot coals. Take the pieces of meat directly out of the marinade, sprinkle with salt and place on hottest part of the grill to sear. Move to less hot part to finish cooking. The pieces will take from 5 to 15 minutes to cook, depending on size. They should be cooked medium, so that the meat is pink and juicy, firm but not hard. Avoid turning the pieces too often. Allow the pieces to rest for a few minutes before slicing.

NOTE. Make a natural sauce ahead of time if desired, using the recipe for Natural Pork Sauce on page 183 as a guide; add a little oregano and mint. The sauce can be enhanced with a few table-spoons of pureed roasted peppers (page 247), if you like.

VENISON

Deer can be hunted in most of the United States, and New England is no exception. White-tailed deer are plentiful, even on the islands off the New England coast. They are surprisingly good swimmers, known to swim miles in the ocean. A few years ago, I witnessed a lone buck swimming from Cuttyhunk Island, Massachusetts, en route to Martha's Vineyard.

In the early days of New England, meat from deer and other game was a vital part of the colonists' diet. Although no longer a necessity, deer still provides families in the more modest rural areas of New England with much appreciated free meat. Moose and bear are also hunted for meat in the northern parts of New England, but I have not included recipes for them because I did not think my readers would have much use for them.

Venison—I use the word to mean deer meat, not, as some European chefs do, to refer to all the larger wild creatures—is very high in protein and low in fat; it is the most healthful of all the meats. It is also quite delicious and, when properly aged, tender and juicy. All things considered, venison is compatible with modern life-styles; it will probably become very popular in years to come. In many parts of the country commercial production of venison is already increasing rapidly to meet demand. The only problem is that venison from farmed deer just does not taste as good as that from the wild. Wild deer feed on grain that is left in the fields, true, but it is not their sole diet, as it is for farmed deer. They also eat berries, and many types of shrubs and grasses. Some of the commercially produced venison resembles beef in flavor. Wild venison has a very distinctive flavor that is all its own.

Venison is deep red in color, with very little outside fat or marbling. Because of the very low fat content, the aging of the meat is crucial. Since the hunting season is during the cold months, it is possible to age the meat outdoors. I recommend a minimum of ten days hanging. The meat should have plenty of cold air circulating around it, and the temperature should be constant, never going above 40 degrees or under 32. It is advisable to remove the tenderloins after four days, as this small exposed piece of meat will become too dried out otherwise. This will be your preview of all the delicious meat to come.

The organs of any animal always taste best at their freshest. Venison liver is especially good if eaten within one day of the kill. It is still good after that, but not quite the same. The heart of the deer is also very special; it too should be eaten as fresh as possible.

Cuts of venison resemble beef in their uses. The loin and rib section, being the most tender, is usually cut into medaillons, steaks or roasts. The top, bottom and eye rounds from the leg can also be cut into steaks or roasts, although they will be a little chewier. Meat from the shanks, breast, shoulder, front legs and other odd pieces is best for stew, sausage or hamburger. Venison, in fact, makes excellent hamburger, provided that you add at least one part pork fat to every four or five parts meat.

I have included only a few recipes for venison, but I urge you to experiment. Try a simple steak with garlic (or other) compound butter, for example. Many of the flavors that work with beef are also excellent with venison. Venison is also good together with fruit; you may want to try some variations on the French classic *grand veneur* (great hunter) sauce using local fruits or berries, as I have used beach plums (page 195). I keep all the fancier cuts that will be used for panfrying, grilling or roasting in an oil-based marinade, which extends the shelf life of the meat as well as flavoring and tenderizing it. The other cuts are best kept refrigerated or frozen.

Roast Venison with Beach Plums

I have found that the best way to roast venison is to cut small roasts from the saddle (loin) or from the leg. A two- to three-pound roast is ample for four to six people. If you have marinated the roast, all that will be needed is salt and maybe a little more pepper. If not, you might like to roll the roast in some chopped herbs and spices along with the salt and pepper.

Venison goes well with many different foods and flavorings. Here are some recipe suggestions to choose from: Braised Sweet-and-Sour Red Cabbage (page 232), Wild Rice Pancakes (page 266), Potato Pancakes (page 251), Gratin of Turnips and Potatoes (page 244), noodles (page 277). An assortment of roasted vegetables, like beets, carrots, parsnips, turnips, Jerusalem artichokes, salsify, potatoes and so on, would also be good.

SERVES SIX TO EIGHT
AS AN ENTREE

1 venison roast, boneless, about
   3 pounds, tied
kosher salt
freshly ground black pepper
vegetable oil or clarified butter
   (page 329)
1½ cups Grand Veneur Sauce
   with Beach Plums (page 195)

1. Preheat the oven to 400 degrees. Tie the roast and season it with salt and pepper. Heat a film of oil or clarified butter in a heavy skillet. When it is very hot, put the venison in the pan and sear it well until all sides are brown. Put the roast in the oven for 5 minutes. Turn the roast and cook for 5 minutes more, until medium rare. Cook it for 2 to 3 minutes less for rare.

2. Remove the roast from the oven and place on a platter in a warm spot; let rest for at least 10 minutes. Finish the *grand veneur* sauce by adding beach plum puree or jelly and heavy cream to the *poivrade* sauce.

3. Slice the venison and spoon some of the sauce on top. Pass the remaining sauce separately.

Marinade for Venison

I am a strong proponent of oil-based marinades. They add flavor, increase tenderness and most importantly extend the shelf life and thus reduce the need for freezing as a means of preserving meat. Venison covered with this marinade will keep up to three weeks in the refrigerator.

MAKES ENOUGH FOR TEN
POUNDS OF VENISON

4 cups vegetable oil
1 medium onion, thinly sliced
1 carrot, peeled and thinly sliced
6 cloves garlic, thinly sliced
4 bay leaves, broken
4 sprigs fresh thyme, chopped
10 juniper berries, cracked
4 tablespoons cracked black
   peppercorns

1. Mix all the ingredients in a pan large enough to hold all the meat. Submerge the pieces of meat in the marinade.

2. Turn the meat in the marinade once a day. Be sure the meat is covered by the marinade.

Poivrade Sauce

Sauces for venison all begin with *poivrade,* one of the classic French sauces. This peppery brown sauce, infused with wine and vinegar, can be finished several ways: with butter alone; with butter and fruit; or with fruit and heavy cream (*grand veneur*). *Grand veneur* is another of the classic French sauces; currant is the fruit traditionally used. I like to make it with beach plums instead, but you could substitute just about any other fruit or berry.

The side dishes you choose to go with the venison determine which sauce to use. For instance, suppose you decide to serve venison steak with fried potatoes—a simple *poivrade* would be perfect. Or say you are serving a side dish with cream in it, like scalloped potatoes —a *poivrade* with fruit would go well but additional cream would make it too rich. If, on the other hand, you are serving a roast from the leg with roasted vegetables on the side, the richness of *grand veneur* sauce would be perfect. Once you have mastered these sauces, you will be able to create many different venison dishes by simply varying one or two ingredients in the sauce in accordance with the cut of meat and your choice of side dishes.

MAKES ONE QUART

4 to 5 pounds venison bones and
   meat scraps, cut in pieces 2
   inches or smaller
2 medium onions, coarsely
   chopped
2 medium carrots, peeled and
   coarsely chopped
2 stalks celery, coarsely chopped
2 tablespoons vegetable oil
1 cup red wine vinegar
1 cup red or white wine
3 cups Reduced Veal Stock
   (page 328)
4 bay leaves
4 sprigs fresh thyme
6 parsley stems
2 tablespoons cracked black
   peppercorns
6 juniper berries
2 tablespoons clarified butter
   (page 329)
2 tablespoons all-purpose flour
salt

For Serving
unsalted butter
beach plum or other fruit puree
   or jelly (optional)

1. Preheat the oven to 400 degrees. Place the bones and scraps in a roasting pan with the onions, carrots and celery. Sprinkle with oil, toss and place in the oven. Brown the bones, scraps and vegetables well, turning occasionally. This should take about 30 to 40 minutes.

2. Transfer the ingredients to a large pot. Deglaze the pan with vinegar; pour the vinegar and scrapings into the pot. Add the wine, stock and 1 cup water and bring to a boil. If the bones are not covered, add more water. Skim any foam from the top and turn the heat down to a simmer. Add the bay leaves, thyme, parsley stems, cracked peppercorns and juniper berries. Simmer, uncovered, for 2 hours.

3. Meanwhile make a roux by mixing the clarified butter and flour in a small pan and cooking slowly, stirring often, until light brown. Allow to cool. After the stock has simmered for 2 hours, add a little of the liquid to the roux, mix to make a smooth paste, then blend the roux into the stock. Cook slowly for 1 hour, stirring once in a while to make sure nothing is sticking to the bottom of the pot. Strain twice, first through a medium strainer, then through a fine (bouillon) strainer. Season to taste with salt. This is a finished *poivrade* sauce. It will keep about 1 week in the refrigerator and longer in the freezer (do not freeze unless necessary).

4. When ready to serve, reheat ¼ cup sauce per person. If you are going to serve the sauce plain, remove from the heat and whip in 1 tablespoon of butter per cup. If you want to add fruit, whip in 2 tablespoons of puree or jelly per cup of sauce, then remove from heat and whip in 1 tablespoon of butter per cup. Always check the seasoning for salt and possibly more pepper.

Grand Veneur Sauce with Beach Plums

MAKES ABOUT ONE CUP

1 cup Poivrade *Sauce (page 194)*
2 tablespoons *Beach Plum Puree
    (page 344) or beach plum jelly*
¼ cup *heavy cream*
*salt and freshly ground black
    pepper*

1. Just before serving, heat the *poivrade* sauce. Remove from the heat and stir in the puree or jelly and cream.
2. Simmer for 5 minutes. Taste and add salt and more pepper if needed.

VARIATION

Substitute currant jelly or another kind of fruit puree or jelly for the beach plum puree or jelly.

Venison Steaks

Only the very best cuts of venison should be used for steaks—the loin, tenderloin, rib and top round. The meat keeps better in larger pieces so cut steaks only a few days before you intend to cook them. Marinate the steaks with the rest of the meat, using the marinade on page 193.

Grill the steaks over a wood or charcoal fire that is quite hot or panfry them in a very hot skillet. Be sure to season the meat with salt and pepper before cooking. When the steak is cooked (rare is best), melt a little garlic butter or other flavored compound butter over it and serve immediately. If you want to serve a sauce, use the *Poivrade* Sauce (page 194) without fruit or cream. Serve with simple garnishes like sautéed green vegetables or a warm spinach and beet salad (page 254) and fried potatoes or Potato Pancakes (page 251).

Venison Goulash

This is one of my favorite stews. Of Central European origin, it is a dish that has long been a part of the American cooking repertoire. This version is in the Viennese style, in which a natural sauce is created without the addition of a lot of excess liquid. It is called *Saftgulasch*, which means natural-juice goulash or stew. This was taught to me by Bruno Elmer, one of my instructors at culinary school long ago. I imagine I have altered the ingredients over the years (until the day I tested the recipe for this book I had always made it from memory), but it does remain true to the original concept. This stew also works very well with beef or veal. Serve this with buttered noodles or spätzle and salad.

SERVES EIGHT TO TEN
AS AN ENTREE

4 pounds venison stew meat
   from the shoulder, breast,
   neck and shank
4 ounces lard
5 medium onions, thinly sliced
   (about 2 pounds)
4 cloves garlic, chopped
4 tablespoons red wine vinegar
2 tablespoons tomato paste
¼ cup sweet Hungarian paprika
1 tablespoon caraway seeds
1 teaspoon dried oregano or
   marjoram
2 bay leaves
½ cup water or Reduced Veal
   Stock (page 328)
salt and freshly ground black
   pepper

1. Trim the meat and cut into large cubes, about 2 inches. The pieces need not be perfectly uniform, as long as they are approximately the same size.

2. Preheat the oven to 325 degrees. Heat the lard in a heavy casserole until it begins to smoke. Add the onions and garlic and cook until they are caramelized (brown). The trick is not to stir the pot often. When the onions are sufficiently browned, add the vinegar and deglaze the pot, loosening any onions that may be stuck to the bottom.

3. Add the tomato paste, paprika, caraway seeds, oregano or marjoram and bay leaves. Cook about 5 minutes, stirring constantly, to expand the flavors. Add the meat and water or stock and bring to a bubbling point. Season lightly with salt and pepper. Cover the pot tightly with a lid or with aluminum foil and place in the preheated oven. After 1 hour, check the stew to make sure the liquid is barely covering the meat. Add a few drops more if needed. Stir well and bring back to a bubbling point. Cover and return to the oven for 1 hour more. At this point the meat should be tender and juicy, but not falling apart. If the meat is at all dry, return to the oven for further cooking. Stir the stew well before serving. The onions should have dissolved almost completely into the sauce, which should appear thick and rich. Check the seasoning.

VARIATIONS

Veal Goulash — Substitute 4 pounds of veal stew meat (shoulder meat is good). Proceed as for venison, but cook only 1 hour.

Beef Goulash — Substitute 4 pounds beef chuck for the venison and cook about the same length of time. Degrease before serving.

Venison Sausages with Sauerkraut

Sauerkraut is a great companion for almost any sausage; I especially love it with homemade venison sausages.

SERVES FOUR AS AN ENTREE

4 ounces country bacon, cut in
  small (1/4 inch) dice
8 Venison Sausages, 4 ounces
  each (page 198)
1 small onion, cut in small (1/4
  inch) dice (1 cup)
1 medium apple, cut in small (1/4
  inch) dice (2/3 cup)
2 pounds homemade or high-
  quality fresh sauerkraut,
  rinsed well and drained
1 bottle (12 ounces) beer
4 juniper berries
1 large bay leaf
1/2 medium potato, finely grated
salt and freshly ground black
  pepper

For Serving
boiled potatoes

1. Fry the bacon in a large frying pan or skillet until crisp. Remove and set aside. Put the sausages in the pan and brown on all sides. Remove the sausages and set aside.

2. In the same pan, fry the onion in the fat that remains. When limp (about 5 minutes), add the apple, sauerkraut, beer, juniper berries, bay leaf and bacon. Mix well, cover the pot and simmer gently for about 1 hour. Then add the grated potato and sausages. Simmer for 10 minutes more. Season with salt and pepper. Serve with boiled potatoes.

Venison Sausages

Use the forequarter, shanks and any other odd pieces of venison for grinding. If you have a smoker, try cold-smoking these sausages for a few hours. Smoked or plain, they are good panfried or grilled, and they go together with the sauces and side dishes suggested for Roast Venison (page 193).

MAKES TWENTY-FOUR 4-OUNCE
SAUSAGES

4 pounds trimmed venison, cut
  in small pieces
2 pounds fatback, rind removed,
  cut in small pieces
1 small onion, diced and sautéed
  in 1 tablespoon unsalted
  butter
6 sprigs fresh thyme, leaves only
6 juniper berries, very finely
  chopped
2 tablespoons cracked black
  pepper
2 tablespoons kosher salt
3 tablespoons freshly chopped
  Italian parsley
1/4 cup ice water

1. Combine all the ingredients *except* the salt, parsley and ice water. Mix well and chill. This can be done a day ahead. Also chill all the equipment that will come in contact with the meat.

2. Pass the mixture through the medium plate of a meat grinder. Keep both the meat and the parts of the grinder well chilled.

3. Add the salt, parsley and water. (If you add the parsley with the salt, you can see that the salt is well mixed in.) Make a small patty and fry it. Taste for salt and pepper; other flavorings are hard to detect properly at this point. Correct seasonings if necessary.

4. Stuff the sausages, following the directions on page 179.

Venison Burgers

Mix venison with fatback (about 3 ounces fatback for 1 pound venison) and grind twice through a medium grinder. Sauté some chopped onion in butter and mix that in. Form into patties and season with salt and pepper. Grill over charcoal and serve with all the traditional hamburger garnishes.

RABBIT

The humble rabbit was one of the many kinds of game that was the mainstay of the colonists' diet. It has remained a popular free food ever since. In the country the tradition of eating rabbit and other game in season continues, but in urban areas rabbit is in demand all year round. Commercially raised rabbits taste very good, although they are not as assertive in flavor as those from the wild. They make up for that in meatiness, which translates into juiciness. The recipes in this book were all tested using domestic rabbits.

Although the rabbit's body is somewhat different in size and shape from other meat animals, it has the same bone structure. Because of the rabbit's size, it is'cut a bit differently. It can also be roasted whole. The rabbit is basically broken down into three parts: the forequarter, the saddle (rib and loin sections) and the hind legs. For stew and a few other preparations, it can be cut into smaller pieces than these. The forequarter, as on all animals, is the least tender part. It is excluded in many gourmet presentations, often being used only to flavor the sauce, but I do use it in many rabbit dishes. The saddle, which is the whole back containing the two loins, is the most highly prized cut. It can be roasted whole (then the meat is removed and sliced) or it can be boned out and the meat sautéed. The hind legs are nice for roasting, sautéing or stewing; they are very meaty. All the meat on the rabbit can be ground for use in pâtés, terrines, sausages and pies. The liver of the rabbit is especially delicious and should be used whenever possible.

Rabbit is usually grouped with poultry because the preparations for chicken (ingredients, flavorings and even methods) can be used almost interchangeably with rabbit. The actual cooking times are different. For roasting, frying and sautéing, rabbit requires a little less cooking time than chicken, but for braising it needs more. Rabbit can be eaten medium rare to medium, but if it is to be well done, it has to be braised. The long cooking time allows the braising liquids to permeate the meat.

Warm Terrine of Rabbit with Prunes and Apples

This is a very coarse terrine, almost resembling a dense stuffing, but the addition of cubed bread makes it rather light in comparison with others. It can be served as an appetizer or even as a small main course for lunch. Be absolutely sure that where this recipe calls for small dice, the pieces are no larger than a quarter of an inch. As with any charcuterie, be sure to keep all the ingredients and equipment well chilled.

MAKES ONE EIGHT-CUP TERRINE

1 rabbit, about 3½ pounds dressed
1 cup Reduced Veal Stock (page 328) and 3 cups of water or 4 cups of water
1 bay leaf
¼ pound dried prunes
about ⅓ to ½ cup cognac or good-quality brandy
1 rabbit liver (or 2 if available)
¼ pound slab country bacon, rind removed and cut in ½-inch pieces
2 tablespoons unsalted butter
1 small onion, cut in small (¼ inch) dice (1 cup)
2 stalks celery, peeled and cut in small (¼ inch) dice (½ cup)
1 apple, peeled and cut in small (¼ inch) dice (1 cup)
4 whole eggs, beaten
6 sprigs fresh thyme, leaves removed and chopped
4 juniper berries, very finely chopped
1 tablespoon salt
½ tablespoon ground black pepper
½ stale baguette (long French bread), crust removed, cut in small (¼ inch) dice (2 cups)
1 pound thinly sliced bacon, for wrapping

For Serving
Cranberry–Onion Jam (page 342) or natural sauce (see Note)

1. Completely bone out the rabbit, removing any sinews and cutting all the meat into small pieces. Chop up half of the bones and put in a saucepan with the stock and water or just water. Use the remaining bones to make a natural sauce, if desired (see Note). Add the bay leaf and simmer slowly, uncovered, for about 2 hours, until the stock is reduced to 1 cup. Strain and reserve.

2. Put the prunes in a small bowl and pour in enough brandy to cover. Set aside.

3. Mix the rabbit meat with the liver and country bacon. The total weight of the combined meats will be about 1½ pounds. Grind twice, using the medium blade. If you are using a food processor, be careful not to overpuree the meat and bacon; it should have somewhat of a coarse texture. Keep chilled.

4. Heat the butter in a sauté pan and add the onion and celery. After 1 minute, add the apple and cook for another 30 seconds. Remove from heat and allow to chill. Pit the prunes and cut in small pieces (½ inch).

5. In a mixing bowl, combine the ground rabbit mixture with the sautéed onion, celery and apple. Add the beaten eggs, the stock, prunes, thyme, juniper berries, salt and pepper. Mix well. Fold in the bread cubes and mix only enough to distribute them evenly. Make a small patty and fry it until cooked. Taste for proper seasoning.

6. Preheat the oven to 350 degrees. Line an 8-cup terrine with sliced bacon. Put the mixture in the terrine and bang on the table, to make sure it is well packed. Cover the top with more bacon.

7. Put the lid or aluminum foil on the terrine to seal it tight. Place the terrine in a deep pan that is slightly larger than the terrine. Pour enough boiling water in the pan to cover about 1 inch of the bottom of the terrine and place in the oven. Cook for 1 hour 30 minutes. To see if it is done, insert a skewer and touch it to your lip; it should be warm and clean.

8. Allow the terrine to rest at least 30 minutes before unmolding and slicing. If you prefer, you can allow it to cool and then warm individual slices (covered with buttered parchment paper) in a low oven when needed. Serve with cranberry–onion jam or natural sauce.

NOTE. To make a natural rabbit sauce, follow the directions for Natural Pork Sauce (page 183). After the sauce is strained, reheat with port wine to taste (about ¼ cup port to 1 cup sauce).

Rabbit Stew with Red Wine, Bacon, Wild Mushrooms and Pearl Onions

This stew is adapted from the classic chicken dish, *coq au vin*. It has plenty of vegetables in it, so all you need is a starch. Buttered noodles are a good match, but my favorite is thick, crusty garlic bread. It is fabulous for mopping up the sauce.

SERVES FOUR TO SIX
AS AN ENTREE

2 rabbits, about 4 pounds each

Red Wine Marinade
1 bottle (750 milliliters) Chianti
    or other dry red wine
4 bay leaves
1 medium onion, finely chopped
6 cloves garlic, finely chopped
4 sprigs of thyme, leaves only

½ pound slab country bacon, cut
    in ½-inch cubes
salt and freshly ground black
    pepper
1 cup all-purpose flour for
    dredging
vegetable oil
2 cups Reduced Veal Stock
    (page 328)
1 pint basket pearl onions
    (¾ pound), blanched and
    peeled
1 pound wild mushrooms, cut in
    bite-size pieces
4 medium carrots, peeled and
    cut into ½-inch cubes
¼ cup coarsely chopped Italian
    parsley

1. Cut up the rabbit as described on page 199. Mix together the marinade ingredients in a pan large enough to hold the rabbit pieces. Add the rabbit and mix well; refrigerate overnight (12 to 24 hours).

2. Preheat oven to 350 degrees. Remove the rabbit from the marinade and allow to drain, reserving the marinade. Render the bacon in a large heavy casserole until it begins to crisp. Remove the bacon and set aside. Season the rabbit pieces and dredge in flour. Shake off any excess. Brown the pieces in the hot bacon fat and remove as they are done. If there is not enough fat left, you may need to add a little oil. When all the pieces are browned, add the marinade and stock; put the rabbit pieces back into the pan. Bring to a boil, skim, and reduce heat to a simmer. Cover and place in the preheated oven.

3. After 40 minutes, remove the stew from the oven and add the pearl onions, wild mushrooms, carrots and bacon cubes. Put back in the oven and cook for 30 minutes more. Check the seasoning. Arrange the stew on a large platter and sprinkle generously with coarsely chopped parsley.

Crispy Fried Rabbit

Suffice it to say that this is my demented version of southern fried chicken. It may not be New England, but it's too much fun to leave out. I like my fried rabbit plain and simple just with lemon wedges, but some people may prefer it with a spicy Rémoulade Sauce (page 333) or mustard sauce. Cole Slaw (page 231) and Shoestring Potatoes (page 250) make good accompaniments.

SERVES FOUR TO SIX
AS AN ENTREE

2 rabbits, about 4 pounds each

Cider Vinegar Marinade
1 cup cider vinegar
1 cup vegetable oil
2 lemons, sliced
1 medium onion, thinly sliced
1 head of garlic, peeled and
   chopped
6 bay leaves, broken
2 tablespoons dried oregano
4 sprigs of fresh thyme
2 tablespoons cracked black
   pepper

For Panfrying
about 2 cups all-purpose flour
salt and freshly ground pepper
cayenne pepper
about 3 cups milk
vegetable oil for frying

1. Since the rabbit will be marinated for at least 2 days and since the liver is best very fresh, remove it and fry it up for a butcher's snack while you are cutting up the rabbits. To cut up a rabbit remove the front legs; cut off the lower part of the leg and reserve it for sauce or discard. Repeat with the hind legs. Using a small cleaver or large heavy knife, cut the hind leg across the bone into 2 pieces. Trim up the saddle (back), removing the belly flap, the neck, and the tail bone of the rabbit (where the legs were removed). Take the long carcass and chop straight across, cutting it into 3 or 4 pieces, depending on the size of the rabbit. Repeat the procedure for the second rabbit. This will give you a total of 9 or 10 pieces per rabbit. (This method is the same as for bone-in stews.)

2. Mix together the marinade ingredients in a pan large enough to hold all the rabbit pieces. Add the rabbit pieces; they should be completely covered by the marinade. Marinate in the refrigerator for at least 2 days, turning the meat twice a day. Leave in the marinade until you are ready to cook.

3. Put the flour in a pan and mix with salt, pepper and cayenne pepper to taste. Taste the flour mix or cook a test piece of rabbit and correct the seasoning. Pour the milk in another pan and have a third pan at hand to put the pieces on. Pour about ½ inch of oil into a deep heavy cast-iron skillet and preheat until hot but not smoking. Working with a few pieces at a time, take the rabbit out of the marinade and place in the milk. Remove from the milk, drain and roll in the seasoned flour. Put the pieces back in the milk and repeat the process. Fry the double-floured rabbit pieces until golden brown on all sides. Continue until all the rabbit is cooked.

7 Eggs, Cheese and Other Dairy Products

Eggs

Hard-Boiled Eggs

Soft-Boiled Eggs with Deep-Fried Potato Skins

Poached Eggs

Poached Eggs on Thin Johnnycakes with Caviar

Scrambled Eggs

Omelets

Shirred Eggs

Quail Eggs

Cheese

Vermont Cheddar Cheese Soup

Seafood Rarebit

New England Cheddar Cheese Pie with Green Onions and Walnuts

Baked Macaroni and Many Cheeses

Grilled Leeks Stuffed with Goat Cheese and Served with a Spring Salad

Aunt Josephine's Farmer's Cheese with Peppers

Ricotta Cheese Filling

Milk and Other Dairy Products

Great eggs, butter, cream and cheese are one of the reasons I love New England. They are an extremely important part of our way of cooking. Farm-fresh cream and butter can do a lot more for a lobster stew than herbs and spices. When using these high-quality everyday products, one begins to understand the beauty of the simple dishes of our region. Without them the authentic character of chowders, seafood stews and other New England dishes can be obscured.

EGGS

"BROWN EGGS ARE LOCAL EGGS AND
LOCAL EGGS ARE FRESH."
—*MARKETING SLOGAN*

Brown eggs are something of an oddity in most places around the country, but New Englanders prefer them. The Rhode Island Red, the New Hampshire and the Plymouth Rock (all obviously of New England origin) are still the most popular chickens for egg production in our region, and all these hens lay brown eggs. I have become so used to brown eggs that I am sometimes startled when I cook in other parts of the country to pick up a white one. It just doesn't feel right. The shell seems frail, and I can't get used to the color. But, of course, white eggs will work just fine in all the recipes in this book.

The egg is more than just a food, it is a phenomenon. It has more uses than any other ingredient in the kitchen. As the great Escoffier once said, "Of all the products put to use by the art of cookery, not one is so fruitful of variety, so universally liked, and so complete in itself as the egg." In any discussion of eggs, the words *complete* and *versatile* crop up time and time again. We have become so dependent on the egg that without it we would have to recreate the art of cooking as we know it today.

In America the egg means the egg of a chicken. Unlike Europe, there are virtually no duck eggs available commercially. In Florida and other parts of the South turtle eggs were once quite popular for baking, but there is a ban now on taking the eggs of this endangered species. Quail eggs are being used more frequently these days. They are useful as appetizers and garnishes, but not practical for baking and other purposes.

"Farm-fresh eggs" is one of those ambiguous marketing phrases. Just what does it mean? Fresh as in not frozen? Farm versus downtown? Having spent four years of my childhood on a farm, I have had some firsthand experience with fresh eggs from free-ranging hens. The difference in the quality of their eggs is striking. Hens that forage on some greens, for example, lay eggs with deeply colored, rich and very flavorful yolks, and they are fresh. Most store-bought eggs are at least a couple of weeks old. For most uses these eggs are fine, but for omelets, fried eggs and other preparations where the egg is the main ingredient, there is no substitute for true farm-fresh eggs; they are heavenly.

Hard-Boiled Eggs

The hard-boiled egg has hundreds of uses in salads, hors d'oeuvres, garnishes and sauces, yet a perfect hard-boiled egg is a rarity. Here is my absolutely foolproof method for hard-boiling eggs.

Find a pot that is just the right size to hold the eggs you wish to boil in a single layer. Cover with cold water. Add a little distilled vinegar and salt to the pot. Put on high heat and bring to a boil. Reduce the heat so the eggs boil gently, not furiously. Continue boiling for exactly 6 minutes and remove from the heat. Allow to stand for 10 minutes, then rinse under cold running water. Peel the eggs (they should peel very easily) or store them in their shells.

Soft-Boiled Eggs with Deep-Fried Potato Skins

Potato skins make fabulous spoons for eating soft-boiled eggs. Serve them on a side dish, on a napkin if you wish, with the eggs cooked to order. Be sure everyone knows what the skins are for. Have the table set with salt, a peppermill and softened butter. Some people like their soft-boiled eggs with hot-pepper sauce.

MAKES FOUR BREAKFAST
PORTIONS

2 medium-size Idaho or other
   baking potatoes
vegetable oil for frying
salt
white vinegar
8 eggs
For Serving
freshly ground black pepper
unsalted butter, softened
hot-pepper sauce (optional)

1. The night before, scrub the potatoes and bake in a preheated 400-degree oven for 40 minutes. Allow to cool, then refrigerate.

2. Cut the potatoes lengthwise into 6 pieces each; trim, leaving about ½ inch of potato attached to the skin. Shortly before serving, start heating the oil to 350 degrees in a pot suitable for deep-frying.

3. Just before serving, fill a saucepan with water, add a little salt and white vinegar, and bring to a slow boil. Gently lower the eggs into the water and check the clock. Time the eggs to your liking. For the classic 3-minute egg, allow 4 minutes so the white is softly set and the yolk warm but still creamy and runny. Remove eggs from water and serve immediately. (The eggs may be cooked longer, as much as 5 or 6 minutes.)

4. While the eggs are cooking, deep-fry the potato skins until golden brown and very crisp. Drain on paper towels and sprinkle with salt and pepper. Serve immediately with salt, pepper, butter and hot-pepper sauce, if using.

Poached Eggs

Poached eggs are most often served on toasted bread or English muffins with a little butter, salt and pepper, but that is only the beginning. You could put them in tartlet shells (page 284) or puff-pastry shells and top them with a light cheese sauce. Or you could use artichoke bottoms, scooped-out baked potatoes or large grilled mushroom caps as a base and top the eggs with a savory sauce made with onions, garlic, tomato or anchovies. Poached eggs served on top of Red Flannel Hash (page 168) are very traditional. Another good dish from the New England repertoire is poached eggs with finnan haddie (page 102) or other smoked fish.

For great poached eggs, the eggs must be very fresh. Then they will have a warm but still runny yolk completely enveloped by the white and a nice oval shape. Here is how I cook poached eggs.

Fill a deep skillet with 2 inches of water. Add white vinegar (2 tablespoons for 4 eggs) and a little salt. Heat the water until it is barely simmering; maintain that temperature throughout. Break the eggs, one at a time, into a saucer or small bowl and slide into the water. Have a bowl of warm water on the side. Simmer for about 4 minutes. When the white is set, remove the egg with a slotted spoon and dip in the warm water to remove the vinegar. Place on a paper towel to drain; trim off any ragged pieces of the white. Serve at once.

NOTE. If you are cooking many eggs, place them in cold water to stop the cooking. Trim and reheat them all at once for 30 seconds to 1 minute in plain salted water.

Poached Eggs on Thin Johnnycakes with Caviar

This is my all-time favorite poached-egg dish. It makes a fabulous breakfast, lunch or late-night treat. It can also serve as a first course for dinner, but it is rich and the rest of the menu should be planned accordingly.

Make 4 Thin Johnnycakes (page 262) and 1 poached egg per person. Fan the johnnycakes around the plate and place a poached egg in the center. Melt a little butter and add some chopped chives and freshly ground black pepper. Spoon the butter over the eggs. Put a large dollop of caviar on top and serve at once. I prefer osetra or beluga caviar.

Scrambled Eggs

Scrambled eggs can be served at virtually any hour of the day or night and can be as plain or as fancy as the occasion and your budget allow. I like all the traditional garnishes—hash browns or home-fried potatoes, bacon or ham—but of these I like Breakfast Sausages (page 180) the best. Nor am I averse to scrambled eggs with truffles: with black truffles it is a great dish; with white truffles it is even better (directions follow the basic recipe).

For good scrambled eggs that are set through but still nice and creamy, allow for carry-over cooking, which occurs after the eggs are removed from the pan. Be sure to use a well-seasoned or nonstick omelet pan for best results. Count two to three eggs per person and about one tablespoon of added ingredients per serving. Heat a well-seasoned or nonstick omelet pan with a moderate amount of butter to medium hot. Break the eggs into a bowl, season lightly with salt and freshly ground black pepper and whisk until smooth and slightly airy. When the butter is bubbling, add the eggs to the pan. Allow the eggs to set a bit, then stir them or shake the pan. Continue until the eggs begin to set up. Remove from the heat and pour on 1 teaspoon of cream or crème fraîche for each egg. Stir gently and serve at once.

VARIATIONS

Truffles — Two nights ahead of time, place the eggs, *in the shell,* in a container with a whole white or black truffle; the eggs will absorb flavor from the truffle. Brush and peel the truffle. Reserve the rest of the truffle for another use or add more to the peelings. Chop the peelings and cook in butter. Add to the eggs as soon as they are put into the pan.

Smoked Fish — Add small boneless pieces of smoked fish such as salmon, trout, whiting, sable, or finnan haddie right before adding the cream.

Bacon or Ham — Add diced pieces of cooked bacon or ham right after the eggs are put into the pan.

Cheese — Grate some Cheddar, gruyère, parmesan, mozzarella or almost any other cheese and fold into the scrambled eggs right before the cream. Mixed cheeses also work nicely.

Herbs — Finely chop a handful of herbs such as parsley, tarragon, chervil and chives (or combine them for fines herbes); stir into the whisked eggs.

Combinations — Combine ingredients; for example: bacon, tomato and cheese; onions, peppers and ham; mushrooms and fines herbes; smoked salmon and caviar.

Omelets

Except for the western omelet (very popular in the East), only a few Americans knew how to make a proper omelet until Julia Child came on the scene in the early sixties. Yet nothing could be simpler, or more versatile. There are countless ways to garnish an omelet and the ingredients can be added several ways for different effects. First, they can be stirred into the uncooked eggs. This is best for fines herbes (or other minced herbs) and for savory cheeses like parmesan or romano; sautéed onion, green pepper and ham are added at this point for a western omelet. Second, and this is the most common way, a filling is placed on the flat omelet before it is rolled. Sometimes a plain omelet is rolled up, placed on the plate and sliced down the middle to create a pocket. This last method is best for loose fillings, like ratatouille.

Always make individual omelets, allowing two or three eggs each and two or three tablespoons filling per omelet. For best results, have the filling ready, work fast and use a well-seasoned or nonstick omelet pan. Beat together the eggs with a pinch of salt and pepper, just until they are blended. Set a well-seasoned or nonstick pan over high heat and add about 1 tablespoon butter. Allow the butter to foam; just as it begins to color, pour in the eggs. Wait a few seconds, then stir the eggs with a wooden spoon with one hand while shaking the pan with the other. Right before the eggs reach the scrambled stage, stop stirring and shaking. Lower the heat and allow the omelet to set on the bottom. At this point add the filling, if using, placing it on the lower third of the omelet. Raise the handle so that the pan is tilted at a 45-degree angle. Pound the handle a few times to make the omelet roll itself up. Invert onto a serving plate.

VARIATIONS

Caviar Make a plain omelet, split it down the center and fill it with crème fraîche or sour cream and top with osetra or beluga caviar.

Seafood Use fresh shrimp, lobster, oysters and the like, plain or cooked in a sauce, as filling. Most often a plain omelet split down the middle works best.

Cheese Almost any cheese can be used in an omelet. Add finely grated sharp cheeses like parmesan directly to the uncooked eggs. Sprinkle grated or sliced Cheddar or mozzarella or other semisoft cheeses over the omelet before rolling. Crumble or spoon cheeses like feta or soft goat cheese onto the omelet before rolling.

Herbs Add finely chopped herbs, fines herbes or others, to the uncooked eggs.

Vegetables Cook vegetables like asparagus, tomatoes, onions, peppers, eggplant, squash and so on in butter and add to the omelet before rolling. Place vegetable stew-type concoctions like ratatouille or Creole sauce in the center of a plain omelet that is split down the middle.

Mushrooms	Sauté any type of mushroom in butter with garlic and add to the omelet before rolling. Or stew the mushrooms in a bit of cream and spoon them into the center of a split omelet.
Combinations	Combine two or more ingredients; for example: lobster, tomato and herbs; ham and mushrooms; asparagus and cheese; creamed leeks with bacon and oysters.

Shirred Eggs

Shirred eggs have a wonderful soft and creamy texture. They are usually baked in a flat dish, and the oven has to be hot enough to cook them evenly from both the top and the bottom. Shirred eggs can also be prepared under the broiler (see the variations at the end of the recipe). Timing is very important as a minute too much or too little can make all the difference; you must also allow for carry-over cooking, which occurs after the dish is removed from the oven. For best results, prepare shirred eggs in individual portions, using a dish just large enough for two eggs. Flameproof earthenware or porcelain dishes are best, but ovenproof glass is quite serviceable.

Preheat the oven to 400 degrees or preheat the broiler to very hot. Break 2 eggs into a saucer or small bowl. Place a flameproof, ovenproof dish over low heat. Add about 1 tablespoon unsalted butter to the dish; when it begins to foam, slide in the eggs. Allow about 30 seconds for the eggs to begin to congeal on the bottom. Tilt the dish ever so slightly and spoon a bit of the butter over the top of the eggs. Season lightly with salt and freshly ground black pepper and place in the preheated oven. Check after 4 or 5 minutes. The whites should be barely set with the yolks still runny but warm and covered with a thin shiny layer of white. Squeeze a few drops of fresh lemon juice over the eggs and serve at once.

VARIATIONS

Brown Butter	Before adding the eggs to the dish, cook the butter until it has a light brown color and nutty aroma. Proceed as with regular shirred eggs, basting the eggs with the brown butter. Sprinkle with a few drops of lemon juice.
Herb Butter	Substitute a compound butter made with lemon and light herbs like parsley, chervil, chives and tarragon for unsalted butter.
Cheese and Cream	Preheat broiler to very hot. Start as for regular shirred eggs, using only ½ tablespoon butter. After the bottom is set, spoon 1½ tablespoons heavy cream on top of the eggs and sprinkle with grated parmesan, romano or sharp Cheddar cheese. Place under the broiler until the cheese is lightly browned and the eggs are set.

Tomatoes, Anchovies and Cheese	Preheat the broiler to very hot. Instead of butter, heat a bit of spicy fresh tomato sauce in the dish. Slide the eggs into the sauce and allow the bottoms to begin to set. Lay 2 anchovy fillets on top of the eggs and sprinkle with grated parmesan or romano cheese. Season with freshly ground black pepper (salt will not be needed) and dot with butter or sprinkle with olive oil. Place under the broiler until the cheese is lightly browned and the eggs are set.

Quail Eggs

As quail has become popular, so have quail eggs found their way to many fine kitchens. Quail eggs vary in color from beige to brown with irregular dark speckles; they are about an inch long. Whole or cut in half, they can be used many ways—in hors d'oeuvres, main dishes, salads and soups. They make very tasty deviled eggs. Quail eggs are stronger in flavor than chicken eggs, and they cook differently. The yolk takes longer to cook than you would imagine. Although quail eggs are sometimes poached or even fried, they are most commonly hard-boiled.

Put the eggs in a pot that will hold them in a single layer. Cover with cold water; add a little salt and distilled vinegar. Place on high heat and bring to a boil; turn down to simmer for 2 minutes. Remove from heat and allow to stand for 6 minutes, then run under cold water. Peel very gently. If not to be used right away, the hard-boiled eggs may be stored in their shells.

CHEESE

In cheese-making, as in wine-making, the craftsman changes a natural food into a finished, manmade product. It takes skill and artistry to create great or even good products, but the craftsman is always limited by the raw ingredient, be that a bunch of grapes or a vat of milk. Great milk explains why New England has long been—and continues to be—an important cheese-making region. For centuries, its lush and fertile rolling hills and valleys have been the home of some of America's first and finest (though small) dairy herds.

Milk is a product of the soil, just like grapes. The flavor of milk varies from month to month, from herd to herd, and from pasture to pasture. In New England the best cheeses are made in June when the milk is scented with the sweetness of the buttercups that cover the meadows. When the milk of several herds, no matter how high the quality, is blended, something is lost. One can still find cheese-makers in New England who use only the milk from their own herd, but the economics of this practice are such that it has become impossible to expand a cheese-making operation and still maintain the integrity of a one-herd cheese.

Although there is a resurgence of certain types of cheese-making in New England, the Cheddar producers are on an artistic downswing. Cheddar is one of the most difficult and most expensive cheeses to make, and even slight variations in milk quality or in the process of cheddaring have profound consequences. The English colonists brought their knowledge of cheddaring to New England, where cheese was made for the first time in the New World. By the time of the Revolution, Cheddar cheese was referred to as Yankee cheese. To this day, English farmhouse Cheddar is the rule that all Cheddars are measured by. The farmhouse Cheddars of England are like single vineyard estate wines. They are only made in summer from the milk of one herd on one specific farm; any other kind is called factory Cheddar. The first factory cheeses in America were made in New England about 1850. They became known as store cheese or rat cheese, terms that are still used in some parts of our region. As far as commercial Cheddars are concerned, our neighbors in Quebec, Canada, win hands down.

Some of the best Cheddar in North America can still be found in Vermont; it's just getting harder to find. For my restaurant, I buy Cheddar in 40-pound blocks from a very small Vermont cheese-maker. His Cheddar is as superb as any English farmhouse cheese. Because of limited supplies, this source is too precious to share, but in the List of Sources there are several good cheese purveyors who sell the finest of Cheddars. Among the high-quality brands of New England Cheddar are Cabot, Plymouth, Crowley (Colby style) and Shelburne Farms.

Gouda and smoked gouda are another type of cheese that has been produced in New England since the 1800s. There are several fine producers, the most notable being Dave Smith of Smith's Country Cheese. This rich and flavorful cheese is not as versatile as Cheddar, but it does have some value as a cooking cheese and is a wonderful table cheese.

Another famous and unique New England cheese is North Pack from New Hampshire. It has a pronounced flavor and is similar to the Canadian Oka and some of the monastery cheeses of Europe.

The newcomers in cheese-making are the producers of soft-ripened cheeses. Drawing their inspiration from the French, these cheese-makers have made remarkable strides in a relatively short time. They are already producing cheeses far superior to the commercial Bries and Camemberts, domestic and imported, that have flooded the American market. Among the best are Craigston Camembert from Wenham, Massachusetts, and Mont-Bert and Mont-Brie from the Guilford Cheese Company in Guilford, Vermont.

Goat's milk cheese is also being produced on a commercial scale for the first time in New England. Goats are well suited to the terrain, and their milk makes wonderful-tasting cheese. There are several people producing a high-quality montrachet-style soft creamy goat cheese, as well as a blue goat cheese. The most notable producers are Westfield Farm in Hubbardston, Massachusetts, and Rawson Brook Farm in the Berkshires.

The last important group of cheeses produced in New England are the fresh cheeses, including farmer's cheese, *fromage blanc,* ricotta, mozzarella, and feta. Farmer's cheese is an old-fashioned small-curd kind of cottage cheese; it can still be found on certain farms scattered about the countryside. *Fromage blanc,* although rare, is produced in limited quantities by some cheese-makers. This creamy, runny fresh cheese is wonderful for dessert, with fresh berries for example. The ethnic fresh cheeses (ricotta, mozzarella, and feta) are more often produced in the city than in the country. These are important cheeses for cooking. The very best ricotta and mozzarella are made in downtown Boston at Purity Cheese, right around the corner from my restaurant.

Many recipes in this book include cheese; those in this chapter feature cheese. In my opinion, though, the most important function of cheese is to be eaten as is; this is the true test of any cheese. Cheese can be a substitute for dessert, an addition to the meal or a meal in itself. The high-quality native cheeses available to us today should be savored with good wine or beer (Cheddar is best with beer). They are a labor of love and they merit a more important place on the American table.

Vermont Cheddar Cheese Soup

This classic New England soup is one of the most nourishing and heart-warming that I know of. It is rich and should be served in small portions as a starter or as a main course for lunch during the cool and cold months of the year. If you are serving it as a main course, you may wish to add some diced cooked ham at the last minute. Another, more elaborate garnish is described at the end of the recipe.

Be extra careful not to boil the soup once the cheese has been added. Once the soup is ready, keep it hot in a double boiler. If there is any left over, reheat it in a double boiler. And remember, the soup will only be as good as the cheese you use.

SERVES FIVE AS A MAIN COURSE
OR TEN AS A STARTER

1 medium onion, diced (1 cup)
2 stalks celery, diced (¾ cup)
1 medium carrot, peeled and
    diced (½ cup)
6 tablespoons unsalted butter
4 tablespoons all-purpose flour
4 cups Chicken Stock (page 327)
1 cup heavy cream
½ pound Cheddar cheese, grated
1 teaspoon Coleman's dry
    mustard
about 1 teaspoon Worcestershire
    sauce
hot-pepper sauce
salt and freshly ground black
    pepper

1. Put a heavy soup pot on medium heat. Cook the onion, celery and carrot in butter until tender (about 5 minutes). Sprinkle the flour on top and cook for another 3 or 4 minutes, stirring constantly.

2. Slowly add the chicken stock, about ½ cup at a time, allowing the soup to thicken each time before adding more. When all the stock has been added, reduce heat to a slow simmer and cook for about 45 minutes or until thick enough to coat a spoon. Strain the soup into another heavy pot, using a coarse strainer. Push through as much of the vegetables as possible.

3. Bring the strained soup back to a very slow simmer. Add the cream, grated cheese and dry mustard. Stir until the cheese is melted and the soup is quite hot, but do not allow it to boil. Season to taste with Worcestershire sauce, hot-pepper sauce, salt and pepper. If the soup appears too thick, thin it with chicken stock, water or cream. Keep the soup hot in a double boiler, if necessary. Serve in warm bowls with toasted country bread on the side.

VARIATION

Garnish the soup with a vegetable *brunoise* and ham. To make the *brunoise*, finely dice about 1 cup onion, celery and carrot combined and sauté in 1 tablespoon butter. Stir in about ½ cup finely diced cooked ham. Mix into the soup just before serving.

Seafood Rarebit

I especially like this dish made with small Maine shrimp. The dish is hearty and perfect for the cold winter months when the shrimp are in season. (For more about Maine shrimp, see pages 34–38.) The dish can also be made with Maine or other crabmeat or with lobster.

SERVES FOUR TO SIX
AS A MAIN COURSE

3 tablespoons unsalted butter
2 egg yolks
1 teaspoon Dijon-type mustard
1 teaspoon Coleman's dry
  mustard
¼ to ⅓ cup ale or dark beer
1 cup peeled raw Maine shrimp
  or cooked Maine crab, picked
  over for shells and cartilage,
  or partially cooked lobster
  meat (see Note)
salt and freshly ground black
  pepper
10 ounces aged Cheddar cheese,
  grated (2½ cups)
about 2 teaspoons
  Worcestershire sauce
hot-pepper sauce or cayenne
  pepper
buttered toast points for serving

1. Melt 1 tablespoon butter in the top of a double boiler large enough for all the ingredients. Add the egg yolks, Dijon mustard, dry mustard and ¼ cup ale or beer. Whisk the ingredients until thoroughly blended. Continue to whisk occasionally until the mixture is quite hot, but do not allow it to boil at any point of the cooking.

2. Melt the remaining 2 tablespoons butter in a separate pan and begin to stew the shrimp, crab or lobster meat. Season lightly with salt and pepper.

3. Add the cheese, a little at a time, stirring constantly. When the mixture is smooth and creamy, season to taste with Worcestershire sauce, black pepper and hot-pepper sauce or cayenne pepper. Fold in the hot seafood, including all the butter and juices. If the mixture seems too thick, add a little more beer.

4. Place at least 4 buttered toast points (triangular or rectangular) in each dish and spoon the hot rarebit over them.

NOTE. About ½ pound Maine shrimp in the shell yields 1 cup peeled shrimp. Other small shrimp can be substituted. Maine crabmeat is sold already cooked and picked; half a pound equals about 1 cup. Other cooked crabmeat can be substituted. The meat from a chicken (1 pound) lobster amounts to about 1 cup meat. Partially cook the lobster as you would for sautéed lobster; consult the chart on page 44 for the correct cooking times.

New England Cheddar Cheese Pie with Green Onions and Walnuts

Back in the 1800s, visitors from Europe were often shocked to see pies served for breakfast as well as lunch and dinner in New England. Cheddar pie was surely a breakfast favorite then, although I think today it is more appropriate to serve it in small portions at lunch, along with salad, or in very small portions as a combination cheese and salad course. The original versions were sweet and dense. I have dropped the sugar altogether and lightened the filling a bit without changing the dish completely. I have seen quichelike recipes for Cheddar pie, but they are not authentic. This is.

MAKES ONE NINE-INCH PIE

½ recipe Thin Butter or Lard
  Crust (pages 284–285)
4 eggs
⅓ cup heavy cream
12 ounces aged Cheddar cheese,
  grated (3 cups)
6 scallions, thinly sliced
salt and freshly ground black
  pepper
hot-pepper sauce
½ cup chopped toasted walnuts

1. Preheat the oven to 350 degrees. Line a 9-inch pie pan with the butter or lard crust. Cover with foil and fill with rice, dried beans or pie beads. Bake for 15 minutes; remove the foil and beans and bake 10 minutes more.

2. Beat the eggs and place in the top of a double boiler along with the cream, cheese and scallions. Heat, stirring constantly, until creamy and hot, but not boiling. Season to taste with salt, pepper and hot-pepper sauce.

3. Pour the mixture into the pie crust and place in the preheated oven. After 10 minutes, sprinkle the chopped walnuts over the top and return to the oven. The pie should be almost completely covered with the nuts. Cook about 20 minutes more or until the filling is set and the top begins to brown lightly. Allow to cool somewhat, but not completely. Serve warm with salad.

Baked Macaroni and Many Cheeses

If you are a real cheese lover, you will undoubtably find yourself at times with a fridge full of cheese tidbits. There is no better use for these scraps than macaroni and cheese and there is none better than that made with lots of different types of cheese. Cheddar, gouda, blue, chèvre, parmesan, gorgonzola, mozzarella or any other cheese can be used in just about any combination. Of course Cheddar is the classic cheese for this dish and if you are buying cheese to make it, you should buy Cheddar; in fact, you will need some Cheddar to make this version work. It is especially important for the top of the casserole. Serve this as a very casual luncheon dish or late-night snack with a little salad to aid digestion.

SERVES FOUR TO SIX
AS AN ENTREE

12 ounces medium elbow macaroni (about 3 cups, uncooked)
6 tablespoons unsalted butter
1 small onion, cut in small (¼ inch) dice (1 cup)
2 tablespoons all-purpose flour
2 cups milk
10 to 12 ounces assorted cheeses (including Cheddar), grated (2½ to 3 cups)
salt and freshly ground black pepper
hot-pepper sauce or cayenne pepper
4 ounces Cheddar cheese, grated (1 cup)
1 cup breadcrumbs

1. Cook the elbow macaroni in a large pot of boiling salted water until cooked through, past al dente but not mushy. Rinse under cold water to stop cooking and drain well. Set aside.

2. Melt 3 tablespoons of the butter in a saucepan over low heat. Add the onion and cook until translucent (about 5 minutes). Add the flour and cook, stirring constantly, for about 3 or 4 minutes. Add the milk a little at a time, allowing the sauce to thicken before adding more. When all the milk has been added, allow the sauce to simmer, very slowly, for at least 20 minutes. Season to taste with salt, pepper and hot-pepper sauce or cayenne pepper. Stir in the assorted cheeses and when the cheese is nearly but not completely melted, remove from the heat and mix with the macaroni.

3. Preheat the oven to 375 degrees. Grease the casserole with the remaining butter, then melt the rest. Pour the macaroni mixture into the casserole. Sprinkle with Cheddar cheese and breadcrumbs and drizzle the melted butter over the top. Bake in the preheated oven for about 40 minutes, until bubbling and crispy brown on top.

Grilled Leeks Stuffed with Goat Cheese and Served with a Spring Salad

In the spring of 1988 I was asked to create a salad and cheese course for 800 people to celebrate the 50th anniversary of the March of Dimes, in Washington, D.C. An all-star cast was assembled by Pierre Franey, and I was determined to put my best foot forward. There must be easier salads in the world to make for 800: this one took four helpers and myself two days of preparation and then it took eight people four hours to put the salad on plates. They were beautiful. To make enough for eight people should take about one hour.

SERVES EIGHT AS AN APPETIZER

2 or 3 large leeks, about 1 inch in diameter
vegetable oil for grilling the leeks
½ pound montrachet-type goat cheese (see Note)
1 egg
2 tablespoons chopped Italian parsley
freshly ground black pepper
salt

Dressing
1 tablespoon finely chopped tarragon
2 tablespoons Dijon mustard
½ cup vegetable oil
¼ cup sherry or other good wine vinegar

mixed lettuce leaves, 4 or 5 per salad, rinsed
12 ounces asparagus, cut in 1-inch diagonal pieces, blanched
2 small carrots, peeled and sliced diagonally, blanched
1 cup fresh shell beans, such as cranberry beans or lima beans, cooked through
1 small baguette (French bread), cut into ½-inch croutons and lightly toasted

1. Trim off the dark green part of the leeks and reserve for other uses. Carefully cut down the full length of the leek, no deeper than the center. Wash the leeks under running cold water to remove all the dirt; shake dry or drain in a colander. Dredge the leeks in oil and place on a preheated grill or under the broiler. Grill the leeks on all sides until they are cooked through and are quite well done. Discard the charred outer leaves and allow the leeks to cool.

2. Set aside the 8 biggest leaves and chop the rest very fine; you should have about ½ cup.

3. Use your hands to mix half the chopped leeks with the goat cheese, egg and parsley. Stop mixing as soon as the ingredients are dispersed; overmixing will cause the cheese to thin out and become watery. Season to taste with pepper and add salt if needed. Put the cheese mixture in a pastry bag. Take a long leaf of leek and wrap it around two fingers to make a small cornucopia. Fill with the cheese mixture. Continue until all are filled. Place the cornucopias on a lightly oiled sheetpan and refrigerate until needed.

4. To prepare the dressing, mix the remaining chopped leeks (¼ cup) with the tarragon, mustard, oil, vinegar, salt and pepper. Allow to stand for at least 1 hour.

5. Shortly before serving, preheat the oven to 375 degrees, then place the well-chilled stuffed leeks in the oven. Cook for 10 to 12 minutes. Fan 4 or 5 lettuce leaves on the bottom of each 8- or 9-inch plate. When the leeks are cooked, place one in the center of each plate. Scatter some asparagus and carrot slices, beans and croutons around each plate. Drizzle a bit of dressing over each salad and serve at once.

NOTE. I like to use Capri goat cheese from Westfield Farm in Hubbardston, Massachusetts; Laura Chenel plain goat cheese is also good.

Aunt Josephine's Farmer's Cheese with Peppers

When I was a young boy, we often visited my Aunt Jo and Uncle Mike Palmere's farm, especially in the summertime, and we were sure to drive off with a carload of tomatoes, corn and fresh eggs. True to her Italian heritage, my Aunt Jo wouldn't think of allowing any visitor to leave on an empty stomach either. Her table reflected her environment: there was never a lot of any one thing, but there were always lots of different things. Lunch at Aunt Jo's might consist of sliced tomatoes with olive oil and vinegar, a green bean salad, roast peppers, homemade pickles (at least two or three kinds), olives, several cheeses, sliced cold meats and, of course, chewy Italian bread. Aunt Jo used to trade eggs for fresh farmer's cheese made by Mr. Jebello, the farmer across the road. She would mix the cheese at the last minute with a dice of peppers from her garden, some coarsely chopped parsley and a bit of salt and pepper. Like all the food she served, it was simple and utterly delicious.

MAKES SIX OR EIGHT SMALL
PORTIONS

12 sprigs Italian parsley
*1 large or 2 small bell peppers,
    green and/or red, cut in small
    (1/4 inch) dice*
*1 pound freshly made farmer's
    cheese (see Note)*
*salt and freshly ground black
    pepper*

1. Pick the leaves from the parsley and coarsely chop them.
2. Mix the peppers and parsley with the cheese and season to taste with salt and pepper. Keep chilled until ready to serve.

NOTE. Several places in New England still make farmer's cheese regularly. Depending on who makes it, it usually has small curds, somewhere between the size of ricotta and cottage cheese; its flavor should be clean, fresh and milky. Freshly made pot cheese or well-drained cottage or ricotta cheese may be substituted.

Ricotta Cheese Filling

Like farmer's or cottage cheese, ricotta can be eaten plain or mixed with vegetables and herbs, but it is most often used as a filling. When it is intended for cannoli, it needs only to be sweetened and flavored with lemon rind, vanilla or garnishes such as candied fruits or chocolate chips. Where cooking is required, some eggs have to be added to bind the cheese (two eggs per pound of ricotta), whether the filling is sweet or savory. This recipe is for a basic cheese stuffing for pasta. It can be adapted to different dishes by adding herbs, like sage or chives, or finely diced and sautéed onions, carrots, or peppers; it can also be mixed with ground meat. The recipe for pasta dough is on page 277.

MAKES ABOUT TWO CUPS FILLING

1 pound fresh ricotta cheese
2 eggs
*2 tablespoons dry marsala or
    sherry*
*1/2 cup finely grated parmesan or
    romano cheese*

1. Mix the ricotta, eggs and wine until smooth and creamy.
2. Fold in the grated cheese and chopped parsley. Season to taste with salt and pepper.

NOTE. Since my restaurant is in an Italian neighborhood, we buy our ricotta cheese around the corner at Purity Cheese, literally minutes after it is made. Commercially made ricotta is usually more watery than the good stuff one finds in such ethnic markets; it also

12 sprigs Italian parsley, leaves picked and coarsely chopped salt and freshly ground black pepper

varies from producer to producer. Even homemade ricotta can vary from one batch to the next. A good filling should be soft but not runny. If it is too loose, add more grated cheese or some white breadcrumbs. If it is too dry, add a little heavy cream.

MILK AND OTHER DAIRY PRODUCTS

I can dimly remember the milk box on the steps, filled with empty bottles waiting to be replaced with full ones in the early morning. That era must have ended sometime during my childhood, for my clearer recollection is of milk from cardboard containers. That change in containers represents a change in the nature and scope of the dairy business as the small dairy has been replaced by large dairy cooperatives that mix, pasteurize and homogenize huge quantities of milk to produce a consistent product. For better or worse, most milk and other dairy products taste virtually the same these days.

A few small high-quality dairies still exist in rural New England; they give their milk the minimum amount of processing. I remember working in New Hampshire a few years back and having heavy cream delivered in glass bottles. There was almost an inch of cream on top, so thick it could be spooned out. I can still get good cream from some farmers in Vermont; it is a lot of trouble because of the freshness factor, but well worth it. Working with this type of milk and cream reminds me that they are not products, they are foods, like apples, and they vary greatly. Some weeks the cream is richer than at other times, and in the summer it is sweeter. It is wonderful to experience these differences.

Such opportunities are rare; usually you have to use what is available. If you are fortunate enough to have a choice, though, you should support the smaller dairies. It costs more for these farmers to operate independently, but their goods are usually well worth the difference in price.

I use whole milk (not skimmed or low-fat) and heavy cream (not whipping or light cream) for cooking because it handles best. The high butterfat content acts as a stabilizer; you will rarely have problems with breaking or curdling when you use heavy or extra-heavy cream.

Crème Fraîche

Crème fraîche is an everyday dairy product in France that is becoming more and more popular in the United States. It is delicious on its own and very useful in cooking. Richer than sour cream and more mellow in flavor, it also reacts differently to heat. Since crème fraîche, unlike sour cream, can be boiled, it can be used to make thick, creamy soups and sauces. Some cheese-makers, like Guilford Cheese in Vermont, and dairy farmers are making crème fraîche, but if you cannot find it, it is easy enough to do at home.

Warm 2 cups of heavy cream to body temperature (test it on your wrist as you would milk from a baby's bottle). Remove from the heat and stir in 2 tablespoons buttermilk. Pour into a crock or glass container, cover loosely with plastic wrap and put in a warm place (70 to 80 degrees) until thickened (24 to 36 hours). Cover tightly and refrigerate. Allow 1 day in the refrigerator for the crème fraîche to develop its tangy flavor. It should keep about 1 week. After the first batch is made, use crème fraîche instead of buttermilk as a starter.

Butter

Butter is made from cream, and it can vary greatly in consistency and flavor. I use homemade sweet butter from Kate's in Old Orchard Beach, Maine, and every night customers comment on how delicious the butter we serve with bread is. I'm sure they notice the difference it makes in the food too, but most people are not attuned to the importance of the quality of the butter that is used in cooking. I guess it's a case of not missing what you've never known. But once you get used to great butter in your food, everything else tastes like margarine (which, incidentally, I never use). Recipes in this book call for unsalted butter to avoid confusion with butter that is labeled sweet but is actually salted, but what I would really like you to use is the freshest, sweetest butter you can find. (For more about butter, see pages 329–330.)

Vegetables

Asparagus
Asparagus and Wild Rice Soup

Asparagus Salad with Maine Crabmeat or Crab Turnovers

Asparagus *Poêlé*

Beans
Green Bean and Mint Salad

Shell Bean Succotash

Boston Baked Beans

Broccoli

Cabbage
Cole Slaw

Hot Cabbage Slaw

Ladies' Cabbage with Potatoes

Braised Sweet-and-Sour Red Cabbage

Ragout of Brussels Sprouts with Bacon, Apples and Walnuts

Corn
Corn on the Cob

Creamed Corn

Sweet Corn and Bread Pudding

Fiddlehead Ferns

Greens
Caldo Verde

Rabes in Garlic and Olive Oil

Mushrooms

The Onion Family
Roasted Garlic

Andy's Favorite Onion Rings

Old-Fashioned Glazed Onions

Grilled Leeks

Parsnips, Turnips and Other Root Vegetables
Brad's Root Soup with Blue Cheese Butter

Parsnip Puree

Parsnip Chips

Maple-Glazed Turnips

Gratin of Turnips and Potatoes

Peas, Snow Peas and Sugar Snaps
Minted Fresh Pea Soup

Petits Pois Simmered in Butter

Peppers and Chilies

Potatoes
All-American Potato Salad

Boiled or Steamed New Potatoes

Garlic Mashed Potatoes

French Fried Potatoes

Freddie's Famous Roast Potatoes

Potato Pancakes

Salad Greens
Mixed Green Salad

Mixed Greens with Red Onions, Green Beans, Blue Cheese and Olives

Parsley Salad

Warm Salad Greens with Sherry–Mustard Vinaigrette

Warm Spinach and Beet Salad with Bacon Dressing

Squash
Liz's Braised Butternut Squash

Tomatoes
Marinated Tomatoes and Arugula with Fried Squid

Without vegetables, food would be pretty boring. They add flavor, texture, color, variety, complexity and good nutrition to any meal. They also aid digestion. The extent to which vegetables improve our health is still being explored. My neighbor Casey Cunningham, a doctor involved in cancer research at Massachusetts General Hospital in Boston, has told me that it is now believed that certain vegetables may actually prevent cancer. One thing is certain, vegetables are good medicine, and every meal should be balanced with fresh vegetables.

Fresh, of course, is an imprecise term, which means different things to different people. When I speak of fresh, what I mean is very fresh, locally grown vegetables, preferably organically grown, whenever it is possible to obtain them. They are superior in flavor and better for you than vegetables that have been sprayed, waxed and gassed to make them last longer and look better. I actually find the imperfections of organic vegetables appealing, a reminder that, like people, each one is a little different. Preservatives that are used on commercial produce give the illusion of freshness to vegetables that have been trucked thousands of miles across the country or shipped across the seas. The reader should be aware of this practice, because unlike packaged foods, these require no labeling. Besides these possibly harmful preservatives, there is a loss in vitamins and nutrients that occurs in some vegetables after harvesting. This deterioration continues as they wait to be sold. There is also a loss in flavor and texture.

The vegetables we have come to consider year-round staples suffer the most from this situation because their acceptable but not wonderful condition has become the norm. Potatoes, carrots, onions and garlic have their glory days just like sweet corn and tomatoes. The flavor of a freshly picked potato is truly unique, very different from the stored potatoes we survive on most of the year. Even with commercial produce there are noticeable differences from season to season. Next May take a closer look at the garlic and onions and compare them with what you get in October. You will find that in the fall these imported vegetables are just a shadow of what they were when picked months earlier. Although it is impossible to cook year-round with locally grown vegetables exclusively, especially in New England, it is possible to learn when to feature different vegetables to create outstanding meals. And that is the single greatest asset a cook can have.

Before trucks, cans, freezers and refrigerators, New Englanders, like people all over the world, ingeniously managed to keep a supply of vegetables, humble though they might be, for most of the year. True, that supply got a little tight toward the end of the winter. The modernization of farming, shipping and storing vegetables was a mixed blessing. Although it provided relief for many people, it had a devastating effect on our tradition of eating locally produced vegetables and on our folk knowledge of the seasons' different bounties.

Although it is no longer necessary for New Englanders to eat root vegetables and cabbage all winter long, they are still the best choice when you consider the trucked vegetables available in our markets during January and February. The full flavor of root vegetables and cabbage lends itself to the hearty meals that are so appropriate for our long, harsh and cold winters. Like generations before us, we should learn to make the best of what is available to us.

As soon as the ground thaws, usually in late March or early April, a new year of fresh vegetables begins with the crop of sweet spring-dug parsnips, which were left in the ground all winter (see page 241). Shortly afterward, fiddleheads, morels, and asparagus appear, followed by an enormous variety of vegetables that last through the summer and into November (every now and then, as late as the first week of December) with squash, pumpkins and root vegetables. Because the growing season starts late in New England, the harvest of summer vegetables often overlaps with fall vegetables, making September and October months of marvelous variety, with combinations of fresh vegetables that rarely coincide in other regions.

Also particular to New England's late growing season is the beneficial effect of frost. Ken Ryan, a dedicated teacher and farmer who provides my restaurant with beautiful organically grown fruits and vegetables for a good part of the year, tells me "the varieties of broccoli, Brussels sprouts, kohlrabi, carrots, parsnips and onions, to name a few, that are grown in New England today owe their unique and sweet flavor to their exposure to frost."

"The harsh and unpredictable weather, over the centuries," says Ken, "has actually helped New England vegetables to evolve into the sweetest and strongest varieties available anywhere in the world today." Some of the finest and most respected seed suppliers in the United States are from New Hampshire, where Ken's farm is located, and Maine.

There is hardly a recipe in this book that does not include vegetables in one way or another. Cooking meat and vegetables or fish and vegetables together enhances both foods and is a more modern and nutritious approach to cooking. In this chapter I have focused on some individual vegetables used in the cooking of this region, offering my thoughts on purchasing and general cooking methods as well as specific recipes.

How to Cook Green Vegetables

The best way to prepare green vegetables like asparagus, green beans, broccoli and peas is to cook them, uncovered, in lots of boiling salted water. I recommend using at least two teaspoons of salt per quart of water. Salt heightens the flavor and helps retain or even improves the color. A large volume of water insures a quick return to a boil, also preserving color, flavor and texture. Cooking time will always vary according to the size and freshness of the vegetable, as well as the purpose it is to be used for. The only sure test is to bite into a piece. If the vegetable is to be reheated, it should be shocked by running under cold water or dipping in ice water. This blanching is the first step of most recipes using green vegetables. If you are going to serve the vegetable right away, drain well, then finish with butter or oil and seasonings.

Steaming is another good method for cooking green vegetables; in fact, many people feel it is a more healthful way to cook them. There is, however, a slight loss of color caused by steaming. I use about one inch of salted water with a steaming rack.

Other methods that are particularly suited to a certain type or size vegetable will be discussed with that vegetable.

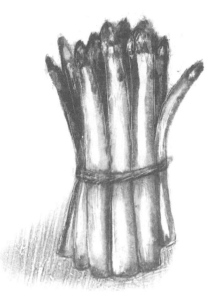

ASPARAGUS

The arrival of asparagus is one of the first and most welcome signs of spring. In New England asparagus usually start coming in at about the same time as fiddleheads in April, giving us our first and long-awaited taste of native green vegetables. Asparagus surely are one of the most loved and most versatile of all the vegetables. They make great accompaniments for fish or meat and are excellent in salads as well as soups. I prefer medium-size asparagus for side dishes and the thinner pencil asparagus for salads, but they can be used interchangeably. Large ones can be quite good when first picked but are more likely to be stringy and sometimes woody.

How to Cook Asparagus

Medium and large asparagus should be peeled gently from below the tip down. Some people tie asparagus in bundles to prevent the tips from being damaged while boiling. The method I use to blanch whole asparagus is to lay the spears flat in an appropriate size pan (a square one is perfect, if you have one) and pour boiling salted water over them at the same time they are put on the heat. This method is less time-consuming than bundling and still allows the asparagus to cook without rolling around. For garnish, cut the spears on the diagonal into one-inch pieces and blanch them in plenty of boiling salted water. Shock in cold water if the asparagus are not to be used immediately.

Asparagus and Wild Rice Soup

Wild rice gives good flavor without masking the asparagus and acts as a thickener as well as a garnish. The sweetened and toasted pecans add even more dimension.

SERVES EIGHT TO TEN
AS A STARTER

2 pounds asparagus
2 medium onions, cut in medium
  (½ inch) dice (2 cups)
2 tablespoons unsalted butter
1 cup wild rice
4 cups Chicken Stock (page 327)

Toasted Pecans
1 tablespoon unsalted butter
½ cup coarsely chopped pecans
1 teaspoon sugar
¼ teaspoon salt

1 cup heavy cream
salt and freshly ground black
  pepper
juice of ½ lemon

1. Wash the asparagus. Cut off the tips about 1½ to 2 inches from the top and set aside for garnish. Roughly chop the stalks.
2. Sweat the onion in butter in a heavy soup pot. After a few minutes add half the wild rice and the chicken stock. Simmer for 30 minutes, then add the stalks. Simmer 30 minutes more.
3. While the soup is cooking, prepare the garnishes. Cut the asparagus tips into ½-inch pieces and blanch in boiling salted water for 1 minute. Shock in cold water and set aside. Simmer the remaining ½ cup wild rice in lightly salted water for about 40 minutes or until cooked through. Drain and set aside.
4. Preheat the oven to 350 degrees. Melt 1 tablespoon butter in a sauté pan. Add the pecans, sugar and salt and toss until the butter is absorbed. Place on a sheetpan and toast in the preheated oven for 8 to 10 minutes.
5. After the soup has cooked for 1 hour, all told, puree in a food mill or food processor. Pass through a medium strainer to remove any asparagus strings.
6. Bring the soup back to a boil and add the asparagus and wild rice garnishes. Add the heavy cream and simmer 5 minutes more. Season to taste with salt, pepper and lemon juice. Ladle into bowls or soup plates and sprinkle with the toasted pecans.

Asparagus Salad with Maine Crabmeat or Crab Turnovers

Not all foods that come into season together combine as felicitously as do asparagus and our native Maine rock crabmeat. You can garnish this salad with either fresh crabmeat or hot turnovers made with fresh crabmeat; both are wonderful.

SERVES FOUR AS AN ENTREE
OR EIGHT AS AN APPETIZER

1½ pounds asparagus, cut into
  2-inch pieces on the bias
1 red onion, thinly sliced
1 cup Sherry–Mustard
  Vinaigrette (page 336)
8 to 10 cups mixed greens
freshly ground black pepper
4 hard-boiled eggs
1 pound fresh Maine crabmeat
  or 16 Maine Crabmeat
  Turnovers (page 41)

1. Blanch the asparagus pieces until tender. Shock under cold running water, drain and refrigerate for at least 30 minutes.
2. When ready to assemble the salad, place the asparagus in a mixing bowl with the sliced onion and the vinaigrette; toss. Add the salad greens, season with freshly ground pepper and toss again, very gently.
3. Carefully arrange the salad greens on plates with the greens mostly on the bottom and the asparagus and onions showing on top. Coarsely chop the hard-boiled eggs and sprinkle over the salad.
4. Garnish the salad with small mounds of fresh crabmeat or with hot crab turnovers.

Asparagus Poêlé

This is the best way I know to extract the full flavor of asparagus. They are steamed in their own juices with the help of only a little butter and a few drops of water. With a little poetic license I call the method *poêlé,* for lack of a better word to describe it. Time the asparagus so they go right from the oven to the table. When you uncover them, a wonderful aroma will fill the room.

SERVES FOUR AS A SIDE DISH

1 pound medium asparagus,
    peeled (see Note)
salt and freshly ground pepper
4 tablespoons unsalted butter

1. Preheat the oven to 350 degrees. Line up the asparagus in a covered casserole or earthenware dish that will hold all of them in no more than 2 layers. Season lightly with salt and pepper and dot with butter. Add 2 tablespoons water and cover tightly.

2. Place in the preheated oven. For medium asparagus allow 17 minutes; for larger ones, 20 minutes. Bring to the table and uncover.

NOTE. This method does not work well with pencil-thin asparagus.

BEANS

With the discovery of the New World came the discovery of hundreds of different types of haricot beans, an important staple of the Indians of both North and South America. Most of the traditional bean dishes of New England (for that matter all of America) have origins in American Indian cookery. Beans come in a kaleidoscope of colors and sizes. Some, like green beans, shell beans and limas, are eaten when young and tender; others, like pea beans, yellow eye and Jacob's Cattle, are allowed to mature fully and are usually dried.

Green Beans and Wax Beans

Green beans are at their peak in summer; the classic Blue Lake green bean is probably the finest variety. French *haricots verts,* which are quite slender and dark in color, seem to be growing in popularity. They are very tender and cook through in minutes. I have seen Chinese green beans as long as two feet at the market, but they are not cooked the same way as regular green beans. They should be deep-fried; then they are delicious, though not the most visually appealing. I have deep-fried regular geen beans, also with good results.

Usually green beans and yellow wax beans are blanched in lots of boiling salted water until tender. Bite one to test. It seems the emphasis on not overcooking vegetables has led a lot of people to undercook them, especially green beans. Most of the time I find this practice to be just as bad.

Blanched green beans and wax beans are excellent in salad or sautéed in butter. They can be seasoned lightly with just a little salt and pepper or more forcefully with ingredients like garlic, onion, tomato concassée (page 337), bacon, fresh herbs, nuts and lemon. Green beans go well with all types of seafood, poultry and meat, particularly lamb.

Green Bean and Mint Salad

Both my grandmother and her sister made this salad every summer with fresh green beans and mint from their gardens. I assume this preparation was passed down from their mother, who emigrated from Rome around the turn of this century. It is utterly simple and very tasty. The salad can be made early in the day, but the lemon should be added only at the last minute, just before serving. Tender young wax beans can be substituted or mixed with green beans if you like.

SERVES EIGHT TO TEN
AS A SIDE DISH

3 pounds green beans and/or
    wax beans
6 branches fresh mint, leaves
    picked and roughly chopped
    (¾ cup)
¾ cup olive oil
salt and freshly ground black
    pepper
juice of 1 lemon

1. Snap the stems off the beans and blanch in lots of boiling salted water until al dente (about 3 minutes). Shock in cold water to prevent further cooking.

2. Combine the beans, chopped mint and olive oil in a large bowl. Mix together and season to taste with salt and pepper.

3. Right before serving, squeeze the lemon juice into the salad and toss. Check the seasoning again.

Shell Bean Succotash

Succotash was an almost universal American Indian dish, consisting as it did of the two most common ingredients to be found in the New World, corn and beans. Nearly every tribe had its own version of the dish, from simple to quite elaborate. Succotash was most certainly served at the first Thanksgiving feast. In New England shell beans, also called cranberry beans or horticultural beans, were favored by the colonists when they adapted this dish.

SERVES EIGHT TO TEN
AS A SIDE DISH

¼ pound slab bacon, cut in
    small (¼ inch) dice
1 medium onion, cut in small
    (¼ inch) dice
1½ pounds shell beans (about 2
    cups shelled) or lima beans
    (see Note)
6 ears of corn, kernels shaved off
    cob (about 2 cups)
½ cup heavy cream
2 tablespoons finely chopped
    chives
salt and freshly ground black
    pepper

1. Render the bacon in a heavy pot or large skillet until it starts to crisp. Add the onion and cook for 5 minutes or until tender.

2. Add the shell beans and 2 cups water. Simmer slowly, adding more water if and when the pot begins to look dry, for 20 to 30 minutes or until the beans are tender and cooked through. Very fresh beans will require less cooking time than older beans.

3. Add the corn and heavy cream and simmer for 5 minutes more. Add the chives and season to taste with salt and pepper. Mix well and serve.

NOTE. Shell beans are usually available in New England markets during the summer and fall. If you cannot locate any, lima beans make a fine substitute.

Boston Baked Beans

The colonists first learned to cook dried beans from the American Indians, who depended on them as a staple food. The Indians of New England slow-cooked beans in underground pits inside deer hides, with maple sugar and bear fat. This dish evolved into cooking beans with salt pork and molasses in a bean pot very slowly, often overnight. The Puritans' belief in minimal work on the Sabbath led to the widespread practice of making beans on Saturday to be eaten on Sunday. Later it became customary for New Englanders to eat baked beans on Saturday. Some diehard Yankees still observe this once very popular ritual.

Here in Beantown we take baked beans pretty seriously and we like them a lot. No self-respecting Bostonian or any other New Englander would ever try to pass off canned beans as the real thing. People would know. You just have to make your own. Like the original Indian recipe, this one uses maple sugar—but it also uses molasses and salt pork like later versions. I have modified the sweetness of this dish to make it more compatible with a lot of different foods. It goes very well with venison and other game. Baked beans also go well with grilled chicken and almost any pork dish. Try them some time with a warm smoked loin of pork. Another interesting way to serve beans is to rebake them inside a baby pumpkin or acorn squash. It is traditional to serve Boston Brown Bread (page 270) with beans.

Many types of beans can be used for Boston baked beans. The only truly authentic bean, some Yankees will tell you, is the pea bean. Others will tell you it is Jacob's Cattle. Still others will tell you it is the yellow eye or soldier's bean or the navy or the Great Northern. I have cooked most all of the types of beans mentioned, and the results were quite similar. This recipe was tested using navy beans, but it will work with any small dried white bean.

SERVES SIX TO EIGHT
AS AN ENTREE

1 pound navy beans, pea beans
 or other small dried white
 beans
½ pound salt pork
1 medium onion, cut in medium
 (½ inch) dice
4 cloves garlic, finely chopped
1 cup tomato concassée
 (page 337)
1 teaspoon salt
2 teaspoons freshly ground black
 pepper
4 tablespoons Coleman's dry
 mustard
⅓ cup maple sugar
⅓ cup molasses
2 bay leaves
3 tablespoons cider vinegar

1. Place the beans in a pot or bowl and cover with cold water. Let stand overnight. The following morning, pick through the beans and discard off-colored or broken ones. Drain the beans.

2. Remove the rind from half of the salt pork and cut into ½-inch squares; cut the other half into ¾- to 1-inch-thick strips (4 or 5 strips), leaving the rind attached. Set aside.

3. Preheat the oven to 250 degrees. Line the bottom of an earthenware crock or bean pot with the squares of salt pork and the onion. Place the beans on top.

4. Bring 1 quart of water to a boil in a saucepan and add the garlic, tomato concassée, salt, pepper, dry mustard, maple sugar, molasses, bay leaves and vinegar. Simmer for 1 minute. Mix well and pour over the beans.

5. Score the strips of salt pork crosswise, about every inch, without cutting through it. This will prevent the strips from curling while cooking. Place the strips on top of the beans and liquid, cover the pot and place in the preheated oven.

6. Bake for 5 hours, checking occasionally (first after 2 hours, then every hour), to be sure the liquid is just barely covering the beans. Add more water as needed. After 5 hours, remove the cover of the bean pot and cook for 1 hour more. Remove the strips of salt pork and stir the pot before serving.

BROCCOLI

Whenever I think of broccoli, I think of my early cooking days in hotels. That is probably why I don't think a lot about broccoli. Hotels used to (probably still do) use a lot of broccoli and cauliflower, because they require less preparation than other fresh vegetables: you just cut them up and cook them; no peeling, no shucking! Broccoli grows well in New England, and many people have it in their gardens. It is good for crudités and as long as it isn't overcooked, it is a wholesome green vegetable with a unique, pleasant taste.

How to Cook Broccoli

The best way I have found to cook broccoli is to cut the stems away from the florets. Peel the stems if necessary and slice them ¼-inch thick on the bias. Cut the florets into small manageable pieces. Blanch the stems and florets separately in boiling salted water; the florets for about 2 minutes, the stems about 5. Shock in cold water and drain. Finish by sautéing in butter or stir-frying with a bit of garlic in oil.

CABBAGE

Cabbage has been a staple vegetable in New England since it was first planted here by the colonists over 300 years ago. This sturdy vegetable, which keeps well when properly stored in a cool dry place, sustained them during the cold winter months. The colonists, who usually boiled cabbage as they had in England, quickly learned other ways of using cabbage, like sauerkraut and cole slaw from the Dutch settlers, for example.

All too often cabbage is limited to serving with meat, particularly beef and pork. In this book you will find several seafood dishes that incorporate cabbage. It goes especially well with lobster, scallops and oily fish like salmon, pollock and bluefish. Poultry and game birds are also delicious with cabbage.

Depending on how cabbage is prepared, it takes on different shades of flavor, from mild when served raw in cabbage salad, to medium when cooked for a hot slaw, to full-flavored when simmered as in New England Boiled Dinner (page 166). I prefer to use Savoy cabbage for cooked cabbage dishes whenever possible. For cole slaw, I use the common green or white head cabbage, available almost anywhere, any time. Chinese and Napa cabbage have a mild flavor and are especially good with seafood (see Nam Tran's Shrimp and Cabbage Salad, page 36). Brussels sprouts and red cabbage are other favorites of mine from the cabbage family.

Cole Slaw

Although no cookout would be complete without cole slaw, it doesn't always have to be served on paper plates. Cole slaw is a fine accompaniment to grilled meats, poultry and fatty fish like bluefish, salmon and pollock. Like potato salad, this is best if made a day ahead.

SERVES TEN AS A SIDE DISH

1 large head of cabbage
   (3 pounds)
1 medium red onion
2 medium carrots
½ cup chopped parsley leaves
1 tablespoon Coleman's dry
   mustard
3 tablespoons Mayonnaise
   (page 333)
½ cup cider vinegar
½ cup vegetable oil
2 tablespoons sugar
salt and freshly ground black
   pepper
cayenne pepper (optional)

1. Cut the head of cabbage in half and remove the core. Cut each half in 3 or 4 wedges and put in a bowl of cold water to soak for at least 1 hour in the refrigerator. This preliminary soaking will soften the flavor.

2. Drain cabbage well and shred very fine. Place in a large bowl. Grate the onion and carrots directly into the bowl. Add parsley. Combine the dry mustard, mayonnaise, vinegar, oil and sugar. Add to the vegetables and mix well. Season to taste with salt and pepper and cayenne pepper, if using. Mix again and chill. Check the seasoning before serving.

Hot Cabbage Slaw

A surprisingly delicious way to prepare cabbage is to sauté it. Shred the cabbage, blanch it in boiling salted water for 1 minute, then sauté it in butter or bacon or goose fat. The fat as well as the garnishes (onions, mushrooms) should be determined by the dish it is going to be served with. That could be anything from cod lobster to goose or pork. (For a more precise recipe, see Warm Savoy Slaw, page 49.)

Ladies' Cabbage with Potatoes

One of the most traditional New England cabbage dishes is a custard widely known as "Ladies' Cabbage." This flan is an embellishment of the original, with onions, bacon and thinly sliced potatoes added. It is especially good with pheasant, Guinea hen and other game birds.

SERVES SIX TO EIGHT
AS A SIDE DISH

1 pound cabbage, roughly
    chopped in 3/4- to 1-inch pieces
1½ pounds Maine or other
    boiling potatoes
¼ pound thinly sliced bacon, cut
    in 1-inch pieces
1 medium onion, thinly sliced
salt and freshly ground pepper
5 eggs
1 cup milk
cayenne pepper

1. Preheat the oven to 350 degrees. Cook the cabbage in a large pot of boiling salted water for 5 to 7 minutes until tender. Drain in a colander and run under cold water to prevent further cooking. Drain well, then place in a large bowl.

2. Peel the potatoes, cut them in half lengthwise, and then cut them across into thin (¼ inch) slices. Blanch in plenty of boiling salted water for 6 to 8 minutes or until the potatoes are cooked through. A few slices may break apart. Drain in a colander and run under cold water to prevent further cooking. Drain well, then add to the cabbage.

3. Fry the pieces of bacon in a large sauté pan until they just begin to color. Pour off some of the fat into a 1½-quart casserole or baking dish and grease the dish. Put the sauté pan back on medium heat and add the onions. When the onions are soft (about 5 minutes), remove from the heat and add the onions and bacon to the cabbage and potatoes; mix together. Season lightly with salt and pepper and spread evenly in the baking dish.

4. Mix the eggs and milk well and season again with salt, pepper and cayenne pepper. Place the dish in a pan with 1 inch of hot water (a *bain-marie*) and place in the preheated oven and bake until the custard is completely set and the top begins to brown (about 30 minutes). Allow to rest a few minutes in a warm place before cutting and serving.

Braised Sweet-and-Sour Red Cabbage

This is classic paired with a pork roast, especially the leg (see Mom's Fresh Ham Sunday Dinner, page 184), or rich-tasting meats like venison or with game birds. Raspberry vinegar is a new, very subtle touch. Grating raw potato in at the end thickens the sauce so that it coats the cabbage and ties all the flavors together.

SERVES SIX TO EIGHT
AS A SIDE DISH

¼ pound slab country bacon, cut
    in small (¼ inch) dice
1 large onion, cut in medium
    (½ inch) dice
2 medium apples, peeled, cored
    and cut into medium (½ inch)
    dice

1. Preheat the oven to 350 degrees. Cook the bacon in a pot suitable for braising, about 4 minutes on medium heat, until it begins to crisp. Add the onion and cook for 4 or 5 minutes more or until soft. Add the apples, cabbage, stock, vinegar and brown sugar.

2. Stir while bringing to a boil, then cover the pot and place in the oven. Cook for about 1 hour. The cabbage should be quite tender. If not, return the pot to the oven for 10 to 15 minutes more.

1 head large red cabbage, cored,
    quartered and sliced (½ inch)
1 cup Chicken Stock (page 327)
¼ cup raspberry vinegar (see
    Note)
½ cup brown sugar
1 medium baking potato, peeled
salt and freshly ground black
    pepper

3. When the cabbage is tender, finely grate the raw potato directly into the pot. Put on medium heat and cook 4 or 5 minutes more or until the potato has turned the braising liquid into a sauce that lightly coats the cabbage. Season to taste with salt and pepper and add a splash of vinegar if necessary.

NOTE. Substitute cider or red wine vinegar for raspberry vinegar if not available.

Ragout of Brussels Sprouts with Bacon, Apples and Walnuts

We almost always have Brussels sprouts as a side dish for Christmas dinner. This rich preparation is an ideal match to rare roast beef *au jus,* popovers and roast potatoes. As a rule you should serve no more than one dish that uses cream in a meal. If you want to have Brussels sprouts but think this ragout is too rich for the rest of the menu, just cook them and toss them in a little butter, then season with salt and freshly ground pepper.

SERVES SIX TO EIGHT
AS A SIDE DISH

2 pints Brussels sprouts (about
    1½ pounds)
¼ pound slab country bacon, cut
    in medium (½ inch) dice
1 medium onion, cut in medium
    (½ inch) dice (1 cup)
2 small apples, peeled, cored and
    cut in medium (½ inch) dice
½ cup Chicken Stock (page 327)
    or water
1 cup heavy cream
1 cup walnut halves, lightly
    toasted
1 tablespoon coarsely chopped
    parsley
juice of ½ lemon
salt and freshly ground black
    pepper

1. Trim and score the Brussels sprouts with an X at the bottom. Cook them, uncovered, in plenty of boiling salted water until tender (about 8 minutes). Drain in a colander and rinse under cold running water to prevent further cooking. Drain well. Unless the sprouts are very small, cut them in half, down the center.

2. Fry the bacon in a large sauté pan on medium heat. When it begins to crisp, add the onion. Cook for about 2 minutes or until the onion wilts.

3. Add the apples, Brussels sprouts, stock or water and cream and simmer for about 5 minutes or until the cream is thick enough to lightly coat the sprouts. Add the walnuts and parsley and season to taste with lemon juice, salt and pepper.

CORN

Sweet corn is unquestionably America's favorite vegetable, and New England is no exception. My fondest memories of summer as a child are the taste of sweet corn on the cob and the ritual of eating it like a typewriter. When the corn was excellent, I could eat three or four ears, even as a child.

Of the many varieties of corn available in New England, the two that are always a sure bet are Silver Queen and Butter and Sugar; I have had others that were also quite good. The key factor is freshness, not variety. If you have never had corn that was rushed from the field and cooked within minutes of picking, then you are really missing something. The sugars in corn turn to starch very quickly, and the character of this vegetable changes considerably.

Corn was readily accepted by the Pilgrims, who learned of the different types and uses from the Indians (see Shell Bean Succotash, page 228, and The Clambake, page 20). Since that time it has never lost its importance in New England cookery. In addition to the few recipes that follow, you will find corn in many other preparations in this book.

How to Cook Corn on the Cob

No vegetable, or for that matter any food, is better than corn on the cob at its best. Here is the right way to cook it.

Bring a large pot of lightly salted water to a boil. Husk the corn and take a bite out of one of the ears. If the corn is very sweet and tender, it will need only to be heated through. In this case add the corn to the water and remove from the heat. After 3 minutes, remove the corn and serve at once. If the corn is not sugary and is a bit starchy, boil it for 5 minutes before removing from the heat. Only tasting the corn will tell you how long to cook it. Overcooking dilutes the flavor and ruins the texture of corn.

I'm not sure if Miss Manners would approve, but the best way to fix up an ear of corn is to roll it over a block of sweet butter, then salt and pepper it to your liking.

Creamed Corn

Whenever I serve corn on the cob, I cook too much. I assume that my guests may eat about three ears each, but they never do. This recipe is so good that you may want to plan to have leftover corn. Wrap the cooked ears of corn tightly in plastic wrap.

SERVES FOUR TO SIX
AS A SIDE DISH

½ cup finely diced onion
2 tablespoons unsalted butter
3 cups shaved cooked corn
1 cup heavy cream
2 tablespoons chopped chives
salt and freshly ground pepper

1. Sauté the onions in butter in a large sauté pan until translucent (about 3 or 4 minutes).

2. Add the corn and cream. Slowly bring to a slow boil (about 5 minutes), then simmer 5 minutes more. Using a fork, mix and mash the corn a bit. Do this a few times over the next 5 minutes. Add the chives and season to taste with salt and pepper.

Sweet Corn and Bread Pudding

At my restaurant, I serve a small piece of this pudding with homemade smoked sausage as an appetizer. You could serve it with chicken or pork; it is a substantial side dish that does double duty as a starch and a vegetable. It could also stand alone as a vegetarian main dish with a simple green salad. The corn naturally sweetens the pudding, so be sure to scrape the cobs after cutting off the kernels, to get every last drop of sugary pulp.

SERVES SIX TO EIGHT AS AN APPETIZER OR SIDE DISH OR THREE TO FOUR AS AN ENTREE

½ loaf white bread, preferably unsliced
3 tablespoons unsalted butter
6 ears of corn, kernels cut off and cobs scraped (about 3 cups)
1 tablespoon chopped fresh parsley
1 teaspoon table salt
½ teaspoon freshly ground black pepper
4 eggs
2 cups milk
3 ounces Cheddar cheese, grated (¾ cup)

1. Preheat the oven to 350 degrees. Trim off the crust and cut the bread into ½- to ¾-inch cubes. You should have about 3 cups, loosely packed. Melt the butter and grease a 9-inch square baking dish with about 1 tablespoon of it. Drizzle the rest over the bread cubes. Toss the bread cubes and place on a sheetpan. Place in the oven until they begin to turn golden brown (12 to 15 minutes).

2. Toss the toasted bread cubes with the corn and parsley. Season with salt and pepper to taste. Spread evenly in the baking dish.

3. Whisk the eggs and milk together and pour over the bread and corn. Let sit about 10 minutes, pressing down lightly on the bread 2 or 3 times so that it absorbs a good amount of the custard.

4. Sprinkle the cheese over the top. Place in the oven and bake until done (about 1 hour). Test by inserting a knife in the center; it should come out clean. If the top is brown and the custard is not completely set, you may wish to cover it loosely with aluminum foil for the last few minutes of baking. Allow the pudding to stand for at least 5 minutes before cutting into squares.

FIDDLEHEAD FERNS

Fiddleheads are one of the first vegetables to appear each year, popping up almost immediately after the ground thaws. They are actually tender young ferns that have yet to uncurl. Prior to making their national debut a few years back, fiddleheads were foraged, not cultivated, and were favored mostly by New Englanders from Vermont, New Hampshire and Maine, and a few "transplants" in the Pacific Northwest. The wild ferns are far superior in flavor to their cultivated counterpart. In early spring fern pickers are likely to come across a few morels, which are sensational paired with fiddleheads. Fiddlehead ferns have a unique flavor that slightly resembles asparagus. They are excellent as a side dish and go well with other vegetables in soups, stews and sautés. The unusual fiddlehead shape makes it a natural choice for garnishing all sorts of dishes. Fiddleheads are excellent sautéed with onions, shallots or leeks. An interesting trio of foraged vegetables is fiddleheads, ramps (wild leeks) and morels. They are also good combined with other vegetables in soup (see page 120) or in a mélange. They can also be added to stews during the last few minutes of cooking.

How to Prepare Fiddlehead Ferns

Fiddleheads have a thin protective layer of light brown "stuff" (for want of a better word), which must be removed. I have found that repeated soaking followed by a double blanching in boiling salted water minimizes the chore of removing it. Put the fiddleheads in a large pot or bowl of cold water and stir around. Change the water and repeat the process a few times until the "stuff" begins to come off. Bring a large pot of salted water to a boil. Add the fiddleheads and blanch for about 1 minute. A lot of the brown stuff will rise to the top of the pot. Skim it off, remove the fiddleheads and drain under cold running water. Clean out the pot, fill it again with salted water and return to a boil. Cook the fiddleheads until tender (about 3 or 4 minutes); drain again and rinse under cold running water. Check each piece, cleaning by hand what did not come off in the water. The fiddleheads are now ready to use.

GREENS

Greens are more associated with the South, where they are extremely popular, than with New England, but turnip and beet greens are not at all foreign to New England. Yankee and southern American cooking both evolved from colonial cooking, and they have more similarities than differences.

Today there are all kinds of greens available to cook with. Mustard greens, collard greens, spinach, kale, chard, beet greens, turnip greens, escarole and broccoli rabe are among the most common.

When buying greens, look for young, brightly colored, perfectly shaped greens that will be full-flavored, yet still reasonably tender. Older greens tend to be stringy and are sometimes overpowering.

The robust flavor of greens demands equally robust foods to accompany them. Most greens go best with pork, lamb, and game birds. On page 175 you will find a recipe pairing calves' liver and mustard greens simmered with onions and bacon. Greens are also great in soups. Bacon, ham, pancetta, salt pork and sausage all have an affinity with greens. The combination is hard to resist.

How to Prepare Greens

Wash all greens well before cooking. Tender, milder greens like spinach, kale and escarole can be sautéed or stir-fried with no prior blanching. Spinach, of course can be used as a salad green. The tender greens from young beets need also be only slightly cooked as in a warm salad or a stir-fry. For the others, use your own judgment. Most greens need to be parboiled in lots of boiling salted water (2 teaspoons salt per quart of water). As with other green vegetables the salt helps retain the color. For some of the very strong greens, like turnip and mustard, I recommend a double blanching. After the greens have been blanched until tender, they can be finished in many ways. For bacon and onion, see page 175; for garlic and olive oil, see page 238. There is certainly room for discovery with these often underutilized vegetables.

Caldo Verde

The first time I saw this soup, I thought it might be Chinese, because of the transparent broth and the extremely thin slivers of green. But as I watched the Portuguese cooks dunking huge chunks of bread into the soup and eating the grilled *linguiça* and *chouriço* sausages that were set on side platters, it wasn't hard to figure out its origins. During the two years that I worked at the Parker House in Boston, where the kitchen staff was predominantly Portuguese, I ate a lot of Portuguese food and learned a lot about Portuguese cooking. This classic soup, which I learned to make from my co-worker and friend, Carlos Santos, is among my very favorites.

What I find fascinating about the soup is that it is better made with water than stock. Some versions do call for chicken stock, but Carlos insisted that stock changes the character of the soup and masks the pure flavor of the potatoes and olive oil. (The Portuguese produce some very fruity and delicious olive oils, which are quite reasonably priced for the quality.) For an authentic *caldo verde*, you must shred the kale very, very fine. The trick is to roll up one or two leaves like a cigar and then cut across with a razor-sharp knife. *Caldo verde* is really a meal in itself when served as I just described. Serve it with a few bottles of Dão or other good Portuguese red wine. Be sure to put out little side plates for the bread and sausage. Dunking the bread in the soup is traditional. Because the bread absorbs so much liquid, the *caldo verde* gets thicker as you eat it. Eventually all that is left is a few spoonfuls of delicious olive oil and kale mashed potatoes. *Caldo verde* can also be served as a starter, without the sausage.

SERVES EIGHT TO TEN
AS A MAIN COURSE

2 pounds Maine or other large
   boiling potatoes
1 cup olive oil
salt and freshly ground black
   pepper
¾ pound kale, stems removed

For Serving
2 loaves crusty Portuguese or
   Italian bread, roasted or
   grilled
2 pounds or more Portuguese
   sausage (linguiça or chouriço)

1. Peel the potatoes and slice thin. Put in a large soup pot with 6 cups water and the olive oil. Add 1 teaspoon salt and bring to a boil. Reduce heat so that the soup boils very gently. Stir with a whip occasionally, to help break up the potatoes. Cook until the potatoes completely dissolve and you have shiny, lightly thickened broth (about 45 minutes). Season to taste with salt and pepper.

2. Wash the kale thoroughly and shred as fine as possible. Add to the broth and simmer for 2 minutes more. Ladle into soup plates and serve at once.

Rabes in Garlic and Olive Oil

Broccoli rabe, also called rappini or rabes (pronounced rah-bees), is a leafy cousin to broccoli, with deep green leaves, thin broccoli-like stalks and yellow flowers. I find it much more exciting than broccoli. It is deliciously bitter and tastes wonderful when slightly overcooked and tossed with lots of garlic and olive oil. Rabes can be served as a side dish, as part of an antipasto or as a salad. My favorite way is to make a sandwich on chewy Italian bread with some rabes and a few slices of cappicola (spicy Italian ham). Rabes are a late crop in New England and are usually not available locally until September. If rabes are not available at your market, try an Italian market. They will surely have it.

SERVES SIX OR EIGHT AS AN
APPETIZER OR SIDE DISH

2 pounds rabes
4 to 6 cloves garlic, finely
  chopped (2 tablespoons)
½ cup olive oil
salt and freshly ground pepper
juice of 1 lemon (optional)

1. Cut the rabes into 2-inch pieces and blanch in boiling salted water until cooked through, not al dente. Drain well.

2. Heat the garlic in olive oil until lightly browned. Add the cooked rabes, toss and season to taste with salt, pepper and lemon juice. Serve hot, at room temperature or chilled.

MUSHROOMS

The enjoyment of mushrooms in New England dates back to the Indians, who foraged for the different kinds of wild mushrooms that grew all over this area. They are among the foods listed as cooked at the first Thanksgiving, but no specific details are given. I suppose they were chanterelles, which can still be found in the wild throughout most of New England in the late summer and early fall. Other mushrooms that grow wild in New England include field mushrooms, trumpets and puff balls, which grow to enormous sizes. Morels can be found in the early spring. Although this region is not as rich in mushrooms as northern California and the Pacific Northwest, there are dozens of varieties of edible mushrooms to be found in New England, if you know where to look and which ones to pick.

Loss of the folk knowledge of mushroom foraging is one of the reasons that until recent years we were reduced to a pitiful one-mushroom culture. People who cannot afford the expensive alternatives, and who do not know enough to risk foraging on their own, still are. Cultivated wild mushrooms, like shiitakes, oyster mushrooms *(pleurottes)* and Roman mushrooms, as well as the woodland mushrooms like cèpes and trumpets foraged by those who have a working knowledge of both fungi and finances, are very costly. For this reason, I use mushrooms more for flavoring and garnishing than as a side dish. You will find many recipes throughout this book that call for moderate amounts of wild mushrooms.

How to Cook Mushrooms

Sauté button or wild mushrooms in a pan large enough to hold all the mushrooms in one layer. Depending on the size of the mushrooms, they may need to be cut into pieces or large slices. Get the pan as hot as possible and then add butter or olive oil. Place the mushrooms so they cover the bottom of the pan. Allow them to sizzle and do not move or shake them. The second you do, they will weep liquid, making it impossible for you to sauté them further. When the mushrooms have cooked for 1 minute and have begun to brown, stir them once briefly, then leave them alone, until they are cooked through. The size of the mushrooms will determine the cooking time. Some experts recommend a minimum of 15 minutes cooking time for wild species, but I think this is far too long. Flavorings like garlic, shallots, onion, chives and tomato, as well as salt and pepper, can be added after the mushrooms are moved for the first time.

Other methods of cooking mushrooms include frying them in a light tempura batter and grilling. Use large mushrooms for grilling. Brush them with garlic-scented olive oil and season with salt and pepper. Place directly on the grill and cook on both sides.

THE ONION FAMILY

No vegetable exceeds the onion in the multitude of culinary preparations it is used for. Like the egg, the onion is not just a food, it is a phenomenon. It is employed universally, in one form or another, in almost every cuisine of the world. There are hundreds of varieties of cultivated and wild onions. A few of the most popular onions used in modern American cookery today are the common yellow onion, red onions, large white onions, white boiling onions, sweet Vidalia onions, red and white pearl onions, leeks, ramps (wild leeks), shallots, scallions or green onions, chives, garlic or Chinese chives, and last but certainly not least, garlic.

Onions are good eaten raw, steamed, boiled, sautéed, stewed, glazed, deep-fried, roasted, grilled, stuffed and almost any other way imaginable. And the onion's flavor to one degree or another is compatible with all meats, fowl, fish and shellfish, and every vegetable. This total versatility is why the onion is often referred to as the "king of vegetables." Scattered throughout this book are scores of recipes using onions. Here they are featured.

Roasted Garlic

The sweet and mild flavor of garlic that has been slowly roasted in the oven is among the greatest of taste experiences. Garlic prepared in this fashion is a terrific accompaniment to roasts like chicken, lamb or beef. The pulp is soft and creamy, as if it had been pureed. Roasted-garlic pulp serves as a condiment for flavoring all sorts of things like pasta (page 278) or potatoes (page 249). When roasting garlic for use as a spread or flavoring, figure that an average head will yield a little more than 1 tablespoon pulp. When serving this as a vegetable garnish, allow one fairly large (not giant) head per person.

To roast garlic, preheat the oven to 325 degrees. Rub each head, skin on, all over with olive oil and then wrap the heads loosely in a large piece of aluminum foil. Place the wrapped garlic in a pie tin or on a sheetpan and place in the oven. Check after 1 hour 15 minutes. The garlic should smell sweet and feel very soft and the skins should be lightly browned when done. It may take up to 1 hour 30 minutes.

Andy's Favorite Onion Rings

One of my best friends, Andy Moes, who, not by coincidence, is also one of the world's great appetites, has an unrestrained passion for all sorts of onions. I have seen Andy eat onion soup, followed by a blue cheese salad with extra red onions, followed by a steak with pearl onions. Andy, who is a morning deejay (The Joe and Andy Family on WROR-FM in Boston), really likes big crisp onion rings; when they are not on the menu, we make them for him especially.

SERVES ANDY OR FOUR OTHERS AS A SIDE DISH

2 large sweet Spanish, Vidalia,
   red or white onions
1½ cups all-purpose flour
½ cup johnnycake meal or white
   cornmeal
salt and ground black pepper
cayenne pepper
2 cups buttermilk or milk
peanut oil for frying

1. Peel the onions and cut across to make slices about ½ inch thick. Separate the rings and reserve the small center piece for stock or some other use.

2. Mix the flour and johnnycake meal together and season to your liking with salt, pepper and cayenne pepper. Put the buttermilk or milk in a bowl.

3. Heat about 3 inches of oil in a deep pot to 350 degrees. Double-bread the onion rings: dip into the milk, drain and then coat with the flour mixture; repeat.

4. Fry the onion rings a few at a time until golden brown. Drain on paper towels and sprinkle with a little more salt, if desired.

Old-Fashioned Glazed Onions

Glazed onions are one of New England's oldest and best-liked vegetable dishes. The old-fashioned method of glazing onions with honey and butter in a hot oven dates back to Colonial times. According to Eleanor Early, a noted expert on New England food, history and culture, George Washington ate glazed onions similar to these in 1790, while visiting the Munroe Tavern, in Lexington, Massachusetts.

As I tested this recipe, I had a daydream about a candle-lit colonial tavern with cold and weary visitors sitting around a long wooden table. The people at the table were quiet and polite. They spoke softly and sipped their little glasses of Madeira. A few spit-roasted pheasants were brought to the table along with boiled turnips and potatoes and steamed brown bread. Then a woman brought out a platter of these onions. The smell filled the room. As she set them on the table, everyone noticed that they were still bubbling.

SERVES SIX AS A SIDE DISH

6 medium onions, about 5 or 6
   ounces each
4 tablespoons unsalted butter
salt and freshly ground black
   pepper
6 teaspoons honey

1. Peel the onions and cut them in half, across. Trim off the bottom so they stand up evenly. Find a baking pan or dish that will hold the onions comfortably.

2. Preheat the oven to 450 degrees. Melt 2 tablespoons of the butter and lightly brush the baking pan. Place the onions in the pan and brush with the remaining melted butter. Season the onions lightly with salt and pepper.

3. Spread about ½ teaspoon of honey over each onion half. Dot the tops of the onions with the remaining butter and place in the oven. Cook for about 45 minutes until the tops are bubbly and the onions have spots of black.

Grilled Leeks

A perfectly grilled leek is one of the finest vegetable accompaniments that I can think of. The inside steams as the outer leaves char, and the flavor of the leek is intensified by the smoky aroma from the grill. (Discard the outer leaves before serving.) There is no trick to this dish, except to buy good leeks and clean them very well; they are often very gritty. Use medium-size leeks that are fresh and tender.

SERVES SIX AS A SIDE DISH

6 medium leeks
¼ cup vegetable oil
salt and freshly ground black
  pepper
1 lemon
¼ cup freshly grated parmesan
  or romano cheese

1. Cut off all but 1 inch of the green part of the leek and discard; the leeks should be about 6 inches long. Make a cut the length of each leek going halfway through, to open it up. Soak leeks in cold water, changing the water a few times, and then hold them one at a time under cold running water to get rid of any remaining dirt.

2. Build a wood or charcoal fire and let it burn down to glowing embers. Dip the leeks in oil and season with salt and pepper. With the cut side facing up, put the leeks on the grill, about 2 inches from the coals. Cook for 5 to 7 minutes or until well charred. Remove the black outer leaves, squeeze a little fresh lemon juice over the top and sprinkle with cheese.

PARSNIPS, TURNIPS AND OTHER ROOT VEGETABLES

Because of the long winters in New England, root vegetables have always been a very important food staple for a good part of the year. Come spring, we all yearn for fresh green vegetables, but looking back at the winter, we have to be grateful for all the beets, celery root, carrots, parsnips, rutabagas, turnips, kohlrabi, salsify, Jerusalem artichokes, potatoes and sweet potatoes that made for some wonderful hearty meals.

Each root vegetable has its own distinct flavor and density, and therefore needs to be handled a bit differently from the others. Almost all are good simply peeled, boiled until tender and tossed with a little butter. Root vegetables also make good purees, alone or in combinations. Roasting and glazing are other methods that can be used for root vegetables. There are many cold-weather dishes in this book, like New England Boiled Dinner (page 166), where root vegetables are an important element of the dish. In this section you will find a few of my favorite recipes where the root vegetable or vegetables are prominent.

Spring-Dug Parsnips

Parsnips are usually harvested after the first frost each year, but it is traditional to leave some in the ground all winter. As soon as the ground thaws, we have our first spring vegetable—the spring-dug parsnip. Spring dugs are the ultimate root vegetable, spicier and sweeter that their autumn counterparts. Dick Fowler, of Fowler's Farm in Westfield, Massachusetts, is the leading producer of parsnips in New England; he leaves about 40 acres of parsnips underground each year. If you find Fowler's parsnips in the spring, you can be sure you are getting real spring dugs.

Brad's Root Soup with Blue Cheese Butter

This pungent and soul-satisfying soup was created several winters ago by Bradford Cole, who was then the sous-chef at my restaurant. Brad grew up in the town of Westfield, Massachusetts, which is New England's largest producer of parsnips. He often joked that this farming village was the parsnip's answer to Castroville, California, the "Artichoke Capitol of the World." Although Boston became Brad's home, he never lost his taste for roots, especially parsnips. Brad Cole died young of cancer, in 1987. He will always be remembered as a great cook by all the people he worked with and cooked for during his eleven-year career in the kitchen. This recipe demonstrates Brad's command of using assertive flavors together to create an unusual balance.

His root soup can be made with one or all of the root vegetables mentioned in the list of ingredients. I like it best when parsnips and rutabagas dominate.

SERVES EIGHT TO TEN
AS A STARTER

Blue-Cheese Butter
3 ounces blue cheese
6 tablespoons unsalted butter

4 tablespoons unsalted butter
1 large onion, thinly sliced
    (2 cups)
½ pound Maine or other boiling
    potatoes, peeled and thinly
    sliced
1½ pounds mixed root
    vegetables (parsnips,
    rutabagas, turnips, Jerusalem
    artichokes, celery root,
    salsify), peeled and thinly
    sliced
4 cups Chicken Stock (page 327)
1 cup heavy cream
juice of ½ lemon
salt and freshly ground pepper

1. To make the blue cheese butter, allow the cheese and the 6 tablespoons of butter to come to room temperature. Mix thoroughly by hand or in a food processor.

2. Heat the butter in a soup pot on medium heat. Add the onion and cook for about 10 minutes.

3. Add the potatoes, root vegetables and stock and simmer slowly for 30 to 40 minutes until the potatoes and vegetables are overcooked and falling apart. Puree using a food mill or a food processor. Let cool and set aside if not using right away.

4. Just before serving, reheat the soup until bubbling. Add the cream and season to taste with lemon juice, salt and pepper. Ladle into soup plates and top each with a dollop of soft blue cheese butter.

Parsnip Puree

The parsnip has always been very popular in New England. Until I moved to Boston, I had never eaten parsnips; now I consider them one of the most underrated of all vegetables. The parsnip has a unique sweet herbaceous flavor, especially the spring dug. I am often asked what spices I use in the parsnip puree at my restaurant and people seem surprised when I answer, "None—just parsnips and butter."

SERVES FOUR TO SIX
AS A SIDE DISH

2 pounds parsnips
½ cup milk
8 tablespoons unsalted butter
salt

1. Peel the parsnips and cut off the very top. Bring a large pot of boiling salted water to a boil. Add the whole parsnips and cook until they are well done (about 10 to 15 minutes). Put in a colander and allow to drain. While the parsnips are draining, heat the milk in a small pot.

2. Combine the parsnips and hot milk in a food processor or blender. Puree and add the butter a little at a time until all is worked in. Season with salt (very little will be needed) and serve hot. The puree can be cooled off and reheated later if desired.

Parsnip Chips

These are some of the best chips you've ever tasted. They are marvelous with grilled poultry, especially quail.

To make them, peel parsnips and slice them lengthwise into thin chips. Heat peanut oil in a pot suitable for deep-fat-frying to 350 degrees. Drop the slices into the oil, a few at a time, and fry until golden brown. Drain well and sprinkle with a bit of salt.

Spring-dug parsnips don't come out as crisp because of their high sugar content. The trick is to lay them on paper towels on a sheetpan and let stand in a warm, dry place for about 1 hour after frying. Serve at room temperature, like potato chips.

Maple-Glazed Turnips

The old-fashioned way to glaze root vegetables was to simmer them with water, butter and sugar. As the water boiled away, a glaze of butter and sugar was formed, which coated the vegetables. But this method left no room for variables like the freshness and size of the vegetables. More often than not, the vegetables, though sweet, were overcooked. A more modern approach is to blanch the vegetables in boiling salted water until done, shock them and then slowly reheat them with butter and sugar. I choose maple as a sweetener, but you may substitute an equal amount of honey or sugar if you desire a more neutral flavor. Because the vegetables are blanched separately, you may vary the shape or even the vegetables to suit your needs. Yams, rutabagas, parsnips, carrots, salsify and Jerusalem artichokes will all glaze beautifully; just substitute an equal amount for the turnips.

SERVES FOUR TO SIX
AS A SIDE DISH

2 pounds purple-top turnips
salt
4 tablespoons unsalted butter
1½ tablespoons maple sugar or
*   2 tablespoons maple syrup*
2 teaspoons chopped fresh
*   parsley*

1. Peel the thick skin off the turnips. Cut into ⅓-inch slices. Cut slices into ⅓-inch-wide strips *(bâtonnets)*, resembling french fries. Cook the turnips in a large pot of boiling salted water, until tender, but not too soft (about 8 minutes). Drain and shock under cold running water.

2. Mix the butter and maple sugar with 1 tablespoon of water in a large sauté pan on medium-low heat. Add the blanched turnips and cook slowly until a glaze forms on them. The pan should be almost dry and the turnips very hot by the time they are finished. Remove from the heat, add the chopped parsley, toss and serve at once.

V A R I A T I O N

Maple-Glazed Yams

Peel 2 pounds of yams or sweet potatoes and cut into *bâtonnets*. Parboil until just tender (about 6 minutes), then drain and shock. Continue as for Maple-Glazed Turnips. Other root vegetables may also be substituted. Parboil only until tender, not soft.

Gratin of Turnips and Potatoes

Scalloped is the term most often used in New England cookery to describe foods cooked in cream or cream sauce. I use the term *gratin* here because this recipe is more in the French style, like *gratin dauphinois*, the famous dish of sliced potatoes baked with cream. I have made this version with both sliced and diced vegetables and feel for this particular combination, diced works best. Rutabagas can be used instead of turnips in this recipe. They are every bit as good and more colorful besides.

SERVES EIGHT TO TEN
AS A SIDE DISH

2 garlic cloves, finely chopped
2 tablespoons unsalted butter
2½ to 3 pounds Maine or other
*   all-purpose potatoes, peeled*
*   and cut in medium-large (½ to*
*   ¾ inch) dice (4 cups)*
2 pounds turnips or rutabagas,
*   peeled and cut in medium-*
*   large (½ to ¾ inch) dice (4*
*   cups)*
4 cups heavy cream
kosher salt and freshly ground
*   black pepper*

1. Preheat the oven to 350 degrees. Grease the bottom and sides of a 9-inch square baking dish with the chopped garlic and butter.

2. Mix the diced potatoes and turnips and spread them evenly in the baking dish.

3. Bring the cream slowly to a boil and season with salt and pepper. You should use approximately 2 teaspoons salt and 1 teaspoon pepper.

4. Pour the cream over the vegetables and cover loosely with foil. Place in the preheated oven. After 30 minutes, uncover the dish and place back in the oven. Cook for 15 to 20 minutes more. The potatoes and turnips should be quite tender and the top golden brown and bubbling.

PEAS, SNOW PEAS AND SUGAR SNAPS

What fiddleheads and asparagus are to spring, peas are to summer. Fresh Atlantic salmon with peas (page 77) is the traditional Fourth of July meal in many parts of New England. It takes a while to shuck fresh peas but it is time well spent. These peas are sometimes called snap peas, not to be confused with Sugar Snap peas. Sugar Snap is a relatively new variety, sort of a cross between a snow pea and a snap pea. Sugar Snaps, which have pretty good-size peas inside, are eaten whole, pea and pod together. Snow peas are all pod, with only tiny seeds inside.

I remember hating peas as a child. My mother used to cook canned peas, and rather than eat them, I would stuff them into my pocket when she wasn't looking. I was reprimanded for doing this, but I got my point across and Mom became less insistent about me eating all my peas. When she switched to frozen peas, I stopped pocketing them. And when I ate fresh peas for the first time, I loved them.

How to Cook Peas

Unless they are very small, shelled peas should be blanched in boiling salted water for about 2 minutes and then shocked. Sugar Snap peas also are enhanced by a quick blanching. Snow peas require no precooking at all. Peas are wonderful cooked in a bit of sweet butter and lightly seasoned. They also mix well with other vegetables, as in a vegetable mélange. I like peas cooked with bits of bacon. Mint goes with peas too. I often sauté them with fresh mint leaves and I also make a great soup with fresh peas and mint. Pea tendrils can be added to salad or quickly stir-fried.

Minted Fresh Pea Soup

I'm not a great lover of cold soups, but I find this one delicious and refreshing. It is also good hot, but it cannot be heated for long periods since its flavor and color change quickly. This is basically a vichyssoise with peas and mint added at the last minute. It can be easily adapted to many different vegetables and herbs by substituting another vegetable for the peas and adjusting the cooking time and flavorings.

SERVES EIGHT TO TEN
AS A STARTER

3 pounds peas, shucked (3 cups)
3 medium leeks, chopped, rinsed
    well and drained
4 tablespoons unsalted butter
4 cups Chicken Stock (page 327)
1½ pounds Maine or other
    boiling potatoes, peeled and
    thinly sliced
6 branches fresh mint, leaves
    picked and chopped (about ½
    cup)
1 cup heavy cream
salt and freshly ground black
    pepper
juice of ½ lemon

For Garnish
unsweetened whipped cream
    (optional)
small sprigs fresh mint (optional)

1. Blanch ½ cup of the peas for garnish; set aside.

2. Sweat the leeks in butter in a soup pot until tender. Add the stock and potatoes and simmer until the potatoes are falling apart (about 30 minutes). Add the remaining 2½ cups of peas and the mint and cook for 2 minutes. Remove from the heat and puree in a food processor or blender until very smooth. Strain if necessary.

3. If you are going to serve the soup cold, cool down as quickly as possible. An ice *bain-marie* (a bucket or bowl filled with ice or ice water) will be very helpful. Stir often to hasten the cooling process. Stir in the cream, season to taste with salt, pepper and lemon juice, add the blanched peas and chill well. Thin down with a little water if necessary.

4. If you are serving the soup hot, heat the base, stir in the cream, add the blanched peas and season to taste at the last minute with salt, pepper and lemon juice.

5. Garnish each bowl of soup, hot or cold, with a small dollop of unsweetened whipped cream and a sprig of mint.

Petits Pois Simmered in Butter

Petits pois are the smallest of the original mini vegetable. Freshly picked and shucked, these tiny peas take very little time to cook; in fact, they just need to be heated through. I season these very lightly and use none of the competitive ingredients like bacon or onions that are good with larger sweet peas. Give yourself plenty of time to shuck the peas; you will need it. Cook them at the very last second and rush them to the table.

SERVES FOUR TO SIX
AS A SIDE DISH

3 to 4 pounds petits pois
4 tablespoons unsalted butter
salt and freshly ground black
    pepper

1. Shuck the peas.

2. Combine the butter and 2 tablespoons water in a 9- or 10-inch sauté pan and bring to a slow simmer, stirring constantly to create a light butter sauce. Add the peas and season right away with salt; it will help to retain the green. Stir the peas for 2 or 3 minutes, just until they are hot. Serve at once.

PEPPERS AND CHILIES

Peppers, another of the New World's great gifts to gastronomy, are exceptionally versatile. They are easy to grow, even in New England, and the taste of a freshly picked bell pepper is one of summer's many delights. As a child, I liked diced peppers from the garden mixed with fresh-made farmer's cheese, a simple little dish that I still enjoy at the height of the pepper season (see page 218).

Since bell peppers come in a wide spectrum of colors, green and red being the most common, but including yellow, purple and chocolate brown, they can add decoration as well as flavor to a dish. In addition, they can be used in all sorts of ways: raw in salads, sautéed with onions (traditional with Italian sausages) and stewed with tomatoes; they can be baked, roasted, stuffed and pickled.

Roasted peppers can be used to garnish antipasto and salads, accompany grilled meat and fish, flavor sauces and relishes and even certain sausages (see the recipe for lobster sausage, page 48). My Italian grandmother kept jars of roasted green peppers in olive oil and garlic, and she always put them out at lunchtime. I loved to stick them in my sandwiches, especially if we were having steak sandwiches.

Chilies have not been an integral part of New England cooking; except for hot Italian peppers, they were not even available until recently. Now they are entering our markets to satisfy the demand created by newcomers from Central America, the Caribbean and Southeast Asia. There are hundreds of varieties of these spicy peppers (some not so spicy), usually with thin walls. They add more than heat to food: they have their own unique flavor, which I am sure we'll be tasting more of in New England if past history is any guide.

How to Roast Peppers

Roasting peppers refers to the traditional method of preparation, but they can also be broiled or grilled, whatever is most convenient. Any color pepper can be used, but red and green are the most useful. Many recipes call specifically for red peppers, and combinations are nice for antipasto and salad.

To roast the peppers, rub them with olive or vegetable oil and place them either directly on the rack of a 500-degree oven with a pan underneath to catch the drippings or under the broiler about 6 inches from the heat or on the grill a few inches from the hot coals. Turn the peppers so that the skins char evenly and so they cook through completely. If the skins do not blacken at least partially, increase the heat or move the peppers closer to the source of heat. When done, remove the peppers from the heat and place in a bowl or pan. Cover with plastic wrap to allow the peppers to finish cooking in their own steam. When the peppers are cool enough to handle, peel off the skin; it should come off easily. Pull out the core and remove the seeds, leaving the peppers whole and intact.

The roasted peppers can be kept refrigerated as is for use in dishes that call for pureed or diced roasted peppers. For antipasto or salad, cover the peppers with good olive oil and add 1 clove garlic, sliced, for each pepper. For long-keeping, place them in canning jars with the garlic and pour in enough olive oil to cover. They can be canned or kept in the refrigerator.

Potatoes are an important crop in northern New England, especially Maine. Whether boiled, steamed, panfried, deep-fried, baked or cooked any other way, potatoes are almost universally loved by New Englanders, and they appear repeatedly in the classic dishes of this region, like chowders, hash and boiled dinner.

Tiny thin-skinned red and white new potatoes are the first to appear each summer. The flavor of these freshly picked potatoes is a revelation—they are so much better than the stored. These very sweet little spuds are best boiled or steamed, as are the larger new potatoes that appear a bit later in the season. Toward the end of summer, thicker-skinned Maine potatoes appear on the market. Maine potatoes have a full flavor and a moderate starch content, which make them an all-purpose potato, good for most uses. French-fried Maine potatoes can be delicious, but high-starch baking potatoes from Idaho and other western states, now available everywhere, are a safer bet for deep-frying.

All-American Potato Salad

Everybody has a favorite recipe for this creamy type of potato salad. This is mine. It's one of those "everything but the kitchen sink" types of recipe, which is not normally my style. But this is the potato salad that I have perfected to my own liking. The salad improves by standing overnight, or for that matter for a few days, so it should be made at least a day ahead. It's so good you will want to have a lot, and it keeps well. This recipe is for ten pounds of potatoes, which serves twenty people. If you want, cut it in half.

SERVES ABOUT TWENTY
AS A SIDE DISH

10 pounds large waxy boiling
    potatoes or Maine potatoes
salt
8 hard-boiled eggs
1 medium onion, cut in small
    (1/4 inch) dice (1 cup)
1 cup chopped scallions
6 stalks celery, peeled and cut in
    small (1/4 inch) dice (2 cups)
1 large dill pickle, finely chopped
    (2/3 cup)
1/2 cup chopped parsley
1 cup Mayonnaise (page 333)
1 cup vegetable oil
3/4 cup distilled white vinegar
2 tablespoons Dijon mustard
freshly ground black pepper

1. Scrub the potatoes and put in a large pot. Cover with water, add 2 to 3 teaspoons salt and bring to a boil. When they come to a boil, reduce the heat to a simmer and cook until well done (about 40 minutes). Pour off the water and place potatoes in a colander to drain. Let cool.

2. Roughly chop the hard-boiled eggs into medium-size pieces, no smaller than 1/2 inch.

3. When the potatoes are cool enough to handle, peel them and cut them into cubes no larger than 1 inch. Place in a large bowl. Add the chopped eggs, onion, scallions, celery, pickle, parsley and mayonnaise. Mix a bit and add the oil, vinegar and mustard. Season to taste with salt and pepper and chill. Check the seasoning again before serving. The salad may need more salt or pepper or even vinegar.

Boiled or Steamed New Potatoes

I like to split boiled or steamed new potatoes in half and toss with unsalted butter and freshly chopped parsley. Depending on what you are going to be serving them with, other mild fresh herbs like dill, chervil and chives can also be tossed with the potatoes.

To boil potatoes, scrub the potatoes and cover with cold water. Add about 1 tablespoon of kosher salt per quart of water and bring to a boil. As soon as the pot boils, turn the heat down and simmer until the potatoes are cooked through. To steam potatoes, scrub the potatoes and put them in a steamer with 1 inch of salted water in the bottom. Cover tightly and steam until the potatoes are cooked through. New potatoes must be fully cooked and very soft in the center to bring out the full flavor, but there is no exact way to time the boiling or steaming of them. Size, starch content and age are all determining factors. The very smallest can take as little as 5 minutes to boil and 10 minutes to steam and the largest can take 45 minutes or more. You must watch and test them as you go.

Garlic Mashed Potatoes

The flavor of these mashed potatoes with roasted garlic is so altogether satisfying and comforting that they could be sold as medicine. I could eat them every day and never grow tired. Grilled steaks and pork chops, roast leg of lamb, smoked pork or other smoked meats, roasted or grilled chicken are all fine matches for garlic mashed potatoes.

SERVES FOUR TO SIX
AS A SIDE DISH

2 pounds Maine or other large
   boiling potatoes, peeled and
   quartered
kosher salt
¾ cup milk
4 tablespoons unsalted butter
2 tablespoons roasted-garlic pulp
   (page 239)
freshly ground black pepper

1. While peeling and cutting the potatoes, bring about 4 quarts of water to a rolling boil. Add about 3 tablespoons of salt and then add the potatoes. Bring back to a boil, reduce heat and simmer, covered, until tender (about 20 to 30 minutes).

2. Drain the potatoes in a colander and allow to drain well, without cooling off too much. At the same time scald the milk.

3. Place the potatoes in a bowl and begin beating with a mixer on medium speed or by hand. Slowly add the hot milk. Add the butter bit by bit and the garlic pulp. Increase the speed of the mixer and whip until the potatoes are smooth and creamy. Season to taste with salt and pepper and serve at once.

VARIATION

Mashed Potatoes   For plain mashed potatoes, simply omit the roasted-garlic pulp.

French Fried Potatoes

Several kinds of deep-fried potatoes come under the general title of french fries. The potatoes you use have to have a high starch content, but you can cut them in various sizes and shapes. Many devices are touted for cutting french fries, but in my estimation the venerable mandoline is still the best. A good sharp knife also works very well.

Except for very thin shoestrings or matchsticks, the potatoes usually need a preliminary blanching in water or oil. Then they can be cooked in one of several different fats or oils or a blend. Almost any high-quality vegetable oil can be used. In general, I recommend peanut oil, but if you have never had potatoes fried in olive oil, you are really missing something. Animal fats like beef suet impart wonderful flavor to fried potatoes, but today the use of those saturated fats is considered to be a frontal attack on the cardiovascular system, most inadvisable. Goose fat, also deemed unacceptable, will provide you with a taste experience I can only describe as heavenly. Try it once before you go. Cut large fries to minimize the fat content. The easiest and safest way to cook french fries is in a deep-fat-fryer with a basket. You can improvise with a deep pot and a skimmer or slotted spoon, but only for small quantities.

SERVES SIX AS A SIDE DISH

2½ pounds baking potatoes
vegetable oil for frying
salt

1. Peel the potatoes and cut into strips ⅜ × ⅜ × 3 or 4 inches. Keep in cold water to cover until ready to fry.

2. Heat 6 inches of oil to 300 degrees in a deep-fat-fryer with a basket or a pot suitable for deep-frying. Dry the potatoes, place in the basket and lower into the oil. Cook for 2 to 3 minutes or until the potatoes begin to turn light yellow. Remove from oil, and drain over the pot. Cool thoroughly.

3. Shortly before serving, reheat the oil to 360 degrees. Plunge a basketful of potatoes into the hot oil and cook until golden brown (about 4 to 5 minutes). Remove from oil, drain over the pot and then on paper towels. Sprinkle with salt and serve immediately.

VARIATIONS

Shoestring Potatoes   Cut the peeled potatoes into strips ¼ × ¼ × 3 or 4 inches. Heat the oil to 360 degrees. Add small amounts of potatoes and stir when they are first added to prevent them from sticking together. Drain over the pot, then on paper towels. Sprinkle lightly with salt and serve at once.

Large Fries   Peel the potatoes or not, as you prefer. Cut into large wedges or rectangles, about ¾ inch thick. This size and shape potato needs to be blanched either in water (see Freddie's Famous Roast Potatoes, page 251) or in oil or fat. Heat the oil or fat to 300 degrees and cook the potatoes, without crowding them, for 4 to 5 minutes or until they begin to color. Drain over the pot and set aside. Shortly before serving, reheat the oil or fat to 340 degrees and cook the potatoes a few at a time until golden brown and crisp. Drain over the pot and then on paper towels. Season lightly with salt and serve at once.

Freddie's Famous Roast Potatoes

Anyone familiar with the food scene in Boston can tell you about Freddie's potatoes. These crispy, garlicky cubes of roast potatoes have been a regular featured dish at many of the restaurants in Boston where Frank "Freddie" King has worked. Freddie, who was introduced to the restaurant business by Lydia Shire, has spent years working in and supervising some of the best dining rooms around the city. During the two years that he served as maître d' at my restaurant, we served these almost every night, usually with roast lamb or chicken.

SERVES SIX AS A SIDE DISH

6 to 8 medium Maine potatoes
  (about 2½ pounds)
1 head garlic
½ cup rendered goose fat,
  melted (see Note)
salt and freshly ground black
  pepper

1. Peel the potatoes and cut into 1½-inch cubes; they do not have to be uniform. Blanch in boiling salted water for 7 to 8 minutes, then drain well.

2. Carefully separate the cloves of garlic, leaving the skin on.

3. Preheat the oven to 350 degrees. Lightly grease a roasting pan, which is large enough to hold all the potatoes in one layer, with goose fat. Add the potatoes and garlic cloves and season with salt and pepper. Drizzle the remaining goose fat over the potatoes.

4. Place the potatoes in the preheated oven and bake for 50 to 60 minutes, turning them about every 10 minutes, until they have a golden-brown crust. Serve as soon as possible (within 10 to 15 minutes).

NOTE. The original recipe for Freddie's potatoes calls for rendered goose fat, but you may substitute 8 tablespoons (1 stick) unsalted butter. Grease the pan and dot the potatoes with butter in Step 3.

Potato Pancakes

There are many ways to make potato pancakes and I do them all. But I keep coming back to this recipe. It is simple, quick and foolproof. These crisp potato cakes can garnish all sorts of poultry and meat dishes; they are also excellent on their own with sour cream and caviar or apple sauce (page 343).

SERVES FOUR AS A SIDE DISH

1 whole egg
½ medium onion, peeled
4 medium high-starch baking
  potatoes (1½ pounds)
2 tablespoons all-purpose flour
salt and freshly ground black
  pepper
vegetable oil for frying

1. Break the egg into a mixing bowl. Grate the onion, using the medium-size hole, into the bowl. Peel the potatoes and grate them, using the largest hole, directly into the bowl. Sprinkle with flour and mix well. Season to taste with salt and pepper.

2. Pour about ¼ inch vegetable oil into a skillet and place on medium-high heat. Divide the potato mixture into 8, to form pancakes that are about 3 inches in diameter and ½ to ¾ inch thick. Place them in the hot oil (they should sizzle) and cook for 5 minutes, until the sides begin to turn dark brown. Do not move them, except to loosen any that stick. Turn the cakes and cook for 5 minutes more. Drain on paper towels and serve at once.

In the past few years the role of the green salad has changed immensely, from a once narrowly defined concept of lettuce, vegetables and dressing to a broader realm that often overlaps with many other areas of cooking. The concept of salad as a separate entity is still valid for many meals, but for others the salad needs to be more closely tied to the other foods being served. In modern salads the greens can be served cold or warmed; they can be mixed or garnished with vegetables, fruit, seafood, poultry or meat. This new way of thinking has redefined not only the salad but also salad greens. Beet greens, young chicory and other strong greens that were not often used in the salads of the past now form the base for warm salads. Because of the changed nature of salads, you will find many composed salads throughout this book.

Another phenomenon in the last few years is the growing variety of greens available. We have come a long way from the days of iceberg, romaine and Bibb; we have learned that any green that tastes good raw can be used in salad. Even in New England we have as many as ten varieties available in the winter, many raised locally in greenhouses and hydroponic farms (see List of Sources, page 358). In summer there may be as many as twenty different lettuces for sale on the local market. And every year there are new ones. Arugula, frisée (curly endive), mâche, Limestone, dandelion, watercress, Oak Leaf and red Oak Leaf, hon tsai tai (oriental spinach), Buttercrunch, red romaine, radicchio, sorrel, Lolla Rossa, Belgian endive, wild field lettuces, the mixture of young lettuce leaves and herbs called mesclun—the list goes on and on. There are far too many to discuss individually, so I'll just make some general observations.

First, match the greens to the vinaigrette or dressing. The flavor of the greens should determine the type of vinegar, oil and herbs and flavorings, if any, that you use. Obviously, strong, spicy greens stand up better to a savory vinaigrette than do delicately flavored greens. Trust your palate. Secondly, use the right types of greens for your salads. If you are making a warm salad, use the heartier, drier greens, like spinach, dandelion, radicchio. Reserve the softer, moister greens like Bibb, Oak Leaf, mâche and so on for a chilled salad. Finally, always clean and store the greens properly. Wash very gently in large amounts of cold water and drain very well, using a towel if necessary to pat the leaves dry. Place a damp towel on top of the leaves and store in airtight containers or plastic bags.

Mixed Green Salad

A simple mixed green salad served separately is an acceptable course in almost any meal. Some restraint should be shown when serving salad and wine together; the vinegar can be quite disturbing to the wine. Dress the salad lightly and use milder types of vinegar, like balsamic or high-quality wine vinegars, or use lemon juice instead of vinegar.

Mix the salad at the last minute. Gently toss chilled greens (several types) with a suitable vinaigrette, using your hands. Use only enough to coat the greens lightly; never douse them. If you want to add other garnishes to the salad, toss the garnish first and then add the greens; this keeps them from bruising. Be creative. Almost anything from your garden is good for salads. You may find a thin slice of melon to be as or even more refreshing than cucumber, for example. See pages 335–336 for vinaigrette recipes.

Mixed Greens with Red Onions, Green Beans, Blue Cheese and Olives

As the lengthy title indicates, this is a colorful mixture. It is also a salad that has been modified from a fairly traditional mix of ingredients.

SERVES FOUR TO SIX
AS A SIDE DISH

1 medium red onion, sliced into
  thin rings
½ pound green beans, picked
  and blanched until tender
1 cup Blue Cheese Vinaigrette
  (page 335)
6 cups mixed salad greens
  (loosely packed), washed and
  dried
½ cup Calamata or other black
  olives, drained
freshly ground black pepper

1. Place the onion rings, green beans and vinaigrette in a large bowl. Toss well, without breaking up the chunks of blue cheese too much.

2. Add the salad greens and toss gently. Serve the salad on individual plates and garnish each with a few olives. Grind a little pepper over each salad.

Parsley Salad

The first time I made parsley salad was for a commemorative birthday dinner at my restaurant, celebrating James Beard's eighty-third. Proceeds from the fund-raiser went to the James Beard Foundation. We used his recipes exclusively for the dinner. Parsley salad was served with chicken stuffed with green-peppercorn butter under the skin before roasting. I liked the parsley salad a lot and soon began experimenting and modifying the recipe. James Beard's parsley salad included garlic, sherry vinegar and parmesan; he recommended serving it with steak and chicken. This adaptation, which I suggest serving with grilled salmon, bluefish or other full-flavored or oily fish, uses milder flavorings, but it is still a very assertively flavored salad.

SERVES SIX TO EIGHT
AS A SIDE DISH

4 tablespoons olive oil
4 tablespoons vegetable oil
2 lemons
4 shallots, finely diced
  (4 tablespoons)
salt and freshly ground black
  pepper
3 large bunches Italian parsley,
  very fresh, washed and leaves
  picked (8 cups, loosely
  packed)

1. Combine the olive oil and vegetable oil in a bowl and grate the lemon rind into the oil, using the finest side of the grater.

2. Juice the lemons and add about 3 tablespoons juice to the oil mixture. Add the shallots and season to taste with salt and pepper. Mix thoroughly.

3. Add the parsley leaves and toss gently. Taste and adjust seasonings. It should be tart.

Warm Salad Greens with Sherry–Mustard Vinaigrette

This is a most practical salad that goes well with all sorts of grilled meats, poultry and game birds, as well as slices of sautéed foie gras, and even some seafood dishes like crab or fish cakes. Mix together some sturdy greens like frisée, escarole, radicchio, spinach, beet greens or endive in any combination. Warm a large sauté pan or two, depending on how much you have, and add just enough Sherry–Mustard Vinaigrette (page 336) to film the pan lightly; add the salad greens. Flip or stir until greens are warmed and have begun to wilt slightly. Be sure to stop before they are cooked. Taste and add more vinaigrette if necessary. Transfer to plates immediately and garnish appropriately.

Warm Spinach and Beet Salad with Bacon Dressing

This warm salad is wonderful by itself or as a garnish for grilled fish or chicken. For this salad the dressing is made in a sauté pan just before serving, and the beets and spinach are dressed and warmed in the pan. Move very fast or you will have a cooked vegetable, not a salad.

SERVES FOUR TO SIX
AS A SIDE DISH

2 medium beets (about 12 ounces)
1 pound spinach
¼ pound slab country bacon, cut in medium (½ inch) dice
1 tablespoon vegetable oil
1 medium onion, cut in medium (½ inch) dice
2 tablespoons raspberry vinegar
salt and freshly ground black pepper

1. Peel the beets and cut into ½-inch-thick sticks the length of the beet. Blanch in boiling salted water until tender (about 8 minutes). Run under cold water, drain and set aside.

2. Pick the stems off the spinach and wash thoroughly in a lot of cold water. If the spinach is at all gritty wash again.

3. Just before serving, heat the bacon in a large sauté pan until it begins to crisp. Add the oil and onion and cook until slightly tender, but not soft (1 to 2 minutes).

4. Add the vinegar and beets and cook for about 1 minute or until the beets are warmed through. Add the spinach and toss quickly; season to taste with salt and pepper. Remove the spinach from the pan as soon as it begins to wilt. Try to arrange this salad with some of the beets on top, but do not fool with it too much. Serve at once.

SQUASH

The squash family includes a large number of vegetables which grow on trailing vines. Soft-skinned squash, like zucchini, summer squash, golden squash, pattypans and others, are easily cooked. Simply slice them and stew or sauté them in a bit of butter or olive oil with seasonings. Garlic, onions, tomatoes, mushrooms, fresh basil, oregano and mint are all good to pair with this type of squash. Most of these soft squash have a mild flavor, so restraint should be used when seasoning. The best time to pick these squash is when they are still small.

The most wonderful feature of the zucchini-type squash is their beautiful edible flowers. They can be added to pasta or risotto, or they can be fried in a light tempura batter. They can also be filled with almost any kind of seafood, poultry, meat, and/or vegetable stuffing, mousse or forcemeat and then fried or baked for an appetizer or garnish.

Hard-skinned squash like acorn, butternut, hubbard and pumpkin are of a different nature and require slower and longer cooking. Their meat is much firmer and denser. Acorn squash are usually cut in half and baked. Butternut is usually diced, then stewed or boiled and pureed. Hubbard squash and pumpkins can be used interchangeably in soups or purees; they are most often used for desserts. Small pumpkins can be baked like acorn squash; they can also be stuffed and baked. For Pumpkin Puree, see page 289.

Liz's Braised Butternut Squash

Elizabeth Laing, my legal counselor and friend, is an avid restaurant-goer, who rarely cooks at home. Her favorite vegetable is butternut squash, so when it is in season I usually make it if I know she is coming. I created this simple dish, which doesn't rely on sweetening for its success, for Liz and others who genuinely love the rich flavor of winter squash.

SERVES FOUR TO SIX
AS A SIDE DISH

*1½ pounds butternut or other
    hard-skinned squash, peeled
4 tablespoons unsalted butter
1 small onion, thinly sliced
salt and freshly ground black
    pepper
1½ cups Chicken Stock
    (page 327)*

1. Preheat the oven to 350 degrees. Trim away any green still on the peeled squash. Cut it into squares about ¾ inch in size. Although they need not be perfect, they should be fairly uniform.

2. Butter a small glass pie or other small baking dish generously. Spread the onion slices on the bottom of the dish and put the squash on top; season lightly with salt and pepper. Dot the top with the remaining butter. Be sure the squash is layered evenly.

3. Heat the stock and season lightly with salt and pepper. Pour over the squash. Cover with aluminum foil and place directly in the preheated oven. After 30 minutes remove the foil and stir. Continue baking, uncovered, for 10 minutes more or until the squash is tender and the liquid has become slightly thickened.

TOMATOES

A lot of Yankees use tomatoes basically for salad, with vinegar and oil or even mayonnaise. But for the Portuguese and Italians who have settled in New England, the tomato is an indispensable ingredient, especially for seafood cookery. Tomatoes and seafood are one of the great classic combinations in cookery.

Maybe it's my Italian heritage, but I use tomatoes freely in my cooking. You will find them in many recipes throughout this book. When tomatoes are in season (August through October and even November), I use them in abundance. The rest of the year I rely on canned or dried tomatoes for stock, soups, and sauces but do not feature tomatoes on their own. The flavorless facsimiles that are available year-round are like zombies, the living dead, hideous creatures with no soul, who come back to haunt us and disgrace the memory of our beloved summer tomatoes.

Sundried or Oven-Dried Tomatoes

An old-fashioned Italian method of preserving tomatoes is to dry them. Drying intensifies the flavor and gives tomatoes a character similar to olives. In the old days tomatoes drying on the roofs of apartment houses in cities and towns along the East Coast were a common sight.

Descendants of the people who once looked down on the Italian immigrants and their relentless effort to maintain their cooking traditions pay astronomical prices for *pumate,* now a hot new item in yuppie markets. Good-quality sundried tomatoes are expensive, especially when packed in olive oil. At the peak of the season, when tomatoes are at their best and yet relatively inexpensive, they can be made for a tenth the price, with no social stigma attached, on the contrary.

To dry your own cut the tomatoes straight down from top to bottom in half. Place them on a rack, skin side down, and sprinkle the meaty inside of the tomatoes generously with salt. At this point they can be sundried or oven-dried. The most important factor in drying is good air circulation. If you are not in a breezy place, a fan will help enormously. Place the tomatoes in the sun and turn them over after half a day. They will probably take at least two days to dry, so turn them twice again the next day. Sprinkle with more salt if necessary. When they are completely dried, seal in airtight containers.

The tomatoes may also be dried in a convection oven. Keep the oven at 150 degrees or as low as possible, and keep the fan on at all times. Turn the tomatoes after eight hours. They will take from sixteen to twenty-four hours to dry. Seel in airtight containers.

To reconstitute dried tomatoes, simmer in plain water until they are tender and have plumped a bit. They can now be used in cooking as is or they can be marinated in olive oil with a few slices of garlic. The tomatoes in oil serve as a nice addition to a salad or antipasto.

Marinated Tomatoes and Arugula with Fried Squid

This is a knockout salad, combining some tried and true flavor combinations in a new way. It is excellent as a luncheon main course, as an appetizer or in a large meal as a combination salad and fish course. Be sure to fry the squid at the very last minute and place it around the salad right before it is served.

SERVES FOUR AS A LIGHT ENTREE
OR SIX AS AN APPETIZER

*12 to 16 thick (½ inch) slices of
ripe tomato (about 1 to 1½
pounds tomatoes)*
½ cup olive oil
⅓ cup aged balsamic vinegar
*2 or 3 cloves garlic, finely
chopped (1 tablespoon)*
*½ cup (loosely packed) fresh
basil, coarsely chopped*
salt and freshly ground pepper
*4 cups (loosely packed) arugula
(6 to 8 ounces), washed and
drained*
*1 pound squid cut into rings
(tentacles included) and fried
(page 33)*

1. Place the tomatoes in a pie tin or other shallow pan and pour the oil and vinegar on top; sprinkle with garlic and basil. Season with salt and pepper and move the tomatoes (don't toss them) so that the ingredients are distributed evenly. Cover and place in the refrigerator for up to 1 hour, moving the tomatoes at least one more time so that they are well marinated.

2. Right before serving, place the arugula in a bowl. Pour some of the marinade on top and toss gently. Divide among individual plates and arrange the tomatoes in the center. Place the fried squid around the tomatoes. Serve immediately.

Pancakes and Fritters, Quickbreads, Bread and Noodles

Tim the Miller's Traditional Johnnycakes
Thin Johnnycakes
Johnnycake Polenta
Brown-Bread Pancakes
Brown-Bread Waffles
Fresh Corn Cakes
Wild Rice Pancakes
Apple Fritters
Corn Fritters
Blueberry Muffins
Cream Biscuits
Boston Brown Bread
Rye Featherbeds
Mark's Whole-Grain Country Bread
Jasper's Breadsticks
Anadama Bread
Pizza
White Clam Pizza

Noodles and Other Pasta
Pasta

Commercial milling of grain in New England began about 1675. By the end of the 1700s, there were scores of mills scattered throughout the region. Huge granite stones, shaped like large wheels, pressed against each other to grind flour or meal from whole grains, particularly corn and wheat. The stone wheels were powered by an even larger wooden wheel, which was turned by the rush of river water. Unfortunately, today most of those mills are occupied by museums, restaurants, antique shops and other, similar enterprises. With the exception of possibly a dozen at most, the old mill is a relic.

The loss of the small mills has had far-reaching effects. With the closing of the small mills, which could no longer compete with the huge grain conglomerates, mostly out of the Midwest, came the end of the era of small grain farmers around New England and other parts of America. The loss of these farms led to the actual extinction of many varieties of corn and other grains.

There are still a few mills left that produce stone-ground flours and cornmeal as it was done in the past. It is a labor of love, and through them we may still get a taste of what bread was like one or two hundred years ago. I urge you to purchase such flours by mail order or at specialty shops, at any price (see List of Sources, page 358). Gray's Mill in Rhode Island, for example, uses unimproved, white-cap flint corn, a true Indian corn that has kept its integrity through the efforts of a few stubborn millers and farmers and the University of Rhode Island. You can make johnnycakes by substituting any white cornmeal for the meal made with this type of corn, but they will not be real johnnycakes.

Another element that is lost through the mass production and distribution of flour and grains is freshness. Although certain types of flours improve with aging a few months, most flours are at their peak right after the milling process. Tasting bread or other cooked forms of freshly milled wheat, rye or corn is a revelation. It is like tasting freshly squeezed orange juice, when all you ever drank before was made from concentrate. Freshness is an important quality that has been forfeited over the years as small, local millers were forced out of business.

The housewives of centuries past were wizards when it came to baking, and they left a legacy of great variety and creativity. Anyone who likes to bake and who understands the properties of the different ingredients can—and does—create his or her own recipes all the time. For that reason alone, there are probably more words written on this subject than any other area of cooking. I have limited myself here to a few favorite recipes, some of them innovative and some New England classics.

FLOURS AND MEALS

The following is a brief review of the different kinds of flour called for in this chapter as well as the one on desserts. Understanding their different properties, virtues and drawbacks is essential to successful baking, especially if substitutions become necessary.

All-Purpose Flour

This is a blend of mostly hard-wheat flour with some soft-wheat flour. Although it is quite useful for culinary preparations such as making roux, dusting, coating, breading, etc., it is only acceptable at best for most baking. I recommend that you use specific flours for specific purposes. In my restaurant, we do not use all-purpose flour at all. For recipes in this book that call for all-purpose flour, bread flour makes an excellent replacement. Store, tightly covered, in a cool, dry place.

Bread Flour

Bread flour or high-gluten flour is made from varieties of hard wheat that are low in starch; these are grown primarily in the northern Midwest in spring. The bran and germ are removed and only the protein-rich endosperm is ground for bread flour. The gluten gives this coarsely textured flour the strength and elasticity needed to make good bread. There is really no substitute for this type of flour in bread baking. Store, tightly covered, in a cool, dry place.

Pastry and Cake Flours

These two flours are very similar, though cake flour is more finely milled. They are made from softer varieties of wheat that have a high starch content; these are usually grown in winter in the southern Midwest and the East. As with bread flour, only the endosperm, which produces a white flour, is used. Pastry and cake flours are low in gluten and have a soft and fine texture that is more suitable for preparations like cakes, where tenderness is a factor. Of the two, cake flour is higher in starch and lower in gluten, but they can be used interchangeably in most cases. They can also be simulated by adding cornstarch to bread or all-purpose flour. (Packaged cake flour already has cornstarch in it.) Store, tightly covered, in a cool, dry place.

Whole Wheat Flour

Also known as graham flour, whole wheat flour, as its name implies, is made by grinding the entire husked kernel of wheat, which is composed of the bran, the germ and the endosperm. Since most of the vitamins and fiber of wheat are in the bran and germ, whole wheat flour is far more nutritious than white flour. White flour, which has a higher gluten content, is mixed with whole wheat when lighter baked goods are desired. Never sift whole wheat flour; sifting removes some of the nutritious bran and germ from the flour. Store, tightly covered or wrapped, in the refrigerator.

Semolina

Semolina is a coarse flour made from durum wheat, the hardest of all types of wheat. Its texture is perfect for making the stiff dough necessary to make good pasta, especially if it is to be dried, but it has few other uses. Although bread flour can be used to make pasta, semolina is far superior in both flavor and strength. Only pasta made from semolina can achieve true al dente texture. Store, tightly covered, in a cool, dry place.

Rye Flour

Rye flour excels in flavor, but is low in protein. For that reason, it must be mixed with wheat flour in most preparations. Rye flour is milled from the endosperm of rye. When rye is ground whole, it is known as pumpernickel. Store rye and pumpernickel flours, tightly covered or wrapped, in the refrigerator.

Cornmeal

Cornmeal is made by grinding whole dried kernels of the hard varieties of corn; it is ground into various consistencies. It is usually sold as fine or coarse; most recipes in this book call for the coarse. Cornmeal also varies in color, depending on the color of the corn. In New England that means yellow or white, but there is also blue cornmeal from a type of blue corn that is native to the Southwest. Cornmeal often needs to be mixed with wheat flour as it is not high in protein and its starches are not fully released unless completely pulverized or cooked for long periods of time. There are, however, some preparations, like johnnycakes, that require only cornmeal. Cornmeal is also useful for breading fish and shellfish for frying. Store, tightly covered, under refrigeration or in a cool, dry place.

Johnnycake Meal

This is a specific type of stone-ground cornmeal made from Indian corn in and around Rhode Island (see List of Sources, page 358). In addition to making the famous cakes, which are its namesake, this meal can be used in many other preparations that call for white or yellow cornmeal. Store, tightly covered, in the refrigerator.

Brown-Bread Flour

A specialty of New England, brown-bread flour is a mixture of whole wheat, rye and cornmeal or johnnycake meal. It can be purchased already mixed (see List of Sources, page 358) or made by simply combining equal parts of wheat and rye flour and cornmeal. It is used mostly for Boston Brown Bread (page 270); it also makes wonderful pancakes and waffles. Store, tightly covered, in the refrigerator.

Tim the Miller's Traditional Johnnycakes

The commercial milling of grain in New England began about 1675 and thrived for almost 250 years. Gray's Mill in Adamsville, Rhode Island, is one of the last stone mills operating commercially in New England. Along with at most a dozen other mills that use traditional grinding methods, Gray's Mill, which was founded during the Civil War, is a living monument to our culinary heritage. Tim McTague, who has operated Gray's Mill since the late seventies, produces freshly milled whole wheat and rye flour, yellow corn and white corn (johnnycake) meal. To free himself from unreliable water power, Tim powers his century-and-a-half-old granite stones with a 1946 Dodge truck. Hardly state of the art, but General Mills' multimillion-dollar operation has never produced flour even close to the quality of Tim the Miller's.

This is Tim's recipe for johnnycakes, which are traditionally served at breakfast. Because they are dense, they should be made small and served sparingly; two or three per person are usually enough. They can be served with butter and maple syrup or with eggs, bacon or sausage. Consult the List of Sources (page 358) for johnnycake meal and other flours.

MAKES SIX TO EIGHT BREAKFAST PORTIONS

2 cups johnnycake meal
1 teaspoon salt
¼ cup heavy cream or milk
butter, vegetable oil or bacon fat
   for frying

1. Mix together the johnnycake meal and salt in a bowl.
2. Bring 2 cups of water to a boil and pour into the meal and salt. Stir well and allow the paste to stand for 5 minutes. Stir in the cream or milk and mix until the paste is smooth.
3. Form small patties about ½ to ⅓ inch thick and 2 to 2½ inches in diameter. Heat a heavy cast-iron skillet to medium-hot. Cover the pan with butter, oil or bacon fat and fry the johnnycakes for about 4 to 5 minutes on each side. Serve hot.

Thin Johnnycakes

I popularized this style of johnnycake about seven years ago, while I was chef at the Bostonian Hotel in Boston. I wanted to create a lighter version of the johnnycakes that I first tasted at the Commons Restaurant across from the church I was married in, in Little Compton, Rhode Island, without changing the integrity of the flavor. Thin johnnycakes served with crème fraîche and caviar are still popular at my restaurant. They are also good with lobster, chicken, eggs, bacon and all sorts of other accompaniments. Try Poached Eggs on Thin Johnnycakes with Caviar (page 207).

MAKES FOUR TO SIX PORTIONS

1 cup johnnycake meal
½ teaspoon salt
1¼ cups milk
1 egg
corn oil

1. Combine the johnnycake meal, salt, milk and egg in a mixing bowl. Whip until completely smooth, then add 2 tablespoons corn oil. Let rest for 10 to 20 minutes to allow the meal to soften.
2. Heat a nonstick or well-seasoned skillet or griddle until medium-hot and season with a bit of oil. Wipe the pan out before adding the batter.
3. Pour or spoon enough batter into the pan so that the johnnycakes spread to about 3 inches in diameter. They should be very thin and have lots of tiny holes. Cook for about 1 minute on each side, until golden brown. Serve hot.

Johnnycake Polenta

Back in colonial times, the Yankees used to make a dish called hasty pudding, a mush made from white cornmeal, which was similar to the rustic Italian dish called polenta, a mush made from yellow cornmeal. Hasty pudding has not made a comeback, but polenta certainly has. It was a natural and logical next step for New England cooks to use johnnycake meal for polenta and call it johnnycake polenta. This is wonderful with game birds, chicken, sausages and venison; it also pairs well with fish, especially when the fish is panfried. Although johnnycake polenta is perfectly good to eat when soft, I prefer to allow it to cool, then cut it into rectangles or triangles and panfry it. Panfrying adds another dimension of flavor from the taste of toasted corn. Its crispness is also a bonus. The polenta should be very smooth and creamy before it is poured into a pan to set. The idea is to have it just thick enough to hold together.

SERVES SIX TO EIGHT
AS A SIDE DISH

1½ cups johnnycake meal
3 tablespoons unsalted butter
about 1 tablespoon salt
freshly ground black pepper
all-purpose flour for dredging
corn, olive or other vegetable oil
  for frying

1. Combine the johnnycake meal with 2 cups water in a heavy saucepan and whisk smooth. Add 4 more cups of water while continuing to whisk to prevent lumps from forming.

2. Place the pot over medium heat and bring to a boil, stirring or whisking frequently to prevent scorching as well as lumps forming. Once the polenta has reached a boil and has begun to thicken, lower the heat to allow the polenta to simmer slowly.

3. Add the butter, salt and pepper and simmer for about 1 hour. Stir frequently; you cannot stir it too often. Be careful not to spatter any on your hand. It is extremely hot.

4. After 1 hour, the polenta should be thick, smooth and creamy. At this point, it can be served as is. If you intend to panfry it, pour it into a 9- or 10-inch baking dish so the polenta is about ½ to ¾ inch thick. It is not necessary to grease the dish; it will not stick. Allow the polenta to set for a while before refrigerating; chill thoroughly.

5. Cut into rectangles or triangles. Heat a large pan with about ¼ inch of oil to medium-hot. Dredge the polenta in flour and place in the hot oil. Cook 4 or 5 minutes on each side, or until golden brown and very crisp. Serve at once.

Brown-Bread Pancakes

My wife and I rarely eat a full breakfast during our busy work days in Boston. But when we drive up to our cottage on Sawyer's Island near Boothbay Harbor in Maine, breakfast becomes almost a defiant gesture. Wild blueberries, lots of them, grow among the juniper shrubs that go down to the water's edge. Many mornings I go out and pick a pint or so and add them to the pancake batter. They are full-flavored and quite small, half the size of cultivated berries, perfect for pancakes. You could add other fruits to the batter as well. The mixture of different grains in the brown-bread flour gives these pancakes a richer flavor than those made with all white flour.

MAKES SIX BREAKFAST
PORTIONS

1½ cups brown-bread flour
   (page 261)
1 cup all-purpose flour
1 tablespoon baking powder
1 teaspoon salt
1 tablespoon brown sugar
4 eggs, separated
1⅔ cups milk
3 tablespoons unsalted butter,
   melted
vegetable oil or butter to grease
   the pan (optional)

For Serving
unsalted butter, softened at
   room temperature
maple syrup, warmed

1. Heat a large cast-iron skillet on low to medium heat until it has reached a hot and steady temperature. The melted butter in the batter usually provides all the fat needed to cook these pancakes, but you may wish to season the pan with a little oil or butter; in that case, wipe out the pan before adding the batter.

2. Sift together the brown-bread flour, all-purpose flour, baking powder, salt and brown sugar in a large mixing bowl.

3. Mix the egg yolks with the milk and add to the flour mixture. Stir until the batter is smooth.

4. Beat the egg whites until soft peaks are formed. Gently fold the egg whites into the batter. While the batter is still streaky and not completely mixed, add the melted butter. Continue folding until the ingredients are blended. Do not overmix.

5. Make the pancakes a few at a time and serve immediately with softened butter and maple syrup.

VARIATIONS

Blueberry Brown-Bread Pancakes

Fold 1½ to 2 cups blueberries into the batter with the melted butter.

Banana Brown-Bread Pancakes

Finely dice 1 large banana and fold it into the batter with the melted butter.

Apple Brown-Bread Pancakes

Fold about 1 cup grated apple into the batter with the melted butter.

Brown-Bread Waffles

Waffles are good for breakfast or dessert. They are just as delicious served with butter and warmed maple syrup as with fresh berries and whipped cream or with ice cream.

MAKES SIX BREAKFAST OR
DESSERT PORTIONS

1½ cups brown-bread flour
   (page 261)
1 cup all-purpose flour
1 tablespoon salt
1 tablespoon brown sugar
2 teaspoons malt powder
   (optional)
4 eggs, separated
2 cups milk
1 tablespoon vegetable oil
⅓ cup chopped walnuts or
   pecans (optional)
3 tablespoons butter, melted

1. Sift together the brown-bread flour, all-purpose flour, salt, brown sugar and malt powder, if using, in a large mixing bowl.

2. Mix the egg yolks with the milk; stir in the vegetable oil. Add to the flour mixture and stir until the batter is smooth.

3. Beat the egg whites until soft peaks are formed. Gently fold the egg whites into the batter. Fold in the chopped nuts, if using. While the batter is still streaky, add the melted butter. Continue folding until all the ingredients are blended. Do not overmix.

4. Heat the waffle iron and pour or ladle on enough batter to spread to the edges. Cook until golden brown. Allow the first waffle to overcook slightly (it may stick) in order to season the waffle iron. Serve immediately.

Fresh Corn Cakes

These are a good match for panfried trout or mackerel—always a memorable breakfast. They can also accompany seafood, chicken or pork at lunch or dinner. Topped with crème fraîche and fresh Maine crabmeat or creamed lobster, they are good as an appetizer.

MAKES TWO DOZEN
TWO-INCH PANCAKES

6 ears sweet corn, shucked
½ medium onion, roughly
   chopped (½ to ¾ cup)
3 tablespoons unsalted butter
1 small red bell pepper, cut in
   small (¼ inch) dice (½ cup)
1 small green bell pepper, cut in
   small (¼ inch) dice (½ cup)
3 eggs
1 cup milk
¾ cup yellow cornmeal
1½ cups all-purpose flour
1 teaspoon salt
1 teaspoon freshly ground black
   pepper
2 tablespoons chopped chives
oil or butter for frying

1. Remove any hairs from the shucked corn. Cut the kernels off the cobs (you should have about 3 cups). Scrape down the cobs to extract the sweet milk from the corn.

2. Combine the corn with its milk and the chopped onion. Pass the mixture through the medium blade of a grinder or make a coarse puree in a food processor.

3. Heat the butter in a large skillet and sauté the peppers briefly. It may seem like too much butter, but it is needed for the batter.

4. Mix the eggs and milk in a large mixing bowl. Add the cornmeal, flour, salt and pepper and mix until smooth. Stir in the corn mixture, peppers and chives.

5. Heat a nonstick or well-seasoned cast-iron pan on medium to low heat until quite hot; allow it to heat for at least 5 minutes before adding the batter. Lightly grease the pan and make the pancakes a few at a time. Transfer to a sheetpan in a warm oven until ready to serve.

Wild Rice Pancakes

Wild rice, a grain native to the Great Lakes region of America and Canada, is another of the American Indian's gifts to our cooking repertoire. It has a special affinity with poultry and game birds. These pancakes are meant to be served as part of a main course, and they suit any food that matches well with wild rice. I recommend you use a nonstick pan with only a little fat for cooking these pancakes.

SERVES FOUR TO SIX
AS A SIDE DISH

¾ cup wild rice (4 ounces)
1 teaspoon salt
1 bay leaf
1 small carrot, cut in small
   (¼ inch) dice (½ cup)
1 large red or green bell pepper,
   cut in small (¼ inch) dice
   (¾ cup)
4 scallions, thinly sliced
3 tablespoons unsalted butter
2 eggs
1 cup milk
1½ cups all-purpose flour
salt and freshly ground black
   pepper
butter, vegetable oil, goose or
   duck fat for frying

1. Combine the wild rice with 2 cups water, the salt and bay leaf in a small saucepan. Partially cover and cook slowly for about 1 hour or until the rice is very tender. Drain off any excess liquid and allow to cool.

2. Sauté the carrot, pepper and scallions in the butter for 2 to 3 minutes. The vegetables should still have some firmness to them.

3. Whisk the eggs and milk together in a large mixing bowl. Add the flour, stirring until smooth. Stir in the rice and vegetables. Season to taste with salt and pepper. Heat a nonstick pan to medium-hot and add a small amount of fat prior to adding the batter. Make pancakes 2 to 3 inches in diameter; cook for 2 to 3 minutes on each side. Transfer to a sheetpan in a warm oven until ready to serve.

Apple Fritters

The smell of my grandmother's kitchen in the morning would wake the dead. An early riser, she would start baking and cooking as soon as the sun came up and within an hour, everyone else would be awake, not because of the noise but because of the intoxicating aromas that filled the house. Apple fritters were a special favorite of my brothers and me. We could eat them as fast as she could make them, but she would keep up with us until we could eat no more. Nina, as we called her, was fanatical about the ingredients she cooked with. Only the most flavorful apples from her favorite orchard were used in her kitchen. There was no need for cinnamon or any other spices; the apples did all the work. This is her simple recipe.

I love these best in the morning, but they also make a fabulous dessert. Try them with homemade ice cream or with Caramel Sauce (page 319). The Chinese dip apple fritters into hot caramel and then quickly into ice water, which hardens the caramel. I have also served these as a garnish for blue-cheese salad. But if you like them plain, as I do, just sprinkle them with a bit of powdered sugar.

MAKES SIX TO EIGHT BREAKFAST
OR DESSERT PORTIONS

2 cups all-purpose flour
1 tablespoon baking powder
½ cup sugar
1 tablespoon salt
2 eggs
⅔ cup milk
4 large firm green or other tart
   apples, peeled, cored and
   sliced ¼ inch thick
2 tablespoons unsalted butter,
   melted
vegetable oil for deep-frying
confectioners sugar for dusting

1. Sift together the flour, baking powder, sugar and salt in a mixing bowl. Mix well.

2. Beat the eggs and milk together and add the flour mixture, stirring until smooth.

3. Fold in the sliced apples and melted butter. Allow batter to stand at least 10 minutes before using.

4. Heat the oil to 375 degrees in a pot suitable for deep-frying. Drop large spoonfuls, the size of a walnut, of batter into the hot oil. Cook the fritters for a few minutes until they are golden brown or even a little darker. Drain onto paper towels. Dust with confectioners sugar and serve at once.

Corn Fritters

These are a delicious side dish to accompany fish, pork or chowder. They are also good as a simple hors d'oeuvre. At my restaurant we serve them with panfried rainbow trout from Maine.

SERVES EIGHT TO TEN AS AN
APPETIZER OR SIDEDISH

3 ears sweet corn
½ cup yellow cornmeal
1½ cups all-purpose flour
1 tablespoon baking powder
1 teaspoon salt
½ teaspoon pepper
¼ teaspoon cayenne pepper
2 thick slices of bacon, cut in
   small (¼ inch) dice
2 eggs
1 cup milk
1 red bell pepper, cut in small
   (¼ inch) dice (½ cup)
1 small onion, grated
1 tablespoon chopped chives
corn or other vegetable oil for
   deep-frying

1. Husk the corn and blanch it in plenty of boiling salted water. Drain and cut off the kernels (you should have about 1½ cups). Set aside.

2. Mix together the cornmeal, flour, baking powder, salt, pepper and cayenne pepper. Sift into a mixing bowl.

3. Cook the bacon until crisp. Add the bacon as well as the fat to the dry mixture. Add the eggs, milk, red pepper, onion, chives and corn and mix well. Chill the batter for at least 1 hour.

4. Heat the oil to 350 degrees in a pot appropriate for deep-frying. Using a serving spoon, drop spoonfuls of batter quickly into the oil so all cook equally. Do not crowd the pot. Check the first fritters. If necessary, the batter can be adjusted slightly (thinned with milk or thickened with flour). Drain fritters on paper towels and serve while still very hot and crisp.

Blueberry Muffins

This is my wife, Nancy's, foolproof recipe for fruit muffins. She likes to split them and toast them and then add more butter.

MAKES ONE DOZEN MUFFINS

5 tablespoons unsalted butter
⅓ cup granulated sugar
1 egg, lightly beaten
1 tablespoon grated orange zest
2 cups pastry flour
5 teaspoons baking powder
½ teaspoon salt
1 cup milk
2 cups whole wild Maine or
  other blueberries
¼ cup light brown sugar

1. Preheat the oven to 375 degrees. Lightly grease 12 standard-size muffin tins with 1 tablespoon butter. Cream the remaining butter and sugar until light in consistency and color. Add the egg and orange zest and beat into the mixture.

2. Mix and sift together the flour, baking powder and salt. Add about a fourth of the flour mixture to the butter-sugar-egg mixture; mix well. Blend in a third of the milk; continue alternating flour and milk, ending with flour. The batter should be smooth.

3. Fold in the berries and spoon the batter into the muffin tins, filling them just a little more than halfway. Sift a small amount of brown sugar over the top of each muffin. Place in the oven and bake for about 30 minutes or until well browned. Stick a skewer into the center of the muffin; it will come out clean when the muffins are done.

VARIATION

Cranberry Muffins Substitute 1½ cups fresh or frozen cranberries, chopped, for the blueberries.

Cream Biscuits

This recipe, which comes from my longtime friend and associate Lydia Shire, has been a standard in my kitchen for almost a decade. I have tried a few other biscuit recipes but have yet to find one better than this. The cream replaces the butter or other fat that is used in most biscuit recipes, and it makes these as moist as can be. Biscuits can be served like bread at any meal, but they are especially good with chowders, baked ham and chicken.

MAKES ABOUT TWO DOZEN SMALL BISCUITS

2½ cups pastry flour
1 tablespoon baking powder
1 teaspoon sugar
1 teaspoon salt
about 1¼ cups heavy cream
4 tablespoons unsalted butter, melted
¼ cup finely chopped fresh parsley

1. Preheat the oven to 375 degrees. Mix together and sift the flour, baking powder, sugar and salt into a mixing bowl. Add the cream slowly and mix until a soft dough begins to form. This may take a little less or a little more cream depending on the amount of starch in the flour and butterfat in the cream.

2. Remove to a lightly floured surface and gently knead until the dough is well formed. Try not to overwork it.

3. Roll out the dough about ½ inch thick. Brush generously with melted butter, then sprinkle with parsley.

4. Fold the dough over, forming two layers with the parsley in the center. The dough should be about 1 inch thick. Using a cookie or pastry cutter, cut into 1-inch rounds and place on an ungreased sheetpan or cookie sheet. Place in the preheated oven and bake until lightly browned, about 12 minutes. Serve hot.

VARIATION

Cheddar Cheese Biscuits

Add 4 ounces of aged Cheddar cheese, finely grated, to the sifted-flour mixture. Mix well to coat the cheese and disperse it evenly throughout the flour. Continue as for Cream Biscuits.

Boston Brown Bread

It is no coincidence that the method used to bake this bread, steaming, is similar to one used by the native Indians of New England, who taught us how to use corn as a grain for bread. The most famous of our region's breads, this wholesome blend of wheat, rye and corn flours is as suitable for our diets today as it was 300 years ago.

MAKES ONE LOAF

1 tablespoon unsalted butter for greasing
1½ cups brown-bread flour (page 261)
1 teaspoon baking soda
½ teaspoon salt
⅓ cup dark molasses
1 cup milk
½ cup dried currants or raisins

1. Preheat the oven to 325 degrees.

2. Generously grease a 1-quart pudding mold or 1-pound coffee can. Combine the flour, baking soda and salt in a mixing bowl. Stir in the molasses and milk. Fold in the currants.

3. Fill the mold or coffee can with batter. It should come up about two-thirds of the way. Cover the top with foil and tie securely with a string to make it airtight.

4. Place in a deep baking pan and fill the pan with boiling water, to come halfway up the side of the mold.

5. Place in the preheated oven and allow to steam for 2 hours, checking the water level after 1 hour. Add more boiling water if needed. Check by sticking a skewer into the bread; it will come out clean when done. Remove string and foil and allow to cool for 1 hour before unmolding.

Rye Featherbeds

The use of potatoes in baking is quite traditional in New England. An old Yankee favorite, featherbeds were little rolls made with potatoes and flour. As the name implies, featherbeds were very light (because of the potatoes). Vermont Chocolate Potato Cake (page 298) also uses potatoes, with the same results. Since these rolls are made with rye flour, they are not strictly speaking featherbeds, but I think they deserve the name—they are just as light and even tastier.

MAKES ONE DOZEN ROLLS

*1 medium (6 to 8 ounces) Maine
    or other all-purpose potato*
*1 scant tablespoon (1 package)
    dry yeast*
1 tablespoon sugar
3 tablespoons vegetable oil
1 teaspoon salt
2½ cups bread flour
1½ cups rye flour
1 egg
caraway seeds
coarse sea salt

1. Peel and boil the potato in lightly salted water. When thoroughly cooked, remove from the pot, reserving 1¼ cups of the potato water. Mash or rice the potato and set aside.

2. Combine the yeast, sugar and ¼ cup of potato water. Mix well and let stand for 10 minutes.

3. Add the oil, salt, potato, bread flour and rye flour to the yeast mixture and begin mixing by hand or machine. Slowly add the remaining potato water (1 cup) slowly. After a soft dough incorporating all the ingredients has formed, remove to a lightly floured surface and knead for 12 minutes or until strong and elastic. If you are using an electric mixer with a dough hook, the kneading will take less time.

4. Lightly butter or oil a large bowl. Shape the dough into a ball and place it in the bowl. Turn the dough once so that it is lightly greased all over. Cover loosely with plastic wrap and place in a warm draftfree spot.

5. Preheat the oven to 375 degrees. Lightly oil a sheetpan or cookie sheet. When the dough has doubled in volume (1 to 1½ hours) turn it out onto a lightly floured surface. Divide the dough into 12 even pieces and shape each piece into a ball. Place the balls on the sheetpan and return to a warm draftfree spot. Allow the rolls to rise for about 20 minutes or until almost doubled.

6. Mix the egg with a bit of water to make an egg wash. Brush the rolls with the wash and sprinkle with caraway seeds and coarse sea salt. Place in the preheated oven and bake for about 25 to 30 minutes or until nicely browned.

NOTE. This dough may also be shaped into breadsticks or loaves.

Mark's Whole-Grain Country Bread

This recipe, developed by my pastry chef, Mark Cupolo, has a few interesting twists to it. Coffee? Cocoa? They are no mistake, as you'll find out when you taste this deeply flavored four-grain bread. It is excellent for sandwiches made with smoked fish, roast beef, bacon and other strongly flavored foods. It is also great for morning toast, with butter and preserves, or with supper in the evening.

MAKES TWO LOAVES

1 scant tablespoon (1 package) dry yeast
1 tablespoon sugar
1/4 cup brewed coffee
3 tablespoons vegetable oil
3 tablespoons dark molasses
2 teaspoons salt
3 cups bread flour
1/2 cup whole wheat flour
1/4 cup rye flour
1/2 cup yellow cornmeal or johnnycake meal
1/4 cup quick-cooking oatmeal
1 teaspoon unsweetened cocoa powder
1 cup water
1 egg

1. Combine the yeast, sugar and coffee in a mixing bowl. Mix well and set aside for 10 minutes.

2. Add the oil, molasses, salt, bread, whole wheat and rye flours, the cornmeal, oatmeal and cocoa powder. Add 1 cup warm water slowly while mixing by hand or machine. When a soft dough incorporating all the flour and grain has formed, remove to a lightly floured surface and knead for about 12 minutes or until the dough is strong and elastic. If you are using an electric mixer with a dough hook, kneading will take less time.

3. Lightly butter or oil a large bowl. Shape the dough into a ball and place it in the bowl. Turn the dough once so that it is lightly greased all over. Cover loosely with plastic wrap and place in a warm draftfree spot.

4. Preheat the oven to 350 degrees. Grease two 9½-inch loaf pans. When the dough has doubled in volume (about 1 hour), turn it out onto a lightly floured surface. Cut in half and shape each half into a loaf. Place each in a loaf pan and return to a warm draft-free spot. If you prefer, shape into 2 large balls or baguettes and place on a sheetpan or cookie sheet. Allow the loaves to rise for 20 to 30 minutes, or until just about double in size.

5. Mix the egg with a bit of water to make an egg wash. Brush the loaves with the wash and place in the preheated oven. Bake for 40 minutes to 1 hour, depending on the shape of the loaves, or until dark brown. Knock on the bottom of the loaf; when you hear a sort of hollow sound, the bread is done.

Jasper's Breadsticks

At my restaurant, we make thick and crusty breadsticks every day. I chose the shape when I opened the restaurant because it takes less time to rise. We had a small work space then, with no proof box, and time was a factor. We have since improved the kitchen, but the breadsticks have become such a tradition that we dare not change them. Besides, we like them.

At the restaurant we improvise a little every day. One of the garnishes we use often is coarse sea salt, lightly sprinkled on top, like pretzels. Served piping hot with fresh sweet butter, the salted breadsticks are hard to resist. You can also use fresh herbs, seeds, spices, cheese, onions, olives, and other vegetables, cracklings, bacon and nuts, alone or in combination, to vary the recipe. Keep the flavors subtle and be sure they complement the other foods being served. Sometimes plain breadsticks are most appropriate.

MAKES TWO DOZEN BREADSTICKS

1 scant tablespoon (1 package)
  dry yeast
1 tablespoon sugar
3 tablespoons olive or other
  vegetable oil
2 teaspoons salt
4½ cups bread flour, sifted
1 egg
coarse sea salt (optional)

1. Combine yeast, sugar and ¼ cup water in a mixing bowl. Mix well and let stand for 10 minutes.

2. Add oil, salt and flour and begin mixing by hand or machine. Slowly add 1½ cups warm water. When a soft dough incorporating all the ingredients has formed, remove to a lightly floured surface and knead for 12 to 15 minutes or until very strong and elastic. If you are using an electric mixer with a dough hook, the kneading will take less time.

3. Lightly butter or oil a large bowl. Shape the dough into a ball and place it in the bowl. Turn the dough once so that it is lightly greased all over. Cover loosely with plastic wrap and place in a warm draftfree spot.

4. When the dough has doubled in volume (about 40 minutes), punch it down. Allow it to rise again for 20 to 30 minutes or until doubled in volume.

5. Preheat the oven to 400 degrees. Lightly oil a sheetpan. Turn out the dough onto a lightly floured surface and roll out about ¾ inch thick in a 12-inch square.

6. Mix the egg with a bit of water to make an egg wash. Brush the entire surface and sprinkle with sea salt, if using. Using a knife or pizza wheel (the perfect tool for cutting breadsticks), cut the dough into 1 × 6-inch strips. Place on the lightly oiled sheetpan and bake in the preheated oven for 15 to 20 minutes or until golden brown.

VARIATIONS

Cheddar Cheese Add 1 cup finely grated Cheddar cheese to dough while mixing. Sprinkle with 1 more cup grated cheese after the egg wash.

Seeds Sprinkle with sesame, poppy, mustard, fennel or caraway seeds, alone or in combination, after the egg wash.

Onion and Poppy Seeds Sauté a finely chopped small onion (about ¾ cup) in butter or oil. Spread over the dough after the egg wash, then sprinkle with poppy seeds.

Fresh Herbs Add picked leaves of thyme, rosemary or marjoram or chopped chives or other herbs to the dough while adding the flour. Use stronger herbs in moderation.

Whole Grain Replace ¾ to 1 cup of the bread flour with johnnycake meal or other cornmeal, whole wheat or rye flour.

Anadama Bread

Whether Anna put too much flour in the cornbread or whether she was just too lazy to make bread at all (the stories vary) legend has it that the name of this traditional New England bread came from her husband's saying "Anna, damn her" all the time. If this bread was a mistake, then it was a good one. The corn adds character and flavor to a yeast dough, while the generous amount of bread flour gives it a light and chewy character not usually associated with cornbread.

MAKES TWO LOAVES

1 scant tablespoon (1 package)
  dry yeast
1 tablespoon sugar
2 tablespoons unsalted butter,
  melted
2 tablespoons dark molasses
2 teaspoons salt
3½ cups bread flour
1 cup yellow cornmeal
1 egg

1. Preheat the oven to 350 degrees. Combine the yeast and sugar with ¼ cup warm water in a mixing bowl. Mix well and set aside for 10 minutes.

2. Add the melted butter, molasses, salt, flour and cornmeal to the yeast mixture. Add about 1 cup warm water slowly as you mix it by hand or by machine. The amount of liquid can vary, depending on the flour. When a soft dough incorporating all the flour has formed, remove to a lightly floured surface and knead for about 12 minutes or until smooth and elastic. If you use an electric mixer with a dough hook, the kneading will take less time.

3. Lightly oil or butter a large bowl. Shape the dough into a ball and place it in the bowl. Turn the dough once so that it is lightly greased all over. Cover loosely with plastic wrap and place in a warm draftfree spot.

4. Preheat the oven to 350 degrees. Grease two 9½-inch loaf pans. When the dough has doubled in volume (about 1 hour), turn it out onto a lightly floured surface. Cut it in half and shape each half into a loaf. Place each in a well-greased loaf pan and return to a warm spot. Allow the loaves to rise for another 20 to 30 minutes, or until just about double in size.

5. Mix the egg with a bit of water to make an egg wash. Brush the top of the bread with the wash and place in the preheated oven. Bake for about 1 hour, or until the bread reaches a deep golden brown color. Knock on the bottom of the loaf; you will hear a sort of hollow sound when the bread is done. Cool on a rack for at least 20 minutes before slicing.

Pizza

Many cooks lose sight of the fact that pizza is bread, and they ruin it with an overabundance of toppings. To make good pizza, all you need to do is make a good dough, top it with a few choice ingredients and bake it in a hot oven until crisp. This recipe comes from Todd English, chef and co-proprietor (with his wife, Olivia) of Olive's, a small and bustling bistro in Charlestown, Massachusetts. Todd is a great cook and dishes up some of the best pizza in the Boston area. (The white clam topping is his too.)

MAKES FOUR TWELVE-INCH PIZZAS

½ tablespoon (½ package) dry yeast
½ teaspoon sugar
1½ cups bread flour
½ teaspoon olive oil
½ teaspoon salt
cornmeal for pans

1. Dissolve the yeast in ½ cup warm water with sugar in a mixing bowl. Let stand for 5 to 10 minutes, until bubbly.

2. Add the flour, olive oil and salt and blend to a smooth dough. Remove to a lightly floured surface and knead until the dough is very strong and elastic, about 12 to 15 minutes by hand, somewhat less with an electric mixer and a dough hook.

3. Lightly oil a large bowl. Place the dough in the bowl and turn to coat dough with oil. Cover loosely with plastic wrap. Let stand in a warm draftfree place until doubled in size (about 40 minutes).

4. Punch down the dough. Turn it out onto the lightly floured surface and divide into 4 even pieces. Roll each into a ball and place on a tray. Cover with a damp towel or plastic wrap and return to a warm draftfree place. Allow them to rise for 1 hour or until just about double in size.

5. Preheat the oven to 425 degrees. Sprinkle several sheetpans with cornmeal. Roll out the dough very thin, place each pizza on a sheetpan and top with ingredients of your choice and place in the oven. Bake for 12 to 15 minutes or until the crust is crisp.

White Clam Pizza

In recent years, Americans have rediscovered pizza and begun to use it as a vehicle for many ingredients other than the old standards, but this new freedom has had some unwelcome consequences, like the cauliflower pizza I saw recently. I myself still like a lot of the traditional Italian-American pizza toppings, and I recommend you not wander far from ingredients like cheese, olives, sausage and other savory foods. Whatever you put on your pizza, I beg you, please, hold the cauliflower!

MAKES ONE TWELVE-INCH PIZZA

12 littleneck clams
2 tablespoons yellow cornmeal
1 ball pizza dough (page 275)
2 cloves garlic, finely chopped
olive oil
2 tablespoons chopped fresh oregano or 2 teaspoons dried oregano
¾ cup grated parmesan cheese
freshly ground black pepper
2 tablespoons chopped Italian parsley

1. Preheat the oven with pizza stones or tiles to 450 degrees. Clean and shuck the clams as directed on page 13 and chop roughly; set aside in their juices.

2. Sprinkle cornmeal on pizza peel (pan). Roll out pizza dough on a floured surface until approximately 12 inches in diameter; place on peel. Rub garlic and 1½ tablespoons olive oil on the dough. Spread clams evenly around the pizza and sprinkle with oregano, parmesan, pepper and additional olive oil if desired.

3. Slide pizza onto stone or tiles and bake for 10 to 12 minutes, until edges are golden brown.

4. Sprinkle with chopped parsley and serve at once.

NOODLES AND OTHER PASTA

Without question, pasta is the world's most versatile food. Nearly every country has its own kinds of noodles and stuffed pasta. Szechwan province in China is famous for more than 400 varieties of noodles, and Italy claims thousands. Before the large immigration of Italians at the turn of the century, traditional New England cooking was limited to egg noodles. Since then, pasta has broken through all ethnic barriers to become a real staple food. Its affinity for seafood makes it very popular in restaurants and in homes in coastal New England especially.

The reintroduction of fresh pasta has been a two-sided coin. On the one hand, it is great for making ravioli, tortellini and other stuffed pastas; on the other it is very often inferior to high-quality dried pasta made from durum wheat or semolina. In my kitchen we use both fresh and dried pasta, depending on what the final dish is. For stuffed pasta, we use fresh dough. For noodles like pappardelle that have an unusual shape or for flavored noodles, like saffron pasta, we also use fresh dough, but we make it from semolina and partially dry the noodles to give them a chewier texture. For many dishes, I prefer to use high-quality dried Italian noodles like cappellini, linguine, penne, orzo, and so on. Luigi Marenzi, whom I worked for in San Francisco back in 1975, always ate dried pasta, although his restaurant offered many homemade pastas. When I asked him why he never ate the fresh noodles, he answered: "Fresh pasta isa for tourists." I have been a skeptic ever since.

Pasta

Making noodles is like making bread. There is a satisfaction that comes from transforming flour into pasta dough that grows as you learn more and more variations. This recipe is for dough that is to be kneaded by hand and then rolled out with a hand-cranked machine, the type that clamps to your table top. Only experience can teach you the proper texture for the dough. Keep it on the dry side and add a few drops of water if necessary. If the dough is too soft, add a little more semolina or flour. I have also included directions for using bread or all-purpose flour. You may want to use this dough until you master the semolina dough.

Once you have learned to work with semolina, however, you will find that it produces the best noodle. Its coarse gritty texture will deceive you at first. The dough will not be smooth after kneading like dough made from bread flour or all-purpose flour. Not until it's been rolled through the machine a few times will it reach a somewhat smooth texture. Semolina's quick-drying properties are a bonus for noodles, but for ravioli and the like you may find it hard to work with. The trick is to keep the ball or sheets of dough wrapped in plastic wrap as much as possible so that the dough is not exposed to air and to work very quickly when it is unwrapped. Recipe directions are for machine-cut noodles.

For hand-cut noodles, roll the noodles into sheets and place them on a work surface. Use a pizza wheel, zig-zag wheel or a knife to cut wide noodles (pappardelle) or 1 × 2-inch rectangles that you pinch in the middle for bowties (farfalle). You can also roll up the sheets and cut crosswise to make fettuccine.

For lasagne, roll the dough into sheets, leaving them somewhat thicker than for regular noodles. Use a pizza wheel, zig-zag wheel or a knife to trim the sheets into 4 × 10- or 12-inch rectangles.

For ravioli, roll the dough into sheets. Cut circles or squares to make half-moon or triangular ravioli in any size. Put a spoonful of Ricotta Cheese Filling (page 218), Crabmeat Filling (page 41), Pheasant Sausage Forcemeat (page 144) or other filling in the middle. Moisten the edges with water and fold the dough over so the edges meet. Use the tines of a fork to press the edges lightly and seal the ravioli. There are also small ravioli makers that use whole sheets of pasta dough; they come with instructions.

MAKES ABOUT ONE AND A HALF POUNDS

Semolina Dough
4 eggs
2 tablespoons olive oil
2½ cups semolina
½ teaspoon salt

Bread or All-Purpose Flour Dough
3 eggs
2½ cups bread or all-purpose flour
½ teaspoon salt

1. For the semolina dough, beat the eggs with the oil; for the flour dough beat the eggs.

2. Combine the semolina (or flour) with salt in a mixing bowl. Make a well and add the beaten eggs in the center. Using your fingers, work the eggs into the flour, from the center out. When most of the flour and eggs are mixed, turn the dough out onto a lightly floured surface and knead vigorously for about 10 minutes. The dough should be very elastic and somewhat smooth. The semolina dough will not appear to be completely smooth.

3. Cover the ball of dough tightly with plastic wrap and allow to rest in a cool place for about 1 hour before rolling.

4. Divide the dough into about 8 pieces. Shape each piece into a rectangle about ½ inch thick, 2 inches wide and 6 inches long. Pass the dough through the thickest setting on the machine. Change the setting so that each pass-through makes the dough a little thinner. Go through the settings until the desired thickness is reached. For most noodles you will want to roll to the next-to-last setting on your machine. The finest setting often makes noodles that are too thin and break easily. (For hand-cut noodles, see page 277.)

5. Once the dough is rolled out into sheets, pass them through the cutting blades to create fettuccine, linguine, or even smaller noodles. Hang the noodles on a rack to dry for 5 to 20 minutes, depending on the thickness and desired consistency of the noodles.

6. Always cook pasta in lots of boiling salted water. Check if it is done by biting into it. Pasta should always be chewy, never soft. It is impossible to give a cooking time. Very fresh flour noodles could take as little as 30 seconds to cook; thick dried semolina noodles could take up to 10 minutes.

VARIATIONS

Saffron Pasta Infuse 1 teaspoon of string saffron in 2 teaspoons of boiling water. Add with the eggs. You may need to add a few teaspoons of semolina or flour to compensate for the extra liquid.

Sweet Garlic Pasta Increase the amount of semolina or flour by ½ cup. Add 3 or 4 tablespoons Roasted Garlic (page 239) with the eggs.

Fresh Herb Pasta Add about 2 tablespoons of picked and finely chopped herb leaves with the eggs. Depending on the foods to be served with the pasta, fresh herbs such as parsley, basil, marjoram, oregano, chervil, chives, thyme, sage or rosemary can be used alone or in combination to flavor the pasta.

Desserts

Pies and Tarts
Thin Butter Crust

Lard Crust

Sugar Crust

Old-Fashioned All-American Apple Pie

Apple–Custard Tart

Cranberry–Streusel Tart

Thanksgiving Pumpkin Pie

Pumpkin Puree

Mincemeat Tartlets

Mincemeat

Deep-Dish Wild Maine Blueberry Pie

More Fruit Desserts
Seckel Pears Poached in Riesling

Gratin of Fresh Berries

Strawberry Shortcake

Peach and Blueberry Cobbler

Sweetened Whipped Cream

Pear Crisp

Strawberry–Rhubarb Crisp

Cakes
Angel Food Cake

Vermont Chocolate Potato Cake

Cranberry–Black Walnut Pound Cake

Pear Upside-Down Spice Cake

Cookies
Mark's Butterscotch Icebox Cookies

Sand Tarts

Mum's Scottish Shortbread

Nancy's Chewy Chocolate Cookies

Puddings and Custards
Maple-Sugar Crème Caramel

Pumpkin Crème Brulée

Indian Pudding

Mark's Indian Pudding Custard

Bread and Butter Pudding with Cranberries

Chocolate Bread and Butter Pudding

Egg Nog Custard

Apple–Butterscotch Tapioca Pudding

Ice Cream
Maple–Walnut Ice Cream

Vanilla-Bean Ice Cream

Wild-Blackberry Ice Cream

Chocolate Ice Cream with White Chocolate Chips

Peach Melba

Sorbet
Cider Sorbet

Concord Grape Sorbet

Cranberry–Champagne Sorbet

Raspberry Sorbet

Dessert Sauces
Raspberry Puree

Custard Sauce

Chocolate Sauce

Hot-Fudge Sauce

Caramel Sauce

Plum–Caramel Sauce

Warm Dried-Fruit Compote

I sing the sweets I know, the charms that I feel.
My morning incense, and my evening meal—
The sweets of Hasty Pudding. Come dear bowl,
Glide o'er my palate and inspire my soul.
—*JOEL BARLOW*

The women of old New England were masters of the art of baking; they were skilled, sophisticated and creative. Their recipes were passed down through the generations and in many cases recorded for posterity. In light of our contemporary life-style—and the setbacks in home cooking that have occurred—it is a good thing these recipes have survived. They document the vast territory of American desserts. The *Boston Cooking-School Cook Book* by Fannie Merritt Farmer, first copyrighted in 1896, clearly shows the range during that era, from the simple puddings and pies handed down from colonial times to more complex desserts like charlottes, soufflés, puff pastry, ice cream and sorbet.

Now many Americans are rediscovering those wonderful desserts. They are turning their backs on the ornamental European desserts that have held the stage for so long and are enjoying the simple desserts of their past. I do not believe that this is a mere exercise in nostalgia; desserts like strawberry shortcake, pumpkin pie, peach cobbler, bread and butter pudding, upside-down cake and vanilla ice cream are timeless classics.

New England has always been famous for its pies, and many other traditional American desserts originated here. Even the French gastronomic writers Henri Gault and Christian Millau, who were not overly impressed on their first culinary exploration of America, had to admit that "you can eat, especially in New England, delicious desserts of American and English origin." *

They were correct to point out the English origins. Many New England desserts are adaptations of early English cookery. The venerable all-American apple pie actually comes from England.

Indeed, the apple itself was brought over by the English colonists. Although we New Englanders can no longer choose among the 150 or so varieties of apple that were once planted here, we still have at least a dozen different kinds available to us, including Jonathans, Pippins, Baldwins, Winesaps, Tompkins Kings, Gravensteins, Macs and early Macs. The Rhode Island Greening, once America's favorite green apple, is still available locally, but even then it is becoming hard to find.

* *Waverley Root and Richard de Rochemont,* Eating in America *(Echo Press, 1981).*

Fruit in general is abundant in New England, and there is an integrity to it that you don't find in large-scale fruit-producing regions. Our strawberries may be small, but what they lack in size, they make up for in flavor. Wild blueberries and raspberries, as well as black raspberries, grow wild and are cultivated in all the New England states; they are especially profuse in the mountains of Vermont and New Hampshire. Nearly all the country's supply of cranberries is produced on Cape Cod, Massachusetts. Gooseberries, currants, mulberries and huckleberries, as well as plums, beach plums, persimmons, quince, many varieties of pear, melons, rhubarb, cherries and Concord grapes are all grown in New England in various quantities.

With all these beautiful fruits at hand, pies are a logical favorite. Eleanor Early, a noted New England travel and food writer, devotes an entire chapter to them in her *New England Cookbook* (Random House, 1954). Fruit also finds its way into cakes, cobblers, crisps, custards and puddings.

In times past, cake baking was considered an essential part of good housekeeping, and the New England housewife knew how to bake all sorts of special cakes. There was a period when Americans took time out for tea in the afternoon. That is still when I enjoy cake the most, in the afternoon with tea or coffee. I find cake is sometimes too heavy after a large meal, though on occasion a beautifully prepared cake makes a lovely dessert.

My favorite sweet is cookies. I believe that any cookie not worth stealing is not worth baking, and at my restaurant we judge the quality of our cookies by how many disappear unaccounted for. Cookies are a wonderful treat with coffee after a fine dinner. In fact, a plate of homemade cookies can be a dessert in itself.

Puddings and custards are also typical New England desserts. These are versatile concoctions that change with the seasons. In winter they might be very plain and simple, like Bread and Butter Pudding or Indian Pudding, which is based on corn, or other puddings based on rice or tapioca; these are often served hot or still warm. In spring they might include fresh maple sugar or syrup or some of the year's first fruits, such as rhubarb or strawberries. Summer puddings include all kinds of wild berries and summer fruits; these are usually served cold. And in fall apples, pears, quince as well as pumpkin and other squash are used.

Oddly enough, frozen desserts like ice cream and sorbet are extremely popular in New England, even in winter. If I am not mistaken, New Englanders are the largest consumers of ice cream per capita in the United States. For sure, ice cream and sorbet often represent half of all the desserts sold in my restaurant on any given night.

Over the years sugar has become identified with dessert, but the word actually refers to a part of the meal. All too often dessert is handled as a separate entity divorced from the rest of the meal. Surely you have eaten in restaurants where you felt you were transported to another place when dessert was offered; I know I have. To avoid this syndrome, the cooks in my restaurant are trained to be bakers; that training makes them more sensitive to the balance that creates a successful meal. They tend to create simple desserts, the kind that are often called "cook's desserts," such as the ones in this chapter. But an appropriate dessert does not even need to be prepared. It can be as simple as sliced fruit or a bowl of berries served with farm-fresh cream, crème fraîche or fresh cheese (*fromage blanc*). An assortment of cheese, with or without fruit, is also a good way to end a meal. Even a selection of dried fruits and nuts is suitable on certain occasions. No matter how simple or how complex the dessert, what is important is for it to be in harmony with the rest of the meal.

PIES AND TARTS

Essentially a pie is fruit wrapped in dough; the other elements—starch, sweeteners, spices and whatever else goes in—are secondary. An understanding of the fruit is therefore essential. Since all fruits vary in water content, sweetness and flavor, you should use recipes as a guide, tasting and analyzing the fruit before you start. It may be particularly concentrated in flavor and texture, in which case very little sugar and starch would be needed to flavor and bind it. So if a particular batch of apples, for example, strikes you as nearly perfect, skip the spices and use a minimal amount of sugar. Or don't bother to make a pie at all!

The pie crust itself is nothing more than fat and flour with a little liquid to hold them together; salt and sometimes sugar are added to flavor the dough. For fat I use butter or butter and lard combined; I do not like shortening, which has no flavor of its own and leaves a greasy film in your mouth. For flour I use pastry flour for its fine texture. You can substitute all-purpose flour if you cannot find pastry flour.

Making a good pie crust is simple—and not so simple. You have to be very careful when you mix the fat into the flour. Keeping them somewhat separate is what creates the layers that make the crust flaky. If the fat is mixed in too much, the crust will be crumbly. You need to work quickly and to keep everything cold, whatever kind of crust you are making.

There are basically three types: Thin Butter Crust, sometimes called 3-2-1 because it is composed of three parts flour, two parts butter and one part water by weight; Lard Crust, which is the classic American pie crust; and Sugar Crust, or *pâte sucrée*, a short crust for open tarts and tartlets. All three can be made by hand; the Sugar Crust can also be made in a mixer or in the food processor.

Thin Butter Crust

This crust is an excellent choice for double-crust fruit pies. For a single-crust pie, simply divide the recipe in half. The dough may also be used for tartlets.

ONE DOUBLE-CRUST NINE-INCH
PIE OR TWELVE TARTLET SHELLS

2 cups pastry flour
½ teaspoon salt
12 tablespoons (1½ sticks)
  unsalted butter, cold
about 7 tablespoons water, ice
  cold

1. Mix together the flour and salt. Cut the butter into pieces the size of a walnut (about 1½ tablespoons). Mix the flour and butter together in a large bowl, using only your hands, until the butter begins to break up.

2. When the flour has just begun to pick up a little color from the butter, add the water, a bit at a time, and mix until the dough starts to come together. Use just enough water to make the dough stick together. Since the exact amount of water needed will always vary, you have to develop a feel for how much to use.

3. Remove the dough from the bowl to a floured surface and knead briefly, just until the dough begins to smooth out. Wrap in waxed paper or plastic wrap and refrigerate immediately. Allow the dough to rest for at least 30 minutes.

4. When ready to roll out the dough, divide it in half. Place one half on a floured surface; return the other half to the refrigerator. To roll out the dough, form each half into a flat circle and quickly roll it out in the shape required. Always roll the dough very thin (about ¼ inch). Line the pie pan with one half and set aside the second half for the upper crust. Refrigerate until ready to use.

5. When assembling the pie, wet the edges where the two crusts join, to form a seal. Using your thumb and index finger, crimp them together. Make vents for the steam to escape.

VARIATION

Tartlet Shells Roll out the dough in one piece and cut out circles 1½ to 2 inches in diameter larger than the tartlet forms. Place the circles in the forms and line with parchment paper or aluminum foil. Add beans, rice or pie beads. Prebake blind at 350 degrees. Cooking time is determined by the final use.

Lard Crust

There is nothing quite like a pie crust made with top-quality lard. Unfortunately, what is available commercially is not always as good as it could be. That is why I like to use some butter with it. If you are able to obtain very high-quality lard, use that, following the same directions. This recipe can be divided in half for a single-crust pie or it can be used for tartlets (follow directions on page 284).

ONE DOUBLE-CRUST NINE-INCH
PIE OR TWELVE TARTLET SHELLS

2 cups pastry flour
½ teaspoon salt
8 tablespoons lard, cold
*4 tablespoons unsalted butter,
  cold*
*about 7 tablespoons water, ice
  cold*

1. Combine the flour and salt in a large bowl. Cut the lard and butter into pieces the size of a walnut (about 1½ tablespoons). Mix the flour, lard and butter together, using only your hands, until the fats break up into smaller pieces.

2. When the flour begins to pick up a little color from the butter, add the water, a little at a time; add just enough to make the dough stick together. The amount of water needed will vary from one time to the next.

3. Remove the dough to a floured surface and knead briefly, just until the dough begins to smooth out. Wrap in waxed paper or plastic wrap and refrigerate for at least 30 minutes.

4. When ready to roll out the dough, divide it in half. Place one half on the floured surface; return the other half to the refrigerator. Form the dough into a flat circle and quickly roll it out into the shape desired. Always roll it out very thin (about ¼ inch). Line the pie pan with one piece and set aside the second one for the upper crust. Refrigerate until ready to use.

5. When assembling the pie, wet the edges where the two crusts join, to form a seal. Crimp them together with your thumb and index finger. Make vents for the steam to escape.

Sugar Crust

Sugar crust makes a good base for open tarts or tartlets. Since it requires less careful handling than a butter or lard crust, it can be made in a mixer as well as by hand.

ONE TWELVE-INCH TART
OR EIGHT TARTLET SHELLS

1½ cups all-purpose flour
¼ teaspoon salt
3 tablespoons sugar
12 tablespoons butter
  (1½ sticks), cold
about 2 tablespoons milk, cold

1. Mix the flour, salt and sugar together in a large bowl. Cut the butter into pieces the size of a hazelnut (about ½ tablespoon) and add to the flour. Using your fingers or an electric mixer, mix in the butter until it is broken up into small pieces and the mixture resembles coarse breadcrumbs. Slowly add the milk, using just enough to make the dough stick together.

2. Remove the dough from the bowl to a lightly floured surface and knead until it is fairly smooth. Do not overwork the dough or it will be tough. Wrap in waxed paper or plastic wrap and refrigerate for at least 30 minutes before using.

3. When ready to roll out the dough, place it on a floured surface and flatten the ball into a circle. Quickly roll out into the desired shape. This dough can be rolled out a bit thicker than that for butter or lard crusts. If making a tart, line the mold. For tartlets, see page 284. Refrigerate until ready to use.

4. This kind of crust is often baked blind (empty). To bake the shell blind, line it with aluminum foil, then fill it with beans or pie beads to help it keep its shape. Prebake at 350 degrees. Cooking time depends on final use.

Old-Fashioned All-American Apple Pie

This pie needs no introduction. It probably doesn't even need a recipe—everyone has a favorite way to make it. Here is mine.

MAKES ONE NINE-INCH PIE

1 recipe Thin Butter Crust
  (page 284)
6 to 8 freshly picked firm and
  slightly tart apples, such as
  Rhode Island Greenings,
  Gravensteins or Granny
  Smiths (about 3 pounds)
granulated sugar (see Note)
ground cinnamon
about 3 tablespoons sifted all-
  purpose flour
3 tablespoons butter, cut in
  small bits

1. Prepare the pie dough, divide in half and roll out each half no more than ¼ inch thick. Line a 9-inch pie pan with one. Keep lined pan and top crust chilled.

2. Preheat the oven to 375 degrees. Peel and core the apples and slice them about ¼ inch thick. Toss with sugar and cinnamon to taste and with the flour. Fill the pie with the apple slices, mounding them somewhat in the center. Dot with butter. Cover loosely with the top crust, using a little water to seal the crusts together. Crimp the edges. Using a fork or the tip of a knife, make several vents in the top crust.

3. Place in the preheated oven and bake for 1 hour or until golden brown. The smell will tell you when it is ready. Serve while still warm.

NOTE. The amount of sugar is determined by how sweet the apples are. It would be a mistake to oversweeten or overseason them.

Apple—Custard Tart

This tart is quite simple, but it has a very sophisticated look to it. As desserts go, it is fairly light and would be a good end to any substantial dinner. Use a tart mold with one-inch-high sides. A cake pan will suffice if you do not have such a tart mold on hand.

MAKES ONE TWELVE-INCH TART

1 recipe Sugar Crust (page 286)
5 to 6 tart green apples, such as Rhode Island Greenings or Granny Smiths (about 2¼ pounds)
2 tablespoons granulated sugar
½ teaspoon ground cinnamon

Custard
1 cup milk
½ cup heavy cream
3 whole eggs
2 egg yolks
¼ cup granulated sugar

simple syrup (page 314) for glazing.

1. Prepare the dough, roll it out and line a 12-inch tart mold with it. Be sure there are no holes or weak spots in the dough. Keep chilled.

2. Preheat the oven to 350 degrees. Line the tart with parchment paper or aluminum foil and fill with beans or pie beads. Bake blind for 15 minutes.

3. Peel, core and thinly slice the apples. Mix the sugar and cinnamon and toss with the apples. Fill the shell with apple slices, reserving the best for the top. Make a circular design on top with the perfect apple slices. Place in the preheated oven and bake for 20 to 25 minutes.

4. While the tart is baking, make a custard by mixing the milk, cream, whole eggs, egg yolks and sugar together; strain. When the tart has baked 20 to 25 minutes, remove and pour half the custard over the apples. Place the tart on a sheetpan and put it back in the oven. Bake for 5 minutes, then add the remaining custard. Fill to the very top, but be careful not to overfill the tart with custard; too much custard will make the tart soggy. Continue baking for 20 to 25 minutes more or until the custard is set. Remove and glaze with simple syrup while the tart is still warm.

Cranberry–Streusel Tart

This dessert combines the flavor of New England cranberries with an Old World streusel topping. It is a fine example of how New England cooks combine their worldly cooking experience with the familiar flavors they love. This dessert was created by Killian Weigand, pastry chef at the Bostonian Hotel and one of the best in all of New England. We worked together for more than five years, and he remains a dear friend and professional associate. I advise you to make the streusel topping well in advance; it will keep indefinitely.

MAKES ONE TEN-INCH FLAN

1 recipe Sugar Crust (page 286)

Cranberry Filling
2 bags (12 ounces each)
   fresh cranberries
¾ cup granulated sugar
1 cinnamon stick
1 orange

Almond Streusel Topping
⅓ cup almond paste
1 cup granulated sugar
6 tablespoons unsalted butter
1⅓ cups all-purpose flour
6 tablespoons unsalted
   butter, melted
2 tablespoons lemon juice
2 teaspoons ground cinnamon

Vanilla-Bean Ice Cream
   (page 311) for serving

1. Prepare the sugar crust and line a 10-inch flan ring. Keep refrigerated.

2. For the filling, combine the cranberries, sugar, cinnamon stick and the zest and juice from the orange. Slowly simmer for 20 minutes until the cranberry mixture becomes thick and heavy. Remove the cinnamon stick and allow to cool.

3. For the topping, combine the almond paste and sugar in an electric mixer or in a mixing bowl with an electric beater and mix until thoroughly combined. The mixture will resemble coarse cornmeal. Add the solid butter and continue mixing until creamy. Add the flour, melted butter, lemon juice and cinnamon. Mix until smooth. Refrigerate until completely chilled and hard.

4. Preheat the oven to 375 degrees. To assemble the flan, fill the flan with the cranberry mixture to within ¼ inch of the top of the crust. This is important to prevent bubbling over. Using the large hole of a grater, grate the streusel topping over the cranberry mixture. Try to distribute it evenly over the entire top. The streusel layer should be about ½ inch thick and will come up over the flan mold.

5. Place in the lower third of the preheated oven. Bake for about 50 minutes or until the top is a rich golden brown. Cool on a rack for at least 30 minutes before serving. Serve warm or at room temperature with ice cream.

Thanksgiving Pumpkin Pie

This pie is almost as traditional as the turkey at Thanksgiving. The Pilgrims almost certainly ate pumpkin at the first Thanksgiving, but it is doubtful they ate it in pie. I have used this very fine recipe many times. It is a bit lighter than other versions.

MAKES ONE NINE-INCH PIE

½ recipe Lard Crust (page 285)
  or Thin Butter Crust
  (page 284)
1¼ cups Pumpkin Puree (recipe
  follows)
¾ cup heavy cream
¾ cup milk
1 cup granulated sugar
3 whole eggs, beaten
1 tablespoon molasses
¾ teaspoon cinnamon
½ teaspoon nutmeg
¼ teaspoon ground cloves
⅛ teaspoon ground ginger
½ teaspoon salt
Sweetened Whipped Cream
  (page 295) for serving

1. Prepare the pie dough, roll it out and line a 9-inch pie pan. Keep chilled. Prepare the pumpkin puree.

2. Preheat the oven to 375 degrees. Combine cream, milk and sugar in a small saucepan and heat slowly over low heat. Do not boil.

3. Combine the pumpkin puree, eggs, molasses, cinnamon, nutmeg, cloves, ginger and salt in a bowl; slowly pour in the hot cream mixture, stirring constantly.

4. Pour into the pie crust and place in the preheated oven; bake for 10 minutes. Turn the oven down to 350 degrees and continue to bake for 30 minutes more or until set. Stick a toothpick into the center of the pie to see if it is done; it should come out clean. Allow to cool. Serve with whipped cream.

Pumpkin Puree

MAKES ABOUT THREE AND A
HALF CUPS PUREE

1 pumpkin, about 5 pounds

1. Preheat the oven to 400 degrees. Quarter the pumpkin and remove the seeds. (Roast the seeds for a snack, if desired.) Cut the pumpkin in chunks. Place in a baking pan with 2 cups hot water, cover with a lid or aluminum foil and bake for 1 hour or until tender.

2. Drain in a colander. When cool enough to handle, scoop out the pumpkin flesh and pass it through a food mill or puree it in a food processor. The puree may be frozen.

Mincemeat Tartlets

Mincemeat is one of the classic New England desserts that hark back to England. It is very popular during winter and especially at Christmastime. Because mincemeat is rich and has a strong flavor, I feel it should be served in small portions. Open tartlets are perfect. Mincemeat is best served hot or warm and tartlets are very easy to heat up, compared to a pie, which can be a bit sloppy to cut and serve while hot. Also, holiday season is a time of abundant desserts, and the small tartlet allows room to try others. Of course, mincemeat lovers can always have two—or three.

MAKES FOURTEEN THREE-INCH TARTLETS

1 recipe Sugar Crust, Thin Butter Crust or Lard Crust (pages 284–286)
2 cups Mincemeat (recipe follows)
2 medium apples, peeled, cored and finely chopped (1½ cups)
Custard Sauce with brandy (page 317) for serving

1. Prepare the dough, roll it out and line the tartlet forms. Keep chilled.

2. Preheat oven to 350 degrees. Line the tartlet shells with parchment paper or aluminum foil and fill with beans or pie beads. Prebake the shells blind for 8 to 10 minutes.

3. Drain the mincemeat and mix with apples. Fill each shell with the mixture.

4. Bake on a sheetpan in the preheated oven until bubbling (about 25 minutes). Cool slightly before serving. Serve with custard sauce.

Mincemeat

In looking through my recipe files, I found this to be the most interesting of my mincemeats, but I cannot recall where or when I got the recipe. I'm sure it is very old, and it certainly is unique, with its use of fresh beef tongue. One innovation I have made in the recipe is not to put apples in the mincemeat until I use it. The results are excellent.

Mincemeat should be made in advance and left to stand for at least one month; it will keep almost indefinitely. This recipe makes about four quarts. If you are a real mincemeat lover, double the recipe; it should keep you going most of the winter.

MAKES ABOUT FOUR QUARTS
MINCEMEAT

1 pound lean beef, such as
    bottom round
1 pound fresh beef tongue
    (see Note)
1 pound suet
4 cups mixed dark and golden
    raisins, chopped
1 cup currants, chopped
½ cup citron, chopped
½ cup candied orange peel,
    chopped
½ cup candied lemon peel,
    chopped
½ cup dried figs, chopped
juice of 1 orange
juice of 1 lemon
1½ cups granulated sugar
1 teaspoon salt
1 teaspoon ground nutmeg
1 teaspoon ground cinnamon
1 teaspoon ground allspice
½ teaspoon ground cloves
2½ cups cognac or other good
    brandy
2 cups sherry

1. Cook the beef and tongue in water until tender, about 1½ hours; remove and drain. When cool enough to handle, peel the tongue, then cut it, the beef and the suet in small pieces. Mix together and grind once through the medium plate of the meat grinder. (The mixture can also be finely chopped with a knife.)

2. Combine with all the other ingredients in a saucepan and simmer until the mixture begins to thicken (about 45 minutes). Remove from heat and pour into a crock. Make sure the mixture is covered with liquid; if not, pour in some additional brandy and sherry. Let cool, then cover with plastic wrap. Put the crock away in a cool place (40 degrees) or refrigerate.

3. Check from time to time to be sure the mincemeat is moist. Add more brandy and sherry as needed. Allow to stand 1 month before using.

NOTE. Cook a whole tongue and use 1 pound for the mincemeat. Use the rest for sandwiches.

Deep-Dish Wild Maine Blueberry Pie

This pie will sweeten the air for miles around. Serve it while still warm, scooped into glass bowls and topped with Vanilla-Bean Ice Cream (page 311).

MAKES ONE DEEP-DISH PIE

½ recipe Lard Crust (page 285)
¼ cup water, cold
½ cup sugar
¼ cup maple syrup
3 tablespoons cornstarch
4 tablespoons butter
4 pints wild Maine blueberries, picked over, washed and drained well
juice of ½ lemon

1. Prepare the pie dough and roll it out about ¼ inch thick in the shape of a deep 12 × 6-inch dish but a bit larger. Keep chilled.

2. Preheat the oven to 375 degrees. Mix the water, sugar, maple syrup and cornstarch in a saucepan. Bring to a boil over medium heat, stirring occasionally. When the mix boils, add half the blueberries. Cook until the blueberries begin to break and the mixture darkens (6 to 8 minutes). Remove from heat and stir in the butter and lemon juice. Add the remaining blueberries and pour into the dish.

3. Quickly cover the dish with the dough. Use a little water to help attach it to the edges of the dish. Make several vents in the crust. Place in the preheated oven and bake for 50 to 60 minutes or until golden brown. The blueberries should be bubbling in the center. Allow to cool down somewhat before serving.

MORE FRUIT DESSERTS

In many cultures, fresh fruit is the most common dessert. During a gastronomic tour I made of China, we were offered ripe fruit to finish most meals. In Szechwan province I tasted the most luscious and fragrant fruits I have ever known. The pears and apples smelled like flowers and were almost honeylike. Wild kiwis, the favorite fruit of the panda (kiwis are called bear pears in China), were much larger and more perfumed than the familiar cultivated ones. Even oranges and bananas were exceptional.

If we Americans were fussier about the fruits we grow and buy, we might also be more inclined to enjoy them on their own. Nothing is more refreshing and satisfying, no dessert more fitting at the end of a large meal than one based on the fruits of the season. A bowl of freshly picked berries or slices of melon, pear or apple are unbeatable. This is the sashimi of desserts, where the talent of the cook is judged by the quality of the raw ingredients chosen, not by technical skill.

For plain fruit, no recipe is needed, only a plate and a knife—and an eye to quality and appearance. Here are a few of my favorite recipes incorporating fresh fruit.

Seckel Pears Poached in Riesling

Seckel pears are quite common in New England. They are tiny, about a third the size of most other pears, and since they have very little core, they are ideal for poaching whole. Peeled with the stems left attached, they are stunning when served standing in small clear glass bowls (three to a bowl) with a bit of the reduced poaching liquid.

This recipe calls for Riesling wine and honey, but if you want to be really extravagant, use a sweet, late-harvest Riesling from California or a good German Auslese. Depending on the sweetness of the wine, little or no honey will be needed.

SERVES SIX

1 bottle good-quality
   Riesling wine
½ cup honey
1 orange, sliced
2 cinnamon sticks
3 whole cloves
10 whole white peppercorns
18 Seckel pears
juice of 1 lemon

1. Combine the wine, 1 cup water, the honey, orange slices, cinnamon, cloves and peppercorns and simmer for 20 minutes.

2. Peel the pears, leaving the stems attached, and place in a bowl with cold water and lemon juice to keep them from turning brown.

3. When the wine has simmered for 20 minutes, add the pears and simmer, uncovered, for about 10 minutes, then remove from the heat; the pears should still be quite firm. Allow them to cool off in the liquid; they will continue to cook by retained heat. Check to make sure they don't overcook; they should be cooked through but not soft. (If the pears seem to be cooked through and the liquid is still hot, remove them and allow to cool separately.)

4. When the pears are cool, remove them from the liquid. Strain it into a saucepan and put back on the heat. Cook down by about a third or until the liquid gains a little body or viscosity. Allow the liquid to cool and return the pears to it. Store in the refrigerator. This keeps for a month but is best the first week.

Gratin of Fresh Berries

This dessert can be prepared in a large shallow baking dish or in individual gratin dishes. There is enough sour cream topping for six individual servings; you may wish to cut back a little if the gratin is to be cooked in one large dish. The best berries for this dish are raspberries, strawberries, blueberries and huckleberries. I like to use at least half raspberries, but you can use any combination of berries in any proportion, according to what you like and what berries are in season.

SERVES SIX

1½ pints fresh berries

Sour Cream Topping
2 cups sour cream
½ cup (packed) brown sugar
1 teaspoon grated lemon rind
1 teaspoon lemon juice

about ¼ cup brown sugar for
   glazing

1. Preheat the broiler. Pick through the berries and place in a 10-inch square baking dish or divide among 6 individual gratin dishes.

2. Mix the sour cream with the brown sugar (½ cup), lemon rind and lemon juice. Spoon the topping evenly over the berries. Sift more brown sugar over the sour cream. Wipe around the dish or dishes; any spots of berries, cream or sugar will turn black under the broiler.

3. Place under the broiler and cook until the sugar starts to caramelize (about 3 to 4 minutes). At this point, the cream will begin to bubble a bit and the berries will be warm. Serve at once.

Strawberry Shortcake

Probably the best loved of all American desserts, shortcake is also one of the simplest—nothing but fresh fruit, whipped cream and biscuits or cake. Its success depends almost entirely on the quality of the ingredients, not on the expertise of the cook. It is the epitome of simple country cooking.

Ideally this dessert is made with berries or other local fruit still warm from the sun, picked that day and never refrigerated. Raspberries, blackberries, peaches, nectarines and most other fruits and berries can be used as well as strawberries. Fruits should be sliced, berries left whole or sliced only if very large. Sometimes, particularly if I am making a whole cake, I like to macerate the fruit in wine or liqueur for a few minutes before assembling the dessert to extract some of the juice and create a very intensively flavored syrup. If you do this, use the wine or liqueur sparingly so that it does not overpower the fruit.

The following recipe is for traditional shortcake; the dough can be made into either a cake or biscuits. The Cream Biscuits on page 269 (omit the parsley) or Angel Food Cake (page 298) are good alternatives to shortcake. In fact, I'm not sure I could decide if I had to which of the three I like most.

SERVES EIGHT

Shortcake or Biscuits
2 cups sifted all-purpose flour
⅓ cup granulated sugar
4 teaspoons baking powder
½ teaspoon salt
8 tablespoons (1 stick)
*   unsalted butter*
1 egg, beaten
⅓ cup milk

3 to 4 pints strawberries
*   (see Note)*
granulated sugar
simple syrup (page 314), sherry,
*   port or other sweet wine or*
*   Grand Marnier or other fruit-*
*   based liqueur for macerating*
*   (optional)*
4 cups Sweetened Whipped
*   Cream (page 295)*
confectioners sugar (optional)

1. Preheat the oven to 400 degrees. Generously butter a 7- or 8-inch ovenproof skillet or an 8-inch cake pan for a whole cake or a sheetpan for biscuits; set aside.

2. Sift together the flour, sugar, baking powder and salt into a mixing bowl. Cut butter into small pieces, about the size of a hazelnut, and add to the flour mixture; mix gently. Add the egg and milk and mix just until the dough sticks together; knead gently.

3. For a cake, transfer the dough to the prepared skillet or cake pan and shape it, patting gently; place in the preheated oven and bake for 20 to 25 minutes or until lightly browned. For biscuits, drop the dough on the sheetpan; bake for 15 to 20 minutes or until lightly browned. Time the baking so that the shortcake or biscuits are still warm when served.

4. While the shortcake or biscuits are baking, hull the strawberries. Set aside a few of the best ones to put on top. Cut the rest of the berries in half if they are very large. Sprinkle with sugar to taste and, if desired, a few drops of syrup, sweet wine or liqueur; set aside. Whip the cream; put it in the refrigerator until ready to assemble the cake.

5. Split the shortcake or biscuits while warm. If you are serving a whole cake, cover the bottom half with berries, preferably macerated, and put a bit of whipped cream on top. Cover with the other layer and top that with the rest of the whipped cream. Decorate with the strawberries that were set aside and serve immediately. If you are using biscuits, put a large dollop of whipped cream on the bottom half of each biscuit (some will run out) and top with fruit. Cover with the top half. Decorate with the strawberries that were set aside. Dust with sifted confectioners sugar and serve.

Peach and Blueberry Cobbler

Here is an old-fashioned but timeless dessert of fruit baked with a biscuit topping. The cobbler formula works beautifully with peaches or blueberries or a combination of the two, as in this recipe. Other fruits (apples, pears, peaches, plums) also make very nice cobblers. Some people like to thicken the fruit mixture, but I prefer to leave it wet, so that the biscuit absorbs some of the liquid while cooking and the rest after serving.

SERVES EIGHT

4 to 6 ripe peaches, sliced (about
   3 cups)
1 pint blueberries, picked over
   and washed
2 tablespoons granulated sugar,
   or to taste
1 recipe Shortcake (page 294)

For Serving
heavy cream or Sweetened
   Whipped Cream (recipe follows)
   or ice cream

1. Toss the peaches and blueberries with the sugar to coat evenly. Place the fruit in a 10-inch square baking dish.

2. Preheat the oven to 350 degrees. Prepare the shortcake and divide into 8 biscuits; cover the top of the fruit with 2 rows of 4 each.

3. Bake in the preheated oven for about 35 minutes or until the fruit is tender and the shortcake lightly browned. Allow the cobbler to cool somewhat before dividing into 8 bowls or plates. Serve warm with cream, whipped cream or ice cream.

VARIATION

Peach Cobbler   Omit the blueberries. Peel and slice 2 to 3 additional peaches, to make 5 cups of fruit. Continue as for Peach and Blueberry Cobbler. (Five cups of apples, pears or plums may also be substituted.)

Sweetened Whipped Cream

Thick farm-fresh cream, not homogenized, is best for whipping. It should be only very lightly flavored with vanilla and sweetened with a little sugar. If farm-fresh cream is not available, buy heavy or extra-heavy cream, not so-called whipping cream, which has the bare minimum of butterfat needed.

MAKES TWO CUPS

1 cup heavy cream
½ teaspoon pure vanilla extract
1 tablespoon granulated sugar

1. Combine the cream and vanilla in a chilled bowl. Beat until the cream begins to thicken.

2. Add the sugar and continue beating until the desired consistency is reached. I like soft whipped cream for most uses.

Pear Crisp

The crisp is a very simple concoction—fruit baked with a crumbly nut, sugar, flour and butter topping. It is a true "cook's dessert" in that once you get the hang of it, you can follow your instinct, combining different fruits and nuts and even sugars. This pear crisp, for example, uses pecans; the Strawberry–Rhubarb Crisp (page 297) uses almonds. Different ice creams can also be used to complement different crisps. An apple and cranberry crisp with walnuts in the topping might be served with Maple–Walnut Ice Cream (page 310), for instance. Try these recipes first and then experiment on your own.

SERVES SIX TO EIGHT

Pecan Topping
1 cup pecan pieces
1 cup all-purpose flour
1 cup (packed) light brown sugar
⅛ teaspoon salt
½ teaspoon ground cinnamon
8 tablespoons (1 stick) unsalted
  butter, cold

8 firm Anjou, Bosc or Bartlett
  pears
2 tablespoons granulated sugar
1 tablespoon all-purpose flour

For Serving
Sweetened Whipped Cream
  (page 295), Vanilla-Bean Ice
  Cream (page 311) or brandy-
  flavored ice cream

1. Preheat the oven to 350 degrees. Toast the pecan pieces in the preheated oven for 6 to 8 minutes or until lightly browned. (This may be done ahead of time.)

2. Combine the flour, brown sugar, salt and cinnamon with the nuts, in a mixing bowl. Cut the butter into pieces the size of a hazelnut (½ tablespoon); add to the flour mixture. Rub the mixture between the palms of your hands, incorporating the butter while keeping the topping crumbly. Set aside in a cool place.

3. Peel, core and slice the pears about ½ inch thick. Toss the slices with the granulated sugar and flour. Place in a 6 × 10-inch baking dish and cover evenly with topping.

4. Place in the preheated oven. Bake for 1 hour or until it is brown, bubbly and crisp. Serve warm. Dish into glass bowls and serve with ice cream or whipped cream.

Strawberry–Rhubarb Crisp

Strawberries and rhubarb are a classic sweet-and-sour combination in many desserts, most notably in pies. It is also a sure sign that spring is here—and in these parts spring never comes a minute too soon.

SERVES SIX TO EIGHT

Almond Topping
1 cup slivered almonds
1 cup all-purpose flour
1 cup (packed) brown sugar
⅛ teaspoon salt
8 tablespoons (1 stick) unsalted
 butter, cold

6 stalks rhubarb
1½ pints strawberries
6 tablespoons granulated sugar
2 tablespoons all-purpose flour

For Serving
Vanilla-Bean Ice Cream (page
 311) or Sweetened Whipped
 Cream (page 295)

1. Preheat the oven to 350 degrees. Toast the almonds in the preheated oven until lightly browned (6 to 8 minutes). Cool and chop coarsely.

2. Combine the flour, brown sugar, salt and almonds in a mixing bowl. Cut butter into pieces the size of a hazelnut (½ tablespoon) and add to the flour mixture. Rub the mixture between the palms of your hands, incorporating the butter while keeping the topping crumbly. Set aside in a cool place.

3. Peel away the thin red outer skin of the rhubarb and trim off the ends. Cut the stalks into ¾- or 1-inch pieces; you should have about 3 cups. Hull the strawberries and cut them in half. Toss the fruit together with the granulated sugar and flour until evenly coated. Place the fruit in a 6 × 10-inch baking dish and cover evenly with topping.

4. Bake for 1 hour or until brown, bubbly and crisp. Serve warm. Dish into glass bowls and serve with ice cream or whipped cream.

CAKES

There is nothing quite so civilized as tea in the afternoon. It is the perfect time to pause for a little homemade cake with a cup of tea or coffee or a glass of sherry or champagne. Whatever cake you serve—angel food or chocolate, upside-down or pound cake—portions should be small, both at teatime and for dessert. I have included here just a few of my favorite cakes. Some of them have strong historical ties to New England, like Vermont Chocolate Potato Cake; others, like Angel Food Cake, are classic American cakes that I happen to like very much.

Different kinds of cakes have different proportions of flour, sugar, butter, eggs, liquid and leavening, not to mention all sorts of other ingredients. The best flour for cakes is from soft or winter wheat, which has less protein (gluten) than hard or summer wheat. Always use cake flour for baking cakes; it is readily available and far superior to all-purpose flour. Sift flour before measuring it; sifting revitalizes and lightens the flour, which becomes packed down during storage. You will notice that for the lightest of all cakes, Angel Food Cake, the flour is sifted three times, once before measuring and twice after. When you add flour to a cake batter, fold it in gently. Overmixing causes the protein in the flour to gain strength, thereby toughening the cake. Keep a thermometer in your oven to check the temperature, and always preheat the oven well in advance. You want it to be ready when you are.

Angel Food Cake

I am a big fan of this classic American cake, whose name refers to its light texture and pure white color. I find the airy, feathery quality very appealing. Even after a substantial meal, it is tempting. It can be served with freshly picked berries and whipped cream (see Strawberry Shortcake, page 294). It can also be served plain or with ice cream or with any number of icings or sauces. I also like this cake because it is practical, using only egg whites as it does. In any good kitchen there are usually egg whites left over, and this is a perfect way to use them up.

The proper handling of the ingredients is crucial to the success of this recipe. Pay extra attention to sifting and folding. I recommend you use parchment paper to line the cake pan. This is a very sticky cake, and the paper will make it easy to unmold. You can bake one large cake or six little ones in three-inch tartlet molds. The large cake should be split in layers; the individual cakes can be served as is. Angel food cake is usually lightly dusted with confectioners sugar to give it an even more heavenly appearance.

MAKES ONE TEN-INCH TUBE CAKE
OR SIX THREE-INCH LITTLE CAKES

1 cup sifted cake flour
1 teaspoon salt
10 egg whites (1⅓ cups)
1 teaspoon cream of tartar
1¼ cups granulated sugar
1 teaspoon pure vanilla extract

1. Preheat the oven to 375 degrees. Line the bottom of a 10-inch tube pan or 6 tartlet molds with parchment paper; set aside.
2. Sift the flour and salt together twice; set aside.
3. Combine the egg whites and cream of tartar in a large mixing bowl. Beat at high speed, gradually adding the sugar. Continue beating until stiff peaks are formed. Add the vanilla.
4. Sift the flour over the beaten egg whites. Roll up your sleeves and fold in the flour by hand (literally), going down from the sides and up through the center of the batter. Gently fold until the flour is barely incorporated. Overmixing will ruin the lightness of the batter.
5. Quickly pour the batter into the prepared cake pan or molds and place in the preheated oven. Bake until done, about 30 minutes for a large cake, 20 minutes for little cakes. Test by lightly pressing the center of the cake; it will spring back when done. Invert the cake pan or tartlet molds and cool completely before unmolding.

Vermont Chocolate Potato Cake

Vermont usually gets credit for chocolate potato cake, but I am sure different versions of this cake have been made all over New England, as well as other regions. The idea of adding potatoes to cake batter appears frequently in old American cookbooks. It sounds like a heavy concoction, but the potato actually produces a lighter cake than one made with flour alone. Most recipes for chocolate potato cake call for melted chocolate, but in this one the chocolate is grated on the smallest side of the grater. The result is a speckled cake, which was dubbed Chocolate Tweed Cake by James Beard because of its appearance. Only a very small quantity of chocolate is used, together with cloves, cinnamon and nutmeg, a combination that gives the cake a complex and somewhat old-fashioned flavor. It is wonderfully light and moist and needs nothing more than a sprinkling of confectioners sugar or cocoa on top, although Chocolate Sauce or Sweetened Whipped Cream could be served on the side.

MAKES ONE TEN-INCH LOAF CAKE

2 medium boiling potatoes
1¾ cups sifted cake flour
2 teaspoons baking powder
1 teaspoon salt
½ teaspoon ground cloves
½ teaspoon ground cinnamon
½ teaspoon ground nutmeg
12 tablespoons unsalted butter
2¼ cups granulated sugar
3 eggs, separated
½ cup milk
2 ounces semisweet chocolate, finely grated
½ teaspoon cream of tartar
confectioners sugar and/or cocoa powder for dusting
Chocolate Sauce, page 318, or Sweetened Whipped Cream, page 295 (optional)

1. Scrub the potatoes and boil in lightly salted water until done; drain in a colander. When cool enough to handle, remove the skins and mash the potatoes. Set aside 1 cup for this recipe; save the rest for another purpose.

2. Preheat the oven to 350 degrees. Lightly butter and flour a 10-inch tube pan; set aside. Sift the flour, baking powder, salt, cloves, cinnamon and nutmeg together; set aside.

3. Cream the butter and sugar, beating until very light and fluffy. Add the egg yolks, one at a time, scraping down the sides of the mixing bowl after each one. Add the mashed potatoes and mix thoroughly. Alternately add the sifted flour mixture and the milk, beginning and ending with the flour. Stir in the grated chocolate.

4. Combine the cream of tartar with the egg whites and beat to firm peaks. Gently fold into the cake batter. Pour into the prepared cake pan.

5. Bake for about 1 hour or until firm to the touch. Test by inserting a skewer; it will come out clean when the cake is done.

6. Cool in the pan on a wire rack for 10 to 15 minutes, then unmold and place on a rack to cool thoroughly. Sprinkle with sifted confectioners sugar and/or cocoa powder. Serve with chocolate sauce or whipped cream, if desired.

Cranberry–Black Walnut Pound Cake

A pound cake is a dense cake that was originally made with a pound of butter, a pound of sugar, a pound of eggs, a pound of flour, and nothing else. Many different flavors and garnishes can be used, but the key to a good pound cake is the butter. Very fresh butter of the highest quality available is called for.

MAKES ONE NINE-INCH LOAF CAKE

¾ pound unsalted butter
1 pound confectioners sugar, sifted
6 whole eggs
1 tablespoon lemon juice
1 teaspoon pure vanilla extract
2 cups sifted cake flour
2 tablespoons grated lemon rind
1 cup black walnut pieces, coarsely chopped
1 cup fresh or frozen cranberries, coarsely chopped
confectioners sugar for dusting

1. Preheat the oven to 300 degrees. Lightly butter and flour a 9-inch tube pan; set aside.

2. Cream the butter and sugar in a mixing bowl, beating until light and fluffy. Add the eggs, one at a time, continuing to beat. Add the lemon juice and vanilla. Now gently fold in the flour, followed by the lemon rind, walnuts and cranberries.

3. Pour into the prepared cake pan and bake in the preheated oven for about 1 hour 30 minutes. Test by inserting a toothpick; it should come out clean.

4. Cool in the pan on a wire rack for 10 minutes, then unmold and place on a rack to cool thoroughly. Sprinkle with sifted confectioners sugar and serve at room temperature.

Pear Upside-Down Spice Cake

Both spice cakes and upside-down cakes are part of New England's culinary heritage. This recipe combines the two, and uses pears, which are plentiful in the region in fall. The best known of the upside-down cakes, though, is pineapple. New England sailing vessels often brought back pineapples from their Caribbean voyages. They were extremely popular even in colonial times, when the pineapple was a symbol of hospitality in New England. Pineapple can be substituted for the pears in this recipe.

An upside-down cake is baked with fruit on the bottom. Then it is unmolded, and the fruit ends up on top. Baking the cake in an ovenproof nonstick skillet makes unmolding, which when not successful can ruin the presentation, almost foolproof. The skillet I use is oval, and it makes for an interesting shape cake. If you do not have such a pan, use a nine-inch cake pan, but be careful when unmolding.

MAKES ONE NINE- OR TEN-INCH
CAKE

6 Bosc, Anjou or Bartlett pears
6 tablespoons unsalted butter
⅓ cup granulated sugar
½ cup (packed) light brown
    sugar

Spice Cake
6 tablespoons unsalted butter
3 tablespoons (packed) light
    brown sugar
2 eggs, separated
4 egg whites
½ cup molasses
1 cup sifted cake flour
1 teaspoon baking soda
½ teaspoon salt
1 teaspoon ground ginger
1 teaspoon ground cinnamon
1 teaspoon ground nutmeg

For Serving
Sweetened Whipped Cream
    (page 295) or Custard Sauce
    (page 317)

1. Peel and core the pears. Cut into ½-inch slices. Toss the pears in a hot sauté pan with 2 tablespoons butter and the granulated sugar until the pears are nicely browned and the sugar is caramelized. Add 2 tablespoons water and remove from the heat. Set aside.

2. Combine the ½ cup brown sugar and 4 tablespoons butter in an ovenproof nonstick skillet and cook over low heat until a syrup forms. Arrange the pears in a circular pattern over the syrup. Do this carefully and artistically; remember, the pears will be on top!

3. Preheat the oven to 350 degrees. To make the spice cake batter, cream butter with brown sugar in a mixing bowl, beating until light and fluffy. Beat in the egg yolks from the separated eggs (add the whites to the others). Stir in the molasses.

4. Sift together the flour, baking soda, salt, ginger, cinnamon and nutmeg. Fold into the batter; do not overmix.

5. Beat the egg whites until stiff peaks form. Fold into the batter a third at a time. Spread the batter evenly over the pears in the skillet. Bake in the preheated oven for about 25 minutes, or until the center of the cake springs back when touched.

6. To unmold, place a serving plate over the pan and turn it, inverting the cake onto the plate. Serve warm or at room temperature with whipped cream or custard sauce.

VARIATION

Pineapple Upside-Down Cake Substitute 1 pineapple for the pears. Peel the pineapple, slice it ¾ inch thick, cut each slice in half and remove the core. Continue as for pears.

There are probably thousands of cookie recipes to be found in the New England repertoire; even the Toll House chocolate chip cookie, perhaps the single most popular cookie in America, was created in Massachusetts. Rather than repeat some of those recipes, which are readily available elsewhere, I decided to include four very special recipes that I have enjoyed many times. None of them are my own. My favorite cookies, you see, are those other people make.

Mark's Butterscotch Icebox Cookies

Mark Cupolo, the pastry chef at my restaurant, makes cookies every day that we serve, compliments of the house, at the end of the meal. Mark makes so many great cookies I couldn't decide which recipe to ask for, so I left it up to him. This is one of his favorites—and mine too.

MAKES FOUR DOZEN COOKIES

¼ cup pecan halves
12 tablespoons (1½ sticks)
  unsalted butter, softened
1 cup (packed) light brown sugar
1 egg
1 teaspoon pure vanilla extract
2 cups sifted pastry flour (see
  Note)
1 teaspoon baking soda
½ teaspoon salt

1. Toast the nuts until just lightly browned, cool and chop fine.
2. Cream the butter and brown sugar in a mixing bowl until light and fluffy. Be sure to scrape down the sides of the bowl. Whisk together the egg and vanilla. Beat into the butter and sugar mixture, again scraping down the bowl to ensure thorough mixing.
3. Sift together the flour, baking soda and salt. Add to the other ingredients and mix until combined. Fold in the chopped nuts.
4. Using plastic wrap, shape the dough into a log about 1½ inches in diameter. Chill for at least 1 hour.
5. Preheat the oven to 350 degrees. Lightly grease one or more cookie sheets. Slice the chilled dough about ¼ inch thick. Place the slices on the prepared cookie sheets and chill for at least 10 minutes.
6. Bake in the preheated oven for 10 to 12 minutes, or until lightly browned. Cool thoroughly on wire racks and store in airtight cookie tins.

NOTE. Pastry flour is preferable, but all-purpose flour may be substituted.

Sand Tarts

During the Christmas season, we always serve small Christmas cookies at the restaurant. Most of the recipes we use are from an old book that I inherited from my grandmother. One evening I had a wonderful conversation with a woman who was quite interested in the origin of some of these cookies. She reminisced about her own grandmother's lovely and delicate Christmas cookies. A few weeks later I received a package of cookies that she had baked using her grandmother's recipes. They were the thinnest and among the greatest cookies I have ever tasted, especially the sand tarts. I wrote her back and told her I had to have the recipe. I have been making them frequently ever since.

As it turned out, this gracious woman, whose name is Margy Bullock, was no amateur in the kitchen. She was the chef for many years at one of New England's most famous restaurants, none other than Alice Brock's restaurant in Stockbridge, Massachusetts. Alice's restaurant, as many of you probably know, was the subject of one of the most popular antiwar ballads of the sixties.

There is no trick to Margy Bullock's recipe; it is simply a perfect balance of ingredients. It is amazing how the slightest adjustments in baking can have such major effects. Use these amounts and follow the method carefully; be sure to roll out the dough as thin as possible.

MAKES SIX DOZEN COOKIES

Cookie Dough
8 tablespoons (1 stick) unsalted butter
1½ cups granulated sugar
1 whole egg
1 egg yolk
2 cups sifted pastry flour (see Note)

Garnish
3 egg whites
6 dozen almond halves
½ cup granulated sugar blended with ½ teaspoon ground cinnamon

1. Cream the butter and sugar by hand or with an electric mixer until light and fluffy.

2. Mix the egg and egg yolk together and beat into the butter-sugar mixture a little at a time.

3. Blend in the flour, being careful not to overmix the dough. Chill the dough for at least 1 hour.

4. Preheat the oven to 350 degrees. Lightly grease several cookie sheets. Roll out the dough paper thin (about ⅛ inch) on a very lightly floured board. Cut or stamp out the cookies. Round (about 2 inches in diameter) is the traditional shape.

5. Lightly beat the egg whites with a little water to make a wash. Lightly brush the cookies with the wash and place an almond half in the center of each one. Sprinkle with cinnamon sugar and place on the prepared cookie sheets. Bake in the preheated oven for about 8 minutes or until lightly browned. Cool thoroughly on wire racks and store in airtight cookie tins.

NOTE. Pastry flour will give a superior texture, but all-purpose flour may be substituted if none is available.

Mum's Scottish Shortbread

You can't get more Scottish than my wife's family. And you won't find better shortbread this side of the Atlantic than you will at the home of my in-laws, Muriel (from Glasgow) and Trevor Thom (from Edinburgh), who presently reside in Providence, Rhode Island. All shortbread recipes may appear to be the same, but not all shortbread is the same. Follow the measurements and procedure in this recipe very carefully, and you'll see what I mean.

MAKES SIX DOZEN ONE-INCH
SQUARES

*½ pound (2 sticks) unsalted
 butter*
*½ cup super fine sugar (also
 called dessert or bar sugar)*
2 cups sifted all-purpose flour

1. Preheat the oven to 300 degrees. Cream the butter by hand or with an electric mixer until fluffy.
2. Add the sugar and beat until very light and foamy.
3. Add the flour and mix until it is all incorporated. Do not overmix. Press into an ungreased 7 × 11-inch glass baking dish. Using the handle of a knife, make slight indentations around the edges. Using a table fork, prick everywhere, about ½ inch apart.
4. Place in the preheated oven and bake about 40 minutes, or until light brown. Cut into 1-inch squares while still warm.
5. Turn off the oven and return the pan to the oven. Let the shortbread crispen until the oven cools. Remove the squares and store in airtight cookie tins.

Nancy's Chewy Chocolate Cookies

One summer my wife and I worked as cooks on a dude ranch high in the Montana Rockies, near Yellowstone National Park. Nancy did most of the baking of desserts and cookies. Everyone loved her cookies, but these particular ones were so popular that it seemed no matter how many she baked, they would all disappear. The recipe doubled three times that summer, so we had to scale it back down for this book—and for this altitude.

MAKES ABOUT THREE DOZEN
COOKIES

*2 ounces unsweetened chocolate,
 grated*
5 tablespoons unsalted butter
2 eggs
*1 cup super fine sugar (also
 called dessert or bar sugar)*
1 teaspoon pure vanilla extract
1 cup sifted all-purpose flour
1 teaspoon baking powder
⅛ teaspoon salt
confectioners sugar

1. Combine the chocolate and butter in a small stainless steel bowl or the top of a double boiler. Place over a pot of simmering water and melt slowly, stirring occasionally with a rubber spatula.
2. Beat the eggs, sugar and vanilla together. Fold into the chocolate mixture and mix well.
3. Sift the flour, baking powder and salt together. Fold into the chocolate mixture. Mix well, being careful not to overmix. Chill the dough for at least 30 minutes.
4. Preheat the oven to 350 degrees. Lightly grease several cookie sheets. Roll the dough into balls about ¾ inch in diameter, then roll them in confectioners sugar. Place on the prepared cookie sheets. Bake in the preheated oven for about 8 minutes. They should appear slightly underbaked. Cool slightly on the cookie sheet, then remove to a wire rack for further cooling. Store in airtight cookie tins or jars.

PUDDINGS AND CUSTARDS

Pudding and custard are simple desserts, easy to prepare. Some, like Indian Pudding, are just a matter of combining ingredients and cooking slowly; others are a bit more complex. Some can be served hot, and almost all can be served cold. Sauces or whipped cream can be used, but they are not always necessary.

Soft-set custard-based desserts, like Bread and Butter Pudding and Crème Caramel, were sometimes referred to as "nervous" puddings in old cookbooks because the center shakes when the pudding is moved. Less "nervous" desserts that are sometimes regarded as puddings, such as Peach and Blueberry Cobbler or Pear Crisp, can be found under the heading More Fruit Desserts in this chapter.

Maple-Sugar Crème Caramel

This has long been a favorite at my restaurant. It is a simple variation on the classic crème caramel. Maple sugar (not syrup) is substituted for plain sugar in both the custard and the caramel. Maple sugar is a powder made from maple sap; it is more useful than the syrup for most baking and cooking. It can be found at gourmet or health food stores or ordered direct from Vermont distributors (see List of Sources, page 356).

SERVES SIX

Maple-Sugar Caramel
1 cup maple sugar
1 tablespoon unsalted butter

Maple-Sugar Custard
4 whole eggs
2 egg yolks
2½ cups milk
1 cup maple sugar

For Serving
Sweetened Whipped Cream
(page 295) and chocolate
shavings (optional)

1. Set out six 6-ounce custard cups or ramekins. Combine ½ cup water and 1 cup maple sugar in a small saucepan. Bring to a boil over medium-high heat. Reduce heat to medium and simmer for 5 minutes or until the syrup looks dark and shiny and is thick enough to coat a spoon. Remove from the heat and whip in the butter. Spoon evenly into the bottom of each cup. Allow to cool; the syrup will thicken.

2. Preheat the oven to 325 degrees. Fill a teakettle with about 1 quart water and bring to a boil for the water bath (*bain-marie*). Combine the eggs, egg yolks, milk and maple sugar. Mix very well so that the sugar dissolves completely.

3. Spoon about ⅔ cup of custard into each cup. Place the cups in a baking pan and fill with enough boiling water to come about halfway up the sides of the cups. Cover loosely with aluminum foil and bake in the preheated oven for about 35 minutes or until set. Check to see if the custard is done by inserting a toothpick into the center; it should come out clean.

4. Chill thoroughly. Loosen the custard with a small knife and unmold onto a colorful dessert plate. Be sure to serve all the sauce from the bottom of the cup.

Pumpkin Crème Brulée

This is a lightly flavored pumpkin custard, prepared in the style of crème brulée or burnt cream. I created it as an alternative to pumpkin pie when Craig Claiborne invited me to cook Thanksgiving dinner at his home in Long Island for a feature in the *New York Times Sunday Magazine*. Since we did this in early September, we really had to scramble for a ripe pumpkin, but we did find one. People expected the custard to be thick like pumpkin pie, but it is light and "nervous," and it was always meant to be that way.

SERVES SIX

1¼ cups milk
½ cup heavy cream
½ cup Pumpkin Puree
   (page 289)
½ teaspoon cinnamon
4 tablespoons molasses
3 whole eggs
5 egg yolks
⅓ cup granulated sugar
¾ cup (packed) light brown
   sugar

1. Heat the milk, cream, pumpkin puree, cinnamon and molasses over low heat until very hot, but not boiling.
2. Combine the eggs, egg yolks and granulated sugar in a stainless steel mixing bowl or the top of a double boiler. Pour the hot milk mixture into the egg mixture a little at a time, whipping constantly.
3. Place the mixing bowl over a pot of boiling water and continue to whisk until the mixture is thickened (about 12 to 15 minutes). It should boil slightly.
4. Spoon the mixture into six 6-ounce custard cups and chill.
5. Just before serving, preheat the broiler. Sift the brown sugar over each cup and place the cups in a pan filled with ice. Place the entire pan under the broiler and cook until the sugar has formed a crisp crust. Serve immediately.

Indian Pudding

This pudding is one of many variations on American Indian dishes. It is also one of the few to acknowledge those origins. Given the Indians' fondness for sweets, this was probably not served as dessert, but rather as part of the meal. Most of the traditional recipes call for either ground cinnamon or ginger; it seems no one could ever decide which was best. I like to use them together. I think this pudding is best served hot with heavy or light cream, but some people prefer it with whipped cream or ice cream.

SERVES SIX TO EIGHT

2½ tablespoons unsalted butter
3 cups milk
5 tablespoons yellow cornmeal
   or johnnycake meal
⅓ cup molasses
⅓ cup maple syrup
¼ teaspoon salt
¼ teaspoon ground cinnamon
½ teaspoon ground ginger
1 egg, beaten
1 cup milk, cold
heavy or light cream for serving

1. Preheat the oven to 300 degrees. Grease a 1½-quart soufflé mold or baking dish with 1 tablespoon butter; set aside. Heat 3 cups of milk in a saucepan until it is close to a boil. Add the cornmeal and reduce heat to low. Stir until the mixture thickens (about 5 minutes). Remove from the heat and add the remaining butter, the molasses, maple syrup, salt, cinnamon, ginger and egg. Pour into the buttered mold or dish.
2. Place in the preheated oven and bake for 30 minutes. Pour the cold milk over the pudding and return to the oven. Cook for 1 hour 30 minutes to 1 hour 45 minutes more or until the top is brown and crisp. Serve hot with cream.

Mark's Indian Pudding Custard

This dish, just recently created by Mark Cupolo, the baker at my restaurant, is lighter than any Indian pudding you ever tasted but is true in flavor to the original dish. Unlike the original Indian pudding, this is best served cold.

SERVES EIGHT

6 cups milk
½ cup yellow cornmeal
2 tablespoons unsalted butter
1 teaspoon salt
1⅓ cups heavy or extra-heavy cream
4 whole eggs
1 cup maple sugar (see List of Sources, page 356)
½ teaspoon ground cinnamon
½ teaspoon ground ginger
½ teaspoon ground nutmeg

For Serving
Sweetened Whipped Cream (page 295)
toasted nuts (optional)

1. Combine 4 cups of the milk, the cornmeal, butter and salt in a heavy saucepan. Bring the mixture to a boil, stirring continuously to prevent sticking or scorching. Reduce heat and simmer, uncovered, very slowly for 30 minutes, stirring often, or until quite thick.

2. Preheat the oven to 325 degrees. Fill the teakettle with about 2 quarts of water and bring to a boil for the water bath (*bain-marie*). Mix the remaining 2 cups of milk, the cream, eggs, maple sugar, cinnamon, ginger and nutmeg together and whisk thoroughly. Keep cold.

3. Remove the cornmeal from the heat and whisk in the cold custard mixture. Mix completely, then strain through a coarse strainer to remove any lumps. Divide among eight 6-ounce custard cups; wipe off any spills or drops on the cups. Put the cups in a baking pan large enough to hold them all. Fill the baking pan with enough boiling water to come about halfway up the sides of the cups. Cover loosely with aluminum foil and place in the oven. Bake for about 40 minutes or until set around the edges and slightly "nervous" in the center.

4. Chill thoroughly and serve right in the cups as·is or with a small dollop of whipped cream. Garnish with toasted nuts, if desired.

Bread and Butter Pudding with Cranberries

In my opinion very few desserts can attain the greatness of a perfectly made bread and butter pudding. At its best, it seems lighter than it really is, and its flavor is rich and delicate at the same time. It has down home appeal, but it can be served at the most formal occasions. It is simple and not so simple. It can be made ahead of time, but to attain the greatness that I spoke of, it should be served while still warm from the oven.

This recipe is a basic formula for an old-fashioned bread and butter pudding with the addition of cranberries. The cranberries give little bursts of tartness that balance well with the smoothness of the pudding. For purposes of cooking and appearance, it is important to cut the bread in uniform rectangles so that it makes perfect rows in the pan. The pudding should be served warm with Custard Sauce or heavy cream.

SERVES SIX TO EIGHT

6 tablespoons unsalted butter, melted
1 day-old baguette (long French bread)
1 cup fresh or frozen cranberries
3 cups milk
6 whole eggs
¾ cup sugar
1 teaspoon pure vanilla extract
Custard Sauce (page 317) or heavy cream for serving

1. Lightly grease or brush a 7 × 11-inch baking dish with a little butter; set aside the rest.
2. Cut the bread into 3-inch sections. Square off the sections by removing the crust. Slice each section lengthwise into 2 rectangular pieces; they should be no more than ½ inch thick.
3. Scatter two-thirds of the cranberries over the bottom of the baking dish. Brush both sides of the pieces of bread with the melted butter and place them over the cranberries in neat rows. Arrange the pieces so they overlap slightly, giving a shingled effect.
4. Preheat the oven to 325 degrees. Mix the milk, eggs, sugar and vanilla and whisk vigorously to make a smooth custard. Gently pour the custard over the bread and cranberries. Let sit for 30 minutes, occasionally pushing down on the bread so that it absorbs as much custard as possible.
5. Sprinkle the remaining cranberries over the top and bake for 30 minutes or until the edges are set and the center slightly "nervous." A toothpick inserted in the center should come out clean and dry. If the pudding is set, but the top is not yet golden brown, remove the pudding from the oven and turn it up to 450 degrees. When the oven is hot, put the pudding back in until it turns golden brown. Or place it briefly under the broiler; watch carefully.
6. Allow the pudding to rest for at least 15 minutes. Cut into squares, using the rows of bread as a guide. Serve with custard sauce or heavy cream.

NOTE. You may omit the cranberries altogether or substitute the same amount of other berries, raisins or currants. Serve with a berry or fruit puree (page 316).

VARIATIONS

Apple-Butter Bread Pudding

Lightly spread the pieces of bread with apple butter instead of buttering them. Omit cranberries. All other ingredients and directions remain the same.

New England Pudding

Substitute common crackers for French bread. Split and lightly butter enough crackers to fill the dish; overlap them as you would the bread. Pour the custard over the crackers and let sit for 1 hour before baking. Other ingredients and directions stay the same.

Chocolate Bread and Butter Pudding

Chocolate bread and butter pudding is more than just another bread pudding, it is an entirely different dessert, substantially creamier and richer, more of a pudding and less of a custard.

SERVES SIX TO EIGHT

4 ounces semisweet chocolate
1½ cups heavy cream
1½ cups milk
⅛ teaspoon salt
6 egg yolks
½ cup sugar
½ teaspoon pure vanilla extract
1 day-old baguette (long French bread)
6 tablespoons unsalted butter

For Serving

Custard Sauce, plain or with bourbon (page 317), Raspberry or Strawberry Puree (page 316) or Hot-Fudge Sauce (page 318)

1. Chop the chocolate into small pieces and place in a saucepan with the heavy cream, milk and salt. Place over low heat and cook, stirring often, until the chocolate has completely melted.

2. Combine the egg yolks, sugar and vanilla in a mixing bowl and gradually whisk in the chocolate cream. Set aside.

3. Cut the bread in 3-inch sections. Square off the sections by removing the crust. Slice each section lengthwise into 2 rectangular pieces; they should be no more than ½ inch thick.

4. Melt the butter and lightly brush a 7 × 11-inch baking dish. Brush both sides of the pieces of bread with butter and place the pieces in the dish. Arrange them in neat rows, slightly overlapping for a shingled effect.

5. Preheat the oven to 325 degrees. Fill a teakettle with water and bring to a boil for the water bath. When the dish is full, gently pour the custard over the bread. Allow to sit for at least 30 minutes, pushing down on the bread occasionally so that the bread absorbs the custard.

6. Place the pudding in a baking pan and fill the pan with enough boiling water to come about halfway up the sides of the pudding dish. Bake in the preheated oven for 30 minutes or until the pudding is set around the edges, but still a little "nervous" in the center. Allow to cool for at least 15 minutes before serving. Cut in squares. Serve with a dessert sauce or puree.

Egg Nog Custard

When Rick Robinson, one of the cooks at my restaurant, told me about his idea for egg nog custard, I replied that I thought that in the process of cooking the egg yolks the true character of egg nog would probably be lost. But he tried it anyway, and it worked. This custard is like the richest, creamiest egg nog you have ever tasted. Needless to say, it is a perfect dessert for the holiday season. And it is quite simple to make.

SERVES EIGHT

1 cup milk
¾ cup sugar
10 egg yolks
2¼ cups heavy cream
2½ tablespoons bourbon
2 tablespoons cognac or brandy
½ small nutmeg, freshly grated

1. Preheat the oven to 325 degrees. Mix, but do not froth, the milk, sugar, egg yolks, cream, bourbon and brandy. Strain through a fine strainer or chinois. Add nutmeg to taste.

2. Pour into eight 4-ounce custard cups or ramekins. Place in a baking pan with a towel on the bottom to keep the cups from sliding. Pour in enough boiling water to come halfway up the sides of the cups and cover with aluminum foil. Bake 20 to 25 minutes or until firm; this is not a "nervous" custard. Chill before serving.

Apple–Butterscotch Tapioca Pudding

Many people wax nostalgic about tapioca, but they still don't cook it very often. The little pearls, which some people call fish eyes, have a wonderful gelatinous texture. This recipe is for individual puddings with caramelized apples lining the bottom of the ramekins. When you unmold them, the apples are on top, like an upside-down cake. They should be served with a little Custard Sauce.

SERVES SIX

½ cup small pearl tapioca (not quick-cooking)
3½ cups milk
¼ teaspoon salt
3 large sweet apples, such as McIntosh or Golden Delicious
6 tablespoons unsalted butter
⅓ cup granulated sugar
1½ cups (packed) light brown sugar
½ cup toasted walnuts or pecans, chopped
Custard Sauce (page 317) for serving

1. Combine the tapioca with the milk and salt in a heavy saucepan. Allow to soak for 2 hours.

2. While the tapioca is soaking, peel and core the apples and cut each apple into 12 pieces. Heat a large sauté pan and toss the apples with 2 tablespoons butter and granulated sugar until the apples and sugar begin to caramelize. The pan must be very hot. When the apples are lightly browned, add 2 tablespoons water and remove from heat. Pour the apples onto a sheetpan so they cool off quickly. Don't lose any of the syrup that is in the pan. Set out six 6-ounce ramekins or soufflé molds. When the apples are cool enough to handle, neatly arrange them on the bottom of each mold. Spoon a bit of the syrup on top.

3. Place the pan of tapioca over low heat and simmer slowly until the pearls become transparent (about 12 to 15 minutes). Bite into one to see if it is tender.

4. A few minutes before the tapioca is finished, combine the 4 tablespoons butter with the brown sugar in a heavy saucepan. Bring to a quick boil for 1 minute. When the tapioca is cooked, stir in this butterscotch mixture and the toasted nuts.

5. Spoon the tapioca mixture into the apple-lined ramekins. Chill for at least 2 hours or up to 24 hours. Loosen the sides of the ramekins with a small knife. Invert the puddings onto dessert plates and spoon a little custard sauce around them.

ICE CREAM

Ice cream is extremely popular in New England. In Boston it is common to see people eating ice cream out of doors at all times of the year, even in the dead of winter.

Ice cream comes in two types. The first is a simple blend of cream and sometimes milk that is sweetened, flavored and then frozen; it is most often used for commercial production and often contains stabilizers. Although this kind of ice cream can be quite good, it is rarely as rich and creamy as ice cream made with eggs. The method I use starts with a custard sauce (crème anglaise) that is flavored and then frozen in an ice-cream machine.

There are unlimited variations on this kind of ice cream. Quantities of cream, if any, can vary as well as the amount of eggs. Some recipes call for whole eggs; I use only yolks. Amounts of sweetener vary less because there is a limit to how much sugar can be added—too much will prevent the ice cream from freezing. The flavors, of course, are just about limitless. Our basic formula for ice cream is three cups of milk, sixteen egg yolks, one and a half cups of sugar and three cups of heavy cream. It may seem like a lot of egg yolks, but that is what makes it so rich and delicious. Depending on the type of ice cream, flavorings are introduced at different times. Some, like maple sugar, liqueurs, extracts and infusions, are added directly to the custard; others, like fruit purees, after the custard has cooled. Most garnishes, like nuts and chopped fruits, are added when the ice cream is partly frozen. Ice cream is very easy to make, providing you have an ice-cream maker. Just be sure the ice-cream mixture is well chilled before putting it in the machine. The greatest benefit by far of making your own ice cream is the chance to eat it just as it comes out of the machine, when it is truly at its peak.

The following recipes for ice cream and sorbet are for a two-quart machine, but they can be adjusted. Ice-cream machines range in technology from a simple hand-crank machine, which requires ice, rock salt and a strong arm, to mechanical marvels that need only to be plugged in and turned on. Italy produces some very fancy machines for making gelato and granita; they are probably the best of their kind, but I have no experience with them. The old hand-crank is really more romantic than practical. What I use is a simple machine made by the White Mountain Company in Vermont. Mine is motorized, but it uses ice and rock salt for its cooling system. Whatever machine you use, remember it is what you put in that determines the quality of what comes out. As always in cooking, the ingredients take the lead.

Store ice cream (and sorbet) in nonmetal containers at about 10 degrees. Allow to come up in temperature to about 25 to 30 degrees right before serving (about 5 to 10 minutes standing at room temperature).

Maple–Walnut Ice Cream

This is a true New England classic, made with walnuts and maple sugar. Maple sugar results when the sap from the maple trees is cooked past the syrup stage to crystal form. It is easier to work with than syrup and more intensely flavored. I use some walnuts to flavor the ice cream and the rest to garnish it. You could substitute pecans for the walnuts if you like.

MAKES TWO QUARTS

3 cups walnut pieces
3 cups milk
16 egg yolks
2 cups maple sugar (see List of
*   Sources, page 356)*
3 cups heavy cream, cold

1. Preheat the oven to 350 degrees and toast the walnut pieces until they are lightly browned. Allow to cool.

2. Heat the milk with 1 cup of walnuts in a heavy saucepan. When the milk is close to boiling, remove from the heat; cover and let steep for 20 minutes. Strain and discard the walnut pieces.

3. Whisk the egg yolks and maple sugar together. Add the warm milk gradually, stirring constantly, until all the milk is added. Return to the saucepan and cook over low heat, stirring constantly, until the custard coats the back of a spoon (170 to 175 degrees).

4. Pour the heavy cream into a large bowl or container. Strain the custard into the cream. Mix well, then chill thoroughly.

5. Freeze according to the directions of your machine. When the ice cream is somewhat frozen but still soft, fold in the remaining 2 cups of walnuts.

Vanilla-Bean Ice Cream

Vanilla ice cream is unquestionably the greatest ice cream of them all. We sometimes take it for granted, but I am sure if it were just invented, it would be the absolute rage in the food world. Vanilla as a flavor is unique, not neutral, but it works so well with so many other flavors that we use it as if it were neutral. There is hardly any fruit, berry or nut that does not go with vanilla ice cream.

Ice cream made with vanilla extract can be good, but it is never as good as that made with vanilla beans. After you steep the vanilla bean in the milk, you need to scrape every bit possible from the bean. Those little specks are the sign of the real thing.

MAKES TWO QUARTS

1 vanilla bean
3 cups milk
16 egg yolks
1½ cups sugar
3 cups heavy cream, cold

1. Split the vanilla bean lengthwise and scrape the seeds into a heavy saucepan. Add the bean pod and the milk. Heat to just below the boiling point and remove from the heat. Cover and let steep for 10 minutes. Remove the bean pod and scrape again to release every bit from the pod. Add the scrapings to the milk and discard the pod.

2. Whisk the egg yolks and sugar together. Add the warm milk gradually, stirring constantly until all the milk is added. Return to the saucepan and cook over low heat, stirring constantly, until the custard coats the back of a spoon (170 to 175 degrees).

3. Pour the heavy cream into a bowl or container large enough to hold all the ingredients. Strain the custard into the cream. Mix well, then chill thoroughly.

4. Freeze according to the directions of your machine.

VARIATIONS

Liqueurs Omit the vanilla bean and add ⅓ to ½ cup brandy or armagnac or a liqueur such as Amaretto, Kahlúa or Grand Marnier after taking the custard off the heat; bourbon is also good used this way. Add vanilla extract to taste (½ to 1 teaspoon). Do not use more than ½ cup of alcohol: too much will prevent freezing.

Infusions For coffee ice cream, steep 1 cup cracked coffee beans in the cold heavy cream. Strain and add the cream to the custard. Lemon or orange rinds can be steeped in hot milk, like vanilla beans. Add vanilla extract to taste.

Extracts Pistachio paste, almond extract, mint extract and so on may be added after taking the custard off the heat. Add extracts carefully, to taste. Use only top-quality pure extracts, not imitation extracts.

Wild-Blackberry Ice Cream

This is Nancy's favorite. Without fail, on our weekend visits to the beach in Little Compton, Rhode Island, we stop at Gray's ice cream stand for some homemade wild blackberry ice cream. If you don't mind a few scratches, wild blackberries are easy to find in our neck of the woods during the summer, and then we make our own. This recipe can be used as a model for any berry ice cream. If you are using less seedy berries, you can fold in a cup or two of whole berries at the very end.

MAKES TWO QUARTS

2 pints wild blackberries
2 cups milk
16 egg yolks
1 cup sugar
2 cups heavy cream, cold

1. Pick through the berries to remove any stems or leaves. Press berries through a medium-fine strainer or a food mill. You should have 2 cups of puree. Set aside.
2. Warm the milk in a heavy saucepan.
3. Whisk together the egg yolks and sugar and add the warm milk gradually, stirring constantly, until all the milk is added. Return to the saucepan and cook over low heat, stirring constantly, until the custard coats the back of a spoon (170 to 175 degrees).
4. Pour the heavy cream into a bowl or container large enough to hold all the ingredients. Strain the custard into the cream. Stir in the blackberry puree. Mix well, then chill thoroughly.
5. Freeze according to the directions of your machine.

Chocolate Ice Cream with White Chocolate Chips

Here's one for unregenerate chocolate lovers. You can substitute semisweet chips for the white chocolate chips, or, if you wish, omit the chips altogether.

MAKES TWO AND A HALF QUARTS

3 cups heavy cream
8 ounces semisweet chocolate, grated
3 cups milk
16 egg yolks
1½ cups sugar
2 cups white chocolate chips, hand-cut

1. Heat the cream and grated chocolate over low heat until the chocolate is completely melted. Mix well and chill.
2. Warm the milk in a heavy saucepan.
3. Whisk together the egg yolks and sugar and add the warm milk gradually, stirring constantly, until all the milk is added. Return to the saucepan and cook over low heat, stirring constantly, until the custard coats the back of a spoon (170 to 175 degrees).
4. Pour the chilled chocolate cream into a bowl or container large enough to hold all the ingredients. Strain the custard into the chocolate cream. Mix well, then chill thoroughly.
5. Freeze according to the directions for your machine. When the ice cream is somewhat frozen but still soft, fold in the white chocolate chips.

Peach Melba

Peach melba is the classic example of how a simple scoop of ice cream can be transformed into a complex dessert, but Americans are no strangers to ice cream desserts—just think of hot fudge sundaes and banana splits. Escoffier's recipe, created to honor the great Australian diva, Nellie Melba, called for topping vanilla ice cream with poached peaches and raspberry puree. We prepare it a bit differently at the restaurant, in summer when peaches and raspberries are in season. You can also create your own concoctions, using either ice cream or sorbet. Some felicitous combinations follow this recipe.

SERVES SIX

3 medium to large ripe peaches
½ pint fresh raspberries
6 large scoops Vanilla-Bean Ice Cream (page 311)
½ cup Raspberry Puree (page 316)
"cigarettes" or other fancy cookies for garnishing (optional)

1. Peel and slice the peaches. Pick through the berries, removing any stems or leaves.
2. Place a scoop of ice cream in a glass bowl or a *coupe* glass or a large martini glass. Pour raspberry puree over the ice cream and surround with the slices of peaches and a few fresh raspberries. Garnish with a "cigarette" or other fancy cookie, if desired.

VARIATIONS

Fresh Figs with Vanilla-Bean Ice Cream and Raspberry Puree

Surround a scoop of Vanilla-Bean Ice Cream (page 311) with quartered fresh figs and spoon some Raspberry Puree (page 316) on top and around.

Vanilla-Bean Ice Cream with Dried Fruit Compote

Spoon some Warm Dried-Fruit Compote (page 320) over a scoop of Vanilla-Bean Ice Cream (page 311). Serve with Sand Tarts (page 302).

Maple–Walnut Ice Cream with Bananas and Whipped Cream

Sprinkle a scoop of Maple–Walnut Ice Cream (page 310) with sliced bananas and top with Sweetened Whipped Cream (page 295).

Wild-Blackberry Ice Cream with Summer Fruits

Surround a scoop of Wild-Blackberry Ice Cream (page 312) with macerated sliced nectarines and plums. Sprinkle with toasted almond slivers.

SORBET

I use the term *sorbet* rather than *sherbet* in deference to the French, whose particular style of making this dessert is quickly—and rightfully—becoming the standard in America. Once you are introduced to the crystal clear, refreshing flavor of good sorbet, you soon forget about milk-based sherbet.

In France and in some restaurants in America, sorbet is served as an intermezzo, a palate-cleanser before the main course. It can be quite nice, especially when you are in France eating real French food, but I have never really been comfortable with this idea. It somehow feels like an affectation, too forced in the context of American cooking. My advice is to stick to sorbet as a dessert. It is a good, light finish to any meal.

Most sorbets are fruit-based, but other flavors like chocolate or even tea may be used. For a good sorbet you need to have a perfect balance of acid (usually lemon juice, which brings up the flavor in other fruits), sugar and liquid. Too much sugar or alcohol can prevent the mixture from freezing. All the recipes in this chapter have been made many times and tested, but if you are creating your own sorbet, you can check the balance by floating an egg in the mixture: if the exposed part of the egg is about the size of a nickel, the proportions are correct.

Be sure the sorbet mixture is well chilled before you put it in the ice-cream maker. Store and serve sorbet as you would ice cream (see page 310).

How to Make Simple Syrup

Most professionals use syrup for making sorbets, and you should too. Your sorbet will be smooth every time. This syrup may also be used for macerating fruit and moistening cakes.

For 4 cups of syrup, combine 2 cups sugar with 3½ cups water in a saucepan. Bring to a boil and continue boiling, uncovered, for 3 minutes or until sugar is dissolved. Cover tightly and store in the refrigerator. It keeps indefinitely.

Cider Sorbet

In New England, autumn means apple cider. People argue endlessly about which apples and/ or which growers make the best cider, but one thing is for sure—there is no shortage of good cider. The quality of the cider will determine the quality of the sorbet, especially in this point-blank recipe, which uses only cider and simple syrup. You can play with the recipe if you like. Add lemon juice or a bit of applejack for a little zing. Substitute hard cider. Or make a spiced cider sorbet by infusing the spices traditionally used in mulled cider. But if you are confident in your local cider, try this recipe as is. It is wonderful and refreshing.

MAKES ABOUT TWO QUARTS

6 cups fresh cider
3 cups simple syrup (page 314)

1. Combine the cider and simple syrup. Chill well.
2. Freeze according to the directions for your machine.

Concord Grape Sorbet

Many Easterners are very fond of Concord grapes, which are among the most flavorful of all grapes, but with their thick skins and large seeds, they are not necessarily the most pleasant to eat. I often find myself reminiscing about eating them right from my grandmother's vines, but the truth is that I would rather have them now in sorbet form.

MAKES ABOUT ONE AND A HALF QUARTS

2 quarts Concord grapes
2 cups simple syrup (page 314)
juice of ½ lemon

1. Remove the grapes from the stems and press through a medium strainer or food mill to remove skins and seeds. Press hard enough to release the deep purple pigmentation near the skin.
2. Combine 4 cups of the grape juice with the simple syrup and lemon juice. Chill well.
3. Freeze according to the directions for your machine.

NOTE. It is advisable to use the egg test (page 314) for this recipe since the sweetness of the grapes can vary greatly.

Cranberry–Champagne Sorbet

It would be tempting—but misleading—to name this pink champagne sorbet because the cranberries give it such a lovely rosy glow. This is a festive sorbet, but it is not necessary to open a great bottle of champagne; any good sparkling wine will do.

MAKES ABOUT TWO QUARTS

2 tablespoons sugar
1 cup fresh or frozen cranberries
1 bottle (750 milliliters)
  champagne or sparkling wine
5 cups simple syrup (page 314)
juice of ½ lemon

1. Put the sugar and cranberries in a small saucepan with ½ cup water. Stir to dissolve the sugar and cook until the cranberries pop.
2. Pour the champagne into a bowl. Strain the cranberries, pressing as much through as possible. You should have about 1 cup juice. Add juice to the champagne; mix and add the simple syrup and lemon juice. Mix well and strain again through a fine strainer. Chill well.
3. Freeze according to the directions for your machine.

Raspberry Sorbet

This recipe can be used as a model for other berry sorbets. Keep in mind that the amount that matters is not the four pints of berries, but the four cups of puree.

MAKES TWO QUARTS

4 pints raspberries
3 cups simple syrup (page 314)
juice of ½ lemon

1. Pick over the raspberries, removing any stems or leaves. Press the berries through a medium strainer or food mill to remove the seeds. You should have 4 cups of puree.
2. To extract every bit of flavor from the berries, add the simple syrup by pouring it over the seeds in the strainer, pushing out every last drop. Mix well and chill.
3. Freeze according to the directions for your machine.

All too often, desserts are offered without the finishing touches that can transform a good one into a great one. A fruit puree or other sauce can add flavor contrast, moisture and color; in a word, dimension. The following basic sauces can be used with puddings, simple cakes and especially ice cream.

Raspberry Puree

Almost any fruit or berry can be pureed for sauce. Straightforward purees of raw fruit and berries are extremely versatile, and they are easy to make. You simply puree the fruit or berries, mix with sugar and lemon juice and strain, if necessary. If you wish, you can add liqueur for more depth of flavor. Besides berries, tropical fruits like mangoes and papayas work very well with this method. A food processor will simplify the process; otherwise you can use a food mill or a strainer. (Some fruits, like apples, cranberries and beach plums, require cooking; since those cooked sauces are most often used with poultry and meat, I have included them in the chapter on basic preparations.)

MAKES TWO CUPS

2 pints raspberries
about ½ cup sugar
juice of ¼ lemon
1 to 2 tablespoons framboise,
kirsch or other fruit-based
liqueur (optional)

1. Pick through the berries to remove any stems or leaves.
2. Put in the workbowl of the food processor and puree until fine. Add sugar to taste and lemon juice. Add liqueur, if desired. Spin around a few more times to mix thoroughly.
3. It is not absolutely necessary, but if you want a more finished puree, strain it. Chill.

NOTE. You may also press the berries through a food mill or medium strainer. Be sure to get every drop. It will not be necessary to strain the puree.

V A R I A T I O N

Strawberry Puree Substitute 2 pints strawberries for the raspberries. Wash and hull the strawberries and cut in half if large. Continue as for raspberry puree, using either a food processor or a food mill or medium strainer. Add sugar and lemon juice to taste. Add 1 to 2 tablespoons fruit-based liqueur (framboise, Grand Marnier, etc.), if desired.

Custard Sauce

This recipe is for a light custard sauce (*crème anglaise*). For a richer sauce, simply add more egg yolks. The sauce may be flavored with liqueur, fruit juice or puree, various spices or different sweeteners, used alone or in combination. Suggestions follow the basic recipe. Match the flavors to the dessert the sauce is going to be served with.

MAKES TWO AND
A HALF CUPS

½ vanilla bean
2 cups milk
4 egg yolks
¾ cup sugar

1. Split the vanilla bean lengthwise and scrape the seeds into a heavy saucepan. Add the bean pod and milk. Heat to just below a boil and remove from heat. Cover and allow to steep for 20 minutes. Scrape the bean again and add any scrapings to the pot. Discard the bean pod.

2. Whisk together the egg yolks and sugar and add the warm milk gradually, stirring often, until all the milk is added. Return to the pot and cook over low heat until the custard coats the back of a spoon (170 to 175 degrees); this will take from 3 to 5 minutes. Strain and chill.

VARIATIONS

Liqueurs   Add about 2 tablespoons brandy, bourbon, rum, Grand Marnier, Tia Maria and so on, after the custard sauce is cooked. Allow for the liqueur by cutting back on the amount of milk.

Fruits   Add about 4 tablespoons fruit puree or juice at the end. Cut back correspondingly on the amount of milk.

Spices   Steep whole cinnamon, allspice, nutmeg, cloves or even coffee (not a spice) or ¼ teaspoon ground spices instead of or in addition to the vanilla bean.

Sweeteners   Replace all or some of the sugar with maple sugar, brown sugar or even molasses.

Combinations   Combine different flavorings, for example, maple sugar and lemon, banana and rum, brandy and spices, strawberry puree and Grand Marnier. The possibilities are infinite.

Chocolate Sauce

Forget about all those intimidating recipes for chocolate sauce you have seen. They are usually sugar-based formulas that require cooking to a certain temperature. They leave a lot of room for problems and inconsistency, and frankly they are usually not too good. My chocolate sauce and hot-fudge sauce (below) are foolproof, providing you use good chocolate. These are basically thin *ganache,* a mixture of chocolate and heavy cream that is usually used for filling and glazing tortes and cakes and that can also be used to make chocolate truffles. The chocolate sauce has a higher ratio of cream to chocolate than the hot-fudge and is intended to be served cold or at room temperature. The hot-fudge sauce must be served hot or warm. Either sauce can be flavored with liqueurs like brandy, chartreuse, Grand Marnier, Tia Maria, cassis, raspberry liqueur, and so on. Simply substitute the liqueur for some of the cream.

MAKES ABOUT TWO CUPS

6 ounces semisweet chocolate
1½ cups heavy or extra-heavy
  cream

1. Chop the chocolate into small pieces and place in a bowl over a saucepan filled with hot water or in the top of a double boiler. Slowly melt the chocolate over low heat, stirring occasionally with a rubber spatula.
2. When the chocolate is melted, stir in the cream until thoroughly combined. Keep the bowl over hot water until this is accomplished. Remove from heat. Serve at room temperature or chilled. Cover and store in the refrigerator.

Hot-Fudge Sauce

MAKES ABOUT TWO CUPS

12 ounces semisweet chocolate
¾ cup heavy or extra-heavy
  cream

1. Chop chocolate into small pieces and place in a bowl over a saucepan filled with hot water or in the top of a double boiler. Slowly melt the chocolate over low heat, using a rubber spatula to stir occasionally.
2. When the chocolate is melted, stir in the cream until thoroughly combined. Keep the bowl over hot water until this is accomplished. Remove from heat and serve. If not to be used immediately, store in the refrigerator and reheat in a double boiler.

Caramel Sauce

Caramel sauce is excellent with apple and pear desserts, as well as with ice cream. Banana also comes to mind as a fruit that would be good with this sauce. Caramel sauce is a little trickier than some others, but if you follow directions carefully, you should have no problems. A sugar thermometer is useful, but not a necessity. Have a small pot of water and a clean pastry brush ready.

**MAKES TWO AND
A HALF CUPS**

1 cup sugar
¼ cup water
½ teaspoon lemon juice
*2 cups heavy or extra heavy
cream*

1. Use a very clean saucepan that is lightly colored inside. You need to be able to see what you are doing. Combine the sugar, water and lemon juice in the pan and put over medium heat to dissolve the sugar. Increase the heat and bring to a boil. Wet the pastry brush and wash down the sides of the pan, to keep them clean of sugar and prevent uneven cooking. Continue to boil and wash down the pan until the sugar reaches a deep golden color (310 degrees). Swirl the pan gently when the sugar begins to color, to ensure even cooking and coloration. Remove from heat.

2. Quickly stir in the cream and return to the heat. Stir constantly until the caramel is completely dissolved and the sauce is smooth. Chill.

Plum–Caramel Sauce

This is an excellent summertime dessert sauce for ice cream, custard or fruit tarts. Choose juicy ripe plums for best results.

MAKES TWO AND A HALF CUPS

10 to 12 ripe plums
1 cup sugar
¼ cup water
½ teaspoon lemon juice
¾ cup heavy cream

1. Pit and quarter the plums and place in a small but heavy saucepan on low heat. Add just a few drops of water to get things started and stew the plums until they are completely falling apart, about 20 minutes. (The time will vary, depending on how ripe the plums are.) Push plums through a food mill or medium strainer and set aside. You should have about 1½ cups of brightly colored plum puree.

2. Combine the sugar, water and lemon juice in a small light-colored saucepan and proceed as in Step 1 of the recipe for caramel sauce (above). When the sugar reaches a deep golden color, remove from heat and stir in the cream.

3. Return the pan to the heat and stir until caramel is completely dissolved and the sauce is smooth. Remove from heat and allow to cool for 10 minutes, then stir in the plum puree. Chill.

Warm Dried-Fruit Compote

This is what I call an adult dessert. It has rich flavors and is boozy, not something the kids would necessarily enjoy. It is excellent in winter with ice cream or a simple buttery pound cake. All three together make a wonderful rich dessert.

Many fruits are available dried. Pears, apricots, figs, prunes, currants, raisins and dates are just a few that could be used for compote. When choosing dried fruit, look for those that most closely resemble their fresh counterparts. Taste each one before cooking to determine its texture. The tougher the fruit, the longer it will need to cook. The compote should be made ahead and allowed to cool, then rewarmed before serving. Since it will keep almost indefinitely, it can be made well in advance.

MAKES ABOUT ONE QUART

3 cups mixed dried fruits
1 cup sugar
½ cup port wine
¼ cup cognac or other good
  brandy

1. Prepare fruits by removing any tough stems or cores. Cut each into ¼- to ½-inch pieces, leaving smaller fruits like raisins or currants whole.

2. Combine the sugar and 2 cups water in a saucepan and boil for 30 seconds. Begin to add the fruits, starting with the firmest. Before adding each new fruit, bring the previous ones back to a simmer. The total cooking time should be no more than 4 minutes.

3. When all the fruits have been added, remove from the heat and stir in the port and brandy. Let the compote cool completely. Store in the refrigerator.

A Few Basics

Water

Salt

Pepper

Herbs and Spices

Stock
Fish Stock

Chicken Stock

Reduced Veal Stock

Butter
Garlic Butter

White Wine Butter Sauce

Goose and Duck Fat

Oil
Aïoli

Mayonnaise

Vinegar
Balsamic Vinaigrette

Tomato–Basil Vinaigrette

Sherry–Mustard Vinaigrette

Lemon–Garlic–Walnut Vinaigrette

Red Onion Vinaigrette

Fresh Mint Sauce

Tomato Sauces
Basic Tomato Sauce

Barbecue Sauce

Pickles, Chutneys, Jams and Relishes
Lightly Pickled Garden Vegetables

Pickled Green Tomatoes

Corn Relish

Cranberry Relish

Cranberry–Onion Jam

Persimmon Chutney

Smooth Apple Sauce

Chunky Apple Sauce

Beach Plum Puree

Spiced Nuts

In organizing this book, I tried to group the different dishes by their featured ingredient. I decided to handle the basic preparations separately, just as we do in professional kitchens. My thinking was that such an approach would make the book more enjoyable for the advanced cook and more helpful at the same time for the novice who is just getting started.

Most of this chapter is intended to serve as a reference to other recipes in the book. For example, stocks are covered here, but the sauces deriving from them are scattered throughout the book. Sauces that are used as components of many dishes, like vinaigrette and mayonnaise, appear here. Basic ingredients, like water, salt, pepper, vinegar, butter and oil, which make such an enormous difference in the outcome of a recipe, are discussed here as well. This is also the place where I catalog some of the homemade standbys of the pantry—the relishes, pickles and preserves that add diversity and a touch of excitement to good cooking.

Fernand Point, one of the outstanding chefs of this century, once said that in cooking "success is the sum of a lot of small things correctly done." *

When cooking is approached from this point of view, it is less intimidating, though no less serious, than it's often made out to be.

WATER

Water is not normally thought of as an important ingredient in cooking, even though it is probably used more than any other food in the kitchen. Water is life-sustaining, and whether it is digested in the form of tea, chowder, pot roast or sorbet, the quality of the water affects the quality of the food, as well as our health.

The days of taking good clean water for granted are over. In many areas (Boston, for one) chlorine levels are unacceptable. In other areas bacteria, lead, radiation and various chemical poisons have contaminated the water we use for drinking and cooking. Have your water tested. If it shows any signs of contamination, use a water-purifying filter. In my restaurant all the water for cooking and drinking is filtered. Another, more expensive alternative is to buy bottled spring water.

---

* Quoted in Ma Gastronomie, *a wonderful memoir incorporating recipes, guest logs and an overview of his restaurant experience as well as other details about the life and times of this great man. An English-language edition was published by Lyceum Books in 1974.*

SALT

In addition to having a flavor of its own, salt brings out the flavor of other foods. For this reason I have recommended the use of it in seasoning almost all the dishes in this book. For baking, curing, pickling and a few other preparations where the exact amount of salt is important, I have specified how much is needed. In other recipes, I have left it to the discretion of the cook. I realize that an excess of salt in the diet is unhealthy and that these days many people are watching their salt intake. Even so, I am against skimping on the salt used in the cooking water for vegetables and pasta.

Because of its acidity, lemon also brings out flavor; when appropriate, I suggest a squeeze of lemon before salting. This often allows for less salt to be used to achieve maximum flavor potential. And, when you use the freshest and best ingredients, you will find they require less salt.

I believe in seasoning food completely before putting it on the table, but overseasoning is a greater sin than underseasoning. You can always add in cooking, but it is well nigh impossible to subtract. I like to use kosher or coarse sea salt because they give more control while seasoning than fine table salt, which lends itself to oversalting. (Sea salt is more acidic and therefore stronger than regular salt and should be used in smaller amounts.)

Be careful when seasoning dishes with shellfish, especially clams and oysters. They often bring enough salt with them for the occasion.

PEPPER

Pepper is undoubtedly the world's favorite spice. Like salt, pepper is recommended for seasoning most dishes in this book; unlike salt, pepper does not bring out the flavor in foods, it complements them. It amazes me how the unique flavor of pepper goes well with so many foods; no other spice can compare.

True pepper is a berry that grows on a vine. Green peppercorns are the unripe berries; they are sold fresh, not dried. Black pepper is picked immature, then dried whole. White pepper is the fully ripened berry, which is husked, then dried. I prefer to use black peppercorns rather than white, with very few exceptions. I find white pepper to be acrid and hot, without the full flavor of the black.

Except in recipes calling for whole black peppercorns, I do not give exact measurements for black pepper. If I used as much as I like, it might be too much for most people. As with salt, the amount of pepper is left to the discretion of the cook. But, please, don't be too discreet!

Buy whole peppercorns that have a strong aroma. Store them in an airtight container and keep it in a cool dry place. Grind the pepper as you need it. Ground pepper loses its flavor very quickly; there is no reason to keep ground pepper in your kitchen or on your table. Buy a good peppermill with an adjustable grinder. It will serve almost every need, from a coarse to a fine grind, and it will last a lifetime.

How to Make Cracked Pepper

The only type of grind that cannot be done in a peppermill is the very large pieces of cracked black pepper, also called mignonette pepper. This texture of pepper is great for seasoning roasts, chops and steaks and is a necessity for mignonette sauce for oysters. I also use this in most sausages, as well as a few fish preparations.

The quickest and easiest way to make cracked pepper is to place a tablespoon or so of whole peppercorns on a cutting board. Place the bottom of a clean sauté pan on top of the peppercorns and roll over them, pressing down firmly on the handle and front of the pan. You could also use a cleaver the same way or use a mortar and pestle. Be careful not to break up the pepper too much.

HERBS AND SPICES

Spices come from the bark, pits, seeds and other parts of various plants and flowers. Herbs are the leaves of plants or the plant itself; most can be used fresh or dried. Cloves and cinnamon are spices; thyme and rosemary are herbs. Both herbs and spices should be used sparingly, as they can overpower the delicate flavors of the foods they are cooked with.

A frequent mistake many cooks make is assuming that when herbs and spices are dried they are not perishable. Unless you are buying loose spices and herbs or drying your own, there is not much you can do to ensure that they are in peak condition, but you can keep them under optimum conditions, that is, stored in airtight containers in a cool and dry dark place. Whenever possible, buy spices like nutmeg, cloves and allspice whole. Grate, grind or pulverize them right before using; their flavors will be more intense. As a rule, you should test any herbs and spices that you have had more than six months, one year at most. Dried herbs and spices lose flavor as they age, and they are often bitter; discard any that are past their prime.

If you have access to fresh bay laurel, juniper berries and other herbs and spices, you should dry them completely and then seal in airtight jars. Replace them the following year when the new crop comes in. Most of the recipes in this book call for fresh herbs. If you wish to substitute dried herbs, use about a third to half as much.

Fresh Herbs

I remember a time not too long ago when fresh herbs, with the exception of parsley, were a novelty, available on a limited basis in the summer months only. Each summer it was a scramble to preserve tarragon, basil, rosemary and chives for winter. I used to pack the basil in olive oil and the tarragon in vinegar and partially dry and then freeze the other herbs.

The introduction of fresh herbs commercially has been a huge success because of their superiority over the dried. Although herbs grown in greenhouses or shipped from Florida and other warm places are not as good as those freshly picked local herbs of summer, they are still very good. Once you have cooked with fresh herbs, it becomes almost impossible to be without them. Thanks to the excellent availability in today's markets, fresh herbs are becoming a standard item for good cooks all year-round.

The best way to store fresh herbs is to wrap them in damp paper, cover tightly with plastic wrap and keep refrigerated. When the herbs begin to turn brown, it is time to discard them.

STOCK

Good stock is an invaluable ingredient in good cooking. It adds flavor and body to soups, sauces and other preparations and often can make the difference between average, good and great food. Stocks are easy to make and if necessary they can be kept frozen—disqualifying any excuse you may think you have for not using homemade stocks in your cooking. Modern cookery has eliminated many of the long-cooked, stock-based sauces of the past in favor of quick pan sauces that are made at the last minute with pan drippings, stock and a little butter. Full-flavored, perfectly made stocks have become more important than ever.

The principles of making stock are simple. Use fresh meaty bones and simmer, never boil, them with water, fresh vegetables, herbs and spices. Skim stocks often to remove impurities (often referred to as scum or foam) as they rise to the top of the pot. If not removed, they will cook back into the stock. Strain stocks and cool down as quickly as possible to prevent bacterial growth. Most stock will keep about one week in the refrigerator. After three days, bring it to a quick boil, strain and quickly cool down again. This will extend its shelf life.

A great stock requires generous amounts of bones and vegetables in its preparation. Use the amounts I give for bones and vegetables, but don't hesitate to add an extra piece of onion, leek, celery or carrot that may be lying around. Be fastidious about following the methods in the following recipes, but don't worry too much about the quantities or the size of diced or chopped vegetables. Stock-making is a frugal art that takes leftover pieces of vegetables, stems from parsley and thyme, broken pieces of bay leaves and extra bones that may be available and transforms them into a kitchen elixir. Remember that everything is strained and discarded at the end. If you save all your usable scraps, you may not need to buy anything to make stock. But use only those vegetables that are called for in the following recipes. Scraps from vegetables that are not listed, such as peppers, can overpower the flavor of the stock or turn it bitter. Mushrooms are not listed because of their expense, but if you have some to use up or a few leftover stems, they will add to the flavor of any stock.

Classically, stock is never salted because it is regarded as only a preliminary preparation, and the finished dish it is used in will be seasoned. But I like to salt my stocks very lightly, unless they are going to be reduced. I feel that by lightly salting the stock toward the end of the cooking, you get a better indication of when the stock has reached its peak of flavor. The salt also acts as a preservative, retarding bacterial growth. I leave the choice up to you.

A FEW BASICS

Fish Stock

Although there are other, easier ways to make fish stock, this method extracts the maximum flavor from the fish bones. It is the only method for fish stock you need to know. The best bones for fish stock are from halibut, sole, flounder or lean white fish. Oilier fish like cod, pollock, bluefish, salmon and swordfish make inferior fish stock. As fish stock cooks for a much shorter time than the other types of stock, chop the vegetables smaller than usual, no larger than one inch.

MAKES ABOUT ONE QUART

2½ to 3 pounds fish bones
2 tablespoons unsalted butter
1 large leek, washed well and
  chopped small
1 medium onion, chopped small
3 stalks celery, chopped small
2 carrots, peeled and sliced thin
3 bay leaves
2 sprigs fresh thyme
4 or 5 parsley stems
½ teaspoon whole black
  peppercorns
1 cup dry white wine
salt (optional)

1. Cut the bones into pieces 2 to 3 inches across. Trim the bones of any excess skin or viscera that may still be attached. Rinse or soak if necessary in cold water to completely remove any traces of blood.

2. Melt the butter in a stockpot on low heat and add the leek, onion, celery, carrots, bay leaves, thyme, parsley stems and peppercorns. Cook for about 5 minutes, stirring a few times.

3. Add the wine and place the fish bones on top of the vegetables. Cover the pot and allow the bones to sweat in the aromatic steam. After 20 minutes, remove the lid and pour in 4 cups water, enough to cover the fish bones.

4. Raise the heat and bring the stock to a boil. Skim the top, then reduce to a slow simmer. Simmer for 10 minutes and remove from the heat. Allow the stock to sit for another 10 minutes. If you like, you can lightly salt the stock.

5. Gently strain the stock through a fine strainer and chill as quickly as possible.

Chicken Stock

Chicken stock is an essential ingredient in most soups. For clear soups, Chicken Broth (page 120) is superior, but for most vegetable and cream soups, the more neutral flavor of stock is better.

MAKES FIVE TO SIX CUPS

5 pounds chicken bones (backs,
  necks, wingtips, etc.)
2 onions, coarsely chopped
4 stalks celery, coarsely chopped
3 carrots, coarsely chopped
4 bay leaves
4 sprigs fresh thyme
5 or 6 parsley stems
2 whole cloves
1 teaspoon whole black
  peppercorns
salt (optional)

1. Rinse chicken bones well under cold water. Place in a stockpot and cover with 8 cups water. Bring to a boil and skim the foam and some of the fat off the top.

2. Reduce to a slow simmer and add the onions, celery, carrots, bay leaves, thyme, parsley stems, cloves and peppercorns.

3. Simmer for 3½ to 4 hours, skimming the top frequently. Add salt to taste, if desired. Gently strain through a medium to fine strainer and chill as quickly as possible.

Reduced Veal Stock

The classical kitchen kept several types of veal stocks and sauces on hand, white and brown, *espagnole*, *demi-glace* and *glace de viande*. In today's kitchen you will normally find only one all-purpose veal stock-sauce. Each chef has a style and consistency of stock that he or she likes to work with. Mine is dark, full-bodied, reduced (but not overly so) and flavorful. Using as much as a third beef bones and a rather large amount of tomatoes gives this stock its rich flavor. The finished stock is very close to being a sauce and requires only a little last-minute cooking and flavoring to become one. It is also useful as a flavor booster in soups and braised dishes, but it is too rich to be used in large quantities for either. When recipes in this book call for reduced veal stock, use only this one for best results.

MAKES ABOUT ONE QUART

7 pounds meaty veal bones,
  sawed into 2-inch pieces
3 pounds meaty beef bones,
  sawed into 2-inch pieces
4 onions, coarsely chopped
4 to 6 stalks celery, coarsely
  chopped
4 to 6 carrots, peeled and
  coarsely chopped
5 or 6 cloves garlic, unpeeled
2 pounds ripe tomatoes or 2
  cans (8 ounces each) peeled
  tomatoes, with juice
4 bay leaves
6 sprigs fresh thyme
6 parsley stems
1 teaspoon whole black
  peppercorns
salt (optional)

1. Preheat the oven to 425 degrees. Put the veal and beef bones in a large roasting pan and place in the preheated oven. When the bones have begun to brown (about 30 minutes), add the onions, celery, carrots and garlic. Continue roasting, turning the bones and vegetables a couple of times, for 30 minutes more or until the bones and vegetables are well browned.

2. Transfer the contents of the roasting pan to a large stockpot. Add 1 cup water to the pan and scrape the drippings and everything else off the bottom of the pan. Be sure to get every bit. Add this to the stockpot, along with the tomatoes and pour in enough water to cover the bones (10 to 12 cups).

3. Slowly bring the stock to a boil and skim the foam from the top. Reduce the heat and simmer the stock slowly for 8 hours, skimming frequently. Add the bay leaves, thyme, parsley and peppercorns about halfway through the cooking (after 4 hours).

4. Strain the stock through a medium strainer into a smaller pot. If time allows, place the pot back on the stove to reduce; otherwise, cool the stock and reduce it the following day. Bring the strained stock to a slow boil and skim. Simmer, skimming from time to time, for about 2 hours or until the stock has been reduced by half. If you wish to refresh the flavor of the stock during this second cooking, add small amounts of the vegetables, herbs and spices that were used in the first cooking, but taste the stock before you add more herbs or spices to avoid overseasoning. Add salt to taste, if using.

5. Strain the stock through a fine strainer and chill as quickly as possible. Keep refrigerated until needed.

BUTTER

Not all butter is created equal, and the quality of the butter you use is very important. I use homemade butter made from fresh cream at Kate's in Old Orchard Beach, Maine. The difference is quite notable. I never buy salted butter because I find the freshest and finest butter is sold unsalted. I also find it easier to deal with salt as a separate entity in cooking. For many preparations, especially sauces, butter goes in last *(monté au beurre)*. It is best to season the sauce before the butter is added since you need to serve the sauce quickly after finishing it with butter. Salted butter complicates this process.

Like all dairy products, butter is perishable and can go rancid. Its quality declines with age. Don't stock up; it's not a good practice.

Clarified Butter

When the milk solids and liquid are removed from butter, what remains is a pure fat called clarified butter, which is used like a cooking oil for sautéing and panfrying (it has too low a burning point to be used for deep-frying). Because clarified butter has had most of the flavor removed, it should never be used in place of whole butter for dishes that do not require extremely high heat. Nor should it be confused with drawn butter (page 330), which imparts the full flavor of butter to other foods. It should be used only as you would use a cooking oil.

To make clarified butter, put pieces of unsalted butter in a double boiler on low to medium heat. When the butter has melted, skim the white milk solids off the top. Carefully ladle the fat from the pot and pass it through a fine strainer into a wide-mouthed container. Be careful not to include any of the liquid that is left at the bottom of the pot: it will cause the clarified butter to spatter as it is heated. Store clarified butter in a covered container in the refrigerator; it will keep almost a month. (One pound of butter yields about three-quarters of a pound of clarified butter.)

Brown Butter

Brown butter *(beurre noisette)* has a wonderfully nutty flavor that is especially good with fish that is dredged in flour and quickly sautéed *(à la meunière* in French). Brown butter is also a good accompaniment for shirred eggs (page 210), calves' brains and many different vegetables.

When serving this with fish, you should brown the butter in the same pan as the fish. After cooking the fish, pour off any excess fat, return the pan to low heat and add unsalted butter (1 to 2 tablespoons per person). Whether you are using a pan fish was just cooked in or a clean pan, the rest is the same. Cook the butter slowly, swirling or stirring it so that it cooks evenly. When the butter begins to foam, pay very close attention: it will also begin to brown. When the butter has a rich brown color and a nutty aroma, remove it immediately from the fire. Add a splash of lemon juice or vinegar to stop the cooking and to flavor the butter. You must work fast as the butter can go from brown to burnt very quickly. Add some chopped parsley, if you like, then lightly season with salt and pepper and spoon over the fish or whatever the butter is to be served with. You can add other garnishes to brown butter, like capers, tomato concassée (page 337), diced lemon, anchovies and herbs.

Drawn Butter

Drawn or melted butter is served on the side with boiled and grilled lobsters as well as with steamers and steamed mussels. It is also good with a whole artichoke. It can be made by simply placing unsalted butter in a small pot in a hot place near the stove or on a slow burner. After it has melted, season lightly with lemon juice, salt and pepper and stir well. Divide among individual bowls for dipping. (For an emulsified butter, add 1 teaspoon of milk for every 4 tablespoons of unsalted butter. Stir as you bring the butter to a slow boil, remove from heat and season lightly with salt and pepper.)

Compound Butters

Compound butters are made by mixing ingredients like lemon juice, herbs, spices, onions, shallots, scallions, anchovies, garlic, etc. with softened butter. Wherever they are called for in this book, measurements and directions are given, but you should feel encouraged to use your imagination and sense of flavor balance to create your own compound butters.

They are most often used to melt over grilled fish, poultry or meat. Other uses include stuffing (like a tarragon butter pushed under the skin of partridge, page 150) and finishing soups and sauces. They can also be spread on bread that is going to be toasted or grilled (garlic bread is a familiar example of this technique).

Compound butter can be used while still soft, right after it is made, or it can be made ahead, formed into a roll with aluminum foil or plastic wrap and kept refrigerated. The compound butter can then be sliced off as needed.

Garlic Butter

MAKES HALF A CUP

8 tablespoons (1 stick) unsalted butter
2 or 3 cloves (or more) garlic, peeled and mashed (1 tablespoon)
2 teaspoons lemon juice
salt and freshly ground pepper

1. Allow butter to come to room temperature.
2. Combine the softened butter, garlic and lemon juice and whip until thoroughly mixed. Season with salt and pepper.

White Wine Butter Sauce

I can't remember who coined the phrase "river of butter sauces flooding the kitchens of America," but it was quite appropriate at the time. The use of butter sauces to cover plates and decorate foods was one of the worst things that came out of nouvelle cuisine, as it was interpreted by American and French-American cooks a decade ago. White wine butter sauce (*beurre blanc*), which we all thought of as pretty chic, has gone the way of most fads, but it should not necessarily be discarded. It can really be quite good when used sparingly. It is best suited to broiled, baked or grilled fish and shellfish.

Many different garnishes can be added to *beurre blanc;* dice or zest of lemon and lime, chopped herbs (alone or in combination), anchovies, mustard, tomatoes and other vegetables are just a few. Stock can also be added to *beurre blanc* during the reducing stage, in order to tie together the sauce and the food it is being served with. In this recipe, the stock can be replaced by more wine. The shallots should be diced very fine since they will not be strained out. Use the measurement for lemon juice or vinegar as a guideline, remembering that different wines have different levels of acidity. Trust your own judgment. Acidity is what makes this sauce palatable; it should predominate.

MAKES ABOUT HALF A CUP

½ cup white wine
¼ cup stock, pages 327–328
(optional)
2 shallots, diced very fine
2 tablespoons heavy cream
6 tablespoons unsalted butter,
cut in small pieces
1 tablespoon white wine vinegar
or lemon juice
salt and freshly ground pepper

1. Combine the white wine, stock, if using, and shallots in a small saucepan. Place on medium heat, bring to a boil and reduce until the pan is almost dry, with no more than 1 tablespoon of liquid left. This will take about 10 minutes.

2. Add the cream and bring to a boil; be careful not to scorch. When the cream looks thick and almost buttery, lower the heat.

3. Add the butter a piece at a time, stirring or whisking constantly, until all the butter has been added and blended in. Remove from the heat and season to taste with vinegar or lemon juice, salt and pepper. Keep warm until ready to serve.

V A R I A T I O N

Red Wine Butter Sauce

For red wine butter sauce (*beurre rouge*), substitute a suitable red wine for the white and red wine vinegar for white wine vinegar or lemon juice.

GOOSE AND DUCK FAT

Goose, duck and other animal fats are extremely flavorful. Goose especially produces a clean, heavenly flavored fat. Of course these fats are not healthful and should be used sparingly— maybe just for very special occasions, like roast potatoes for Christmas.

How to Render Goose, Duck and Other Animal Fats

Cut the pieces of fat into cubes no larger than 1-inch. Take a heavy pot that is large enough to hold all the fat you plan to render with the fat at least 2 inches below the top of the pot. Add 2 or 3 tablespoons water to the bottom of the pot and place a single layer of fat in the bottom. Turn the heat on low and stir occasionally while the water evaporates and the fat begins to render. Now add all the remaining fat. Allow the fat to simmer very, very slowly, stirring occasionally. The fat should be barely hot enough to render; if it is any hotter it will scorch and be ruined. When the liquid fat has come up over the solid fat and the solid fat has shrunk to a third its original volume (about 1 hour), turn off the heat. Allow the fat to cool but not harden. Ladle the fat through a strainer into a glass jar. Keep refrigerated.

Oils pressed from various vegetables, seeds and nuts serve two purposes in cooking—frying and flavoring. Although oil imparts flavor to fried foods, the most flavorful oils are not used for frying. The fruitiest or nuttiest oils are generally the ones that are most gently pressed and least refined. These are often made from expensive ingredients like olives, walnuts and so on. Even if cost were not a factor, the very qualities that give the oil its rich flavor make it unsuitable for frying. Because these oils are hardly or not at all refined, their smoking point is too low for frying. The best oils for frying are those that have been at least partially refined, like safflower, corn and, my favorite for most frying, refined peanut oil. These are usually lower in price as well. Small quantities of the more expensive oils, like first-pressed olive oil, walnut, hazelnut and unrefined peanut oil, can be added to other oils to enhance their flavor, but mostly they should be reserved for vinaigrettes or for finishing dishes. Sesame oil and Chinese hot-chili oil, two very flavorful oils, are mainly used in small quantities for frying and stir-frying.

When you are using the finest oils in salads, keep the dressing simple, in order to feature the oil as well as the lemon or vinegar. Salad dressings with lots of mustard, garlic and other assertive flavorings do not require the use of extra-virgin olive oil or other expensive oils; still they should be made with only the highest quality pure vegetable or seed oils. A blend of oils can also work very well.

Aïoli

Aïoli is one of my favorite sauces. For garlic lovers it can be used like mayonnaise, as a sauce for cold meats and fish, for sandwiches, and for dressing pasta and other salads. I also use it to rub on fish or meat before grilling and to finish sauces (the mushroom ragout on page 171, for example) and soups. Because I use it in so many preparations, I have simplified the recipe, omitting the bread that is typical of the classic Provençal aïoli. This is a quick and easy version, which is really a garlic mayonnaise.

MAKES ONE AND A HALF CUPS

2 egg yolks
6 cloves garlic, finely chopped
¾ cup olive oil
¾ cup peanut oil
1 tablespoon lemon juice
salt and freshly ground black
pepper

1. Whisk together the egg yolks and garlic in a large mixing bowl. Add the olive oil, a few drops at a time, until the aïoli begins to thicken.

2. When the olive oil has been incorporated, add a few drops of water (¼ teaspoon). Whisk in the peanut oil, a bit more rapidly. When all the oil has been incorporated, add the lemon juice and season to taste with salt and pepper. Keep refrigerated.

Mayonnaise

Mayonnaise is basically an emulsification of oil and egg yolks, and you can change the flavor dramatically by varying the type of oil, from corn to peanut to olive oil. To a lesser degree, the final result also depends on what acid is used (vinegar or lemon or lime juice) and how much and how sharp the mustard is. Different garnishes can be added to make different mayonnaise-based sauces. Mayonnaise is so simple to make, using a simple technique to combine staples of every kitchen, and it is such an important part of home cooking that it always surprises me that more people don't make their own. With a little practice, you can make it as easily by hand as by machine.

MAKES ONE AND A HALF CUPS

2 egg yolks
1 teaspoon Dijon mustard
1¼ cups vegetable oil
1 tablespoon white wine vinegar
    or lemon juice
salt and freshly ground black
    pepper

1. Whisk together the egg yolks and mustard in a small bowl. Add the oil, drop by drop, until the mayonnaise begins to thicken.

2. When half the oil has been incorporated, add a few drops of water (¼ teaspoon). The water helps to stabilize the emulsification. Whisk in the remaining oil, a little more rapidly. When all of the oil has been added, whisk in the vinegar or lemon juice and season to taste with salt and pepper. Keep refrigerated.

VARIATIONS

Tartare Sauce The most famous of the mayonnaise-based sauces, in America at least. Add 1 tablespoon chopped onion, 1 tablespoon chopped parsley, 2 tablespoons chopped dill pickle and 1 teaspoon or more lemon juice to the Mayonnaise.

Tartare Sauce with Green Tomatoes Substitute 2 tablespoons chopped Pickled Green Tomatoes (page 340) for the dill pickle in the Tartare Sauce.

Herb Mayonnaise This is terrific with cold poached lobster, crab or fish. Add 2 tablespoons finely chopped shallots, 1 tablespoon chopped chives, 2 teaspoons chopped parsley, 2 teaspoons chopped chervil and 2 teaspoons chopped tarragon to the Mayonnaise. Use other herbs, like basil or mint, when they are compatible with the dish being garnished.

Rémoulade Sauce This is an excellent cold sauce for all types of hot and cold seafood. Add 1 finely chopped hard-boiled egg, 1 tablespoon chopped capers, 1 tablespoon chopped cornichon or dill pickle, 1 teaspoon chopped parsley and a dash of hot-pepper sauce or cayenne pepper to the Mayonnaise. Add a small amount of chopped onion (1 tablespoon) and chopped anchovy (1 fillet) as well, if you wish.

VINEGAR

Vinegar is made through a process known as acetic fermentation, which can happen naturally or be induced by the use of a so-called mother. Wine and cider are the most common base for making vinegar, but any other liquid that has gone through yeast fermentation, such as rice wine, can be transformed into vinegar. Basic vinegars can be flavored with herbs, spices, flowers, fruits, citrus rinds, and so on, to create additional flavor variations.

Vinegars vary greatly in quality. Cider vinegar, which is especially important in New England cookery, runs the gamut from nondescript and overly acidic to beautifully well balanced and fruity. The best apple cider vinegars can be purchased from small cider producers. Most health food stores carry at least one good cider vinegar. Distilled white vinegar is useful for cooking eggs and for cleaning, but has very few other applications.

The best American wine vinegars are usually produced in small quantities and are not that easy to find. Often the best bet for top-quality wine vinegars are the French and Italian ones, usually found in gourmet food shops. Champagne vinegar is among the greatest and most dependable of the white wine vinegars. Balsamic vinegar, from Modena, Italy, is one of, if not the greatest of, the red vinegars. Its sweet syrupy quality is unmatched for salads, as well as for cooking. Another excellent wine vinegar is made from sherry; it is excellent for salads and in cooking, and it can be found in most gourmet food shops.

Vinaigrette

As the role of salad has changed in modern cookery, so has the role of vinaigrette. Still used to dress green salads and cold vegetable salads, it now is also used to dress warm salads and grilled meats and fish. It has become a substitute for compound butter, serving the same purpose of adding flavoring and moisture, without the cholesterol.

When you make a vinaigrette, always match the oil and the vinegar with each other and with the food it is to be served with, and always use the highest quality of both. The type of oil and vinegar used also determines the ratio. For example, an aged balsamic vinegar would require far less oil to offset its acidity than would cider or champagne vinegar.

Basic vinaigrette is made with anywhere from one to three parts oil mixed with one part vinegar and seasoned with salt and pepper. Additional flavorings and garnishes might include shallots, onions, scallions, garlic, tomatoes, anchovies, capers, pickles, mustard, cheeses, sweeteners, spices and fresh herbs such as tarragon, basil, thyme or parsley. More exotic variations use fruit rinds, wine, chopped eggs, green tomatoes, and various fruits and vegetables. I usually make vinaigrette by mixing as I go, dipping the lettuce I will be using and tasting. Provided you have a fairly good palate, it is easy to mix vinaigrettes without using a recipe. Always let the vinaigrette stand for at least one hour to allow the flavors to blend and mellow. In many cases vinaigrettes can be kept in the refrigerator for days or even weeks; bring back to room temperature before using. In addition to the following recipes, you will find various vinaigrettes scattered throughout the book.

Balsamic Vinaigrette

MAKES ONE CUP

½ cup aged or regular balsamic
vinegar
¼ cup vegetable oil
¼ cup first-press olive oil
1 shallot, finely chopped
salt and freshly ground pepper

Combine the vinegar, vegetable oil, olive oil and shallot and mix well. Season to taste with salt and pepper.

VARIATIONS

Herb Vinaigrette

Add 2 or 3 tablespoons chopped fresh basil, tarragon, chervil, marjoram, mint, parsley and/or chives, alone or in combination, to the Balsamic Vinaigrette. Mix well.

Blue Cheese Vinaigrette

Crumble 4 ounces good-quality blue cheese, like a French Roquefort or a Maytag from Iowa, by hand or break it up with a fork. Add to the Balsamic Vinaigrette along with 1 teaspoon finely chopped garlic. Mix well without breaking up the cheese too much. Keeping the ingredients cool will help.

Tomato–Basil Vinaigrette

This dressing is particularly good for salads with lots of garden vegetables like green beans and tender young zucchini or other summer squash. It is also good for cold pasta salads. It should be made well in advance of using.

MAKES ONE AND A HALF CUPS

2 tablespoons finely chopped
shallots
1 tablespoon Dijon mustard
3 branches fresh basil, leaves
picked and coarsely chopped
(3 to 4 tablespoons)
½ cup extra-virgin olive oil
½ cup tomato concassée
(page 337)
¼ cup vegetable oil
¼ cup red wine vinegar
salt and freshly ground black
pepper

1. Combine the shallots, mustard, basil and olive oil in a mixing bowl. Mix well to disperse the mustard throughout.

2. Add the tomato concassée, vegetable oil and vinegar. Stir well and season to taste with salt and pepper. Allow at least a few hours for the flavors to combine. Mix well again before using.

Sherry–Mustard Vinaigrette

This vinaigrette is especially good with the firm and full-flavored greens that are typically used in warm salads. The mustard helps keep the dressing emulsified; this is especially helpful in making warm salads, which must be mixed so quickly.

MAKES ONE CUP

1 tablespoon Dijon mustard
2 tablespoons finely chopped
   shallots
2/3 cup peanut oil
1/4 cup sherry wine vinegar
salt and freshly ground pepper

Combine the mustard and shallots in a mixing bowl. Whisk in the oil, drop by drop. When half of the oil is incorporated, alternate drops of vinegar and oil, continuing until completely mixed. Season to taste with salt and pepper.

Lemon–Garlic–Walnut Vinaigrette

This vinaigrette takes lemon juice instead of vinegar. The assertive flavor of the three main ingredients makes this a perfect dressing for strong and bitter greens like endive, frisée and watercress. The absence of vinegar and the presence of walnut oil also makes it more compatible with wines than most.

MAKES ONE CUP

2/3 cup walnut oil
3 tablespoons lemon juice
4 cloves garlic, finely chopped
1 shallot, finely chopped
salt and freshly ground pepper

Combine the oil, lemon juice, garlic and shallot and mix well. Season to taste with salt and pepper.

Red Onion Vinaigrette

This vinaigrette is especially good for topping grilled fish and smoked fish. Try to make it about two hours ahead. That way the onions will have time to wilt to the point of perfection and to flavor, color and sweeten the vinaigrette, yet still be crunchy.

MAKES ONE AND A HALF CUPS

1 medium red onion, sliced into
   very thin rings
1/2 cup peanut oil
1/4 cup champagne vinegar
1/2 teaspoon sugar
salt and freshly ground black
   pepper

Place the onion rings in a mixing bowl. Add the oil, vinegar and sugar; season to taste with salt and pepper and stir. Do not break the onions. Place the bowl in a cool place and stir once in a while. The onions will eventually wilt and be covered by the liquid.

Fresh Mint Sauce

This old-fashioned, English-style mint sauce lies somewhere between a flavored vinegar and a vinaigrette. It is traditionally served with roast or grilled lamb. It is also an outstanding accompaniment for baby goat.

MAKES ABOUT THREE CUPS

1 cup champagne vinegar or
good white wine vinegar
½ cup sugar
6 branches fresh mint, leaves
picked and finely chopped
(2 cups)
10 shallots, finely chopped
(½ cup)

1. Combine the vinegar, ½ cup water and sugar and mix until the sugar is dissolved. Add the chopped mint and shallots and mix well.
2. Store in a tightly sealed glass container. It will keep indefinitely.

TOMATO SAUCES

I use tomatoes lavishly when they are in season, and you will find many sauces embellished with tomatoes throughout this book. Included here are recipes for a couple of all-purpose tomato-based sauces, as well as directions for tomato concassée, a very useful preparation to have at your fingertips.

Tomato Concassée

Though not, strictly speaking, a sauce, tomato concassée is an important basic preparation called for many times in this book. Prepare only as much as you need; it does not keep well. (One large tomato will make about ½ cup concassée.) Use tomatoes that are ripe but still firm.

Bring a pot of water to a boil and have another pot or bowl of ice water at hand. Core the top of each tomato and score the bottom by making a little X; do not cut into the flesh. Drop the tomatoes in the boiling water. After 20 to 30 seconds, you will see the skin begin to wrinkle. Remove the tomatoes and shock in the ice water to prevent further cooking. Peel the skins with a paring knife; they should come off easily. Quarter the tomatoes and remove the seeds and juice. Dice the flesh. The size depends on the recipe.

Basic Tomato Sauce

Here is an all-purpose, Neapolitan-style tomato sauce that can be used for many of the traditional Italian-American pasta and vegetable dishes. This basic sauce, which is vegetarian, can also be simmered with pork, sausages, chicken, meatballs or pieces of beef (please, no ground beef—ground pork is much better). When it is going to be used with fish and shellfish, it can be simmered with a little clam or mussel juice or fish stock. I use a combination of fresh tomatoes and tomato paste, which adds to the intensity of the tomato flavor. I brown onions and carrots to get the sweetness needed to balance the acidic tomatoes. Commercial sauces of this kind usually add sugar to achieve a balance. Sealed in airtight containers, this sauce will keep for weeks in the refrigerator.

MAKES TWO QUARTS

4 tablespoons olive oil
2 bay leaves
2 medium onions, cut in small
    (¼ inch) dice
2 medium carrots, peeled and
    cut in small (¼ inch) dice
12 cloves garlic, finely chopped
4 pounds ripe tomatoes, peeled,
    quartered and seeded
    (about 8 cups)
1 can (6 ounces) tomato paste
¼ cup coarsely chopped fresh
    basil leaves
salt and freshly ground
    black pepper

1. Heat the olive oil with the bay leaves in a heavy saucepan. When the bay leaves begin to brown, add the onions, carrots and garlic. Cook over medium heat, until the vegetables are a nice brown color (about 15 minutes)

2. Add the tomatoes, crushing them between your fingers right into the pot. Add the tomato paste, 1½ cups water (rinse out the tomato-paste can twice) and the basil. Bring to a boil and season lightly with salt and generously with pepper (at least 1 teaspoon). Reduce to a simmer and cook for 45 minutes to 1 hour. You may leave the sauce as is (chunky) or pass through a food mill for a finer texture.

Barbecue Sauce

Like Italian tomato sauce, Southern barbecue sauce has become an American standard. Brush this sauce on ribs, chops, steaks or chicken, and cook them over a hot wood or charcoal fire. This recipe was developed by Stan, the sous-chef at my restaurant, who hails from Savannah, Georgia. Make lots: it will keep for months in the refrigerator in tightly sealed jars.

MAKES TWO QUARTS

½ cup corn or other
  vegetable oil
2 large onions, coarsely chopped
  (2 cups)
2 carrots, peeled and coarsely
  chopped (⅔ to 1 cup)
12 cloves garlic, finely chopped
1 tablespoon finely chopped
  ginger
2 bay leaves
2½ pounds tomatoes, peeled,
  quartered and seeded
  (about 4 cups)
1 cup apple cider vinegar
1 cup brown sugar
2 cans (6 ounces each)
  tomato paste
1 teaspoon hot-pepper sauce
1 tablespoon Worcestershire
  sauce
2 teaspoons Coleman's
  dry mustard
salt and freshly ground
  black pepper
cayenne pepper

1. Heat the oil in a large pot and add the onions, carrots, garlic, ginger and bay leaves. Cook on low heat, until tender (about 20 minutes).

2. Add the tomatoes, vinegar, brown sugar and tomato paste. Rinse out the cans with 1 cup water and add to sauce. Add the hot-pepper sauce, Worcestershire sauce, dry mustard and a bit of salt and pepper. Simmer for about 1 hour.

3. Pass the sauce through a food mill or puree coarsely in a food processor. Adjust seasoning with more salt and pepper and cayenne pepper, if desired.

At different times of year you may wish to capitalize on the abundance of seasonal foods like cranberries, persimmons, corn and the like. By using various methods of cooking, along with natural preservatives like sugar, salt and vinegar, you can put up your favorite foods for use in the months ahead. Here are a few of my favorites.

Lightly Pickled Garden Vegetables

This pickle is for an assortment of firm vegetables; always use some onions. The brine is light and uncooked: it is meant to flavor the vegetables and extend their life, not completely preserve them. In fact, they are great the next day and at their best the first week.

MAKES ABOUT FOUR QUARTS

4 to 5 pounds of mixed garden vegetables (see Note)
½ cup cider or white wine vinegar
½ cup sugar
1 tablespoon salt
4 bay leaves
1 tablespoon peppercorns
4 sprigs fresh dill
4 sprigs fresh thyme
2 sprigs fresh tarragon

1. Peel the vegetables if necessary and cut in 1-inch chunks. Place in crocks or canning jars.
2. Combine 5 cups water with the vinegar, sugar, salt, bay leaves, peppercorns, dill, thyme and tarragon and mix well. Pour over the vegetables. Seal and refrigerate; it will keep in the refrigerator for months.

NOTE. Choose among the following vegetables: cucumbers, carrots, celery, fennel, cauliflower, peppers and onions. Green vegetables, like peas and green beans, do not work well in this recipe.

Pickled Green Tomatoes

Green tomatoes are great fried or baked in pies; they also make marvelous pickles. This sweet-and-sour-style pickled tomato is excellent with sandwiches or as an alternative to cucumber pickles in Tartare Sauce (page 333). It makes a wonderful sauce for clams (page 14).

MAKES ABOUT FOUR QUARTS

12 green tomatoes (4 to 5 pounds)
2 cups white wine vinegar
1 large onion, quartered
6 cloves garlic, crushed
4 tablespoons kosher salt
6 tablespoons sugar
1 tablespoon mustard seeds
2 tablespoons peppercorns
6 bay leaves

1. Cut the tomatoes in half or quarters so that they are uniform in size. Place the pieces in a crock or canning jars large enough to hold them.
2. Combine 6 cups water with the vinegar, onion, garlic, salt, sugar, mustard seeds, peppercorns and bay leaves in a large pot and bring to a boil. Pour the mixture over the tomatoes. When the liquid has cooled, seal the containers and refrigerate. Allow at least three days for the tomatoes to brine. They will keep indefinitely refrigerated in airtight containers.

Corn Relish

This is an old-fashioned highly seasoned relish that I adapted from my grandmother's recipe. Sealed tight and refrigerated, it will keep months; sterilized, it will keep indefinitely. I find it handy to keep around for quick meals or snacks.

MAKES SIX PINTS

16 ears of corn, husked
2 cups cider vinegar
1½ cups sugar
1 tablespoon salt
2 tablespoons mustard seeds
1 tablespoon turmeric
1 teaspoon celery seeds
2 tablespoons Coleman's
    dry mustard
1 teaspoon ground ginger
1 teaspoon ground allspice
1 tablespoon cornstarch
2 red bell peppers, cut in small
    (¼ inch) dice (1 cup)
2 green bell peppers, cut in small
    (¼ inch) dice (1 cup)
1 large onion, cut in small
    (¼ inch) dice (1 cup)

1. Cook the corn on the cob as directed on page 234 and shave off the kernels (you should have about 8 cups). Set aside.

2. Combine 1 cup water with the vinegar, sugar, salt, mustard seeds, turmeric, celery seeds, dry mustard, ginger, allspice and cornstarch. Bring to a boil and add the diced peppers and onion. Simmer for 10 minutes on medium heat.

3. Add the corn and cook for 5 minutes more. Spoon into pint jars and seal. Keep refrigerated.

Cranberry Relish

No Thanksgiving dinner would be complete without cranberry relish. It can be made in large batches if you want to make enough for the winter.

MAKES THREE CUPS

2 oranges
1 cup sugar
2 teaspoons lemon juice
2 teaspoons fresh ginger, cut in
    fine julienne
1 bag (12 ounces) fresh or frozen
    cranberries
½ teaspoon freshly ground
    white pepper

1. Peel 1 orange and cut the zest (orange part only) into very fine julienne, as thin as possible; set aside. Squeeze both oranges for juice; set aside.

2. Combine the sugar and lemon juice in a small sauté pan. Heat up slowly and continue cooking until the sugar begins to caramelize. If necessary, wash down the sides of the pan by brushing with a little water to keep the sugar from burning.

3. When the sugar is caramel colored, add the julienned ginger and orange zest. Cook for about 1 minute, then add the cranberries, orange juice and pepper. Continue to cook on medium-high heat, stirring frequently, for about 5 minutes or until the cranberries are slightly broken but not mushy (frozen cranberries will take about 7 minutes). Remove from the heat and let cool.

Cranberry—Onion Jam

This jam is an excellent accompaniment to cold roast meats, like venison and pork, and meat pâtés, like the rabbit terrine on page 200. The trick to making this is to caramelize the onions thoroughly. If this is not done properly, you may find the jam needs more sugar.

MAKES ABOUT TWO PINTS

2 tablespoons vegetable oil
2 pounds sweet white onions, sliced as thin as possible
1/4 cup cider vinegar
1/3 cup sugar
2 cups cranberries
salt and freshly ground black pepper

1. Heat a large sauté pan on high heat and add the oil, then add the onions. Let the onions cook without stirring for 5 minutes. Stir the onions and continue cooking. Cook for 20 minutes or however long it takes for them to reach a deep brown color. Stir only to prevent scorching. The less the onions are stirred, the faster they will caramelize.

2. Add the vinegar, sugar and cranberries and continue cooking for 8 to 10 minutes more or until the cranberries have dissolved. (If frozen cranberries are used, it will take somewhat longer.) Season moderately with salt and pepper and remove from the heat. Let cool. Divide among jars, seal and keep refrigerated.

Persimmon Chutney

A pair of persimmon trees, one male and one female, was often given as a housewarming gift in colonial times. Originally from China, the persimmon grows only as far north as southern New England. There are numerous types of persimmons, most of them bearing fruit late in October. Persimmons are inedible until they are completely ripe and very soft; store them in a cool and dry dark place until they are. They will be very sweet without any astringency. I like to preserve persimmons in the form of a spicy chutney, which is excellent with ham and other smoked meats or cold roasts. Tightly sealed, this concoction will keep for up to two months in the refrigerator, so don't be afraid to multiply the recipe to suit your needs.

MAKES ABOUT TWO PINTS

about 1 1/2 pounds persimmons
3 to 4 limes
1 piece fresh ginger (about 2 inches)
1/2 cup sugar
2 ripe pears or apples, peeled, cored and cut in medium (1/2 inch) dice
1 small red bell pepper, cut in medium (1/2 inch) dice
1/4 cup golden raisins
1/4 cup black raisins or currants
salt and freshly ground black pepper
cayenne pepper
cider vinegar

1. Squeeze the pulp out of the persimmons, discarding the stems and skin; set aside. You should have 2 cups or a little more. Peel 2 of the limes and cut the zest (green part only) into very fine julienne (slivers); set aside. Squeeze as many of the limes as you need to make 1/2 cup of juice; set aside. Cut the ginger into very fine julienne (slivers).

2. Combine the lime juice and zest, ginger and sugar in a large saucepan. Bring to a boil, then add the pears or apples, pepper, golden raisins and black raisins or currants. Reduce the heat and simmer until the pears or apples become soft. Add the persimmon pulp and bring back to a boil. As soon as the mixture boils, remove from the heat. Season to taste with salt, pepper, cayenne pepper and vinegar; the chutney should be spicy, sweet and sour, all at the same time.

3. After the chutney has cooled, transfer to glass jars. Seal tight and store in the refrigerator. Allow a few days for the flavors to develop.

Smooth Apple Sauce

This smooth apple sauce is good for all kinds of apples, but especially the softer, sweeter types, like McIntosh and Empire. This is pure apple sauce, no sugar or spices; the results depend wholly on the apples being used. If, however, you are not satisfied with the results, you can finish it off with some sugar and cinnamon or nutmeg. The sauce will have a slightly pink appearance due to the contact with the skins during cooking. This sauce will keep for one month in the refrigerator; sterilized, it will keep indefinitely.

MAKES THREE PINTS

5 pounds soft sweet red apples

1. Wash the apples and then cut each into 6 or 8 pieces, leaving the skins and cores attached. Place in a large heavy saucepan and add ½ cup water. Place on medium heat and cover tightly.

2. After 20 minutes, stir the apples and lower the heat to a slow simmer. Cover and cook for another 30 minutes, or longer if necessary, until the apples are very well done (mushy). Remove from heat and let stand until the apples cool a little. Push through a food mill or medium strainer; allow to cool completely. Transfer to airtight containers and store in the refrigerator. Serve cold.

Chunky Apple Sauce

Firmer, tarter apples, like Gravensteins, Rhode Island Greenings and Granny Smiths, are best for a chunky apple sauce. They require a little sweetening.

MAKES THREE TO FOUR PINTS

6 pounds tart firm apples
½ cup sugar
½ teaspoon ground cinnamon
¼ teaspoon ground allspice
3 tablespoons unsalted butter

1. Peel, core and cut the apples into medium (½ inch) dice.

2. Combine the apples, sugar, cinnamon and allspice with 1 cup water in a large copper or stainless steel pot. Bring to a boil, then reduce the heat to a simmer. Stir often to prevent scorching. After about 15 minutes, mash about half the apples in the pot with a fork. Continue to cook and stir for 10 minutes more.

3. Remove from the heat and stir in the butter. Allow to cool, then store, tightly sealed, in the refrigerator. Serve at room temperature or reheat and serve warm.

Beach Plum Puree

Beach plums grow wild along much of the New England coast. Most people make jelly, which can be excellent, but I like to make puree, using only enough sugar to preserve the plums. The puree is especially good with venison (pages 192–198) and other game preparations. It can also be used for desserts and confections.

MAKES TWO CUPS

2 pounds wild beach plums,
   stems removed and washed
1 cup sugar
juice of ½ lemon

1. Place the plums in a large saucepan and add the sugar, lemon juice and ½ cup water. Bring to a boil, then reduce the heat to a simmer. Cook for 20 minutes, stirring and mashing occasionally, until you have a thick mixture.

2. Push the mixture through a medium-fine strainer. Transfer to a glass jar, seal tight and refrigerate. This will keep up to 1 month in the refrigerator.

Spiced Nuts

These nuts are great for snacking or for a crispy garnish for salads, as in the salad of grilled duck with cranberries on page 129.

FOR ONE POUND OF NUTS

1 pound pecan or walnut halves
2 tablespoons unsalted butter
⅓ cup Worcestershire sauce
6 dashes hot-pepper sauce
kosher salt

1. Preheat the oven to 300 degrees. Combine the nuts with the butter, Worcestershire and hot-pepper sauce in a large sauté pan. Place on medium heat and cook, stirring, for 5 minutes or until all the liquid is absorbed.

2. Spread the nuts on a sheetpan lined with parchment paper and bake for 20 minutes. The nuts should be dry and thoroughly heated through. Sprinkle with a moderate amount of salt (to taste) immediately after removing from the oven. Allow to cool completely. Store in the cupboard in an airtight container.

Seasonal Menus

The essence of good cooking is the balancing of good local ingredients to create a satisfying meal. The menu is all-important. Every component of every meal should create contrasts, with no repetition, and should always suit the occasion, be it formal or informal. The time of year, place where you live, the people you are feeding, and the limitations of time and space (your kitchen) are the key elements in creating a great menu. A great dish, like New England Boiled Dinner or Vermont Cheddar Cheese Soup, can be an abomination if served on a hot summer day. Likewise, a light and refreshing steamed bass can leave your guests wanting on a sub-zero night in February. The quality of the preparation of any dish is rendered meaningless when it is taken out of context.

For several reasons this concept is particularly important to the recipes in this book. New England is a cold place most of the year, where a steaming bowl of chowder can be as appropriate in May as it is in January. Most of New England's classic dishes are cold-weather dishes; many of the recipes in this book are cold-weather recipes. The great foods of summer are light and simple, often self-explanatory and usually improvised; the hearty foods of the colder months are usually more complex. Without apologies, I offer here some recipes that are quite rich; I can only hope that you will take them in the spirit from which they come and use them accordingly.

In emphasizing the richer foods of the cool and cold months, I do not wish to create an image of New Englanders as people who eat salt pork and heavy cream all the time. We don't. It is important, even in the coldest months, to balance heartier dishes with lighter ones in any given menu and on any given day. It is never appropriate to stuff your guests, and with family it is especially important to balance the foods they eat on an ongoing basis.

The following menus demonstrate how and when many of the recipes in this book would be used in New England. They highlight some of the important foods of each season. With a few exceptions, the dishes in these menus can be found in this book; the few that are not are those that need no explanation. You will have no problem recreating any of these menus. In some cases they are intended for special occasions. In trying to highlight as many dishes as possible, I have made some of these menus quite elaborate. For Thanksgiving, for example, I list seventeen different dishes, all appropriate for the holiday. For other special occasions or for the simple two- or three-course meals that are most common at home, you may want to scale down the menus to suit your needs. They are meant to be suggestive and to serve as a guide.

I have not given beverage recommendations, but a brief overview of this subject follows the menus.

JANUARY

A Stormy Winter's Night Raw Cape Scallops with Lemon, Onions and Capers

New England Boiled Dinner
(brisket, cabbage, turnips, parsnips, potatoes and beets)

Fresh Horseradish and Mustard Pickles
Pear Crisp

A Hearty Luncheon Thin Wedges of Cheddar Cheese Pie with a Mixed Green Salad
Fresh and Smoked Haddock Chowder
Tropical Fruit Salad and Sand Tarts

Sunday Brunch Red Flannel Hash with Poached Egg

or

Old-Fashioned Salt-Cod Cakes with Bacon

Toasted Whole-Grain Country Bread with Sweet Butter
and Preserves

Cranberry Muffins

FEBRUARY

A Valentine Dinner for Two Wellfleet Oysters with Osetra Caviar

Grilled Nantucket Quail (one each) served with Warm Salad
Greens with Sherry–Mustard Vinaigrette

Panroasted Lobster with Herbs and Grilled Shiitake Mushrooms

Vanilla-Bean Ice Cream with Warm Dried-Fruit Compote

Dinner by the Fire Broiled New England Shellfish
(clams, oysters, mussels and periwinkles)

Lucky's Log-Seared Skirt Steak with Gratin of Turnips
and Potatoes

Endive and Watercress Salad with Blue Cheese Vinaigrette
Pear Upside-Down Spice Cake

MARCH

A Family Dinner   Maine Shrimp Bisque

Roast Capon with Oyster Stuffing
Braised Butternut Squash and Glazed Onions
Mashed or Roasted Potatoes

Indian Pudding Custard

Lunch on a Blustery Day   Warm Spinach and Beet Salad with Bacon Dressing
Seafood Rarebit with Lobster, Crab or Shrimp
and Toast Points
Vermont Chocolate Potato Cake with Hot-Fudge Sauce

A Yankee Breakfast   Poached Finnan Haddie with Egg Sauce
Homemade Breakfast Sausages and/or Rashers of Bacon
Toasted Boston Brown Bread with Sweet Butter

APRIL

Easter Sunday Dinner   Chicken Broth with Morels and Wild Rice
Asparagus Salad with Mustard Dressing and Maine Crabmeat
Turnovers

Mom's Fresh Ham
Braised Sweet-and-Sour Red Cabbage
Potato Pancakes and Apple Sauce

Featherbeds and Cheddar Cheese Biscuits

Strawberry–Rhubarb Crisp with Ice Cream
Chocolate Bread and Butter Pudding

Chicken Dinner   Some of the Last Great Oysters of the Season with Jasper's
Mignonette
Mixed Greens with Balsamic Vinaigrette
Five-Spice Roast Chicken
Fiddlehead Ferns and Spring-Dug Parsnip Puree
Maple-Sugar Crème Caramel

The First Cookout Stuffed Quahogs

An Assortment of Cold Vegetable Salads

Barbecued Cuts of Baby Lamb or Goat

Fresh Mint Sauce

Grilled Leeks and Potatoes

Fresh Fruits, Angel Food Cake and Ice Cream

A Seafood Dinner Periwinkles with Escargot Butter

Shad Roe Wrapped in Bacon and Grilled with Wilted Spinach, Red Onions and Oranges

Half-Crispy Black Sea Bass with Scallion Puree and Sautéed Spring Vegetables

Fresh Berry Sorbet and Cookies

J U N E

A Rainy Afternoon by the Shore: Steamers and Clam Fritters
Lunch Turns to Dinner
Cups of Fish Chowder with Common Crackers

Boiled Chicken Lobsters with Drawn Butter

Mixed Green Salad and Steamed New Potatoes

Deep-Dish Blueberry Pie

Simple and Elegant Supper Smoked Trout with Red Onion Vinaigrette

Grilled Sweetbreads with Bacon, Corn Relish and Mixed Green Salad

Wild-Blackberry Ice Cream

J U L Y

Fourth of July

Mussels Steamed with White Wine and Garlic

Salad of Cold Poached Salmon with Fresh Peas

Lobsters, Chicken and Homemade Veal Sausages on the Grill

Green Bean and Mint Salad

Potato and Other Cold Salads

Strawberry Shortcake

While the Sun Goes Down

Marinated Tomatoes and Arugula with Fried Squid

Barbecued Bluefish with Smoked Shrimp Butter

Cole Slaw

Corn on the Cob

Gratin of Fresh Berries

Fisherman's Breakfast

Tinkers and Bacon

Blueberry Brown-Bread Pancakes

Cantaloupe or other Sweet Melon

A U G U S T

The Clambake

Soft-Shell Clams

Fresh-Picked Mussels

Rock Crabs

Maine Lobsters

Portuguese Sausages

Silver Queen or Butter and Sugar Corn

White Boiling Onions

Sweet Potatoes and New Potatoes

Drawn Butter, Lemon Wedges, Salt, Pepper and Hot-Pepper Sauce

Homemade Breads and Rolls

Peach Cobbler

Deep-Dish Blueberry Pie

Watermelon and Other Fresh Fruits

A Light Supper

Bluefin Tuna Carpaccio

Garden Tomatoes with Maine Crab

Homemade Breadsticks and Sweet Butter

Fresh Nectarines and Plums

SEPTEMBER

The First Cool Nights   Gravlax-Style Bluefish with Mustard–Dill Sauce
Salad with Garden Vegetables
Lobster and Corn Chowder with Corn Fritters
Apple–Custard Tart

A Proper Dinner   Salad of Grilled Duck with Cranberries and Spiced Nuts
Haddock Braised with Saffron, Fennel, Tomatoes and Mussels
Sweet Garlic Pasta
Pumpkin Crème Brulée

A Favorite Dinner   First of the Season Oysters on the Halfshell

Pork Rib Chops with Clams and Garlic Sauce

Potatoes Fried in Olive Oil

Fresh Fall Berries

OCTOBER

Simple Lunch or Dinner   Lightly Pickled Garden Vegetables and Mixed Green Salad
Indian Summer Chowder with Smoked Chicken or Poussin, Sweet Potatoes and Corn
Pear Crisp

An Autumn Dinner   Oyster, Ham and Wild Mushroom Tartlets

Breast of Pheasant, Hunter Style
Johnnycake Polenta

Cider Sorbet

Hunter's Dinner   Pheasant Ravioli en Brodo
Breast of Wild Duck with Bitter Greens and Turnips
Cranberry–Streusel Tart

Dinner in Boston   Oyster Stew

Boston Scrod with Boiled Potatoes and Mixed Green Salad

Seckel Pears Poached in Riesling

New England Thanksgiving   Wild Maine Belon Oysters with Apple Cider Mignonette

Cape Cod Littleneck Clams with Horseradish and Lemon

Fresh and Pickled Vegetables

Common Crackers

Chunky Lobster Stew with Tomalley Croutons

Roast Vermont Turkey with Giblet Gravy

Roast Saddle of Venison with Beach Plum Sauce

Country Sausage and Sage Dressing

Cranberry Relish

Maple-Glazed Yams

Sautéed Wild Mushrooms and Grilled Leeks

Mashed Potatoes

Boston Brown Bread

Anadama Bread

Old-Fashioned All-American Apple Pie

Thanksgiving Pumpkin Pie

Maple–Walnut Ice Cream and Homemade Cookies

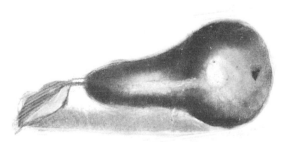

A Holiday Cocktail Party—All Seafood

Raw New England Shellfish on Ice
(sea urchins, cape scallops, Wellfleet oysters and littlenecks)

Stuffed Quahogs

Baked Oysters with Leeks and Pancetta

Grilled Lobster Sausages

Shrimp Toasts

White Clam Pizza

Brandade de Morue

Squid and Olive Salad

Seafood Fritto Misto (scallops, clams, whitebait) with Rémoulade Sauce

Spiced Nuts, Shortbread and Chocolates

A Special Holiday Lunch

Thin Johnnycakes with Crème Fraîche and Osetra Caviar

Mussel and Ham Bisque

Warm Salad with Lobster, Foie Gras and Papaya

Egg Nog Custard

Small Christmas Dinner

Oysters with Caviar

Lydia's "Chinese" Christmas Goose

Glazed Onions and Turnips

Ragout of Brussels Sprouts with Bacon, Apples and Walnuts

Potatoes Roasted in Goose Fat

Endive Salad with Lemon-Garlic-Walnut Vinaigrette

Mincemeat Tartlets and Scottish Shortbreads

Beverages

I tend to take the Chinese approach toward beverages: if you enjoy a particular beverage with your food, then it is suitable. Wine is obviously a great choice for most meals, but we Americans tend to oversimplify our wine selections with food. At my restaurant the popular choice for white wine is California Chardonnay; for red, California Cabernet Sauvignon. Without delving into this too deeply, let me say that although Chardonnay and Cabernet Sauvignon are excellent grape varietals, they are only two of the many to choose from. Shellfish, especially raw shellfish, and fish go well with Sauvignon Blanc, Sémillon Blanc and our own Eastern varietal, Vidal Blanc. With game birds, Riesling and Gewürztraminer are usually a good choice, and it is okay if they are a little on the sweet side. Champagne, as you probably know, is acceptable with almost any food. And sherry pairs very well with certain seafoods, especially the shellfish stews. Red wines are all too often restricted to drinking with meats, but the lighter ones are great with most seafood and even the richer (bigger) reds can successfully accompany seafood, providing it is not too mild in flavor. With venison, lamb and beef it is usually best to choose a hearty red wine. Of the red varietals, Merlot, Sirah and Zinfandel can make good substitutes for the standard Cabernet Sauvignon and Pinot Noir. The choices are overwhelming, from the different varietals to the different wine-making regions around the world. There are simply too many interesting matches of food and wine to limit oneself to choices that have become almost clichés. The subject of pairing food and wine is exhaustive; it can be a lifelong pursuit. (I know, it is one of mine.)

In New England we are starting to develop many respectable wines, and I encourage people from all regions to try their local wines. Sakonett Vineyards in Rhode Island and Crosswoods Vineyards in Connecticut (see List of Sources, page 358) are in the forefront of vinifera wine-making in New England. In addition, there is a tradition of making wine from fruit other than the grape that dates back to colonial times. There seems to be a renewed interest in these fruit wines, and production is increasing all around New England. One of the leaders of this movement is Jack Partridge of Nashoba Vineyards in Bolton, Massachusetts. His dry wine from apples (especially Gravensteins) can be surprisingly well suited to lighter foods; his dry wine from blueberries is quite sophisticated, suitable for drinking with game and other red meats. The other fruit wines (pear, plum, peach, etc.) are more of a novelty and are not serious considerations at the dinner table except possibly with dessert. (See List of Sources, page 358, for New England fruit wines.)

Another viable fruit product is sparkling (hard) cider, which has been around for centuries but is being made commercially in New England for the first time. This type of cider is refreshing and can be excellent with more casual foods, like cold meats and salads; it is also quite good with raw oysters.

Beer is another beverage that pairs well with many of the foods of New England, in some cases better than wine. I can't imagine a piping hot bowl of steamers without an ice-cold draft beer to accompany them. And Cheddar cheese is better complemented by beer than by wine. I am not what you would call a big beer drinker, but I truly enjoy it with certain foods. There are several small new boutique breweries in New England that produce delicious and rich European-style beers. Samuel Adams, brewed by the Boston Beer Company, is among the most popular.

If I seem to have skirted the subject of beverages, it is in order to reinforce my original statement: if you enjoy a particular beverage, then it is suitable. The classic food and beverage combinations, although tried and true, tend to be dogmatic, bordering on the dull. Use some restraint, but not too much. What you eat and drink is your choice. Have fun!

List of Sources

If you can't find johnnycake meal, maple sugar, common crackers, sea urchins or cob-smoked ham where you live, you will find them here. These are some of the purveyors that I use; all are top-notch. Most will mail order, but a few are either too small or too big. The smaller ones are listed for the sake of my fellow New Englanders, who may find themselves near to these producers. A few of the larger purveyors have assured me that they will assist you in finding the retailers in your vicinity that distribute their products. The best fruits and vegetables are usually the ones that grow nearest to you, but for many dishes, like johnny-cakes, there is no substitute for the real thing. I'm sure you will find all of these wonderful people kind and helpful. New England has hundreds of dedicated food producers; I extend my apologies to the many who are not included in this list.

For a more in-depth guide to New England foods, I highly recommend *The Tasty Side of New England* by Beth Hillson (The Stephen Greene Press, 1989).

CHEESE AND OTHER DAIRY PRODUCTS

Cabot Farmers' Cooperative
　Creamery
Main Street, Box 128
Cabot, Vermont 05647
(802) 563-2231
*Cheddar cheese (several types),
sour cream, butter*

Craigston Cheese Company
45 Dodges Row, Box 267
Wenham, Massachusetts 01984
(617) 468-7497
Camembert-style cheese

Crowley Cheese, Inc.
Healdville, Vermont 05758
(802) 259-2340
Colby cheese

Guilford Cheese Company
R.D. #2, Box 420
Guilford, Vermont 05301
(802) 254-9182
*soft-ripened cheeses,
mozzarella*

Kate's Butter
P.O. Box 79
Old Orchard Beach, Me. 04064
(207) 934-5143
homemade butter

The Plymouth Cheese Corp.
P.O. Box 1
Plymouth, Vermont 05056
(802) 672-3650
*curd-style Cheddar, old-
fashioned relishes and pickles*

Purity Cheese
55 Endicott Street
Boston, Massachusetts 02113
(617) 227-5060
fresh ricotta and mozzarella

Rawson Brook Farm
P.O. Box 345
New Marlboro Road
Monterey, Mass. 01245
(413) 528-2138
plain and flavored goat cheeses

Shelburne Farms
Harbor Road
Shelburne, Vermont 05482
(802) 985-8686
handmade Cheddars

Smith's Country Cheese
20 Otter River Road
Winchendon, Mass. 01475
(617) 939-5738
gouda and smoked gouda

State of Maine Cheese Co.
75 Front Street
Rockland, Maine 04841
(207) 596-6601
various Cheddars

York Hill Farm
York Hill Road
New Sharon, Maine 04955
(207) 778-9741
goat- and cow-milk cheeses,
romano-style cheese

CONDIMENTS
VINEGAR, HONEY, JAM AND PRESERVES, MAPLE PRODUCTS

Black Lamb Herb Farm
90 Sawyer Hill Road
New Milford, Conn. 06776
(203) 354-5634
cider vinegar and cider jelly

Chicama Vineyards
Stoney Hill Road
West Tisbury, Mass. 02575
(508) 693-0309
vinegars and wine

Concord Spice and Grain
84 Thoreau Street
Concord, Massachusetts 01742
(617) 369-1535
vinegars, oils, spices, dried
fruits, organic products and
various other condiments and
foods

Dan Johnson's Sugar House
70 Ingalls Road
Jaffrey, New Hampshire 03452
(603) 532-7379
maple syrup

Ellis Enterprises
419 North Main Street
Brewer, Maine 04412
(207) 989-6565
wild blueberry honey, assorted
honeys

Green Briar Jam Kitchen
6 Discovery Hill Road
East Sandwich, Mass. 02537
(508) 888-6870
beach plum jelly, various jams
and preserves

Maple Grove Farms of
  Vermont
167 Portland Street
St. Johnsbury, Vermont 05819
(802) 748-5141
maple sugar and syrup

Nervous Nellie's Jams and
  Jellies
Sunshine Road
Deer Isle, Maine 04627
(207) 348-6182
wild Maine blueberry conserve,
various jams and preserves

Wickford Apiaries
107 Chatworth Road
N. Kingstown, R.I. 02852
(401) 295-5383
honey from mixed blossoms

FISH AND SHELLFISH

Cape Cod Shellfish and
  Seafood Company
33-35 Boston Fish Pier
Boston, Massachusetts 02210
(617) 423-1555
Wellfleet and other oysters,
Cape Cod clams, various other
seafoods

Cotuit Oyster Company
P.O. Box 563
Cotuit, Massachusetts 02634
(508) 428-6747
Cape Cod oysters and clams

Downeast Seafood Express
Box 138, Route 176
Brooksville, Maine 04617
(207) 326-8246
lobsters, rock crab, sea scallops
and various other seafoods

Ducktrap River Fish Farm
R.F.D. #2, Box 378
Lincolnville, Maine 04849
(207) 763-3960
excellent smoked seafood of
every description, including
Eastern salmon and their own
farmed trout

Ipswich Shellfish Company
14 Hayward Street
Ipswich, Massachusetts 02938
(508) 356-4371
soft-shell clams and various
other seafood

James Hook and Company
15-17 Northern Avenue
Boston, Massachusetts 02210
(617) 423-5500
Maine and Canadian lobsters,
some other shellfish

Marblehead Lobster Company
Beacon and Orne Streets
Marblehead, Mass. 01945
(617) 631-0787
mail-order lobsters

Mitchell and Winter, Caspian Caviars
Highland Mill, P.O. Box 876
Camden, Maine 04843
(207) 236-4436
outstanding Maine seafoods: Maine shrimp, scallops, sea urchins and other exotic items, also very fine sturgeon caviars.

Red Wing Meadow Farm, Inc.
187 North Main Street
Sunderland, Mass. 01375
(413) 665-3295
fresh brook trout and other fish

Steve Connelly Seafood Company
10 Newmarket Square
Boston, Massachusetts 02118
(617) 427-7700
with plants on Nantucket and Gloucester; complete range of New England fish and shellfish: Nantucket cape scallops, groundfish from Georges Bank; also smoked fish, finnan haddie

MEAT, POULTRY AND GAME BIRDS

Boyajian, Inc.
P.O. Box 26
Belmont, Massachusetts 02178
(617) 876-5400
poussin, turkeys, fresh foie gras and other specialty items

B & B Pheasantry
701 Methuen Street
Dracut, Massachusetts 01826
(508) 458-2841
fresh pheasants

East Meadow Farm
Nantucket, Mass. 02554
(617) 228-0255
quail, mallard ducks

Gaspar's Sausage Company
P.O. Box 436
N. Dartmouth, Mass. 02747
(508) 998-2012
Portuguese linguiça *and* chouriço

Glen Echo Farm
Box 1
Spofford, N.H. 03462
(603) 363-4510
natural spring lamb, piglets

Green Acres Turkey Farm
566 West Street, Route 121
Wrentham, Massachusetts 02093
(617) 384-2441
organic turkey, chicken, geese

The Harrington Ham Co.
Main Street
Richmond, Vermont 05477
(802) 434-3411
cob-smoked hams, country bacon and other smoked specialties

John Dewar and Company
753 Beacon Street
Newton, Massachusetts 02159
(617) 964-3577
specialty meats, venison, game birds

Lovejoy Brook Farm
R.F.D. #1
Chester, Vermont 05143
(802) 875-3159
natural goats and baby lambs; also calves

Pheasant Hill Farms
P.O. Box 129
Cohasset, Massachusetts 02025
(617) 545-1356
pheasant, quail, mallard ducks

Pine Acres Rabbitry
229 East Main Street
Norton, Massachusetts 02766
(508) 285-7391
fresh rabbits

The Pork Schop of Vermont
P.O. Box 99
Hinesburg, Vermont 05461
(802) 482-3617
natural smoked hams, bacon and other smoked products (no nitrates)

Salumeria Italiana
151 Richmond Street
Boston, Massachusetts 02113
(617) 523-8743
pancetta, prosciutto and other Italian specialties

Smokehouse, Inc.
15 Coventry Street
Roxbury, Massachusetts 02119
(617) 442-6840
custom smoked meats, poultry and sausages, no nitrates

Sugar Hill Farm, Inc.
Smith Hill Road
P.O. Box 50
Colebrook, Conn. 06021
(203) 379-9649
organic mature lamb

GRISTMILLS AND COMMON CRACKERS

Gray's Grist Mill
P.O. Box 422
Adamsville, R.I. 02801
(508) 636-6075
true Rhode Island johnnycake meal and brown-bread flour, various pancake and muffin mixes

Kenyon Corn Meal Company
Usquepaugh
West Kingston, R.I. 02892
(401) 783-4054
johnnycake meal, brown-bread flour, other grains

Morgan's Mills
R.D. #2, Box 115
Union, Maine 04862
(207) 785-4900
organic wheats, rye, oats, buckwheat, barley

The Vermont Country Store
P.O. Box 3000
Manchester Center, Vt. 05255
(802) 362-2400
common crackers and many other regional specialties

VEGETABLES, HERBS, FRUITS AND NEW ENGLAND WINES

A & M Orchards
38 Eldridge Road
Harvard, Massachusetts 01451
(508) 456-8408
several varieties of apples and other fruits

A. Russo and Sons
249 Lexington Street
Watertown, Mass. 02172
(617) 923-1500
specialty produce: fresh vegetables, herbs and fruits

Bluebird Acres
714-747 Parker Street
E. Longmeadow, Mass. 01028
(413) 525-6012
many different apples, some heirloom varieties including Rhode Island Greenings, Winesaps, Kings, Snows, etc.

Crosswoods Vineyards
75 Chester Maine Road
N. Stonington, Conn. 06359
(203) 535-2205
vinifera wines of excellent quality

Delftree Corporation
234 Union Street
North Adams, Mass. 01247
(413) 664-4907
shiitake mushrooms, available year-round

Diamond Hill Farms
P.O. Box 96
Rockport, Maine 04856
(207) 236-2396
organic and hydroponic lettuces and vegetables

The Fresh Connection
Massachusetts Department of Food and Agriculture
Leverett Saltonstall Building
100 Cambridge Street
Boston, Massachusetts 02202
(617) 727-3018
newsletter listing various producers during the appropriate seasons

Greene Herb Company
1415 Lancaster Avenue
Lunenburg, Mass. 01462
(508) 534-3412
fresh herbs and flowers

Herbal Gardens
96 Litchfield Road
Litchfield, N.H. 03051
(603) 881-7276
beautiful organic vegetables, herbs and flowers

Meadowbrook Herb Garden
Route 138
Wyoming, Rhode Island 02898
(401) 539-7603
herbal teas and dried herbs, organic

Nashoba Valley Winery
100 Wattaquadoc Hill Road
Bolton, Massachusetts 01740
(508) 779-5521
old-fashioned New England fruit wines, orchard fruits

Sakonett Vineyards
162 West Main Street
Little Compton, R.I. 02837
(401) 635-4356
tasty vinifera wines including Vidal Blanc

Walker's Roadside Stand
Little Compton, R.I. 02837
(401) 635-4719
excellent vegetables and lettuces, large selection

Wilson Farm
10 Pleasant Street
Lexington, Mass. 02173
(617) 862-3900
high-quality vegetables, pumpkins and fruits

Index